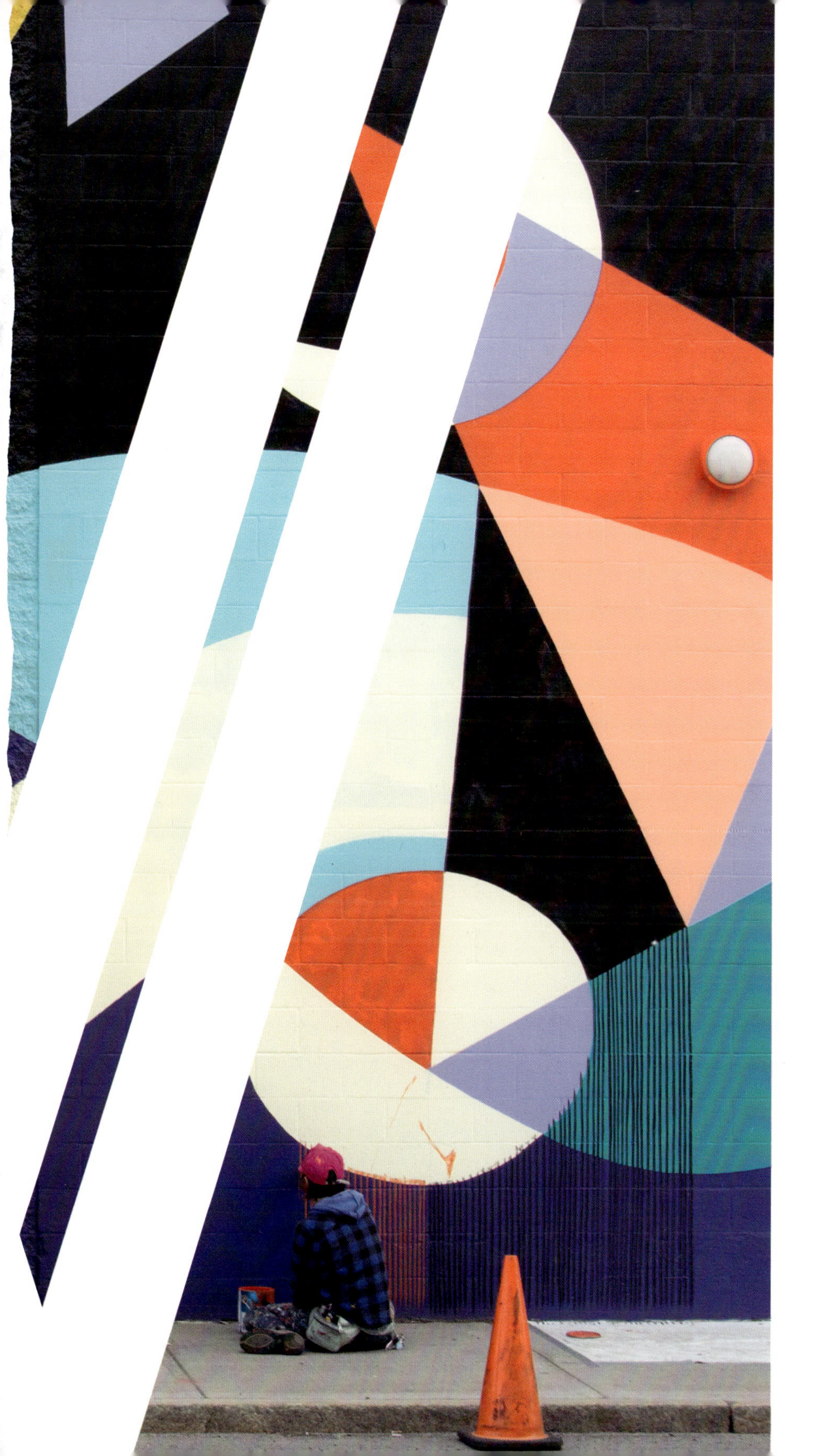

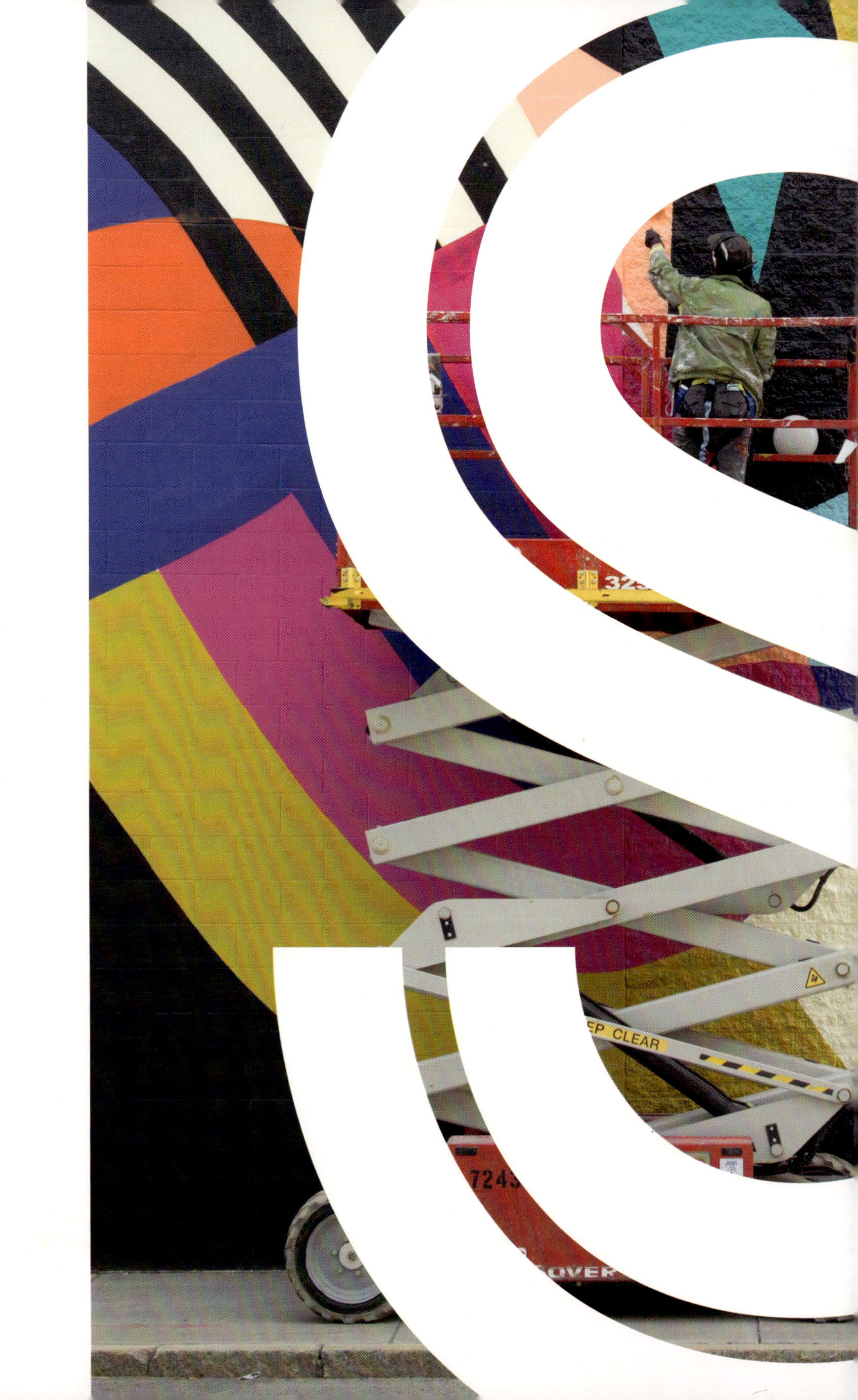

Hi–Vis

Ten Years of Public Art at the Buffalo AKG Art Museum

Essays by
Zack Boehler,
Eric Jones, Aaron Ott,
and Janne Sirén

Edited by
Matt Connolly and
Pam Hatley

Texts by
Julia Bottoms, Amanda Browder, Hillary Waters Fayle, Futura 2000, Maya Hayuk, Monet Alyssa Kifner, Aaron Li-Hill, Bunnie Reiss, Casey Riordan, Rachel Shelton, Shasti O'Leary Soudant, and Edreys Wajed

Buffalo AKG Art Museum
in association with
D Giles Ltd

BUFFALO AKG ART MUSEUM

g

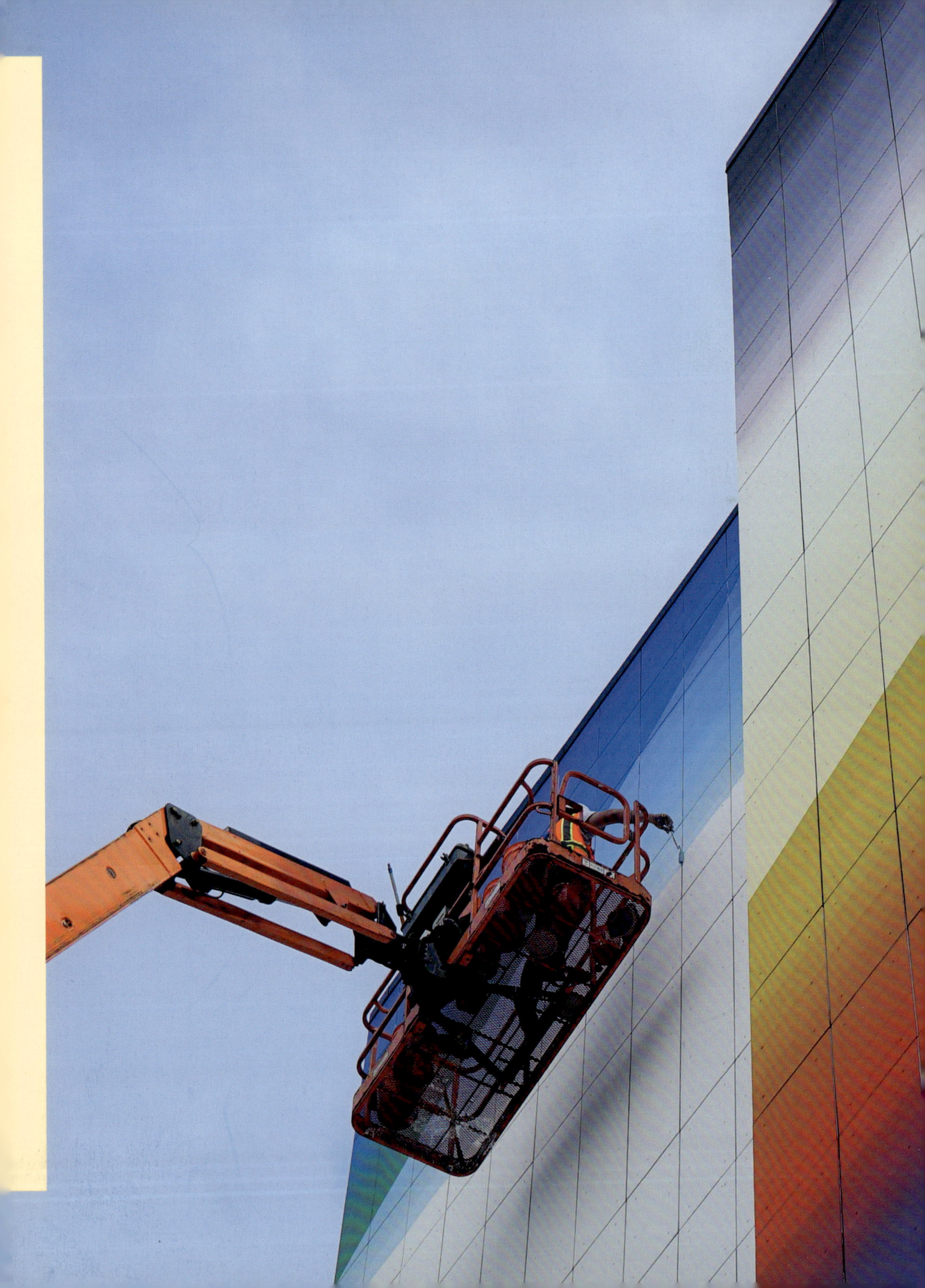

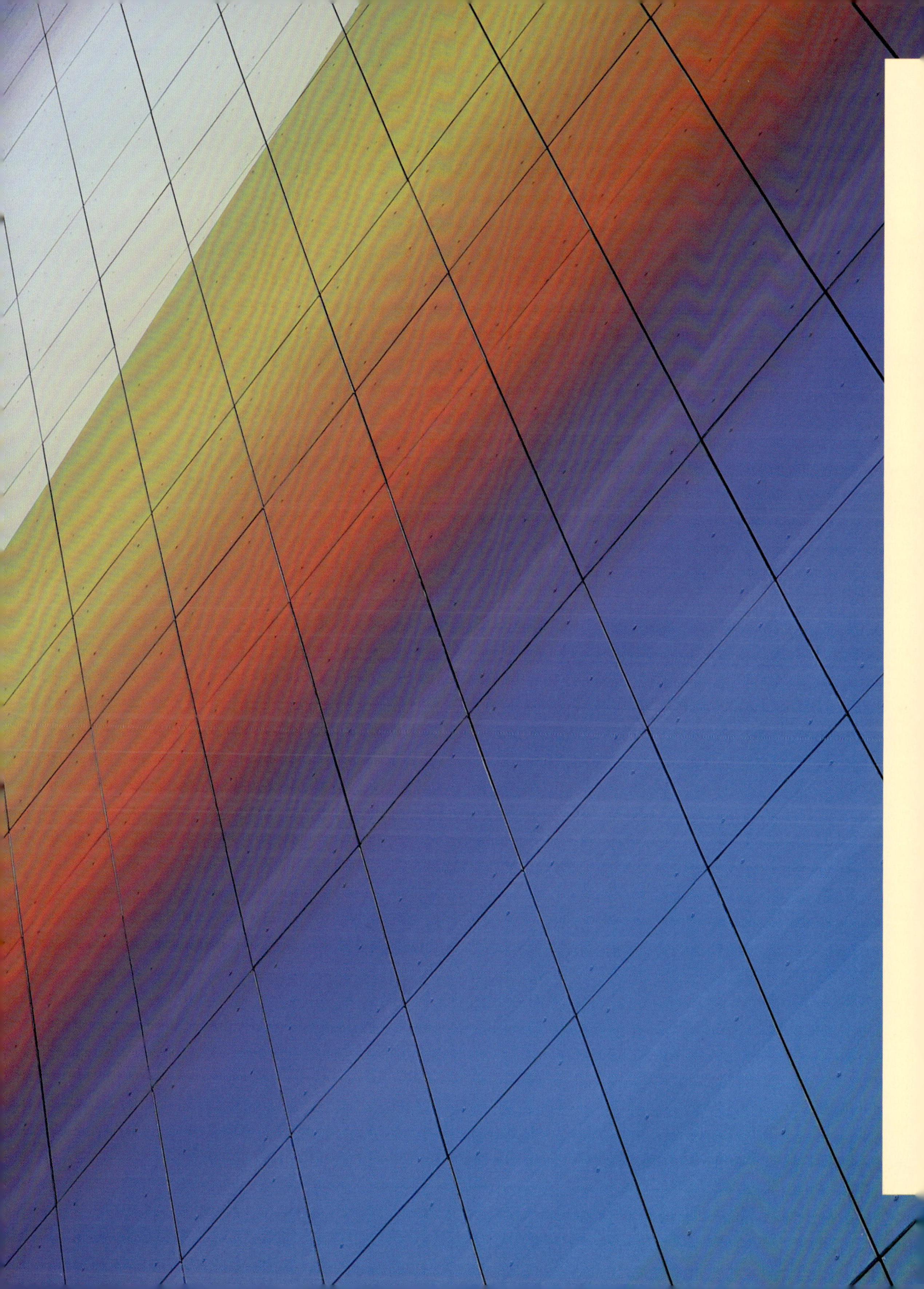

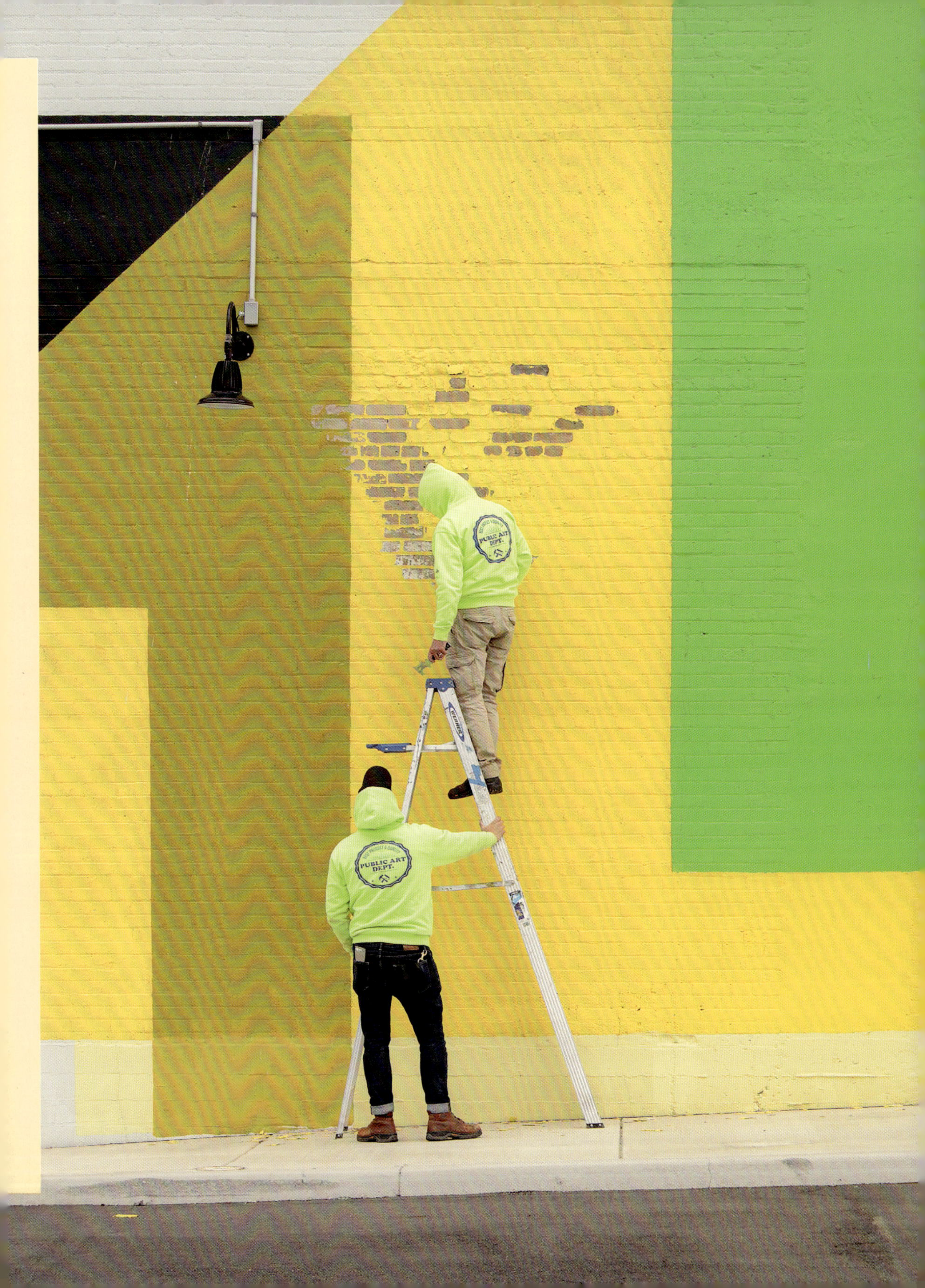

Contents

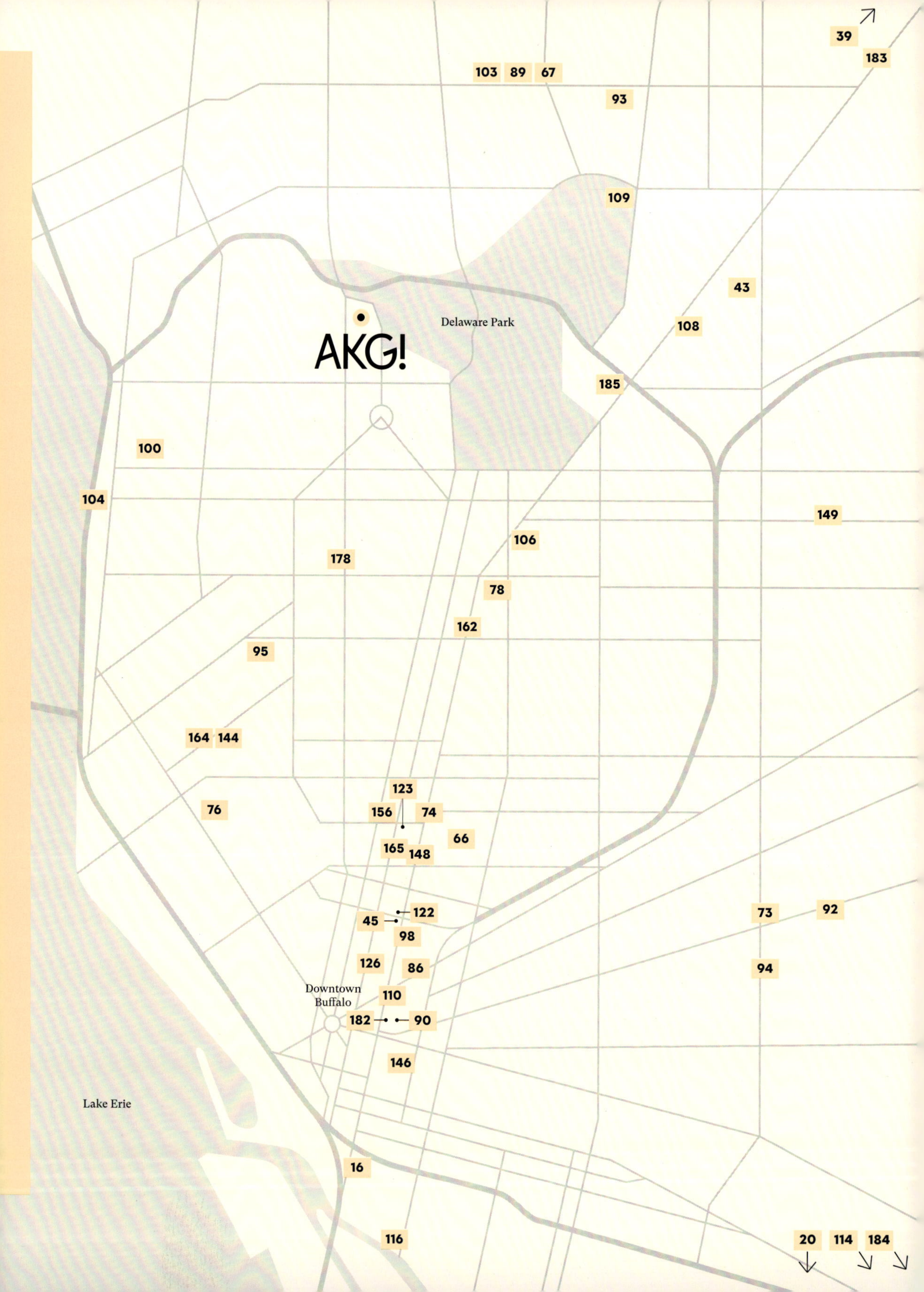

39
183
103 89 67
93
109
43
108
Delaware Park
185
AKG!
100
104
149
106
178
78
162
95
164 144
76
123
156 74
66
165 148
122
45
98
73 92
126
86
94
Downtown
Buffalo
110
182 90
146
Lake Erie
16
116
20 114 184

Locations

Highlighted projects are on view

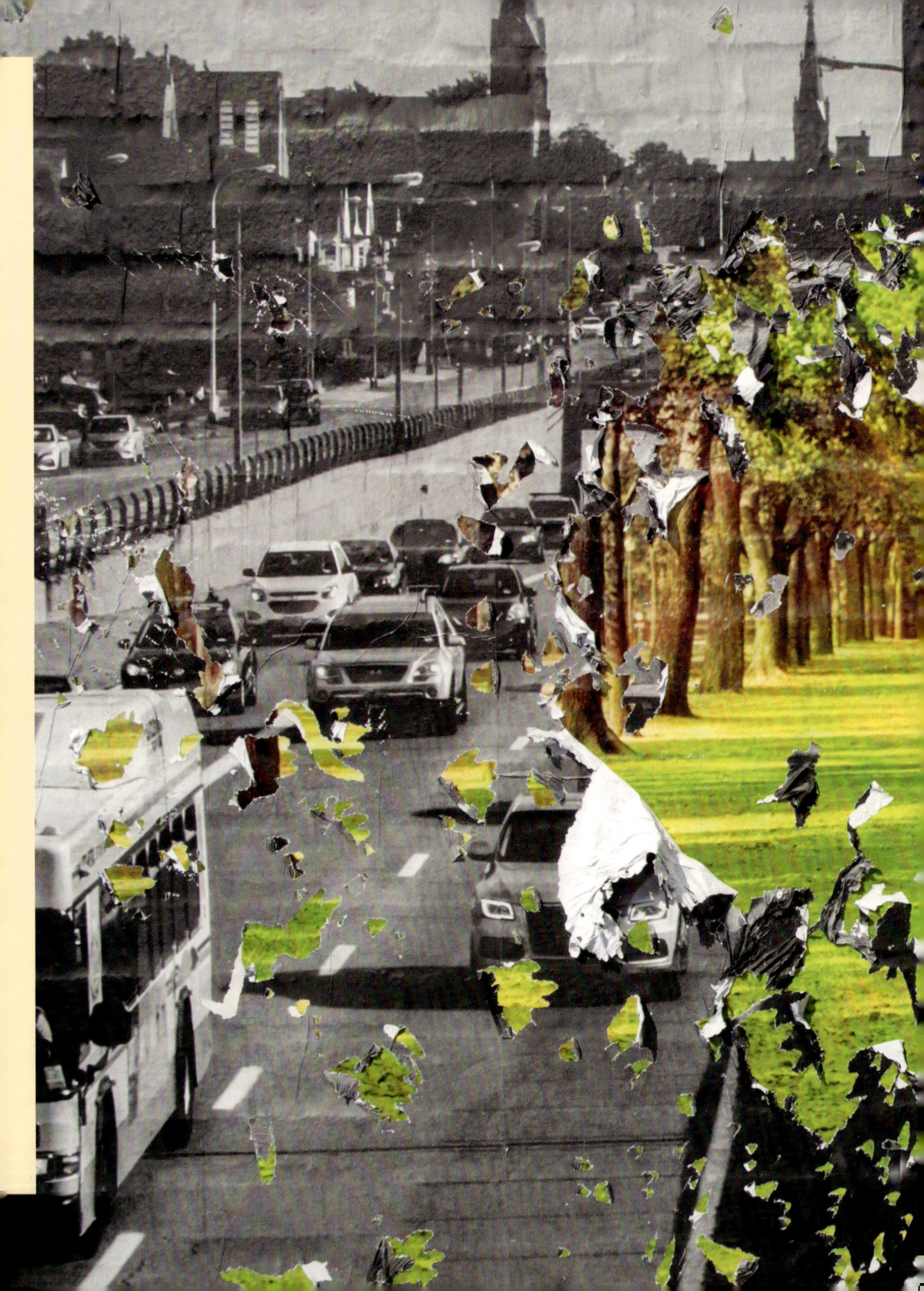

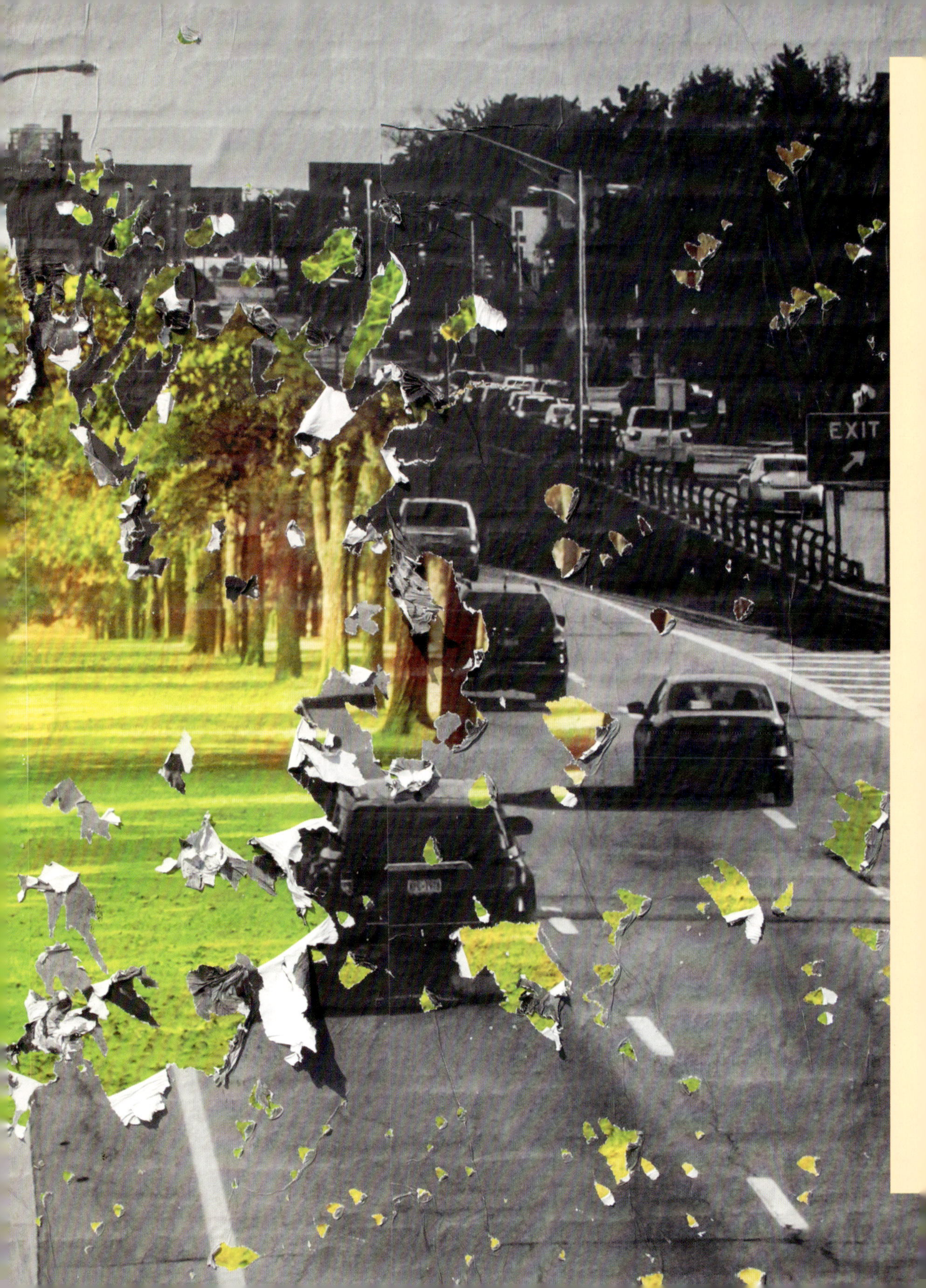

EXIT

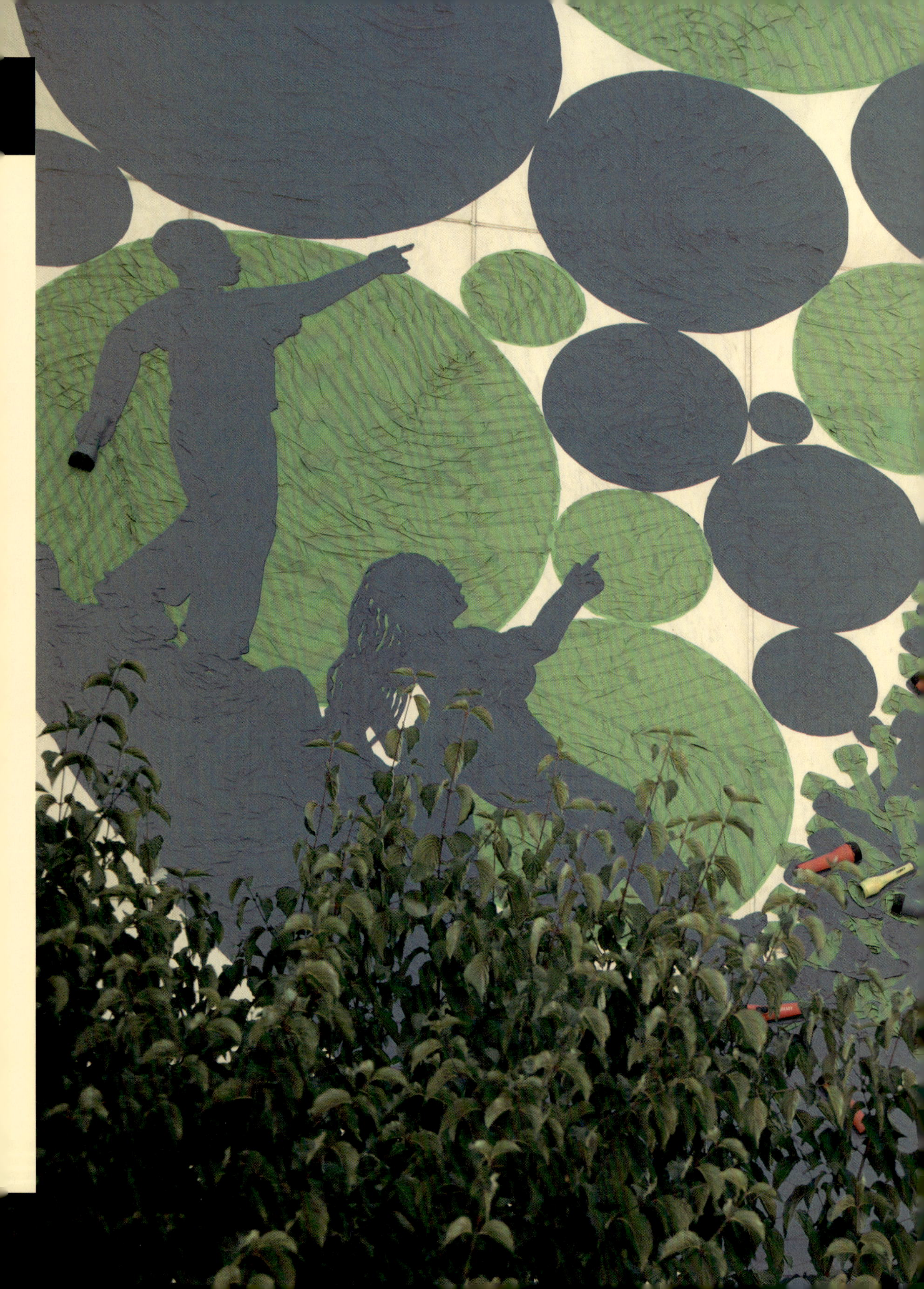

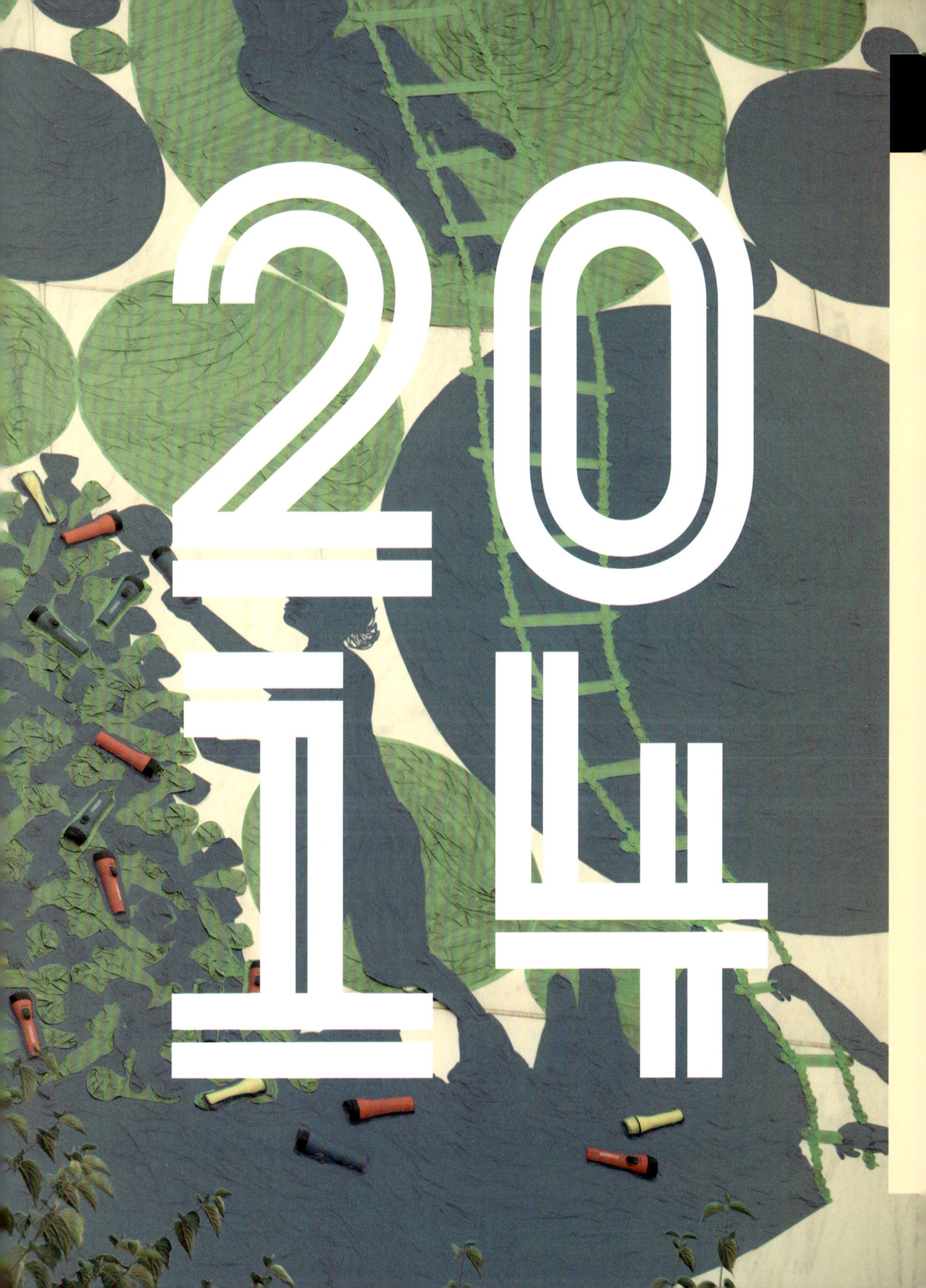

2014

You Are Beautiful

Matthew Hoffman

Various locations throughout Erie and Niagara counties

Forty-four billboards
Dimensions variable

In 2014, over the Labor Day weekend, billboards mysteriously began to appear across Erie and Niagara counties bearing a simple, enigmatic message: "You Are Beautiful." As more billboards and then stickers emerged, members of the public connected the works to the museum and the artist. *You Are Beautiful* is an extension of a project that Hoffman began as a graffiti-style self-affirmation scrawled on an underpass in Chicago.

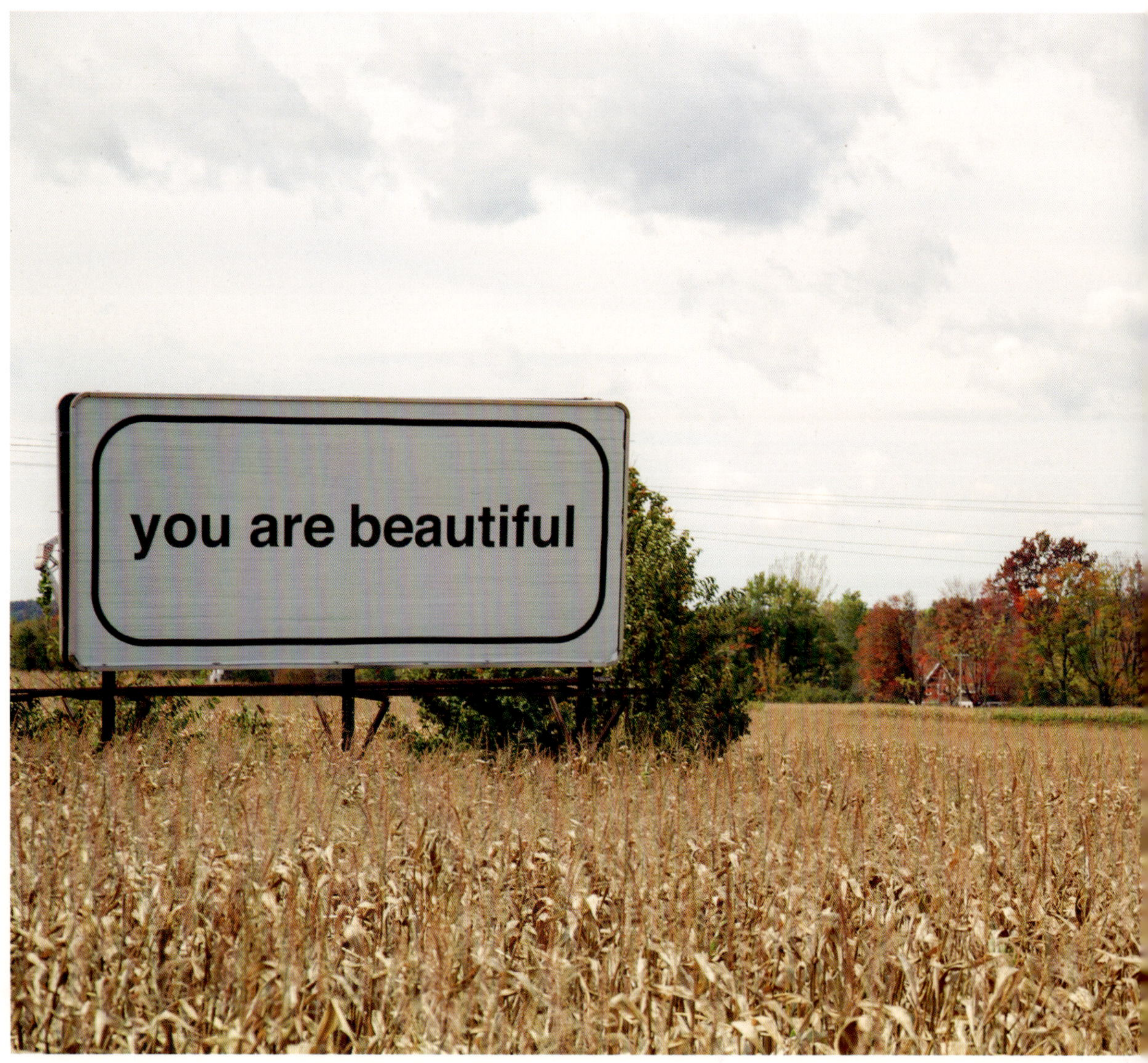

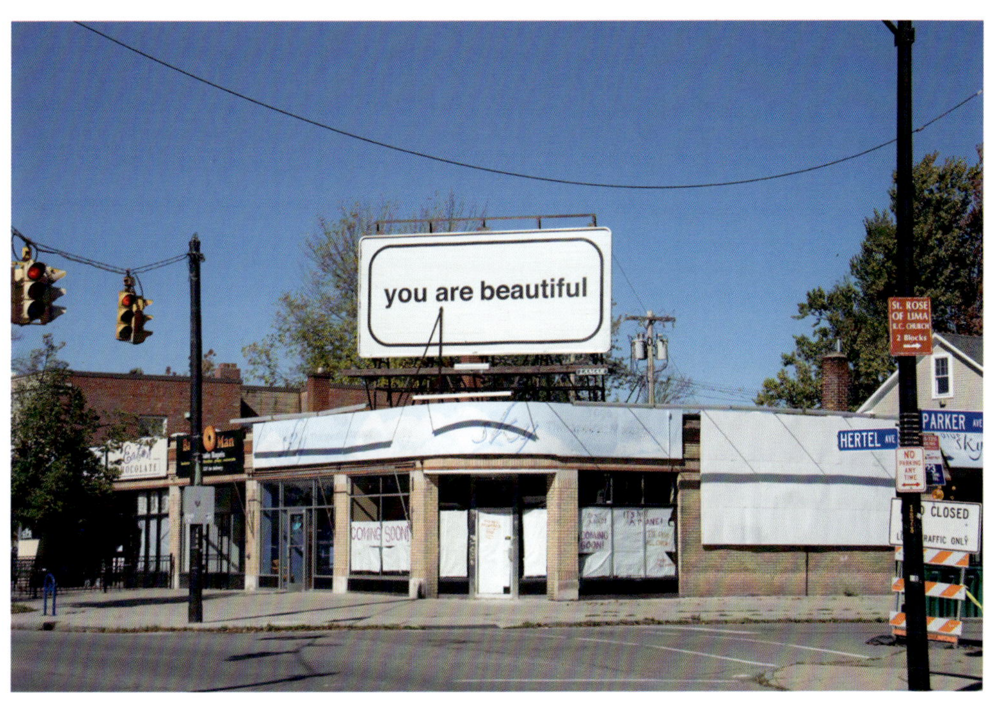

you are beautiful
COMING SOON!
HERTEL AVE
PARKER AVE
St. ROSE OF LIMA R.C. CHURCH 2 Blocks
NO PARKING ANY TIME
CLOSED
TRAFFIC ONLY

Shark Girl

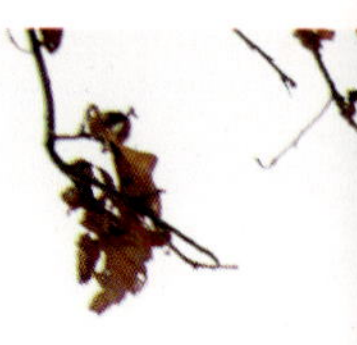

Casey Riordan

Canalside

Fiberglass and paint
60 × 60 × 36 inches
(152.4 × 152.4 × 91.4 cm)

There are days I forget about Shark Girl, and that I am her creator. She exists outside of me and has her own life. She brings me joy when I think about her, which is ironic because she was born from existential dread. Shark Girl developed in the pages of my sketchbook in 2004, as a self-portrait full of self-doubt about my art and at odds with the temp job I was working. By day, I catalogued outdated paper files at a corporate real estate firm in Chicago, preparing them to go to a contracted shredding company. By night, I made small drawings and watercolors of I can't remember what. In between, I rode the subway and drew in my sketchbook; drew and drew and drew. Shark Girl made her way out of the sketchbook and into my gallery work that year and, due to good fortune, she has not left my practice.

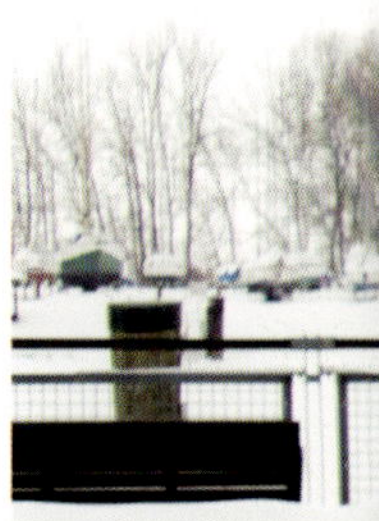

Creating work for an exhibition, an artist has control in manipulating the feelings of an audience. I spent almost a decade trying to bring the viewer into my melodramas. Public art changed that in a day's time. My Shark Girl sculpture that lives in Buffalo was originally installed along the Ohio Riverfront in Cincinnati. She faced the water and gazed blankly, indifferent to her environment. My intent was for the viewer to sit with Shark Girl, in sympathy and solace. Passersby saw that as a missed opportunity. By sundown on the day she was delivered, someone had turned her around and pushed her almost ten feet to the side. This added bridges and riverboats to the composition, so that person could sit with Shark Girl and smile and take a picture: create a memory. It was then I gave up control and did not return her to my intended site.

The second decade of Shark Girl's life has been a delight. I get to live vicariously through her, like a proud parent. She receives love and affection and is visited daily by tourists, families, children, co-workers, parties, dogs, and couples getting engaged. Shark Girl is a destination. She is a star. She has fans who make fan art. She has her image tattooed on fans' bodies, and people dress up as her for Halloween. She has met celebrities, appeared on the JumboTron at a professional hockey game, and has even run for president. Shark Girl is in profile pictures, on dating sites, on the news, in the paper, on top-ten lists, and has a social media account that I did not create. Shark Girl brings people joy, and I feel their joy.

Upon reflection, what I mistook for autonomy, I now see as isolation. Once thinking she spontaneously sprung from air, Shark Girl was born of my fear and tears. Shark Girl is an antidote for depression. Shark Girl saved me from myself. Viewers saved me from myself. Others can give us what we need if we risk letting them in. Public art is a facilitator of connection.

—CASEY RIORDAN

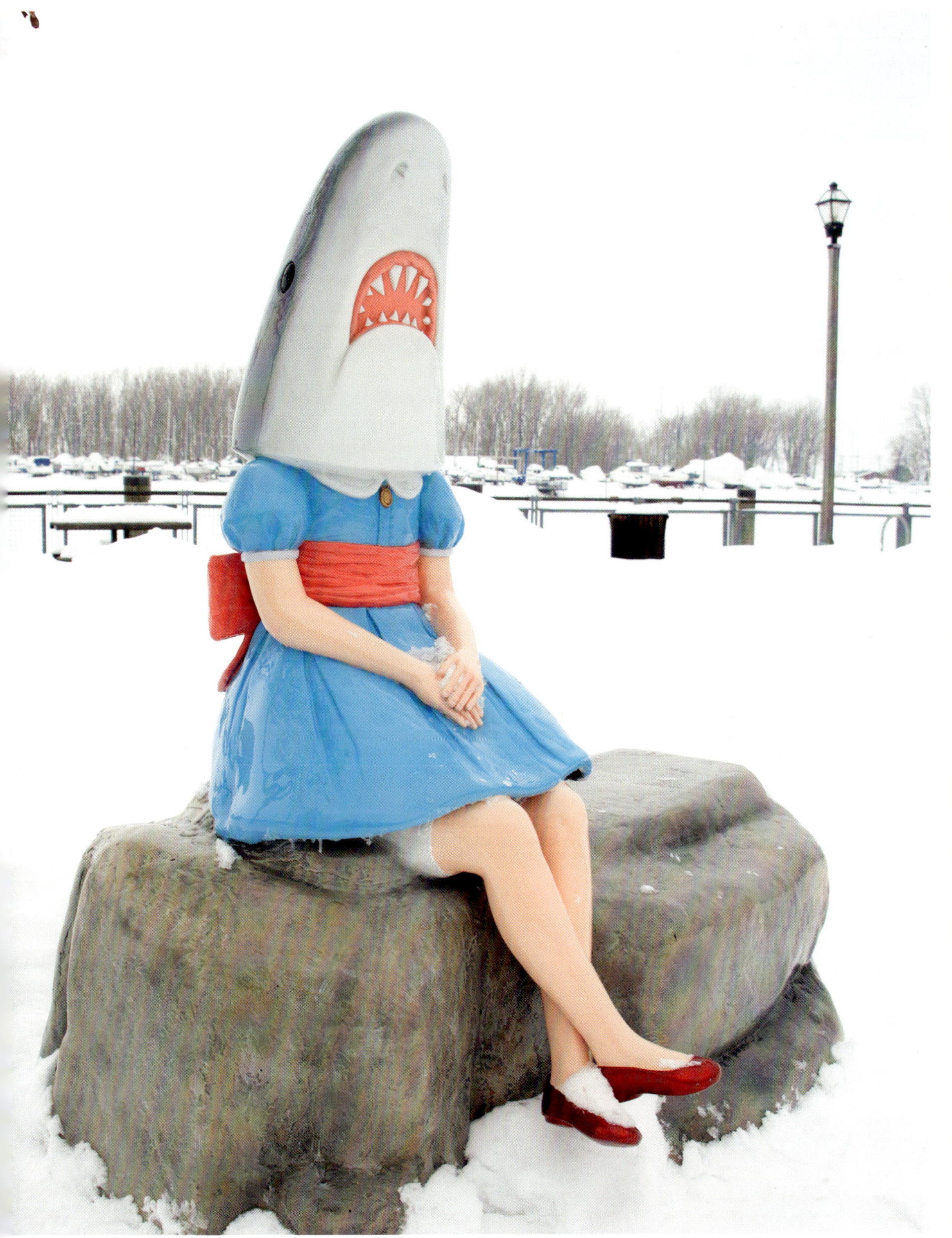

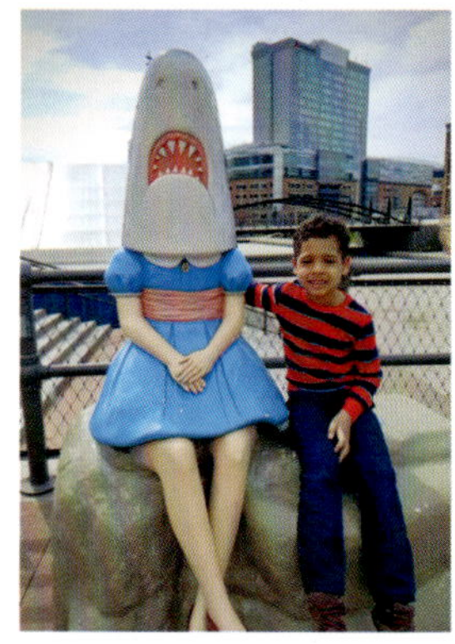
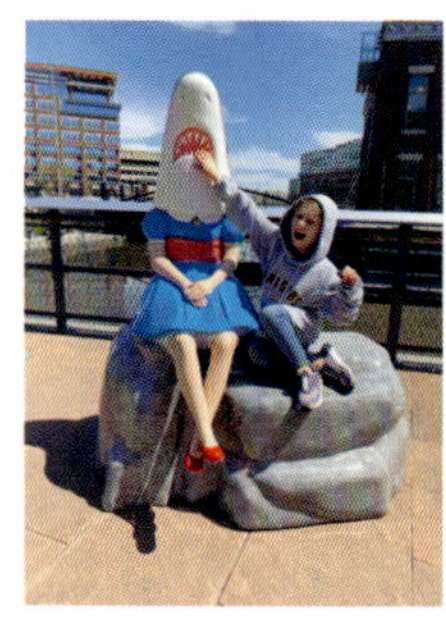
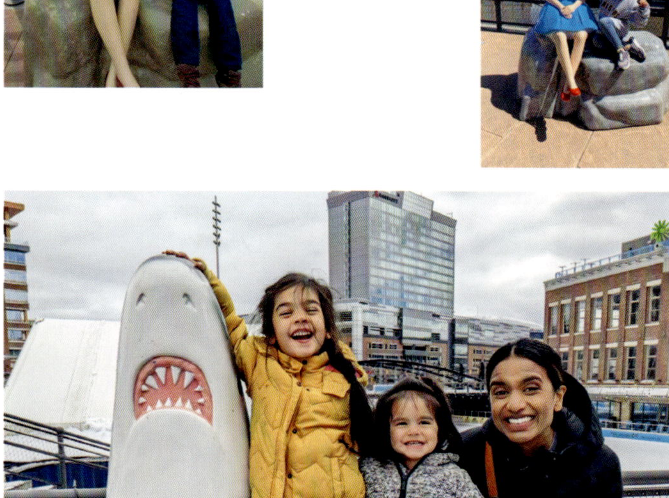
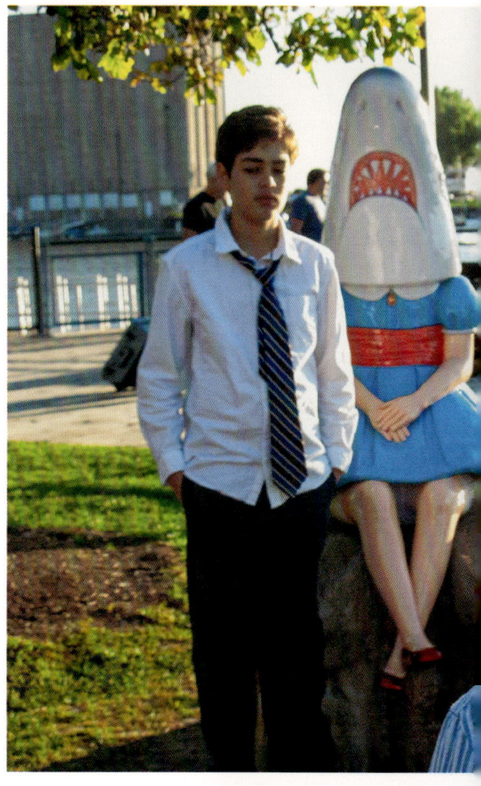
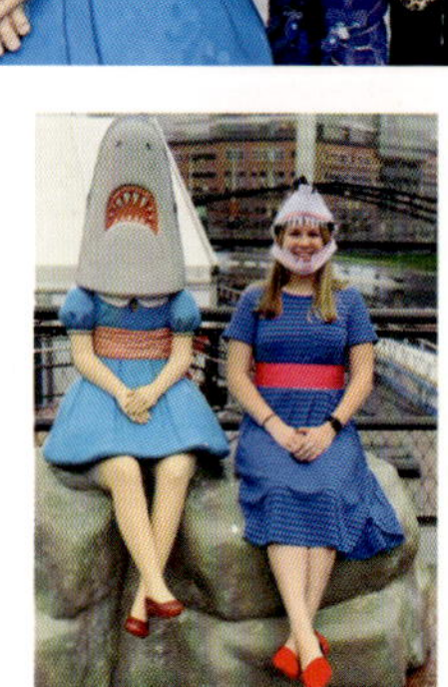
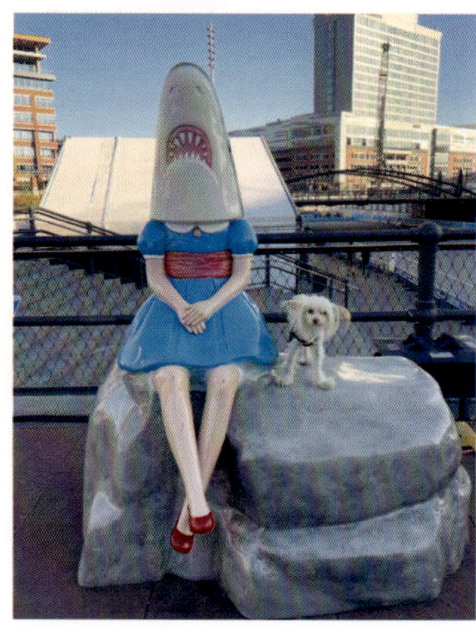
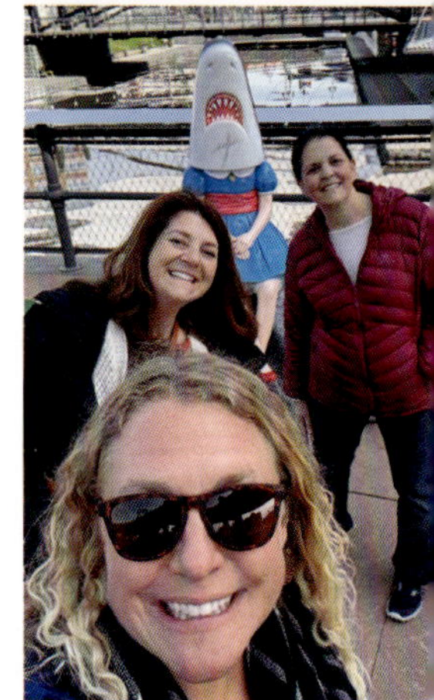
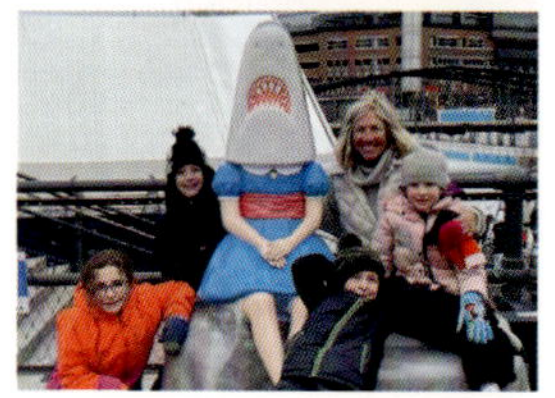

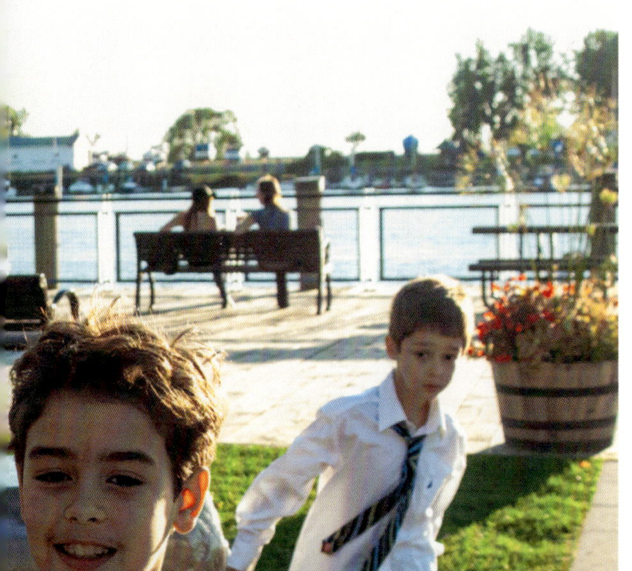

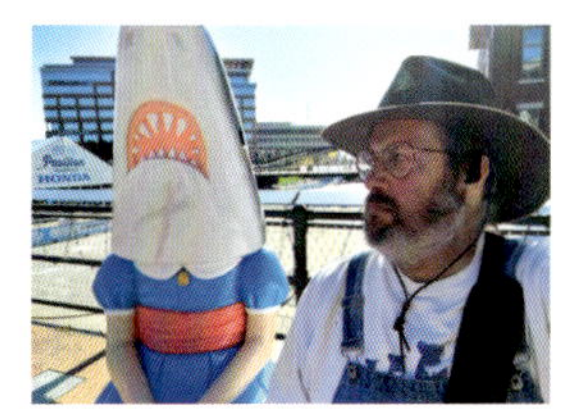

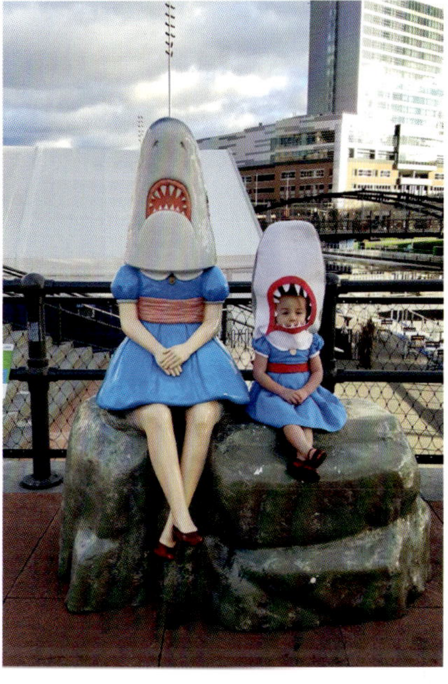

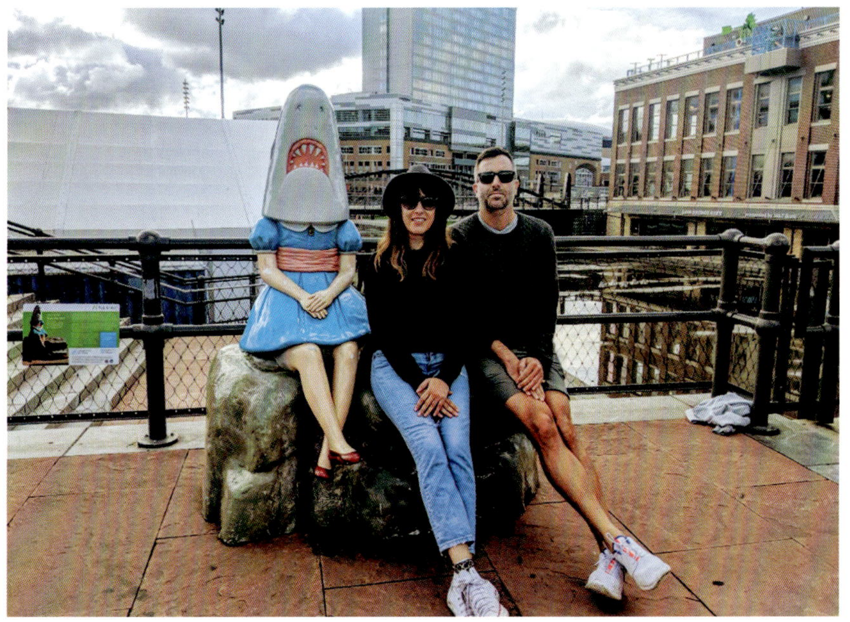

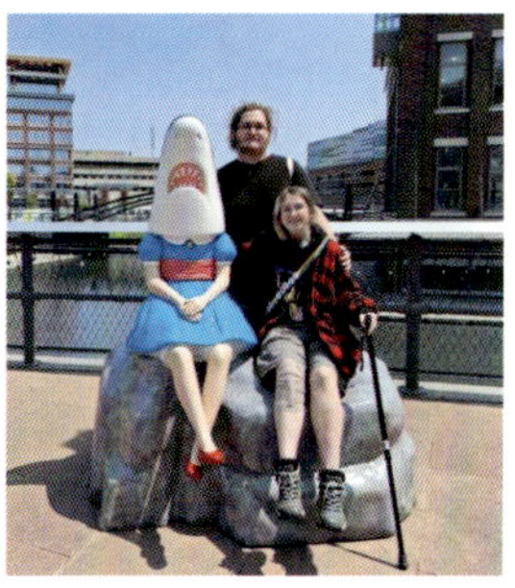

Hamburg Arena Painting

Charles Clough

Hamburg Public Library

Acrylic on canvas
6 feet 3 inches × 16 feet
8 inches (1.9 × 5.1 m)

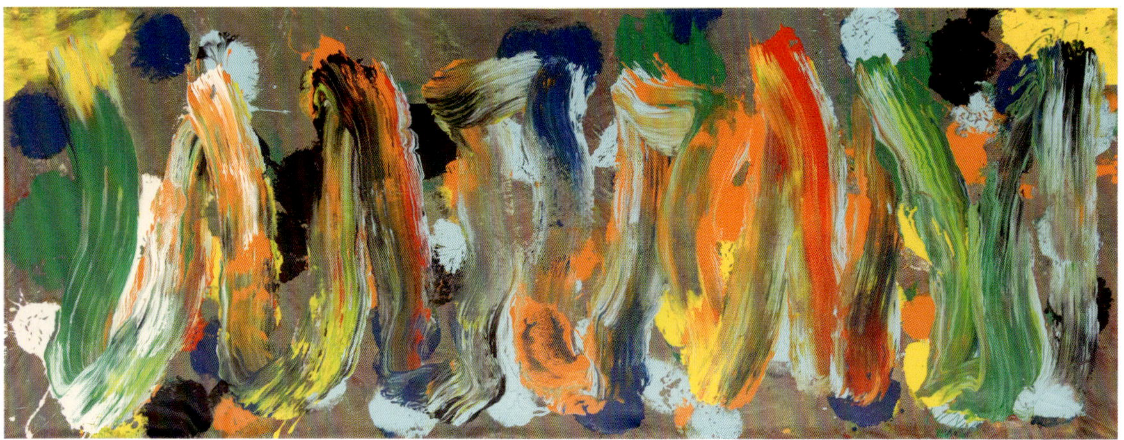

Over the course of eight hours, 168 participants and volunteers gathered in the Swan Auditorium at Hilbert College in Hamburg to add their marks to this work by pouring or splattering a variety of colors onto the canvas, then smearing, pushing, and scraping the paint using Clough's giant and distinctively crafted "paintbrushes" called Big Fingers.

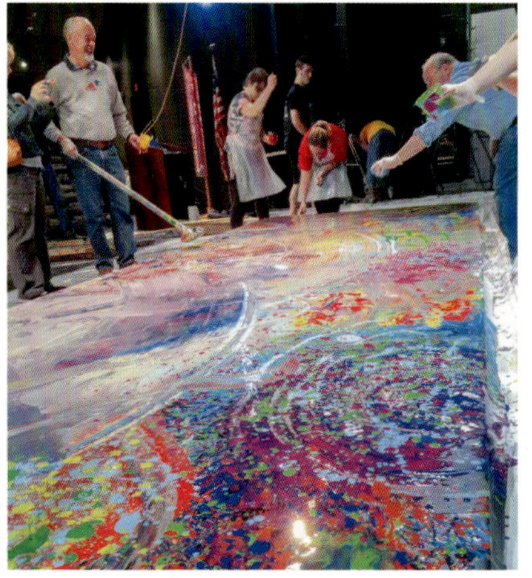

Buffalo Caverns

Tape Art

Central Library, Buffalo & Erie County Public Library

Green and blue painter's tape Variable: approximately 50 feet at highest point × 150 feet (15.2 × 45.7 m)

From August 17 to 22, 2014, artist collective Tape Art created a mural on the north wall of the Central Library using low-adhesive drawing tape. Passersby were invited to watch, and even contribute to, the creation process. The temporary mural was on view for just eight days.

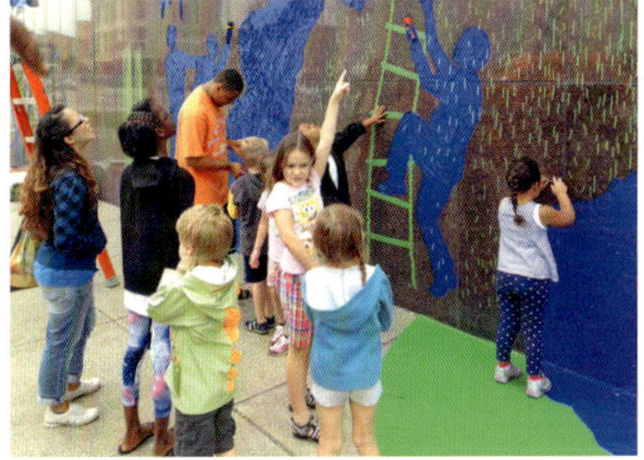

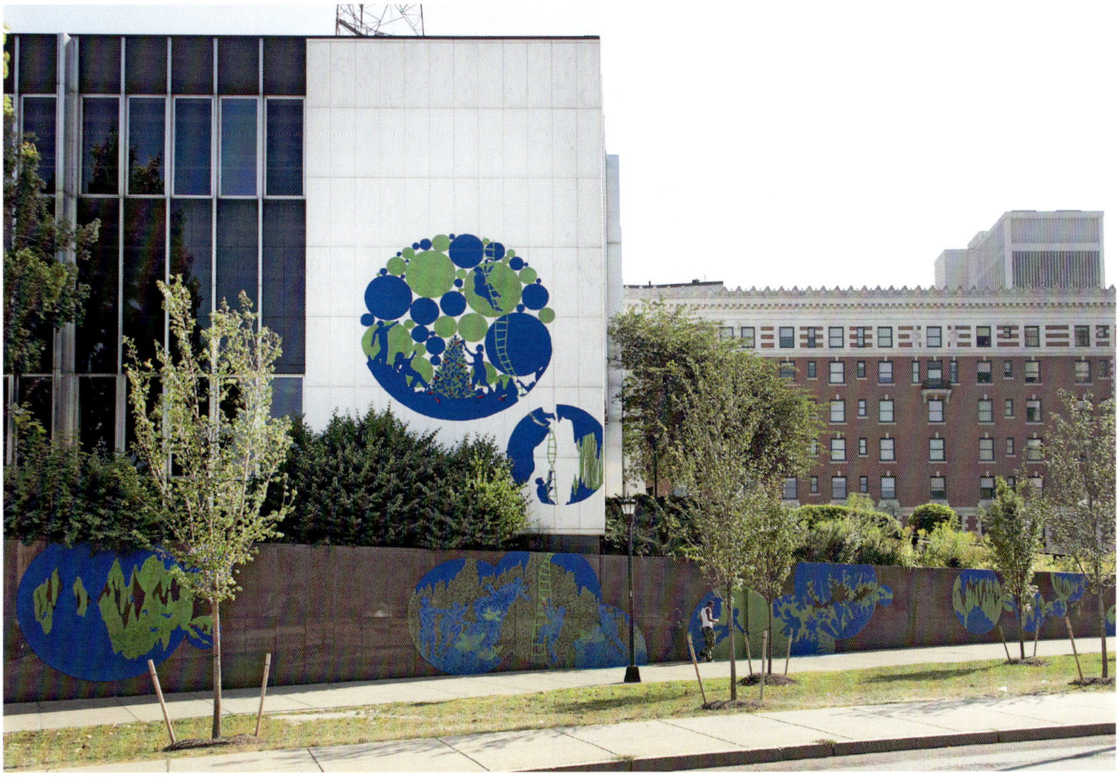

Art Unbound: Catalyzing Creativity Beyond Museum Walls

JANNE SIRÉN
Peggy Pierce Elfvin Director

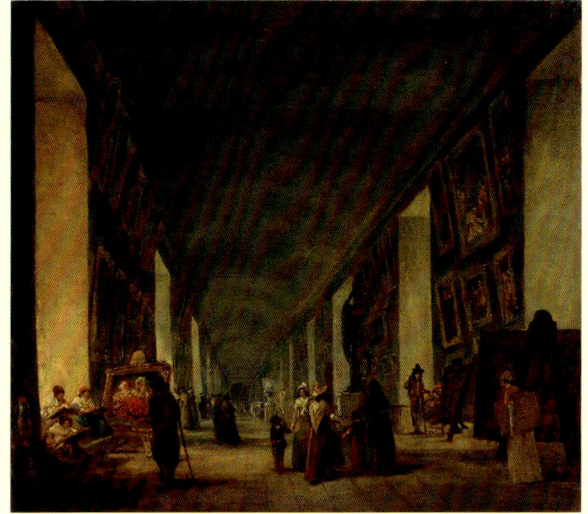

Ever since the world's first public art museum, the revolutionary Louvre, opened its doors to visitors in 1793, art museums have functioned as cornerstones of the public sphere—that nebulous space where collective identities are molded, ideas are debated, and points of view are expressed (above).[1] Increasingly since World War II, they have also operated as subjects of public trust.[2] Whether or not they are public institutions in the eyes of the law or according to their articles of incorporation—in the US, most art museums are private nonprofit enterprises—people tend to regard art museums as such, as incarnations of an amorphous collective sensibility that supersedes national identity. Even in the US, with its diverse cultures and decentralized governmental system, art museums are perceived as having both unifying and universalizing agency. According to a 2021 report by the American Alliance of Museums, "the public continues to regard museums as highly trustworthy—ranking second only to friends and family, and significantly more trustworthy than researchers and scientists, NGOs generally, various news organizations, the government, corporations and business, and social media." Further, "for respondents who had visited a museum in the past two years, museums are the number one trusted source of information."[3] Being *public* and

being *trustworthy* lie at the very core of what being a museum is all about.

If art museums are thought of as public institutions, what then is public art? Wouldn't *all* art be public to some extent? Once it leaves the hands of its maker, under what conditions does a work begin to accrue a patina of "publicness"? Consider, for example, Michelangelo's *David*, one of the most well-known and frequently reproduced artworks in the world (below). In June 1504, soon after its completion, *David* was installed next to the entrance to Florence's town hall, the Palazzo della Signoria, also known as the Palazzo Vecchio. This 12,500-pound marble statue, the preeminent symbol of Florentine ingenuity and prowess, stood there in all its glory for centuries, defiantly glaring at the enemies of Florence, real or imaginary, long after its power had been eclipsed by other Italian cities. In 1873, due to preservation concerns, *David* was moved indoors, to the Galleria dell'Accademia di Firenze, where the Renaissance masterpiece has since been a magnet for tens of millions of adoring visitors.[4] *David*, in summary,

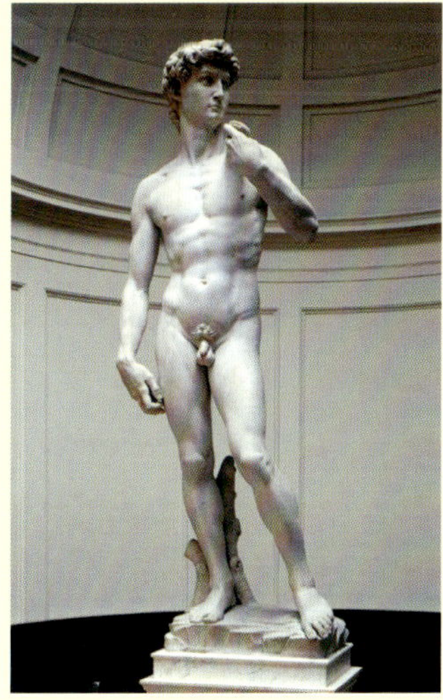

↖ Hubert Robert. *The Grand Gallery of the Louvre between 1794 and 1796*, 1794–96. Oil on canvas, 145 ⅝ × 161 ⅜ inches (370 × 410 cm). Musée du Louvre, Paris.

← Michelangelo. *David*, 1501–4. Marble, 16 feet 11 inches (5.16 m) high. Galleria dell'Accademia di Firenze.

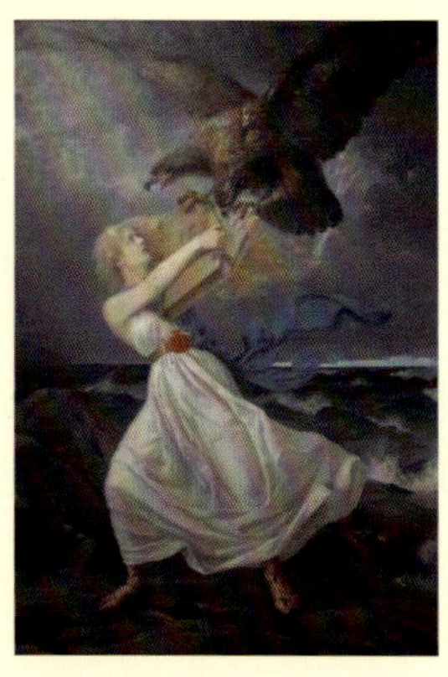

is a pronouncedly public artwork, and certainly its public patina is deeper than that of the artist's drawings, which are rarely, and if then only briefly, displayed due to their sensitivity to light.

Like artworks, art museums and the initiatives and programs they foster also have their distinct histories and paths of becoming. Before we turn to Buffalo and its unique platform for connecting art and people—the decennial of which this publication celebrates—let's take a detour through Helsinki and its public art collection, which served as a source of inspiration for the Buffalo AKG's Public Art Initiative.

A common slogan in Finland is "art belongs to everyone" ("*taide kuuluu kaikille*"). It's a statement that might raise some philosophical eyebrows in places where art has historically been thought of more as a private commodity or a luxury good than as a quintessential cornerstone of civic society. In Finnish public discourse the very notion of art as a privately owned and managed asset class is controversial. Somewhat unexpectedly, given how short the runway of Finnish art history is, the country's systemic attachment to democracy, freedom, and the rule of law is powerfully manifest in its cultural arena. In fact, during periods of Russification, when Finland's legal system was threatened by Russian imperialism, artists were among the first to rush to the barricades, creating artworks expressing devotion to autonomy and the rule of law. A case in point is Eetu Isto's *The Attack* of 1899 (above), in which a double-headed eagle, the heraldic

symbol of the Russian Empire, tries to claw Finland's lawbook from the hands of the Finnish Maiden, the personification of the nation. Finns are attached to their laws and statutes, and they also envision culture and art in a diversity of media as something that defines them.

A paradigm-defining example of Finland's secular theology of art is found in the mission of the Helsinki Art Museum—"Making Helsinki more fun through art"—and specifically in its approach to collection development, management, and display. HAM's collection consists of approximately 10,000 artworks in various media dating primarily from the early twentieth century to the present. New acquisitions are almost exclusively works by living artists. Most museums of modern and contemporary art around the world typically display a small percentage of their collections at any given time, while preserving the bulk of their holdings in climatized storage facilities. In contrast, one quarter of HAM's collection is on permanent display in its host city's public buildings. Additionally, nearly three hundred public artworks from Helsinki's public art collection, which is managed by HAM and ranges chronologically from late eighteenth-century memorials to recent installations, are

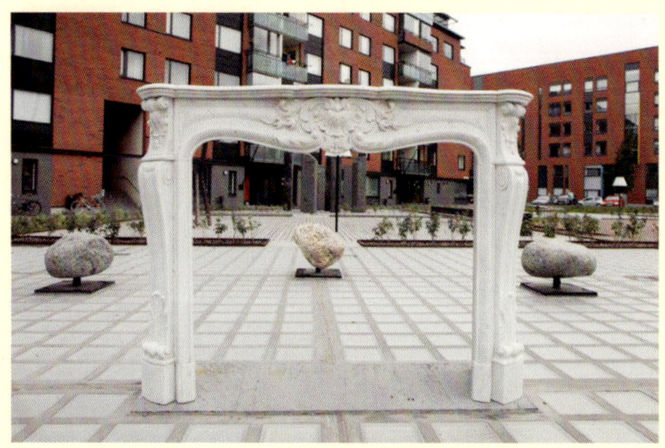

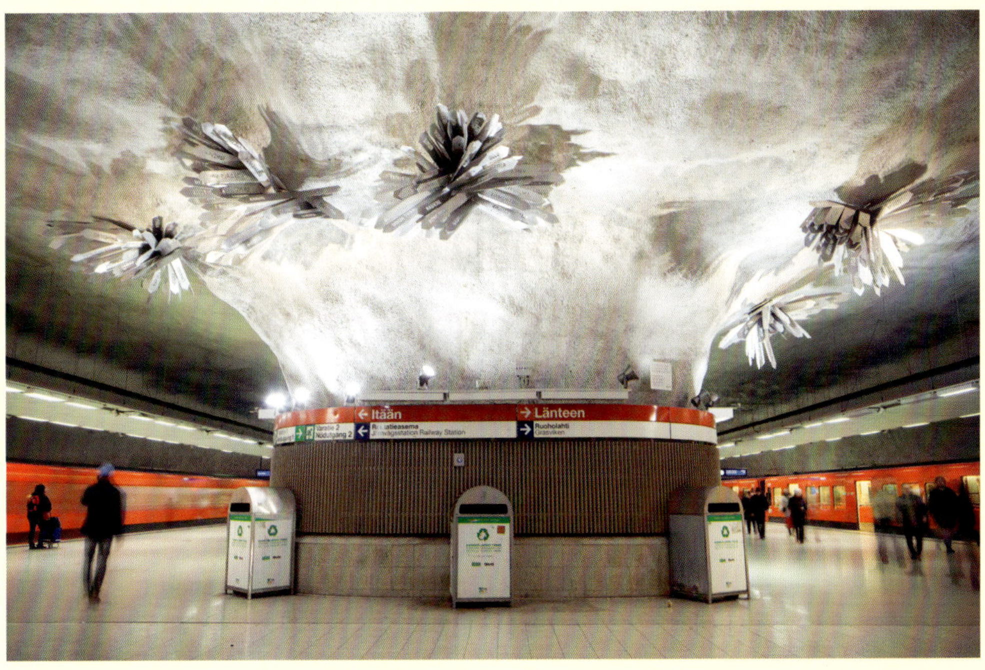

↖ Eetu Isto. *The Attack*, 1899. Oil on canvas, 78¾ × 55⅛ inches (200 × 140 cm). Suomen kansallismuseo, Helsinki.

↙ Robert Wilson. Tapio Wirkkala Park, 2012. Helsinki. HAM Helsinki Art Museum.

↑ Otto Karvonen. *Roots of the City*, 2013. Aluminum, dimensions variable. Kamppi metro station, Helsinki. HAM Helsinki Art Museum.

located in parks, streets, and squares around the city (below left). In recent decades, HAM's Public Art Department has also commissioned more than two hundred site-specific artworks in semipublic indoor spaces, including schools, daycare centers, and libraries.

The Director of HAM, a position I held from 2007 to 2013, works as the head of a department within the civil service of Helsinki, coordinating efforts with other departments in order to address one lofty goal: to make Helsinki an interesting place to live for its residents, notably, in our case, through the agency of public art. Creating public art is different than acquiring a typical artwork. It requires long lead times, often with extensive planning and collaboration with interior designers, architects, and city planners.

HAM, in short, navigates the constraints of a gallery space—ubiquitous in the museum field—differently than most of its peer institutions. It regards Helsinki's outdoor and indoor spaces, the halls and walls of the buildings that belong to the City of Helsinki—of which there are many—as de facto extensions of its own (above). HAM's approach to collection management and display is echoed in its organizational structure. Its curators have three primary areas of focus: special exhibitions, development and preservation of the fine art collection, and public art, which is overseen by curators who specialize in this field. Collectively, this group of curators advances HAM's vision of itself as a "city-wide museum" that "offers surprises in the cityscape":

> HAM is strongly involved in the everyday life of Helsinkians, and together we find new ways of looking at life in Helsinki and beyond. HAM builds international interest in Helsinki. It is the most popular museum in Finland and reaches new audiences. HAM defines what an art museum can be.[5]

Defining what an art museum can be is, of course, something that all of us who work in the field think about. The question sits at the center of our forward-looking aspirations and strategic planning; it keeps us on our toes as we seek to remain relevant and foster trust in an ever-changing and divisive environment. This question, and specifically the search for a model that borrows the public spirit of a European art museum such as HAM but that infuses it with the dynamism inherent in the funding structure of an American museum, were top of mind in 2013 when I moved from Helsinki and a lifetime appointment as Director of the Helsinki Art Museum to Buffalo to lead the Buffalo AKG Art Museum (at that time the Albright-Knox Art Gallery). And I came prepared with the experience of tackling the unique challenges of public art.

One of the things that struck me upon my arrival in Western New York was that while many Buffalonians spoke about their hometown museum, the sixth oldest art museum in the United States, with pride and a general sense of awareness of its importance, they also felt that the museum exuded an air of elitism and therefore was not really their domain. "The last time I visited the museum was on a school trip years ago," was a common refrain I heard in countless casual interactions I had with fellow Buffalonians. By contrast, parks in Buffalo, as in many other cities, are preeminent public spaces that not only feel accessible but are tangibly just that. The AKG is located within a celebrated and well-utilized Frederick Law Olmsted park (page 28), yet it was clear to me that many viewed the museum as near the park, but not a part of it.

Thinking about the challenges that might arise within the Western New York community if Buffalo's flagship museum tried to realize its long-standing ambition of expanding its footprint, and the obvious obstacles that its perception of "being elitist" would pose to a community-wide capital campaign, I started to think about how to deconstruct these aspects of the museum's identity. How could we change the identity of the place that is home to one of the world's great collections of modern and contemporary art; how could we create a sense of shared ownership without actually relinquishing the art from the museum's ownership and control; how could we increase physical and psychological access to art while creating a platform for shared artistic and curatorial experiences? Public art became the solution to breaking down the museum's walls without demolishing them.

As someone who believes very much in decentralized organization and in empowering leaders, I was looking to hire a curator to take up the initiative and run with it, someone who, if given the platform, could build a public art program. This person not only had to be knowledgeable and passionate about contemporary art and living artists; they would also need the ability to interface with a plethora of individuals, organizations, and neighborhoods. I could tell from his first interview that Aaron Ott had the passion and the charisma to walk into uncharted territory with courage and create something new.

With the strong endorsement of then Board President Leslie Zemsky, my team and I were able to obtain the support of Erie County and its Executive Mark Poloncarz and the City of Buffalo and its Mayor Byron Brown. Within months of my arrival, a partnership was forged between a private museum and two government entities, the county and the city, that have distinct and sometimes unaligned priorities and areas of operational focus. This partnership between unlikely partners, entering its eleventh year, has resulted in the creation of more than sixty artworks around Buffalo and Erie County, and the chapters of this book celebrate that new landscape of art. Public art has become Buffalo's twenty-first-century cultural glue.

The presence of these artworks in different public places in our community, with a focus on neighborhoods historically deprived of any cultural investment, has also changed people's perceptions about their art museum: the former ivory tower is now our *Common Sky* (below). What once was viewed from a distance as a bastion of impenetrable privilege is today regarded and experienced as a museum of and for the people. One might even argue that the AKG's capital campaign, now fully completed, owes its success, at least in part, to the museum's Public Art Initiative, which has become a magnet for fresh ideas about "collective doing" and a communal esprit de corps. Public art has created access and trust, and access and trust have resulted in new and even unexpected sources of funding. And it certainly is true that the spatial poetics of the new Buffalo AKG, its architectural identity conceived by Shohei Shigematsu and his team at OMA, was

Museum visitors enjoy a silent disco under Olafur Eliasson and Sebastian Behmann's *Common Sky*.

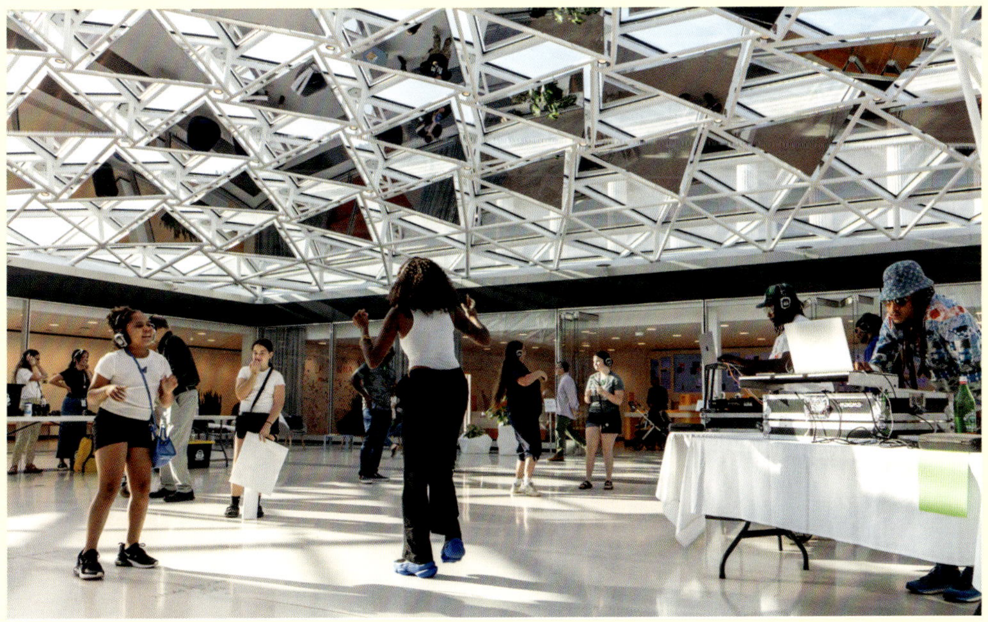

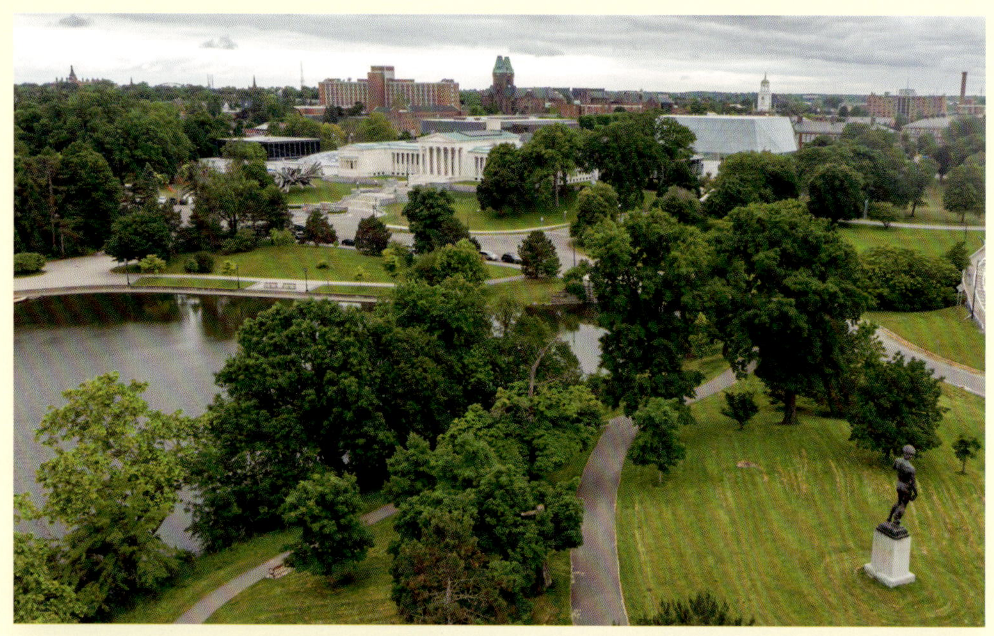

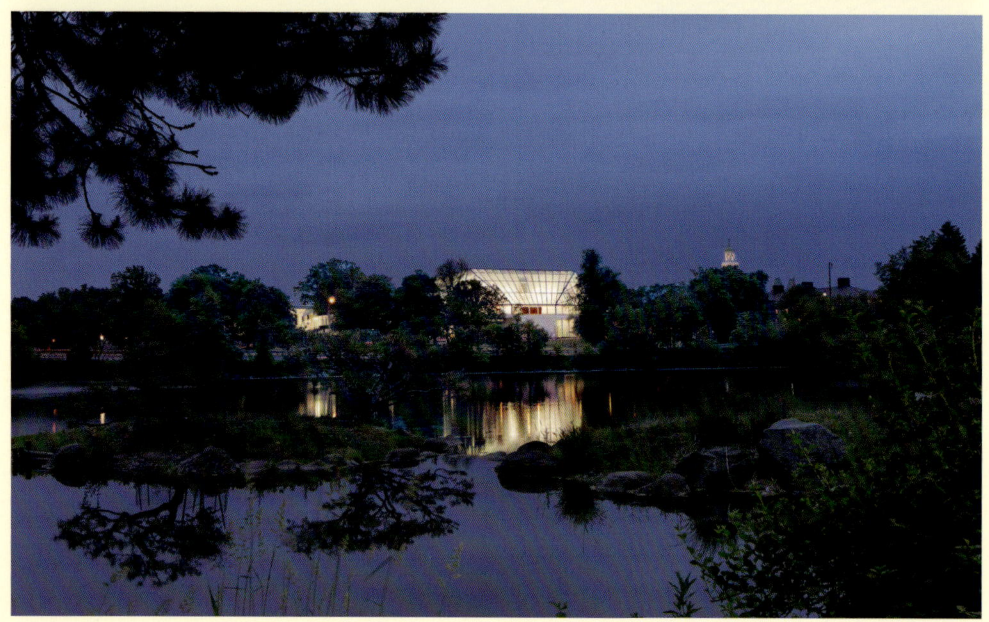

informed by principles and values that underlie the museum's Public Art Initiative: transparency, joyfulness, legibility, physical approachability and accessibility, relation to the surrounding cityscape and existing built environment, and relevance to the local community (left). In tandem, these qualities project upon both the Buffalo AKG and its Public Art Initiative a sense of welcome and ultimately, when activated by people, a proposition of radical commitment to community.

It is not easy to change people's opinions, thoughts, and feelings about each other or their institutions. Art has that transformative potential. For that potential to be released, human agency and ingenuity are required. As my fellow authors explain in this volume, it is not public artworks alone, those material artifacts, that change lives and uplift the human spirit; rather, minds are moved and collective moments of cultural magic happen through the public art process, in which artists, curators, and a multitude of communal voices become a chorus of co-creators. From the cacophony of the public sphere, synthesis is born. Change happens when we do things together, and doing things together is an area of curatorial expertise at which the Buffalo AKG's Public Art team—Curator of Public Art Aaron Ott and Public Art Project Coordinators Zack Boehler and Eric Jones—excels. In their work, fundamental principles of brilliant mission command come to life: Aaron, Zack, and Eric just need "what" and "why;" they have no fear of the "how." Therein lies the success of the Buffalo AKG Art Museum's Public Art Initiative, to date the only one of its kind in the United States.

1   For a history of the Louvre as the world's first public art museum, see Andrew McClellan, *Inventing the Louvre: Art, Politics, and the Origins of the Modern Museum in Eighteenth-Century Paris* (Cambridge: Cambridge University Press, 1994).

2   For essays on art museums and public trust, see James Cuno, ed., *Whose Muse?: Art Museums and the Public Trust* (Princeton, NJ: Princeton University Press, 2004).

3   "Museums and Trust 2021," American Alliance of Museums, https://www.aam-us.org/2021/09/30/museums-and-trust-2021/.

4   Today, a copy of Michelangelo's *David* is on view outside the Palazzo Vecchio, and the original is on permanent display at the Galleria dell'Accademia di Firenze.

5   Helsinki Art Museum website (www.hamhelsinki.fi), accessed February 2024.

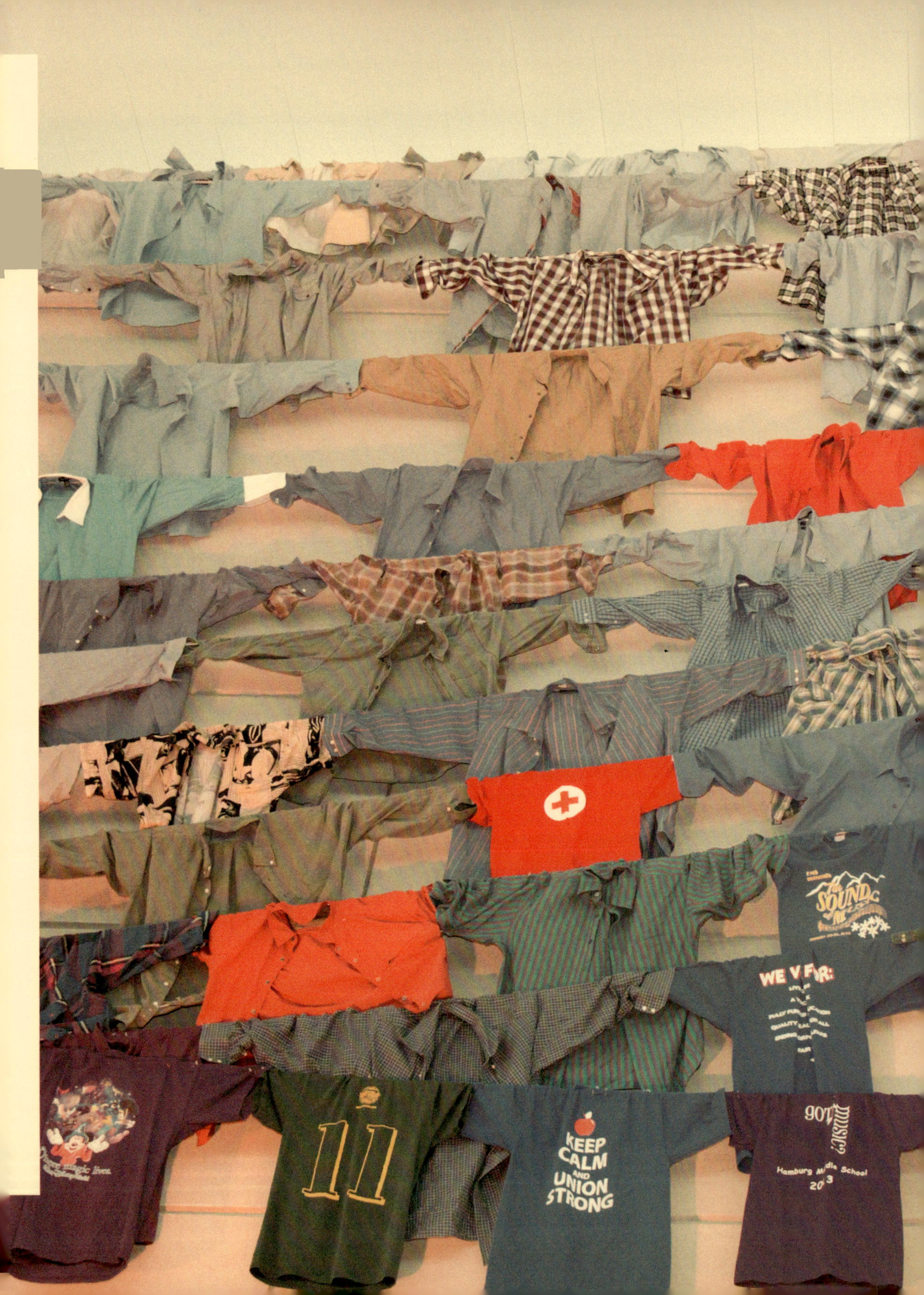

the SOUND
of the
WE V FAIR:
KEEP
CALM
AND
UNION
STRONG
Hamburg Media School
2013

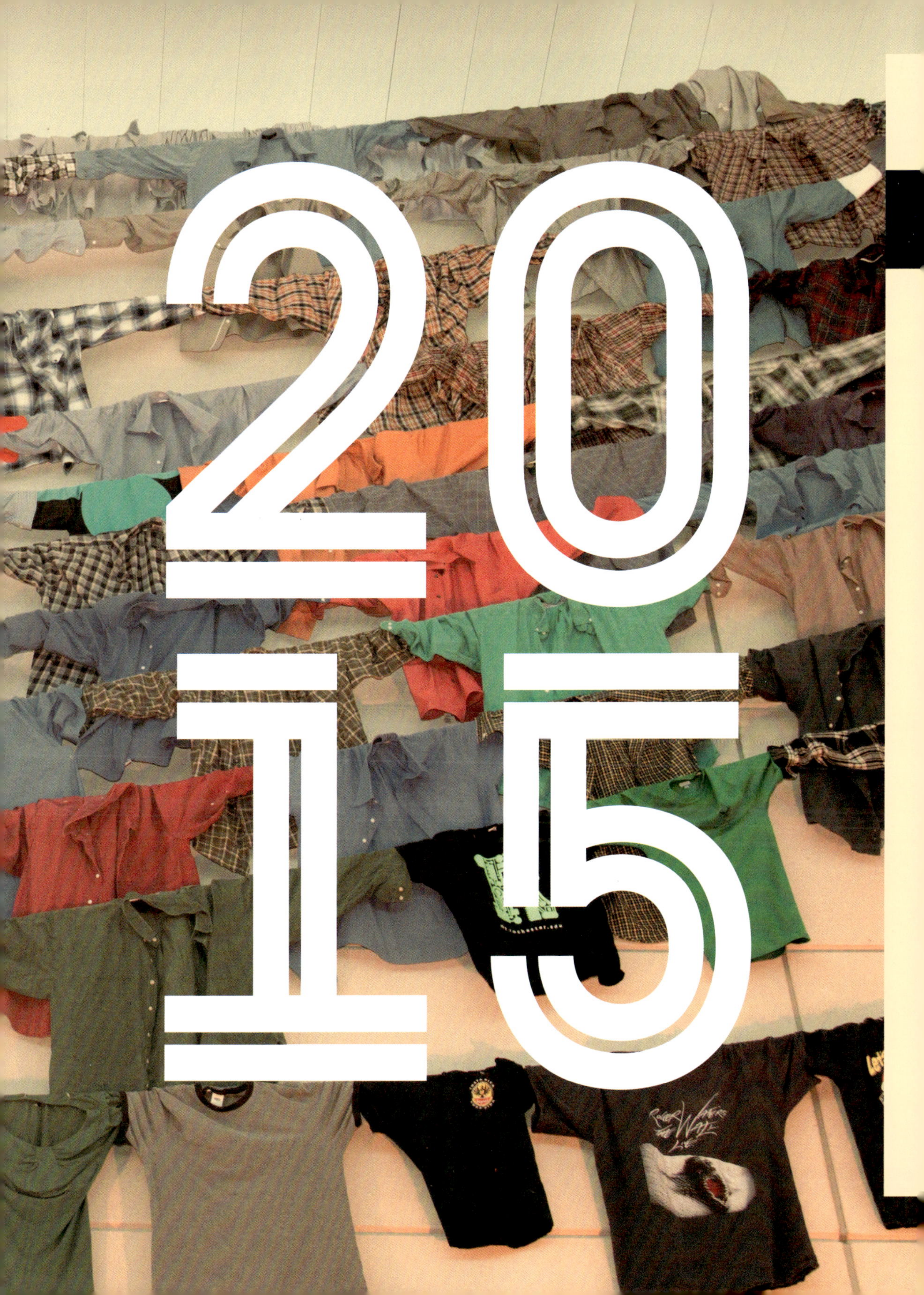
20
15

Silent Poets

Jaume Plensa

Canalside

Polyester resin, stainless
steel, and light element
Each overall: 26 feet 3 inches ×
5 feet ¼ inch × 4 feet
3 ⅝ inches (8 × 1.5 × 1.3 m)

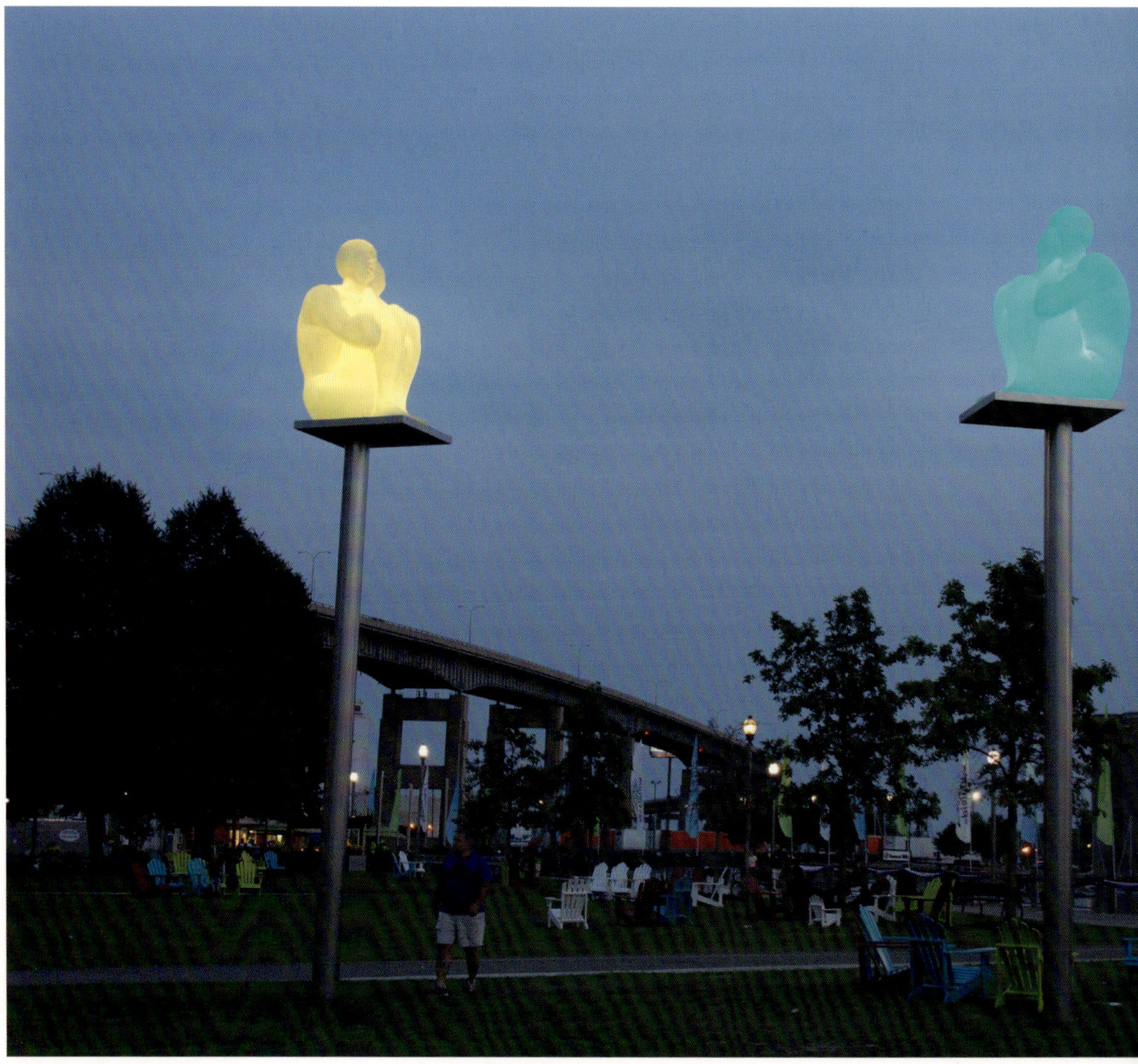

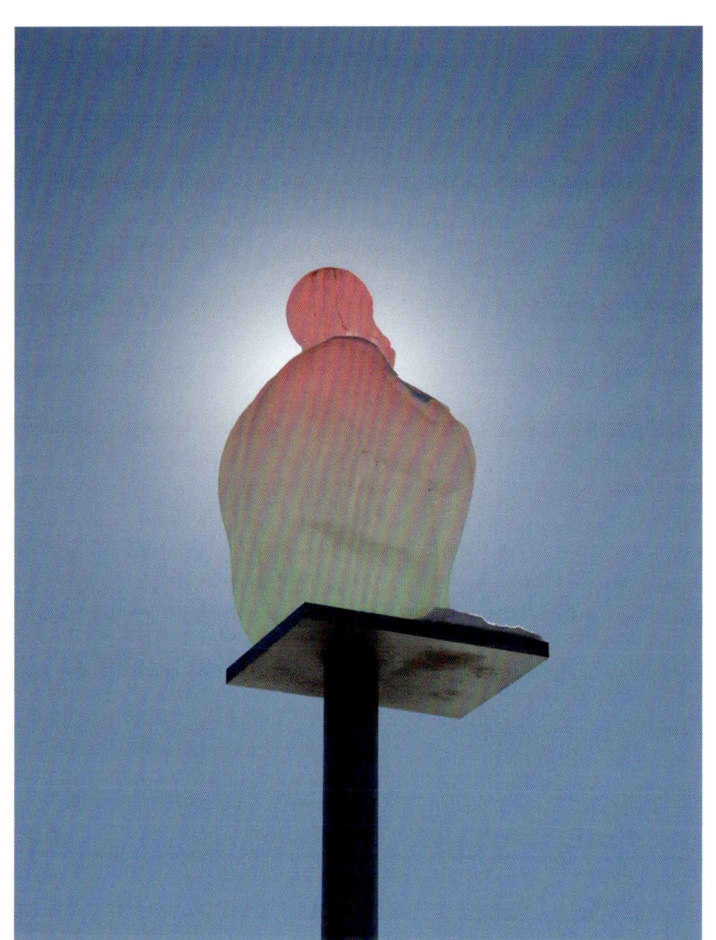

We Share a Dream

Kaarina Kaikkonen

Buffalo Niagara
International Airport

Donated apparel, rope,
and wire
Two elements, each overall:
17 feet 6 inches × 138 feet
(5.3 × 42.1 m)

In summer 2015, the people of Western New York donated more than one thousand shirts for Kaikkonen's monumental public work. Assisted by a team of local volunteers, Kaikkonen attached the shirts at the sleeves. The final work was installed above the ticketing area in the lobby of the Buffalo Niagara International Airport.

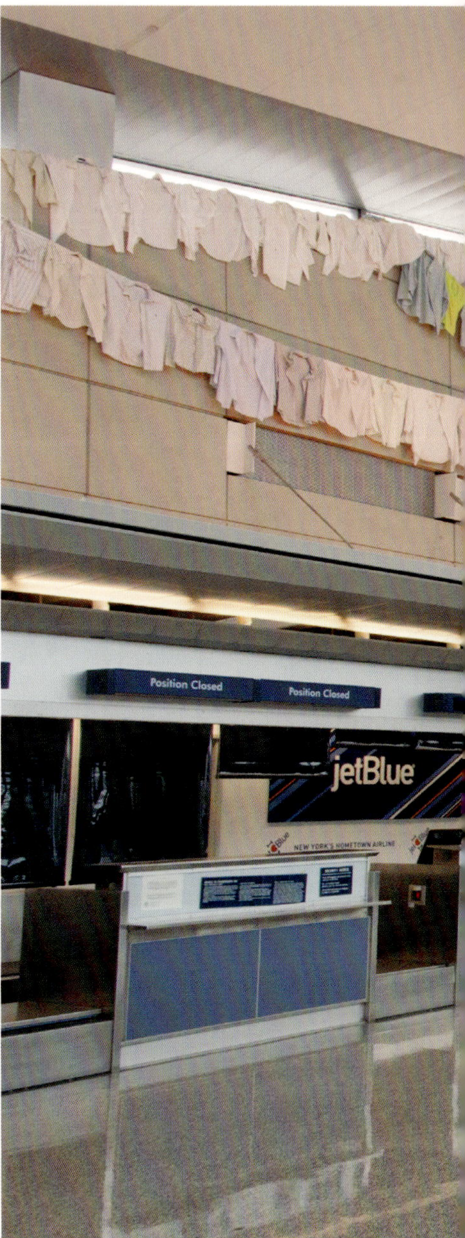

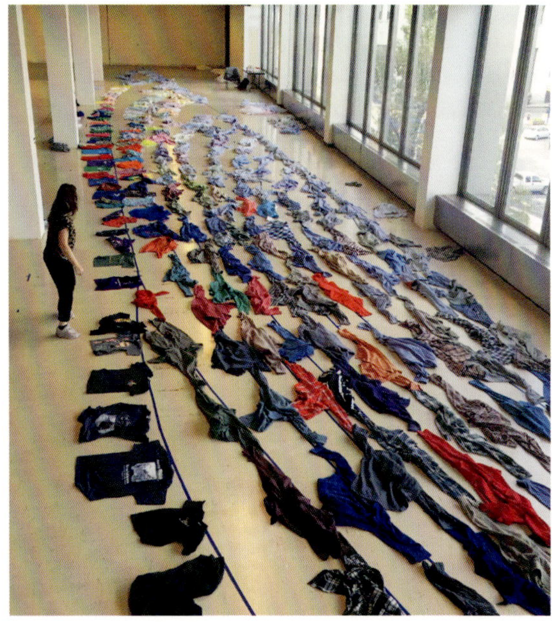

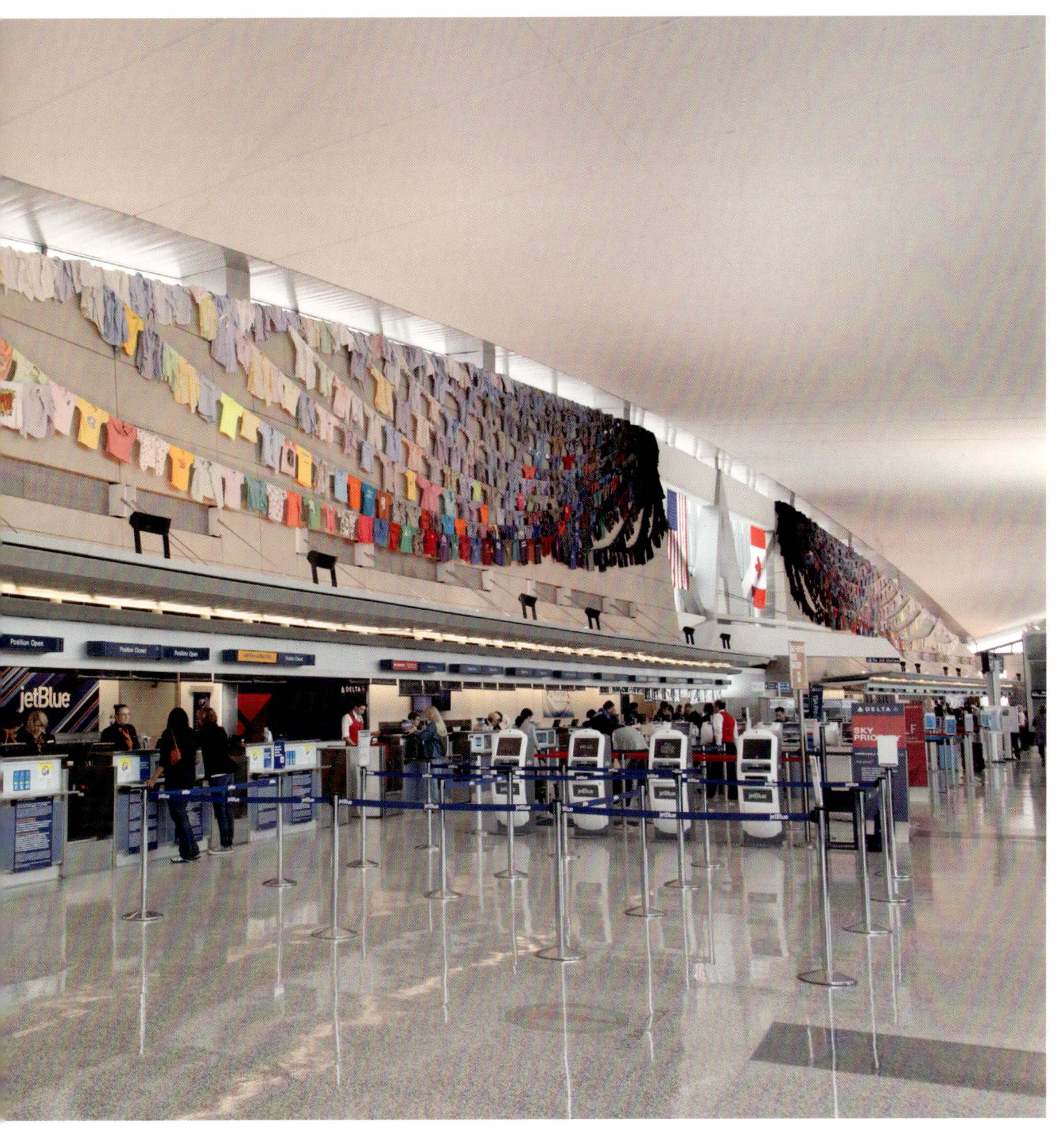

ReWilding New York (Community Seed Stations)

Jenny Kendler

Martin Luther King, Jr. Park, Buffalo

Broadway Market

Mattie's Restaurant

Matt Urban Hope Center

Urban Roots Community Garden Center

Orchard Park Public Library

Clarence Hollow Farmers Market

Explore & More Children's Museum (East Aurora)

Charles E. Burchfield Nature & Art Center

Ellicott Island Bark Park

Repurposed news boxes with vinyl flower wrap, seed packets, postcard mailer; planter and internal shelving made from reclaimed barn siding 36 × 19 × 16 inches (91.4 × 48.3 × 40.6 cm)

As part of an effort to revive our ecosystem with plant life indigenous to the region and provide food sources for monarch butterflies and other pollinators, packets of native wildflower seeds were distributed in Community Seed Stations, donated and repurposed newspaper boxes placed throughout the region, where the seeds were free to take.

Kendler also developed *Milkweed Dispersal Balloons* (right). With a specially designed mobile food cart, she and others passed out biodegradable balloons filled with the seeds of the milkweed plant, the sole source of food for monarch caterpillars. Visitors to the various food cart sites were encouraged to take the balloons home and pop them outside in their own neighborhoods.

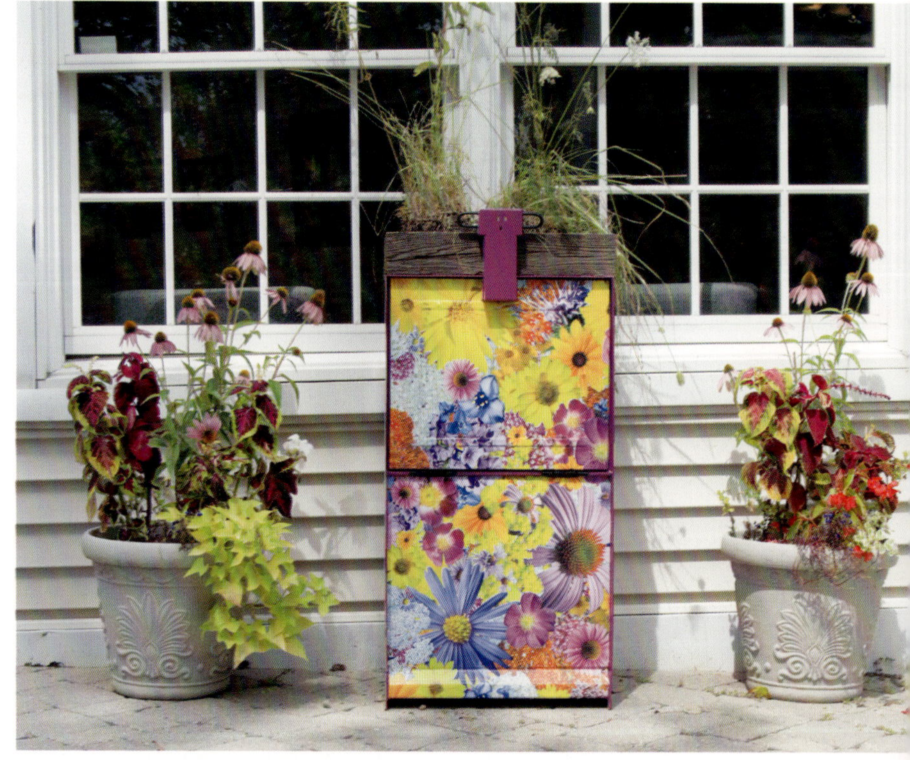

Milkweed Dispersal Balloons

Jenny Kendler

Elmwood-Bidwell
Farmers Market

Insectival at Tifft
Nature Preserve

Sunday in the Park
at Charles E. Burchfield
Nature & Art Center

Food Truck Tuesday
at Larkin Square

Garden Walk Buffalo

Food Truck Rodeo
at the Buffalo History
Museum

Performance involving
mobile food cart, bio-
degradable latex balloons,
milkweed seeds,
and orange hemp twine
Dimensions variable

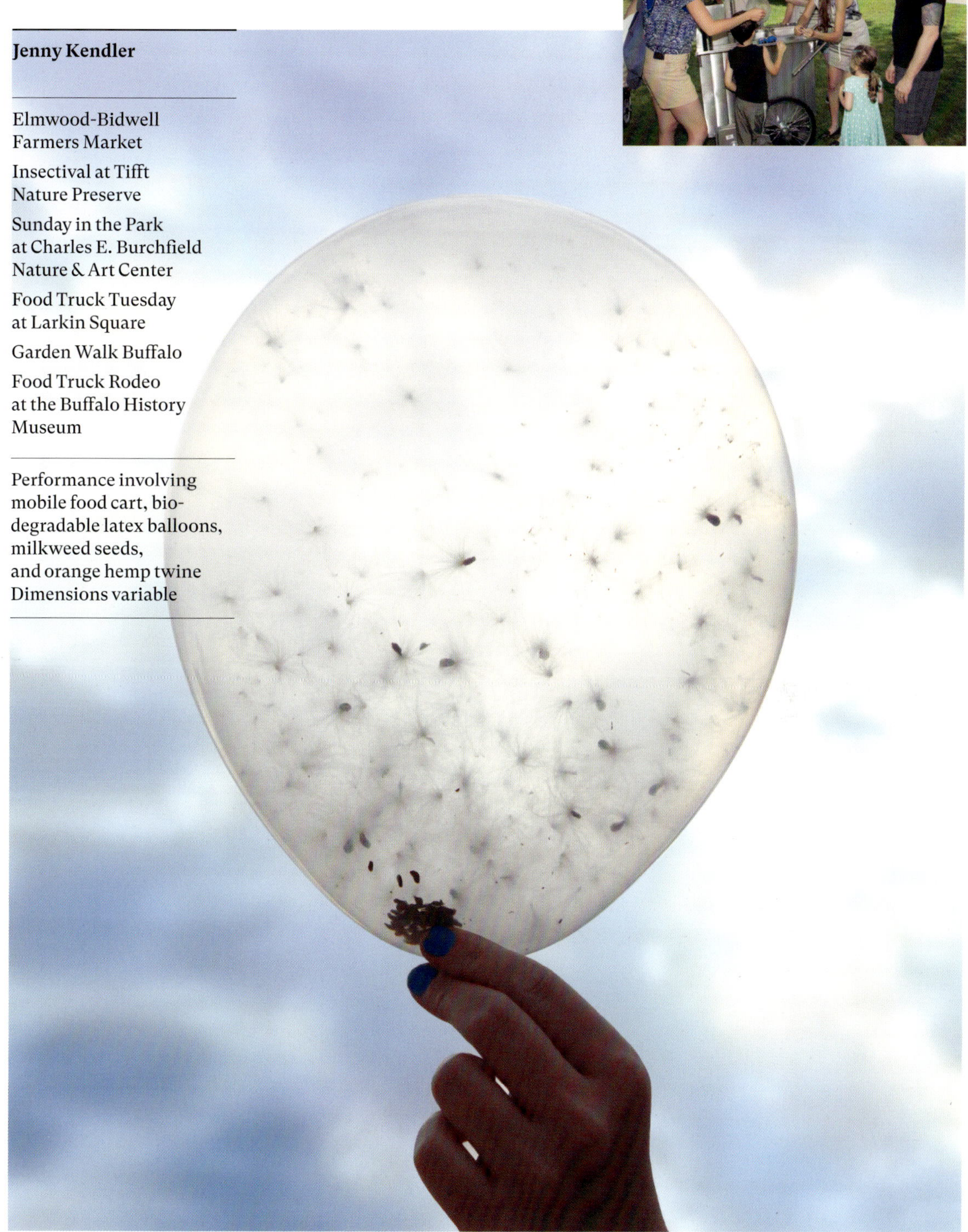

Shayne Dark:
Natural Conditions

Shayne Dark

Buffalo and Erie County
Botanical Gardens
May 22–October 4, 2015

Eighteen sculptures of
various materials
Dimensions variable

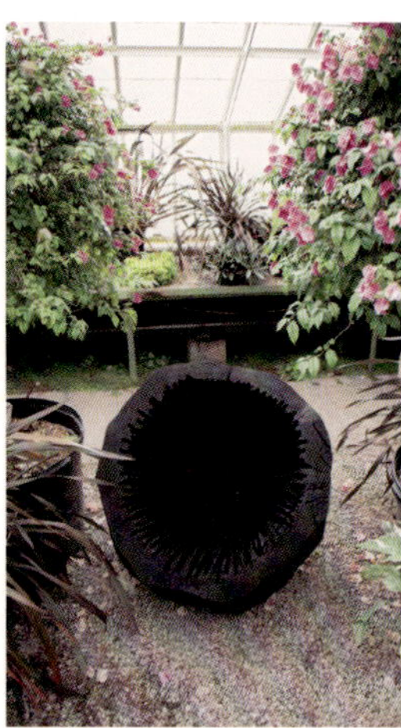

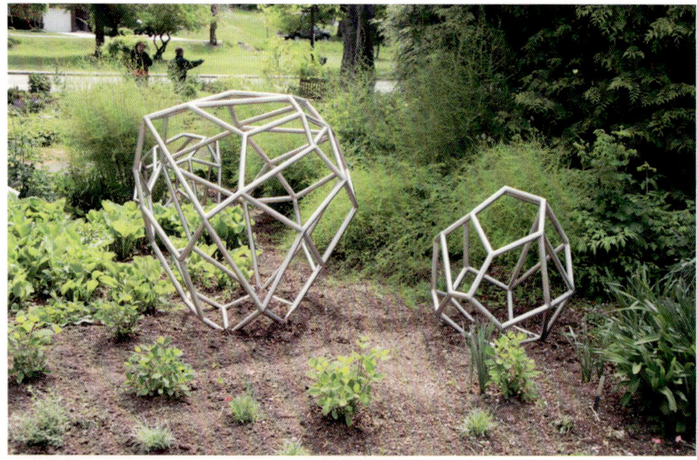

Installation
views of *Shayne
Dark: Natural
Conditions:*
↑ *Fracture Zone
#2–4*, 2015.
→ *Critical Mass 1*,
2015.
↗ *MacLachlan
Woodworking
Museum #3.*

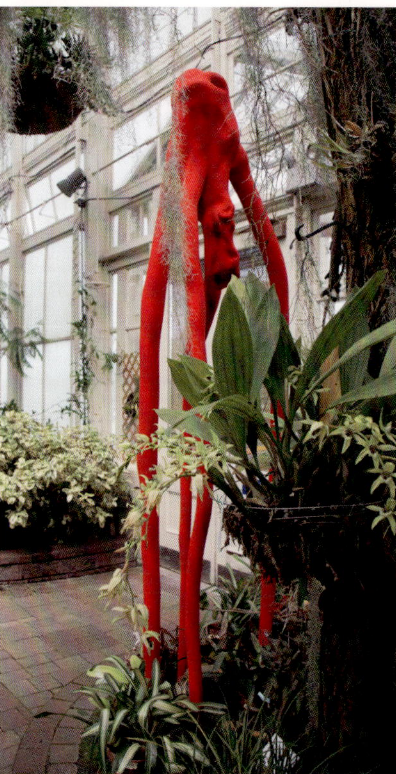

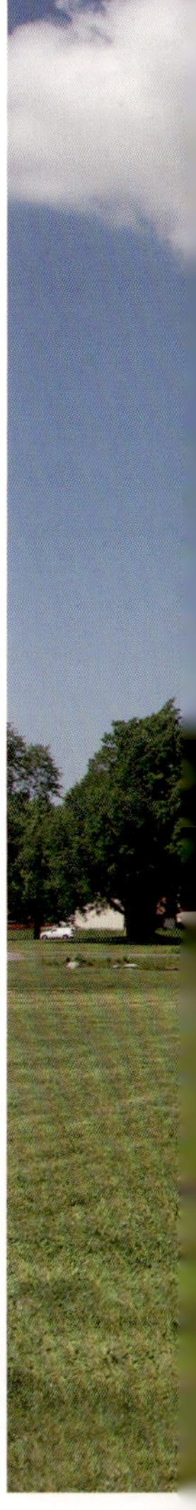

*Shayne Dark: Natural
Conditions* was an exhibition at the Buffalo and
Erie County Botanical
Gardens that integrated
Dark's work into a natural
setting, drawing aware-
ness to beauty and design
inherent in nature.
From September 14–19,
2015, Dark took up a
residency at the Gardens,
where he sourced local
organic material at the end
of its lifecycle to create
a site-specific installation.
This was also the original
site of Dark's *Tanglewood*
(right), now permanently
installed at Bassett Park.

Tanglewood

Shayne Dark

Bassett Park

Cedar and paint
Dimensions variable;
current installation 240 ×
120 × 120 inches (609.6 ×
304.8 × 304.8 cm)

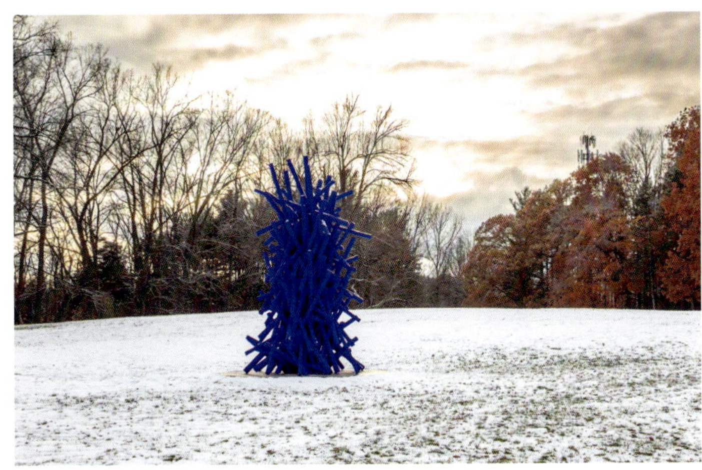

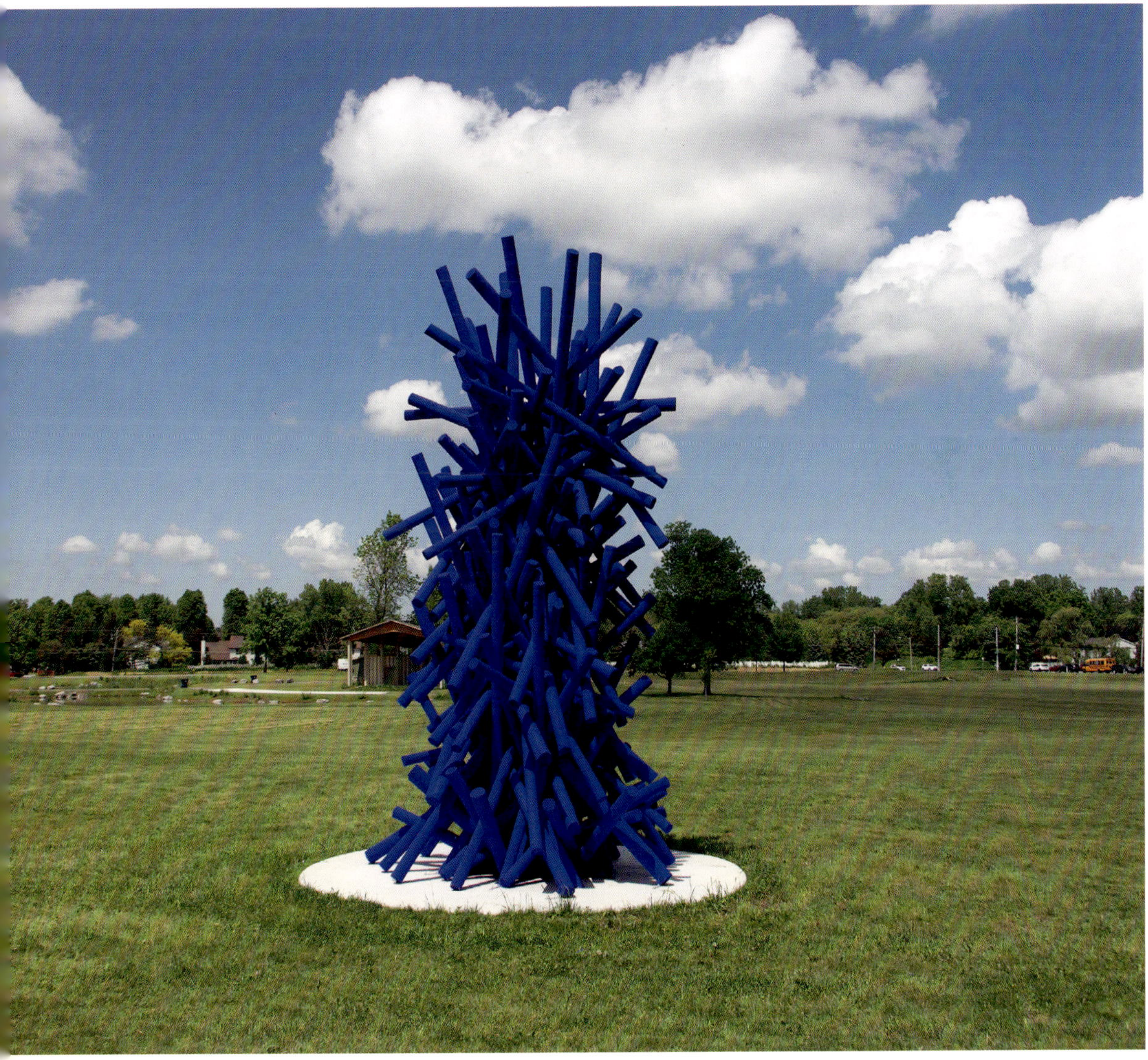

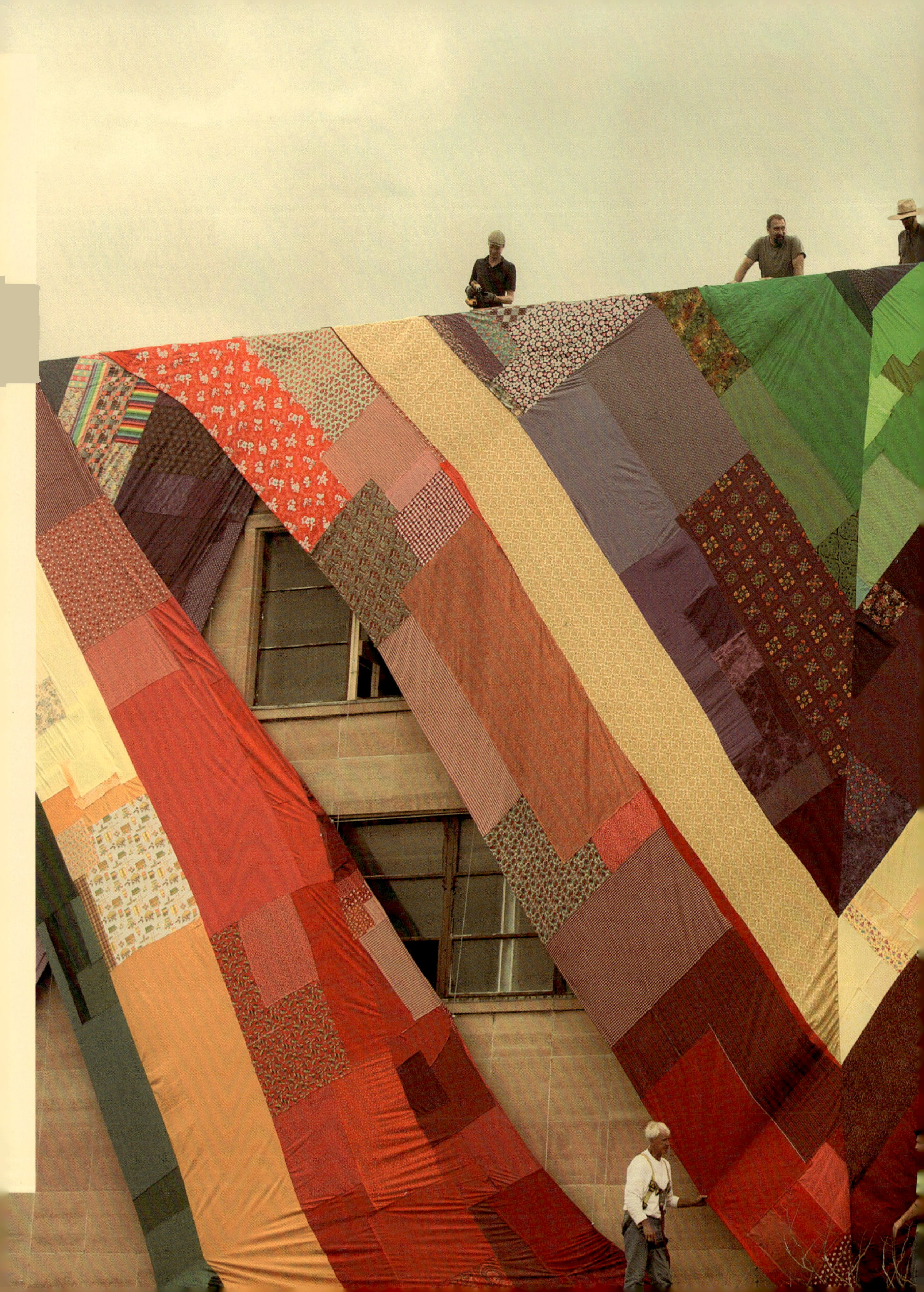

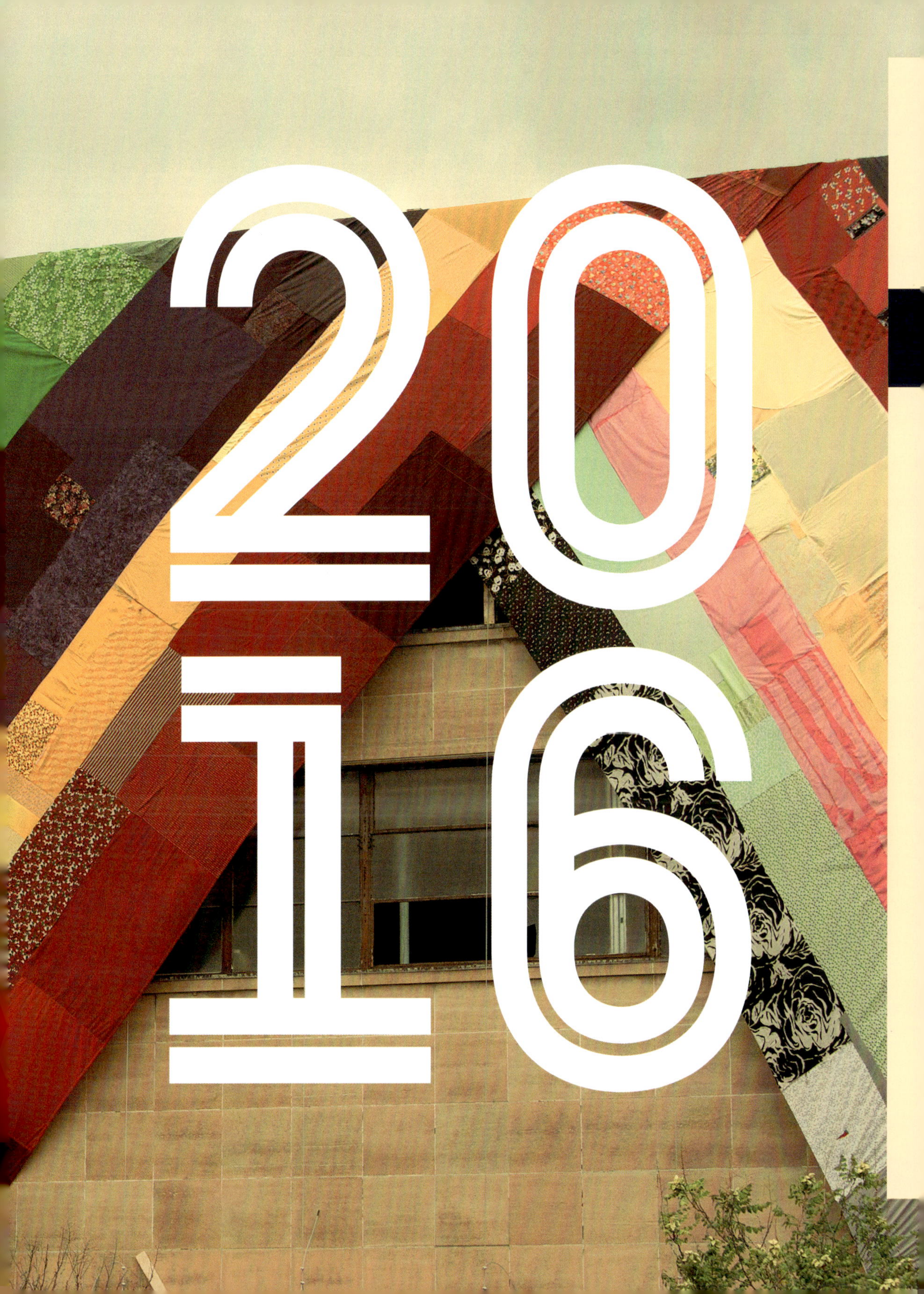
2016

Locus Amoenus

Roberley Bell

Tifft Nature Preserve

Chain link with powder
coating, welded and forged
polychrome steel urns,
weathered cast-plaster
birds with tree trunk,
and concrete animal forms
Dimensions variable

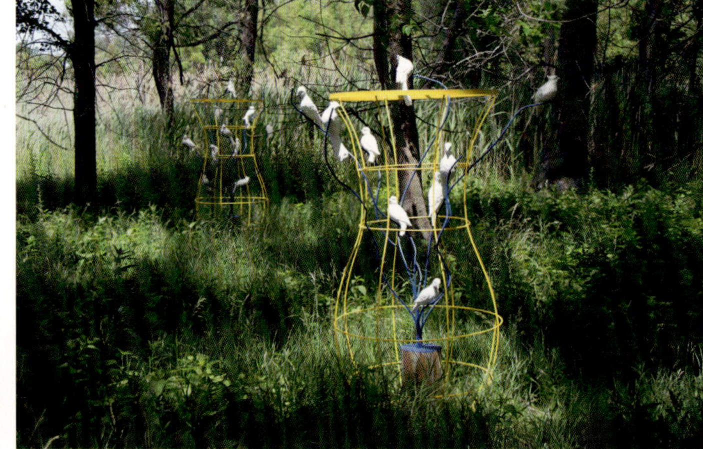

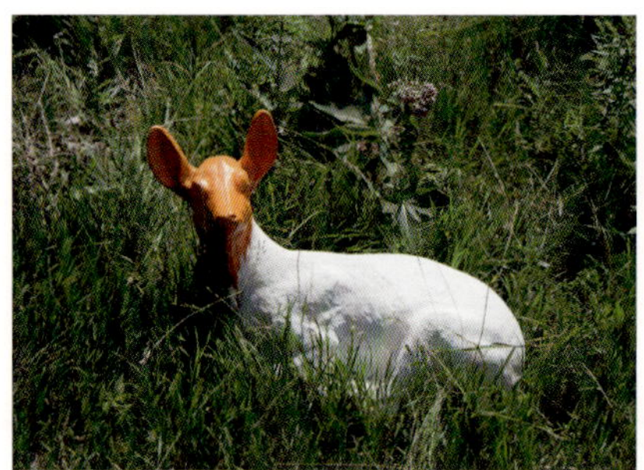

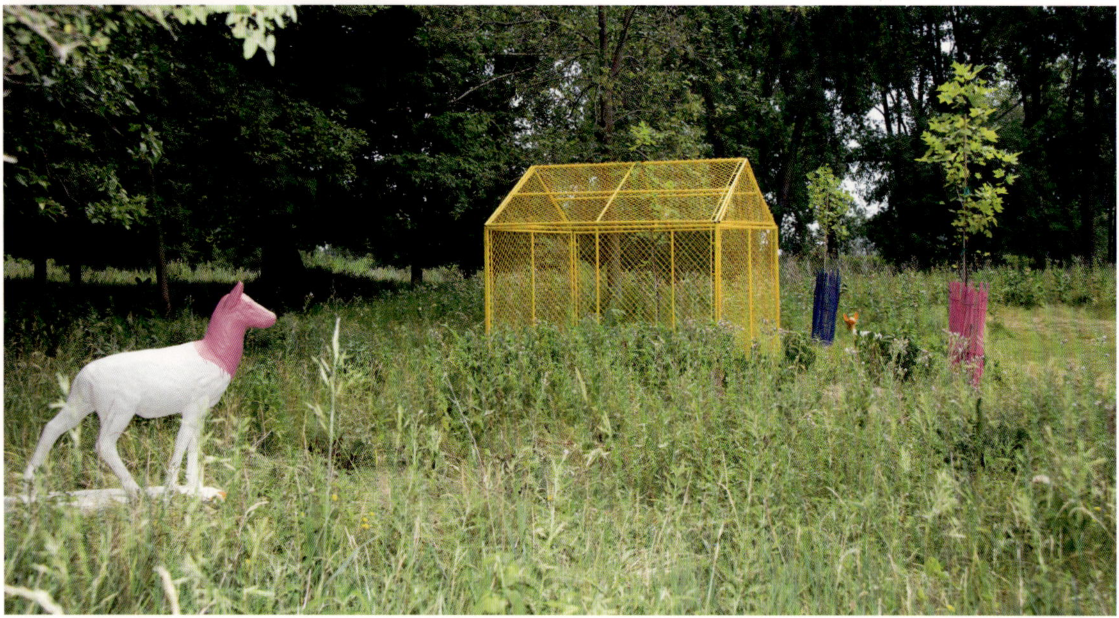

72 Jewett

Daniel Galas

Koch Metal Spinning,
72 Jewett Avenue, Buffalo

Acrylic paint
Approximately 28 × 200
feet (8.5 × 61 m)

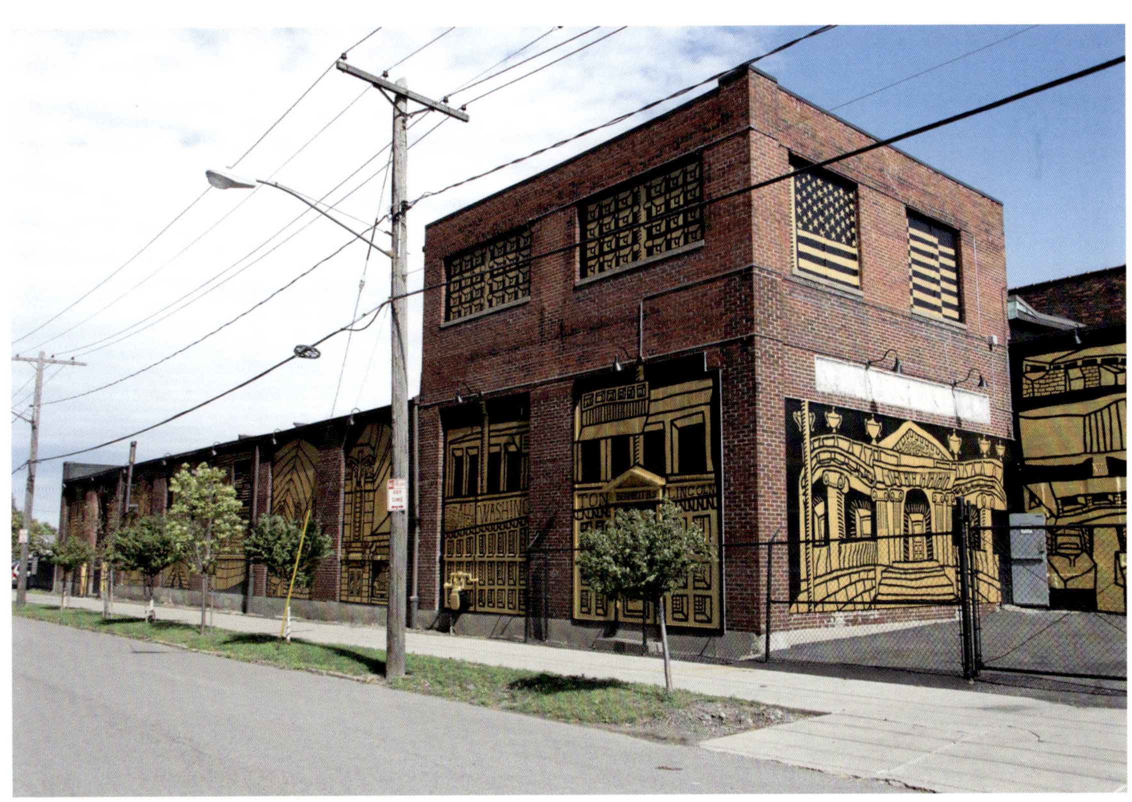

Dream Keepers

Alice Mizrachi

Buffalo Center for Arts
and Technology, 1221 Main
Street

Acrylic and spray paint
30 × 80 feet (9.1 × 24.4 m)

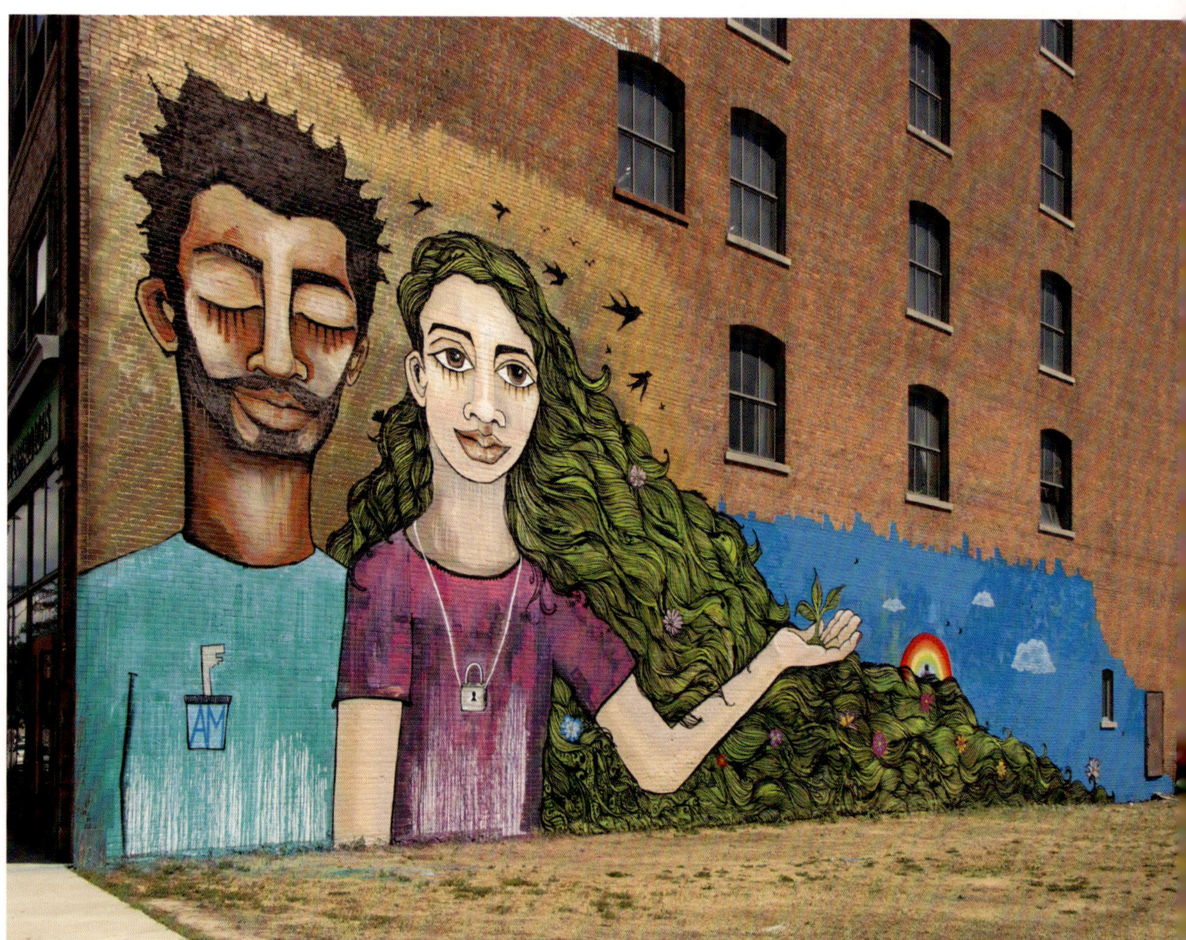

Noodle in the
Northern Lights

Jessie and Katey

45

Shea's 710 Theatre

Acrylic paint
Approximately 32 × 240 feet
(9.8 × 73.2 m)

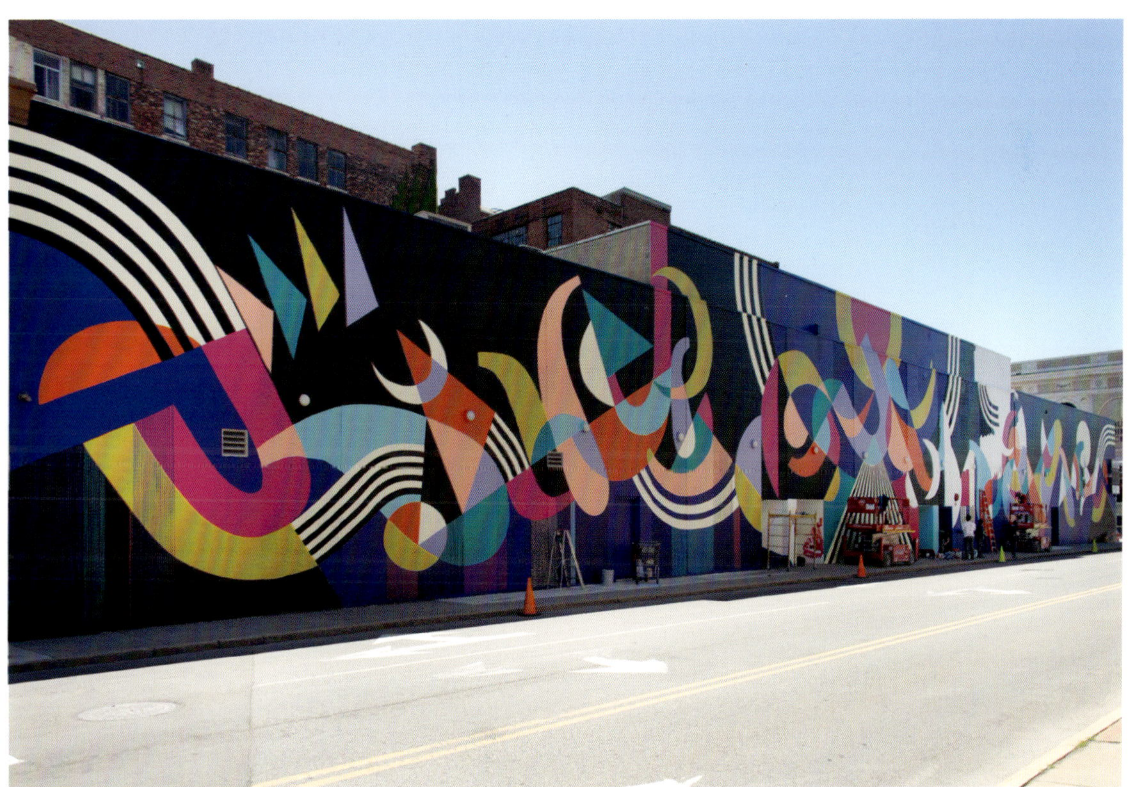

Spectral Locus

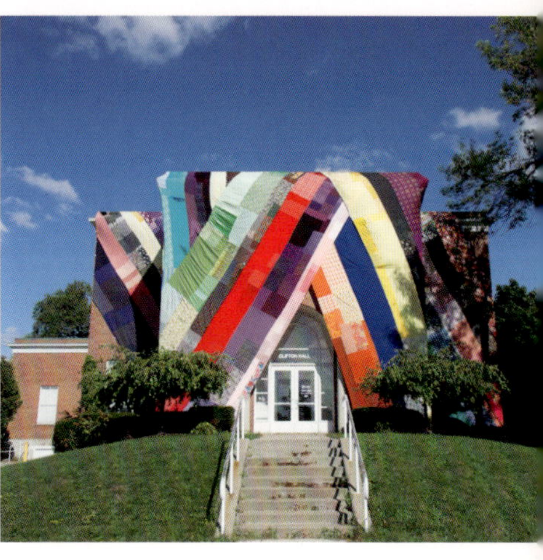

↑ Clifton Hall
→ Former Eckhardt Building
↘ Former Richmond Avenue Methodist Episcopal Church

Amanda Browder

Former Richmond Avenue Methodist Episcopal Church, 467 Richmond Avenue

Former Eckhardt Building, 950 Broadway Avenue

Clifton Hall, Buffalo AKG Art Museum, 1231 Elmwood Avenue

Donated fabric and steel cable
Dimensions variable

In spring and summer 2016, Browder asked for donations of non-stretch fabrics with bright colors and bold patterns. She then welcomed the Western New York community to join her for public sewing days to cut, craft, and sew together giant swaths of the donated fabrics. The results were draped over three buildings in Buffalo.

Spectral Locus was built in three phases: obtaining donations of fabric, organizing volunteers to sew, and installation. So at the outset my biggest concerns were: will the community provide donated fabric, will inspired volunteers show up and, finally, is there engineering expertise somewhere in the community? As the project took shape, all these concerns vanished as hundreds of people touched the project in some way.

These uncertainties of community engagement actually energize this work. Without knowing the eventual results, the art becomes less commercial. It's wholly based on collaboration and emerges from the community organically. In a sense, everyone is a participant observer: me, volunteers, institutional representatives, even the thousands of passersby. All immersed in the cultural moment of the city.

This piece was the start of a new chapter of my work as an artist. Notably, with the support of the Buffalo AKG Art Museum and a National Endowment for the Arts grant, we were able to scale the project to a larger size. This meant more buildings, more ways to interact with the community and to connect more people to the contemporary art world.

The fabric donations were more than I could have hoped for. Colorful and filled with local history, many came with touching stories of families donating their most precious textiles as a way to pay tribute to their family history. An elderly mother of one family had dementia but loved to find fabric and had made some hand-stitched pieces that were in the donation pile. In the turret of the church, I placed her 30-foot-long hand-stitched vine with hopes that the family would bring her to see her design. I was inspired by imagining her creativity nurtured by a life of interacting with fabric.

I learned that the Buffalo volunteers are unique, caring, and curious people. People of all abilities, ages, and backgrounds from the community showed up to the sewing days. Volunteers often shared detailed life stories, revealing a city with a personality that was both historic and evolving. *Spectral Locus* was a project that offered an opportunity for the stories and the personal histories to be woven into the textures, patterns, and colors of the pieces.

The work was designed for three buildings: the former Richmond Avenue Methodist Episcopal Church, the former Eckhardt Building, and Clifton Hall at the museum. The buildings were located in different neighborhoods, thus extending the work across a broad urban landscape. The installations of the completed pieces were complex, and each building posed its own issues. What made it happen was two brothers with two cranes. The brothers were legendary fifth-generation pipefitters, and with their help and humor, all three locations went up smoothly.

When we finished installing the piece, we had parties celebrating our collaborative accomplishment. Although the *Spectral Locus* pieces were only up for two weeks, they are not forgotten. *Spectral Locus*, like a medieval tapestry, will never be cut up or repurposed. In addition, it will live on in thousands of memories and serve to remind us that the materials of a material world are always challenging us to create anew.

—AMANDA BROWDER

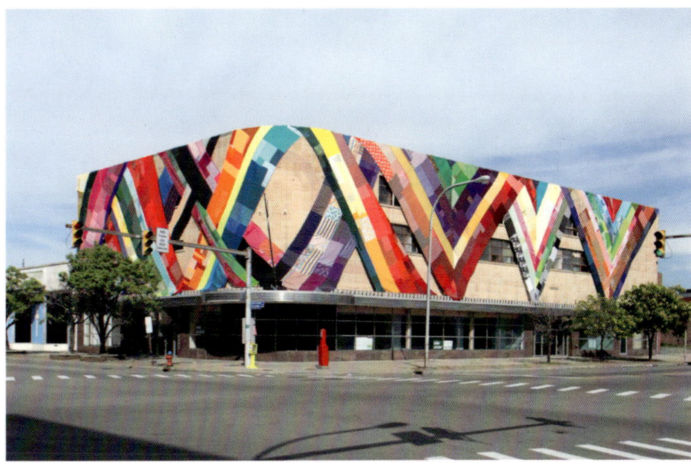

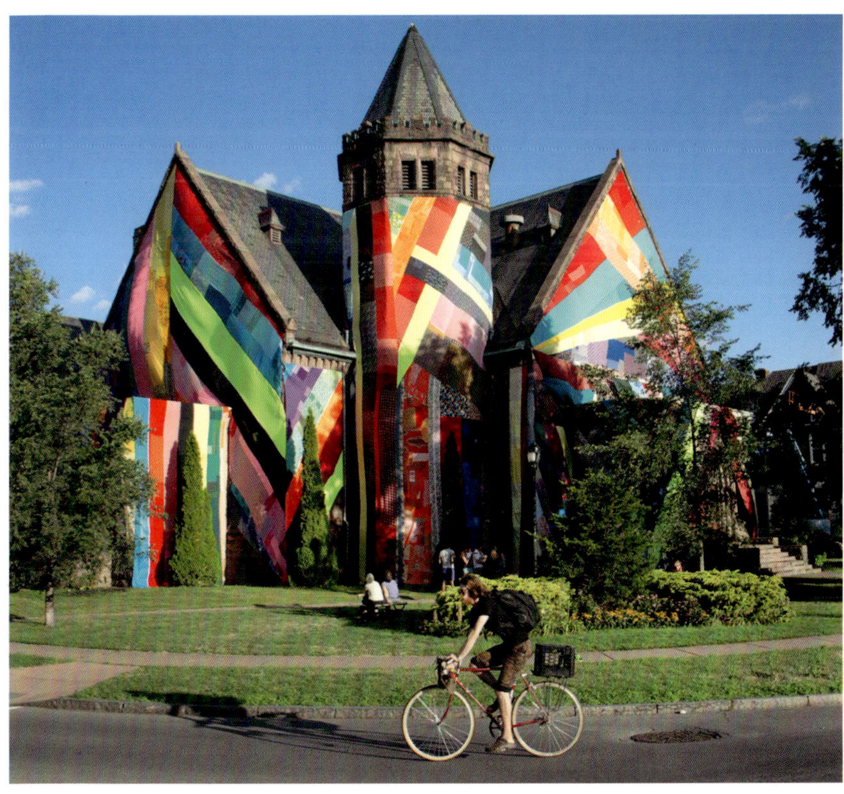

Collective Ambition: Launching the AKG Public Art Initiative

AARON OTT
Curator of Public Art

When I was asked to join the Buffalo AKG Art Museum (then the Albright-Knox Art Gallery) in 2014 as their inaugural Curator of Public Art, I defined my curatorial philosophy as one rooted in generosity. I was confident in constructing something foundationally built on collaboration, community, and dialogue. I knew at the time that the Public Art Initiative at the AKG would be unique, that no other North American museum had yet dedicated its institutional expertise to public art on such a broad civic scale.

I still did not realize how much of our work would be novel. I definitely did not plan on how many of my initial meetings and conversations would feel like faith-based experiences; my common refrain in the early days was "trust me"—not always the most reassuring statement from an out-of-towner. Now, as we reflect on the work we've accomplished over the last ten years, I am thoroughly humbled and honored to have created something that has wildly exceeded our collective ambition.

The Buffalo AKG is the only museum that sustainably bridges public/private gaps with the placement of public art, using our rich history as the longest operating modern and contemporary art museum in America. We work cooperatively with partners at the county and city levels, broadly connecting with our community audiences in the Western New York region. The results over the past ten years have been wide-ranging, including sixty installations, interventions, collaborations, and commissions with more than eighty artists. These dynamic installations are now among the most recognizable elements of our shared landscape.

Not One Kind of Thing

As producers and commissioners of public works, there are a lot more variables beyond our control than there would be inside a museum. But what we yield in control over those variables, we gain in public discussion. For our own initiative, this is illustrated most evidently with *Shark Girl* by Casey Riordan (below left and page 16), notably, and perhaps especially because the work was among the very first we placed. *Shark Girl* was—much to my relief—overwhelmingly loved, but, in the beginning, there were vocal detractors who thought the whimsy of the work did not rise to the seriousness of museum engagement.

For the uninitiated, *Shark Girl* is exactly what she sounds like, the fantastical and ridiculous combination of a great white shark head atop a little girl's frame. Picture Jaws meets Alice in Wonderland. Part of *Shark Girl*'s inherent charm rests in the unexpected juxtaposition of symbols of innocence and terror.

I had no idea at the time that the creation of a Buffalo icon was upon us. An artwork that deals in awkwardness, loneliness, and existentialism, even when it is also hilarious, is not the most logical candidate for a beloved public work. The

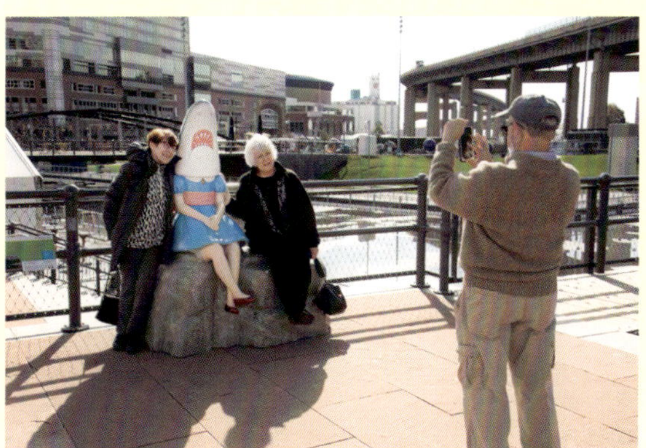

Casey Riordan's *Shark Girl* began "working" almost as soon as it was installed.

public's take on the work was immediate and, if you'll indulge me, profound. Even detractors were at least still generous in their assessment—sometimes. One local said, "I don't like *Shark Girl*, but I love what she's done," meaning that what the work did was encourage a dialogue in public space about the value of place.

This singular installation represents a primary element of our success—when the museum is the producer, this has a unique influence on civic dialogue and to the success of a work that might not otherwise have found such gravity or attention. The inherent authority of the museum carries into public space and adds an organic underlying meaning-making to those spaces as a result.

In the early stages of our installations, we had no context *other* than our museum to lean on. I'll admit that was a bit frightening. How would we provide something to our public that was not one note, not one kind of thing? How could we remain in dialogue as we produced projects? If *Shark Girl* was a convenient accident with the best possible reaction, we would still need to be purposeful with our messaging, our content, and our conversations moving forward. From the beginning, I was certain that we would find an anchor in Matthew Hoffman's *You Are Beautiful*.

What Is Beautiful?

You Are Beautiful, or *YAB* for short (above right and page 14), started out as a street art project in Chicago with a handful of stickers—black text on a silver ground saying simply "You Are Beautiful." For me, Hoffman's sentiment represented the core of how I wanted to curate and how I wanted to be in dialogue with our public—it encapsulated the generosity I sought. *You Are Beautiful* is a remarkably flexible statement, one that can be interpreted as personal or shared, inward or outward, capturing a single moment or encompassing everything around you. The fluidity and plasticity of Hoffman's work appealed to me from the get-go, and I worked hard, and maybe even a little maniacally to get the project off the ground.

We had many false starts. I tried to produce a several-hundred-foot-wide *YAB* sign on a building that was in bankruptcy. Later, I tried to develop

a smaller (still several-hundred-foot) sign that would grow vines and flowers throughout the structure, only to find out that the location was a former landfill that had regulations on what could be planted (very little) and what could be anchored (even less). The number of iterations we explored and the patience the artist granted me still boggle my mind.

In hindsight, billboards seem obvious. They kept the basic structure of the work—printed black text on a silver background—and gave us the flexibility to place it throughout the entire county and even into adjacent ones. It was still gigantic and bold and legible and would result in exactly the kind of dialogue we were after.

For us, the message *was* the art, and any alteration would degrade it, so we set about placing the work unaltered and unannounced. We wanted the work to be found, and in discovery we wanted the natural curiosity of its placement to stimulate engagement. I have faith, which has only grown since, that the mere existence of artwork in public is rewarding enough that connection is the natural outcome—and further, that when the connection is later found to be a museum, it is all the more valuable.

And yet, it was more rewarding than I could have imagined. We placed forty-four billboards throughout Erie and Niagara counties, and we also distributed, for free, more than 150,000 *You Are Beautiful* stickers. People did the research, made the connection, and they shared their experiences with us.

In the early days of the installation, we would regularly hear from our public, in exchanges that went something like this: "What does that sign mean?" After all it is essentially contextless—it refers to no product or place, no institution or affiliation, and is expansive and associational. We would turn the question back to our audience: "What does it mean to *you*?" The delightful truth is that it doesn't matter how they responded. That's the whole point. An impromptu discussion about what beauty means for someone in a given moment is profound, and we remain thrilled that so many people engaged in those discussions, most of which we will never hear, never directly participate in, but which remain immeasurably valuable, nonetheless.

The first year of our initiative would host two more participatory projects: Tape Art's *Buffalo Caverns* installation at our downtown public library (page 21) and Charles Clough's *Hamburg Arena Painting*, which would later be installed in a library in Hamburg, a town in Erie County south of Buffalo (page 20). These projects would serve similar purposes that were different from the

previous two: getting the community involved in the direct production of the work. Providing spaces where anyone and everyone is authorized to act as a cultural producer is, to my mind, deeply important, arguably even necessary for the maintenance of a robust cultural-civic environment. The Tape Art installation coincided with the placement of *YAB* billboards and the installation of *Shark Girl*, and the works all played off each other: participatory, sculptural, interactive, dialogic.

Tape Art is exactly what it sounds like. This Providence, Rhode Island, troupe led by Michael Townsend produces mural-style installations made entirely of painter's tape. Their work is meant to be impermanent, which often means it is removed immediately upon completion—evocative of but decidedly less precious than the Buddhist tradition of creating and then destroying sand mandalas. The approachable nature of the material—everyday painter's tape—and, in our case, the fact that a significant portion of the mural was produced at ground level on the Central Library's marble facade—made the work interactive for people of any skill level (below). With Tape Art, the barriers to participation are as close to zero as possible, and because the stakes are so seemingly low, a lot of people joined in. There

<hr>

↖ Matthew Hoffman's *You Are Beautiful* was made into stickers as well as billboards to proliferate his message.

→ Kristen Carbone, then the Executive Director of Tape Art and formerly a curatorial assistant at the AKG, at work.

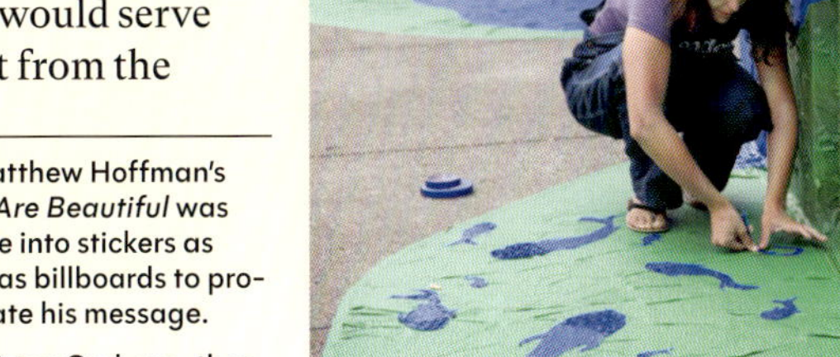

is brilliance in this modality; by proving that it's no big deal to participate, the action and therefore the outcome becomes very important to people.

The impermanence of *Buffalo Caverns* also served a specific purpose for our burgeoning initiative. I knew that the work would not last long. In fact, I argued with Townsend to let us keep the work up after completion for longer than they had ever allowed: a whole eight days. What happened was what I *hoped* would happen. If someone walked by and disliked the work (we learned quickly that there are always a few), we were able to assure them that in short order the work would disappear and engage them in dialogue about what they would like to see instead. For those who loved the work and were inevitably sad to see it go, we explained its temporary nature but likewise asked more questions about what they might like to see next, or with more permanence. Both data sets were extremely informative in our early days and would influence the way we worked moving forward.

I can honestly say that in the earliest years of our initiative I didn't spend much time absorbing the *effects* of our work. I was much more interested in listening to collective desire where I could find it and responding in ways that I thought a museum could: by adding depth and dialogue, then by letting the public take over. The works that we produced in our second year were not groundbreaking in and of themselves. We worked in an airport, we worked with county cultural partners at our botanical gardens, we roamed the city and county with more participatory works. You don't need a museum to do this kind of work, but what I've come to realize over time is that museum involvement tends to demand discernment and contemplation and add layers of complexity and interest. When that richness is mixed with sustainability and long-term commitment, these kinds of engagements start to matter beyond themselves, becoming part of a tapestry of cultural importance and meaning-making that only museums can support.

Buffalo is a city that, in terms of population and size, sits between St. Louis, Missouri, and Toledo, Ohio. Put differently, the only city in America *smaller* than Buffalo with an NFL team is Green Bay, Wisconsin. The scale of a museum's reach is not limited to its local audiences, but where public art is concerned, especially on a practical level, scope and impact will be measured by how people engage with the work, and in communities like ours, a museum makes that direct engagement all the more impactful.

Absurd Mathematicians

Most of the works we produce are commissioned, meaning we work with artists to produce new art for our audiences. This is a challenge for everyone involved. For artists, whether they are local or not, challenges begin straight away: with numerous desires from the public, budgetary restraints, and from all of the conceptual and practical limitations that abound at installation sites. At the AKG, we pride ourselves on being an artist-centered organization. This means that we take it upon ourselves to support our artists through these challenges.

Good people doing good work can accomplish great things. In 2015, I was lucky to hire Eric Jones as our first Project Coordinator. Eric had worked previously in art centers and understood what I was after, bringing a nuanced mix of educational acumen and community-mindedness to our initiative. Little did I know how much I needed his assistance.

On Eric's second day on the job, he jumped into a Bobcat when no one from Shayne Dark's studio—and certainly not I—could figure out how

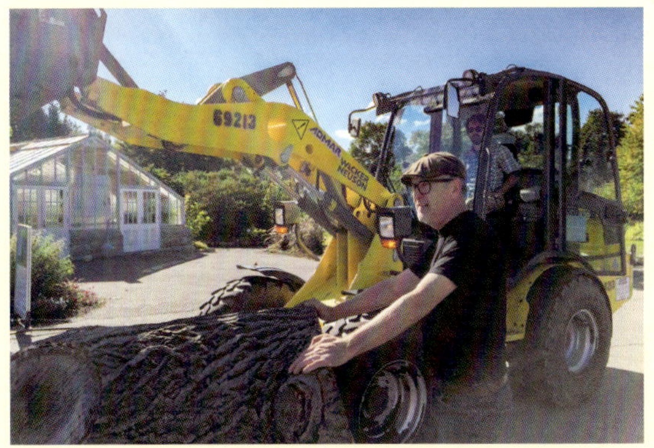

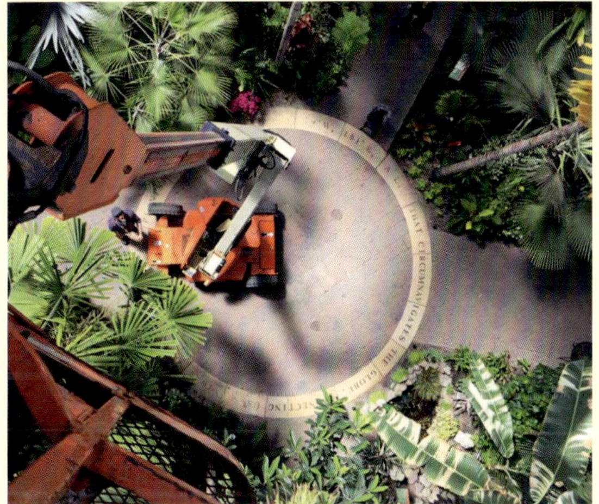

to operate the machine during our installation of *Natural Conditions* at the Buffalo and Erie County Botanical Gardens (above left and page 38). I can't imagine trying to get Dark's heavier-than-expected works of painted ironwood through these sensitive environments without Eric. I certainly wouldn't have slept well at night if he hadn't been there to confirm how to safely hang Dark's *Windfall*, consisting of twenty-nine applewood stumps, from the Garden's rotunda (middle left).

For another project shortly thereafter, Eric would solve absurd mathematical problems regarding the gravitational pull of a 180-foot parabolic wire carrying an unknown amount of weight along the curved wall above the ticket kiosks at the Buffalo Niagara International Airport. He did all of this knowing that we'd have to first manage the collection of donated clothing solicited by the artist that would form the body of Kaarina Kaikkonen's *We Share a Dream* (page 34), attach and engineer the work entirely offsite, and then install it during evening hours at the airport, from 10 pm to 4 am, over the course of only three nights (below left).

My gratitude for this kind of work is eternal, and it is indicative of the kind of work *required* for public art. Real world conditions are *never*

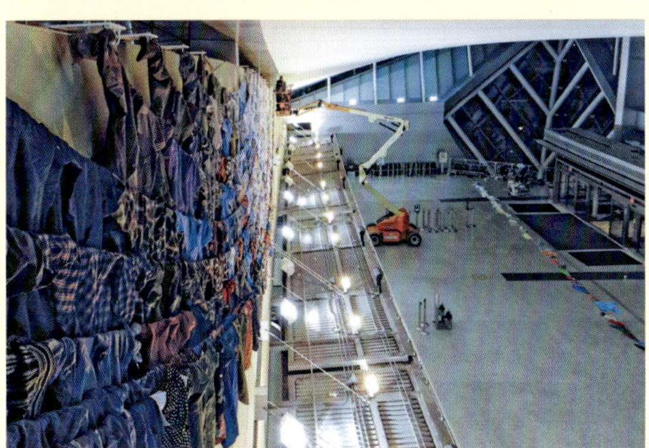

ꜛꜛ Shayne Dark's impressive work required heavy machinery to install—and the confidence to use it.

ꜛ Eric Jones pilots a Bobcat with one of Dark's tree stumps.

← Another engineering feat: hanging the 180-foot wire that supported Kaarina Kaikkonen's work in the Buffalo Niagara International Airport.

museum conditions. We encounter a built environment that is often not what we expected. In outdoor conditions, weather delays are sometimes welcome reprieves from punishing installations, but more often than not such delays are anxiety-inducing, with looming delivery deadlines, artist travel schedules, and public unveilings.

Mercifully, from Joy

An unexpected outcome of our work is that we've also learned how to manage making people cry—mercifully—from joy. This first happened in 2016 with Amanda Browder's multi-site installation *Spectral Locus* (page 46). After months of once again collecting donations from the public to source our materials and after months of community sewing programs led by the artist herself, we finally set about installing her building-sized works. After figuring out the logistical complications of hanging an installation on a building without actually touching the facade at her first site, we moved to our second of three locations. The church on Buffalo's West Side at Richmond and Ferry Street presented wholly different challenges than our first. Here we *could* attach to the building but only at mortar joints, not into the historically protected sandstone nor the fragile roof. When we finished, Browder walked through an intersection for a view of the whole installation and began crying (above). This startled me, and I asked if she was okay. She simply responded in astonishment, "It's standing!"

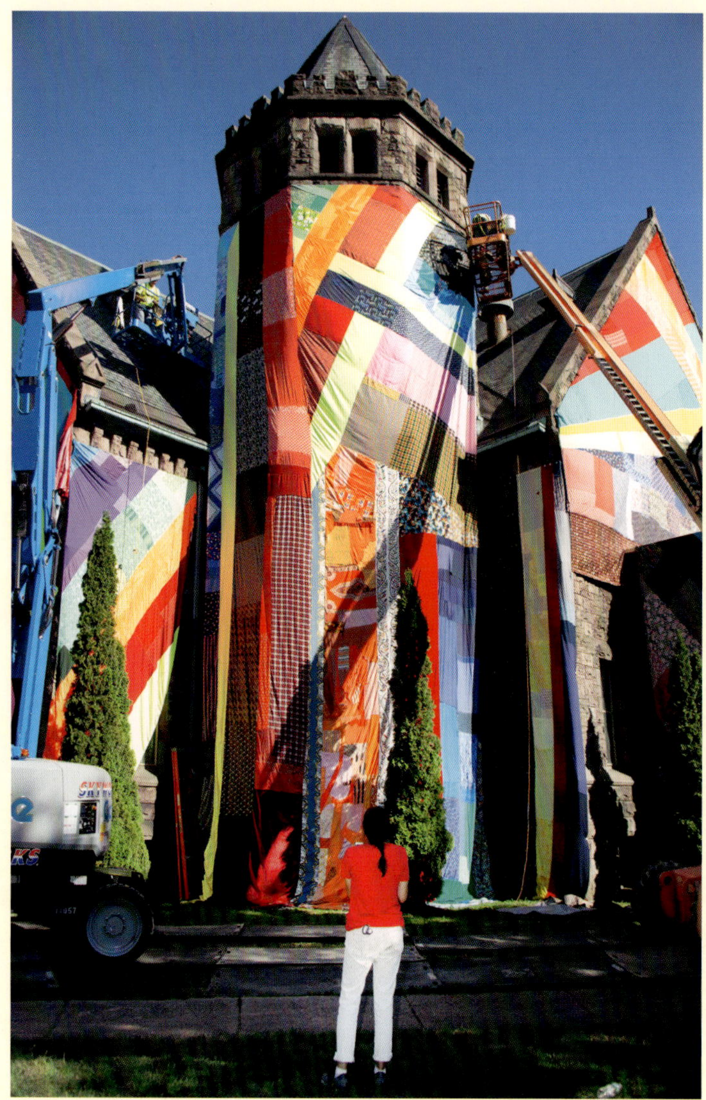

↑ A moment of joy as Amanda Browder's installed work exceeds her expectations.

→ Artist Shasti O'Leary Soudant taking a brief rest as her work is installed overnight at an NFTA station.

Unlike most other projects for the artist, the restrictions on how we could use the building made her beholden to the physical and formal design of the church. Where Browder's work normally seeks to disrupt and disguise architecture, here the two melded together in harmony. It had never happened quite like this for her before, and it stood as a significant moment in her career.

The next year there was also a lot of crying. In 2017, we installed Shasti O'Leary Soudant's sculpture *Gut Flora* at the Niagara Frontier Transportation Authority's Allen Street Station (below and page 74). The transit station was being updated and renovated to accommodate a new suite of buildings at the Buffalo Niagara Medical Campus. In keeping with a tradition set in 1984 by the NFTA and led by the visionary curator and gallerist Nina Freudenheim, every station of the NFTA's subway has public art integrated into the site. With the rebuild, the NFTA remained dedicated to that long-standing cultural commitment. O'Leary Soudant shed tears of joy when her work was completed, too. This installation represented the artist's first permanent sculptural work and resulted in a significant shift in her studio practice, which is increasingly dedicated to public spaces.

That year also saw the installation of *The Freedom Wall*, easily our most significant and important work to date as far as our local audience is concerned. In the early days of the initiative, we were tasked with asking ourselves a set of questions that would establish the circumstances for good installations. Reductively, I often boiled them down to the practical matters of artist, location, and funding, and I would go about trying to answer at least two of those variables before tackling a third. But I was, in a situation of my own making, forced to learn the hard way there was much more to consider.

Listen. Learn.

The backstory is important here. In 2016, our initiative produced our first-ever mural with Jessie Unterhalter and Katey Truhn, a duo from Baltimore. Jessie and Katey have built a practice based on playful and vibrant geometric abstractions. The site on Tupper Street between Pearl and Main Streets is along one of the most heavily trafficked portions of our downtown, and tens of thousands of people see the work on an average day. We consciously decided to go big and make an impact, not just with content and composition, but literally with scale.

Mural-making is an approachable way to create artwork in public spaces. As a museum, we wanted to set the bar high in terms of the quality of the work, but also the quality of production. Jessie and Katey crushed the biggest wall of their career at the time with *Noodle in the Northern Lights* (page 45). Their bold color combinations, filtered through their shared interest in textiles and natural patterns, complement some of the

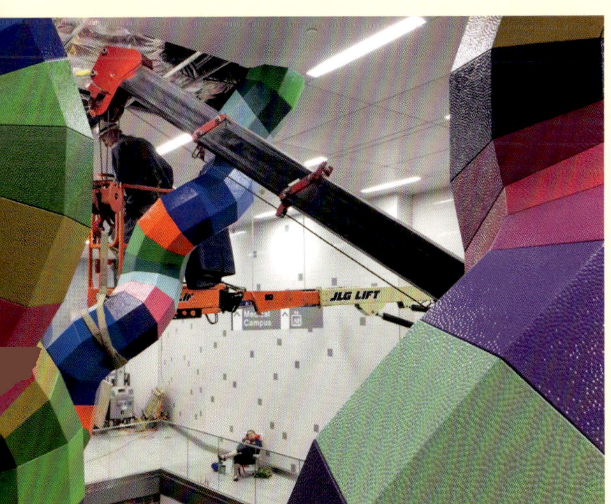

strongest holdings in the AKG's permanent collection, which includes some of the greatest examples of abstract painting in the world. The response to the work was predictable: public affection for a transformational work of art… followed by questions and criticism about local representation.

And so our team trained our eyes on the landscape for local artists and locations that could yield meaningful opportunities. The NFTA's Cold Spring maintenance station for their bus fleet offered an ideal confluence of rich possibilities. The site walled off an entire city block with precast concrete. The wall was constructed with slabs that gently vary in height and width between structural support columns. The architectural result is an inherent framing device.

The site sits at the corner of Michigan Avenue and East Ferry Street in Buffalo. Ferry Street gets its name from its eastern terminus, Freedom Park (formerly Broderick Park) on Unity Island. That island reaches into the Niagara River at one of the narrowest points between the United States and Canada, and historically it served as a site for the harrowing crossing of people fleeing enslavement. This section of river is dangerous, with extraordinarily fast-moving, thrashing white waters. It makes clear the desperation of those who braved the crossing, which in the best of circumstances would have included Underground Railroad assistance in the form of rafts clandestinely ferried across the treacherous span.

The Michigan Street African American Heritage Corridor, dedicated in 2007, is anchored at its southern point by the Michigan Street Baptist Church. That 1849 building also became a legendary Underground Railroad station, providing freedom seekers sanctuary before their crossing to Canada. But the intersection of Michigan and Ferry, a full two miles north of the church, was lesser known and less visible as an entry point into the historical corridor.

Additionally, the site is adjacent to Buffalo Public School 192, the Buffalo Academy for Visual and Performing Arts, and the Historic Bethel African Methodist Episcopal Church, the oldest Black church in Western New York, whose establishment in 1831 predates the incorporation of Buffalo by a year. Lastly, the intersection is just one block east of Main Street in Buffalo, a notorious dividing line between Black and white populations in a devastatingly segregated city.

As someone not native to Buffalo, I began learning about the region's history with the Underground Railroad and our city's influential leaders in the struggle for civil rights and human rights in our country. I had never heard of Mary Talbert before my arrival in Buffalo, but I would soon learn of her legacy as the founder of the Niagara Movement, a precursor of the NAACP. I would learn of her relationship with Frederick Douglass and how together they fought for women's suffrage and women's rights long before they were won, long before they were the norm in American politics. I would further learn about Reverend J. Edward Nash Sr., the leader of the Michigan Street Baptist Church, and the bold risks he and his compatriots took to save lives. As I pondered what it would look like to produce a statue or portrait or any kind of representation of Mary Talbert or Reverend Nash, I wondered how people would recognize the work. What would compel them to investigate the work and how would it be received as celebratory? It was too important to get wrong.

The stakes were even higher given the city's history. In 1983 a bronze bust of Dr. Martin Luther King, Jr. was unveiled in Buffalo's MLK Park. Created by John Woodrow Wilson, the figurative work objectively does not look much like the subject. This was reportedly the artist's intent: not to make a simulacrum of Dr. King, but to make a symbolic representation, a sort of everyman version in which we might all recognize in ourselves and in our community that same capacity for change that King inspired. The reception was anything but positive. The image of Dr. King is sacrosanct in America, and the sculpture presented by Wilson was seen by many as a failure of skill and intent. Had the work been presented inside a museum, with all that a museum offers by way of contextualization, it might have fared better; it certainly would not have become the lightning rod that it did. In public space, however, the public has the final word. The work still stands today, but to many it's a symbol of disrespect, even injustice, given the weight of what it should represent.

I knew about this work when I started thinking about *The Freedom Wall* (page 78). I even privileged a central part of my original concept on imagery of Dr. King. I thought, if there were a painting of Mary Talbert on a wall, people may not recognize it. But if that same image were directly next to a painting of Dr. King, people would immediately recognize him and intuitively start building the connections. And so, armed with the knowledge that literal representation was of utmost importance, I set about trying to see who in our local community had artistic facility and sensitivity for portraiture. I had already met the extraordinarily talented Buffalo artist Chuck Tingley and highly regarded his figurative work. I asked him to provide me with some examples. I asked him to paint Dr. King, James

Baldwin, and Angela Davis. I wasn't thinking about content yet; I felt I just needed to prove we could answer the question of fidelity.

I am no Civil Rights historian. From the beginning, I was interested in learning with our community. I hadn't known about Mary Talbert prior to living in Buffalo. It stood to reason there was more I didn't know that was just as valuable to our broader community and to our shared histories. The architecture of the NFTA wall, wrapping around Ferry and up Michigan, provided twenty-eight precast "frames." I decided to poll our community and engage in a dialogue almost exclusively on Buffalo's East Side about our

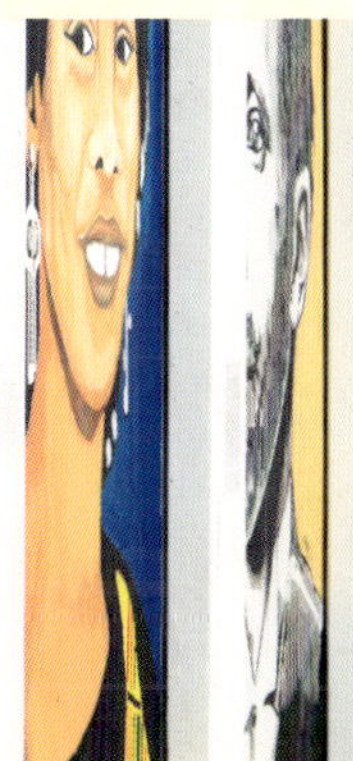
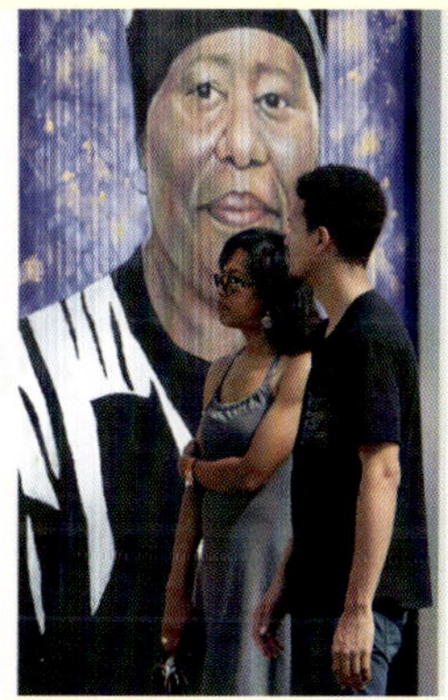
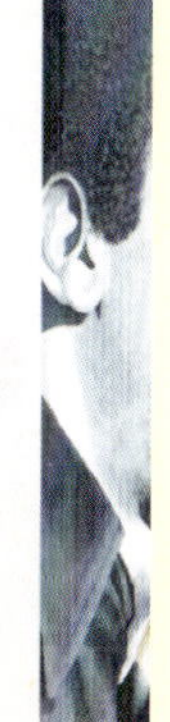
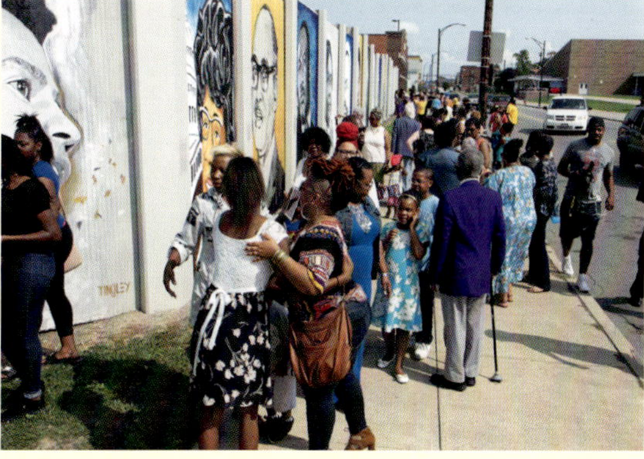

Quiet moments of reflection intermix with joy and celebration as *The Freedom Wall* is unveiled.

citizens' lived experience with civil rights related to Buffalo specifically, and to our nation. Tingley delivered astounding paintings of King and Baldwin, and before he could complete Davis (whom he would eventually go on to paint for the final installation), I was confident that the question of veracity was answered. It was time to host public meetings about content.

Those first few meetings were disastrous. It was made abundantly and at times fiercely clear during our initial meetings that Black authorship and Black talent meant more than I had allowed. Though I had been seeking feedback and authorship for the content, I had ignored the fact that the meaning of the content was itself dependent on the producers. It was clear that Black artists needed to be involved if the project were to move forward.

The frank fact of the matter is that I over-privileged the notion of fine portraiture and in doing so blinded myself to the question of actual representation; that is, who was responsible for painting these portraits, and whose story is it to tell? It is decidedly *not* the story for this white cis hetero male to tell, that much is certain. And though Tingley is Vietnamese American, our community argued that he was not qualified to be the lone artist in charge of the project.

Though our community conversations were filled with passion, I was nonetheless given the grace and time to answer the legitimate and heated concerns that were raised. Our community introduced us to local artists I had not known prior to our meetings. I met John Baker, a staunch advocate for local Black representation. I deepened my relationship with Edreys Wajed, who faced the project with a direct honesty that clarified our collective mission. And I met Julia Bottoms, a jaw-dropping talent, then in her twenties, who immediately convinced us

that the project was finally viable and that we could adapt and answer our community.

There are many cautionary tales associated with this project. But if there is any takeaway, it is that the power of listening and the power of including the public in the creative process from the earliest stages are some of the most important determinants of success. We learned the hard way, and I continue to say what remains the truth for me, which is that *The Freedom Wall* represents the most difficult and easily the most important learning and growing experience of my life.

Tingley would remain on the project, joined by Baker, Bottoms, and Wajed. The result is seven portraits each: by a Black woman in her twenties, a Vietnamese American man in his thirties, a Black man in his forties, and a Black man in his sixties, all of whom lived in Buffalo and all of whom were graduates of SUNY Buffalo State University. It went from a myopic, if well-intentioned, project to one that is broadly repre-sentative due entirely to our public's participation and their determination for a better outcome.

I mentioned tears earlier. They flowed again as the portraits took shape. The public regularly visited the site during production. We heard stories of people who purposefully altered their commute to watch the daily progress. The portraits were selected from community input as originally intended and included, in addition to national figures, Buffalonians such as Dr. Lydia T. Wright, the first Black pediatrician in Buffalo, and Minnie Gillette, the first Black woman elected to the Erie County Legislature. The wall is not a memorial and includes living figures such as Al-Nisa Banks, the owner, editor, and pub-lisher of *The Challenger*, one of the largest African American newspapers in the state of New York, and Alicia Garza, one of the cofounders of the Black Lives Matter movement.

Curators, especially in contemporary museums, like to believe we know creative culture and are therefore informed about our respective publics, but often our developed-but-niche knowledge does not necessarily translate to knowledge of community. In fact, the opposite is generally true: through specialization, we are more insular than we imagine. I own the mistakes that were made in the process of my work. In truth, I continue to hold them close, as a way to stay mindful as I move forward with new projects.

Looking back on it, I am astonished at the work we completed in 2017. Mercifully, that year we were joined by our second Project Coordinator, Zack Boehler, who, on his second day, helped run that heated public meeting about *The Freedom*

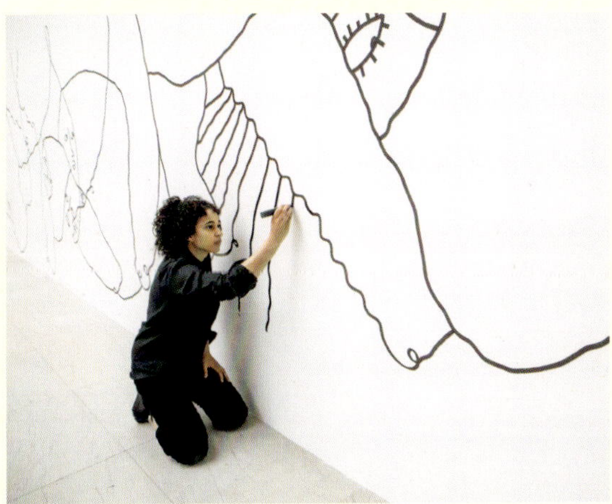

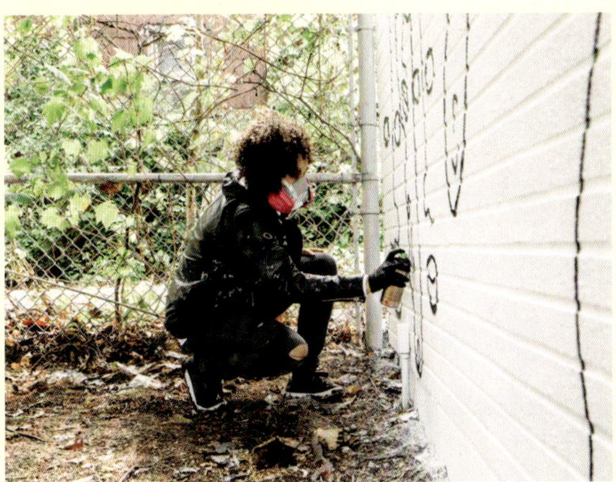

Wall. Zack exudes poise and calm, an asset in the passion-based spaces of public art debate. The educator in him welcomes dialogue and a sense of comradery towards a common goal. Zack also added critical experience with sculpture to our team, extending our ability to consider ever-more complex installations. He is an artist favorite in an artist-centered organization, and his ability to creatively problem-solve on the fly while honoring the artist's intentions is unparalleled. His confidence in our mission and in our public is something that still moves and motivates me to this day.

That same year, we produced our first murals on Polytab. Polytab is a nonwoven cloth that allows mural-making to become mobile in a process that was first pioneered by the Philadelphia Mural Arts Program. We also hosted our first ever crossover installation of work in the museum, with Shantell Martin's inspiring exhibition *Shantell Martin: Someday We Can* in our Sculpture Court (above left and page 70), and *Dance Everyday*, a gigantic mural on Buffalo's East Side, near what would later become the museum's satellite location during our campus expansion (below left and page 72). If we started the initiative with the goal of just getting good work in public, Martin's exhibition was an artery that ran from public space back to the museum through these simultaneous interventions. As such, her work remains one of the most important inflection points in the development of our initiative.

By the end of 2017, we had produced work that connected us deeply with our community in new ways. We had collaborated on authorship, on content, on production, and on location. This work solidified our commitment to community and broadened our ambition for commissions and collaborations moving forward. As a global arts organization, our initiative attracted more and more national and international attention and talent. The following years would offer us the ability to match our exceptional local talent with artists from around the world.

Growth and Harmony

In 2018 we would again present public work connected to an exhibition. We extended *Robert Indiana: A Sculpture Retrospective* (June 16– September 23, 2018) by installing the artist's *ONE through ZERO (The Ten Numbers)* (page 88) concurrently at Buffalo's Outer Harbor, about

eight miles from our campus and in a dramatically different, waterfront environment.

Partnering with other organizations, as we did with the Erie Canal Harbor Development Corporation, the operator of the well-established, popular destination Wilkeson Pointe, where we placed Indiana, can yield expansive audience engagement. However, in early conversations with any partner, even the most enthusiastic among them, we are often speaking different languages towards a common but potentially unknown and amorphous public art outcome. The first steps always involve figuring out how to reach a shared understanding. Sometimes this takes years. Not often, but sometimes, it takes mere months.

The genesis of Louise Jones's *Wildflowers for Buffalo* (page 90), the largest mural of her career at the time, was essentially happenstance. I was walking out of our downtown public library with my child, and we paused on the promenade to enjoy the small garden spaces they nurture there. Together we pondered, as we shifted our gaze from the foreground of the garden to the large blank wall of a building just beyond, what it might look like to have flowers grow onto the side of that building. I took a photo on my phone and texted it to Jones (left). She agreed that it would be a great look and said yes, she would be our artist. Within weeks we had a plan with our partners at Ciminelli Real Estate Corporation, and within months we had a finished work, at the time also the largest we had ever commissioned.

Large can mean many things and offer many opportunities. Our 2020–22 project *Cobblestone Commons* (page 116) gave us the option of offering mural opportunities along a 300-foot expanse to local artists, including Obsidian Bellis, Monet Alyssa Kifner, and Karle Norman, who would

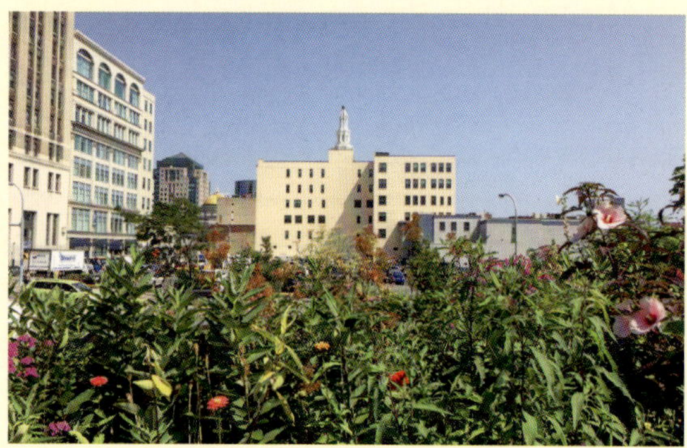

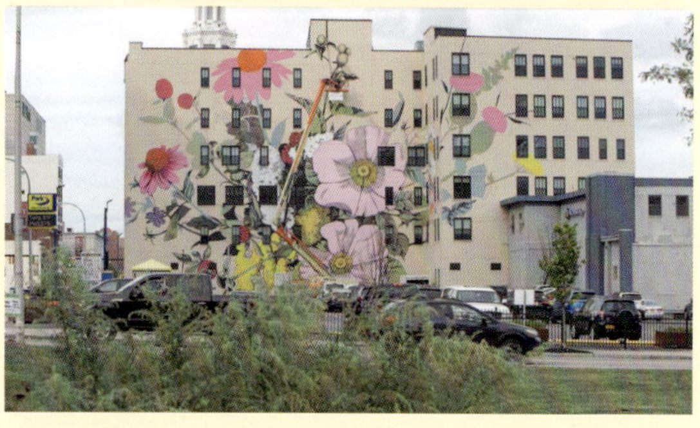

Louise Jones's
Wildflowers for Buffalo,
from idea to reality.

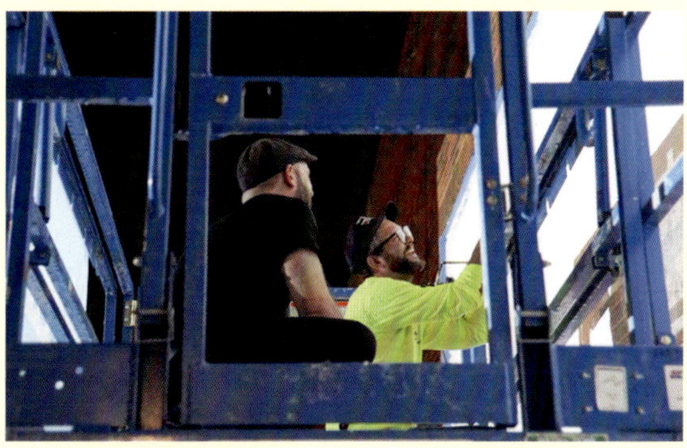

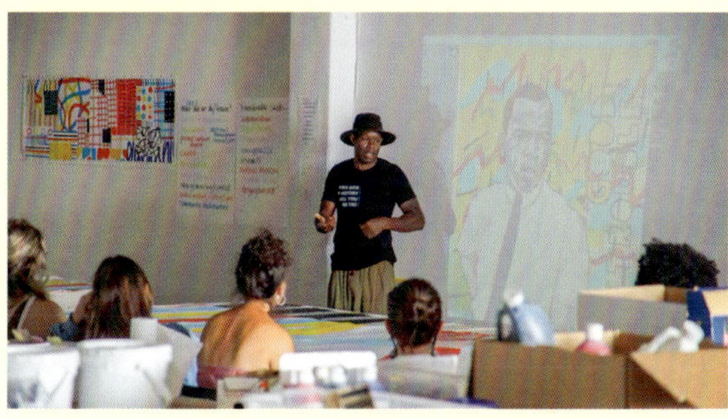

make their public art debuts alongside national and international talent. Our team loves working with artists on their first-ever public works. In those instances, we are often teaching artists what we've learned, offering our insight into best practices and tricks of the trade. In special cases, like with *Cobblestone Commons*, our team learns something as well, as we did with the different techniques that Jason Brammer, Thomas Evans, and Miriam Singer used during their respective installations. It is exceedingly rewarding to create situations in which we continue to learn and can add to our local artists' experience as they meet talent from outside our region, hear of new opportunities, ask questions about development, and generally share in the bond of working so closely together. I hear from some colleagues at museums, "That's not what we do," referring to working with new and emerging artists, especially when it means literally teaching them how to accomplish an outcome they've never attempted before. My response is, "No, that's just not what you've *done*." I don't believe I've seen a mission statement that denies any museum the opportunity to take some chances on young, emerging, and local talent, even when their explicit stated mission, like the Buffalo AKG's, is globally oriented.

AKG as Catalyst

It is impossible to pick favorite projects or favorite artists from the past ten years. It has been rewarding to see careers form and blossom because of the direct action our museum has taken. Certainly, artists like Julia Bottoms or Edreys Wajed don't owe their success to us. Thriving as an artist is an unbelievably difficult task, and there's no one thing that is responsible for that achievement. But we take pride in their successes, having recognized early on undeniable talents deserving of our attention and of public appreciation.

It is also rewarding to provide access to works that our public, especially local audiences, would not otherwise be able to view. Jun Kaneko's work is such an example (page 124). Producing some of the world's largest single-fired ceramic objects, Kaneko is an unparalleled visionary. Practically speaking though, because his work is gigantic, sometimes topping thirteen feet tall and thousands of pounds each, those works pose significant challenges to ship and handle. Thus, if you live in Omaha, Nebraska, where

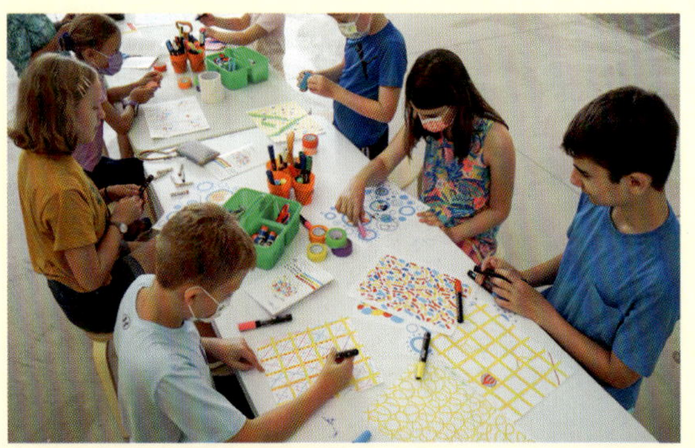

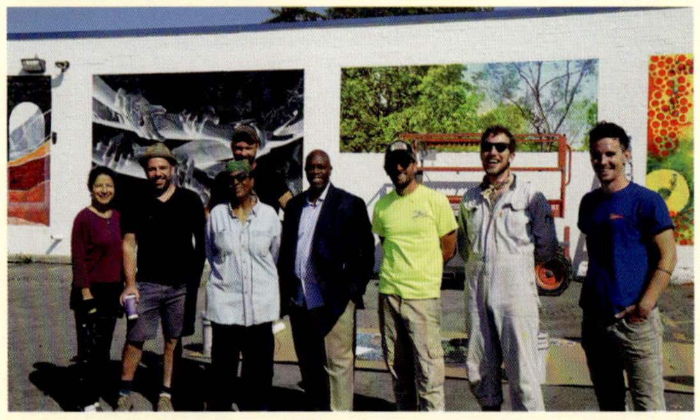

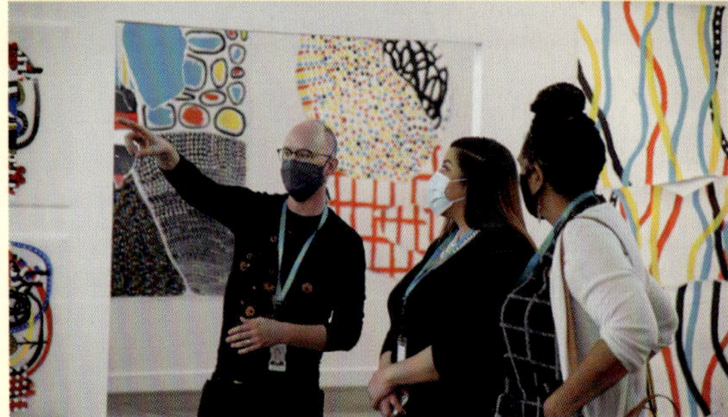

Participatory and experimental, Albright–Knox Northland showed what the Public Art Initiative could look like in a gallery space.

← Visitors create art in the exhibition space.

↙ Resident artists and members of the Public Art team pose in front of the murals as they go up on the wall.

↙↙ Aaron Ott (left) points out features of the Tullet exhibition to museum staff.

Kaneko's studio is located, there is the luxury of familiarity through proximity. But in Western New York, you may have never seen these astounding works, let alone conceived that ceramic sculptures could withstand, and frankly thrive in, a Buffalo winter. We get the chance to introduce our public to works like these.

As our initiative evolves, we are also engaging more intentionally with architects and designers. Specifically, Cannon Design constructed two buildings, one at 201 Ellicott Street in downtown Buffalo and one on D'Youville University's campus on Buffalo's West Side, that purposefully included facades designed to accommodate murals. Josef Kristofoletti painted nearly 7,000 square feet of the 201 Ellicott building entirely with a four-inch brush (page 146). Maya Hayuk came to D'Youville with her assistants and adapted her signature techniques to accommodate specific materials that the surface demanded, unusual for her practice (page 144). Both projects have been internationally recognized for the profound ways they help, advance, and beautify the communities they serve. The D'Youville site received an additional intervention from our initiative, with installations of handwoven pillows by Coryn Kempster and Julia Jamrozik (page 164). These pillows, the result of a series of workshops the artists held with high school students from the neighboring BPS 198 International Preparatory School, were produced by artisans from Stich Buffalo, an organization founded to empower refugee and immigrant women through the sale of their handcrafted goods.

Forward Focus

A lot happens in ten years—certainly more than this written account could hope to hold. While I was privileged to start an initiative from scratch, our institutional mandate from the time I joined in 2014 focused primarily on campus expansion, a long-identified necessity for our museum. This would ultimately result in the closure of our main campus in late 2019 to begin construction on what would become the current-day AKG. Though not explicitly part of the Public Art Initiative, what would become Albright-Knox Northland, our satellite site from 2020 to 2022, during construction, took significant cues from the structure of public art, showcasing participatory, experimental, and commission-based works.

We closed our Northland doors in 2022 and opened our AKG doors in 2023. The new museum sets the stage for the next series of adaptations and evolutions of our initiative. In 2014, we needed to define public art at the AKG for the first time. Between 2014 and 2019 we grew, matured, learned hard lessons, and transformed. From 2019 to 2023 we concentrated on responding to our communities, to our collective challenges, and to losses both small and devastating. We continued to grow, but, significantly, it was our roots that grew deeper and stronger.

Now, as we look forward to what is to come, as we consider the forms of engagement most pressing for our audiences, as we think of the dynamism we can add to our production, we are faced again with necessary adjustments and adaptations. As we engage with this fact, I realize our evolution will be constant. Change is inherent in the work of public art. Our future will ask us to pivot and respond, to engage and react as we have learned to do, but more and more it will ask us to think and act with intention, as the thought leaders and catalysts that we have become.

If the AKG has exhibited the art of our time since its inception in 1862, we remain committed to carrying that torch into the future. In history, no other "ism" in art, no other movement, has persisted or adapted in the way that public art has. Public art, always a reflection of its time, has been a form of cultural conversation and civic intervention for thousands of years. Shifts in governments, borders, cultures, and various technologies have all affected how we engage with and interpret our shared landscapes. In a world where our lives are dictated by technological mediation, I believe that what will matter most are the ways in which our public spaces foster relationships, reward our social nature, and reawaken our respect for self, space, and humanity. The positive disruptive power of public art is unparalleled in recalibrating our awareness and is among the most powerful and engaging ways that we have to tell our own stories and to retell them with others. As we commit to future growth, we also devote ourselves intentionally and enthusiastically to you, our public. We don't know what you will fall in love with next, but we are excited to make it together and know the process will be just as magical and moving as it has been in our first ten years.

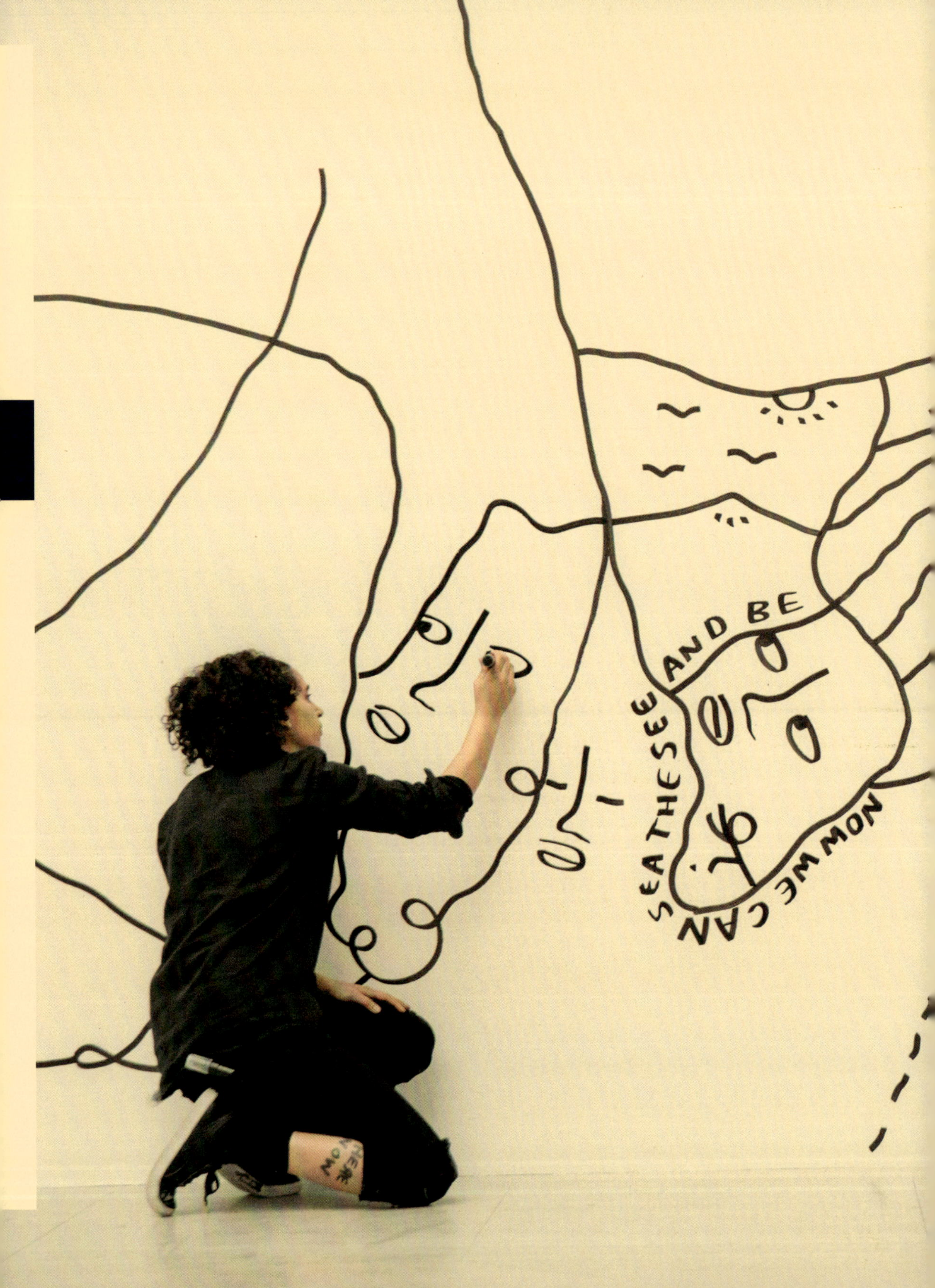

SEA THE SEE AND BE
NOW WE CAN

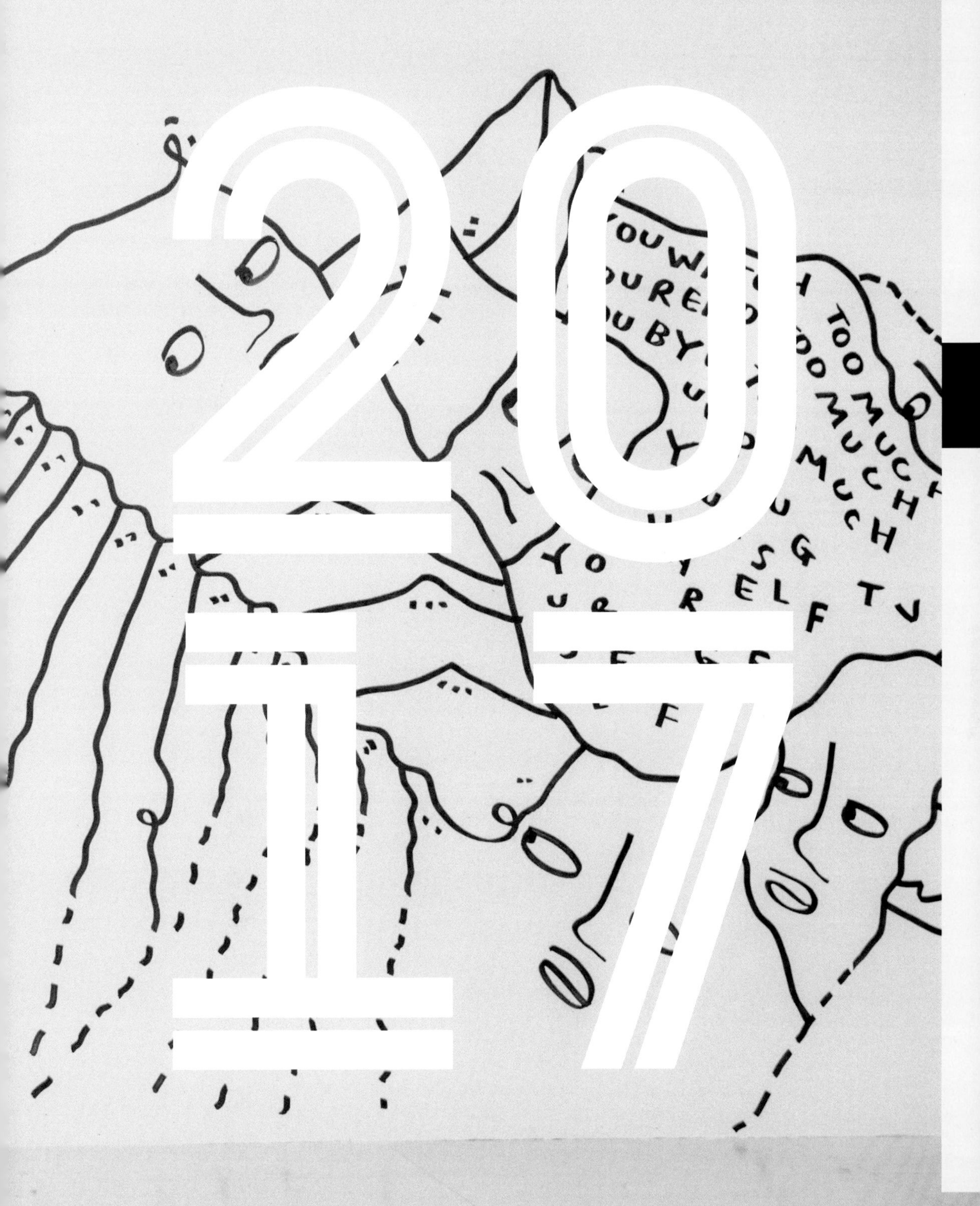

2017
YOU WATCH
YOU READ
YOU BUY
YOU
TOO MUCH
TOO MUCH
MUCH
YOURSELF

Walk Through

Beverly Pepper

---

87 Carlton Street, Buffalo

Stainless steel and baked
enamel
Two elements:
32 × 30 × 87 inches
(81.3 × 76.2 × 221 cm) and
30 × 30 × 87 inches
(76.2 × 76.2 × 221 cm)
Overall: 65 × 63 × 87 inches
(165.1 × 160 × 221 cm)

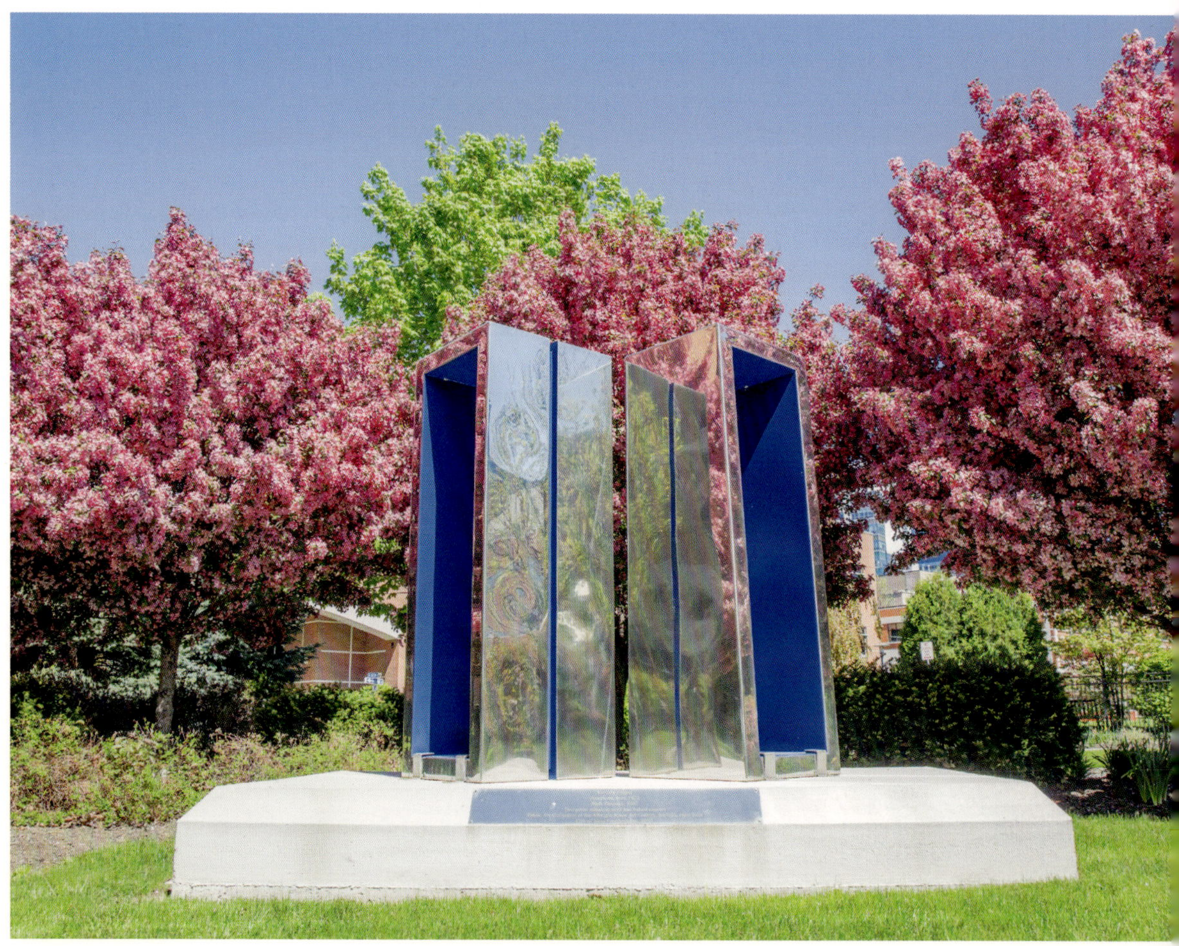

Magic Buffalo

Bunnie Reiss

Joe's Deli, 1322 Hertel Avenue, Buffalo

Acrylic paint
22 × 42 feet (6.7 × 12.8 m)

In 2017, Reiss created *Magic Buffalo* on the east and west walls of Joe's Deli on Hertel Avenue. In the intervening years the mural on the building's west-facing side was damaged. In 2022, Reiss returned to Buffalo to complete a new mural. Now visitors can see the east wall of her mural from 2017 along with the new mural on the building's west side.

↓ Reiss's 2017 mural.
↓↓ The repainted mural in 2022.

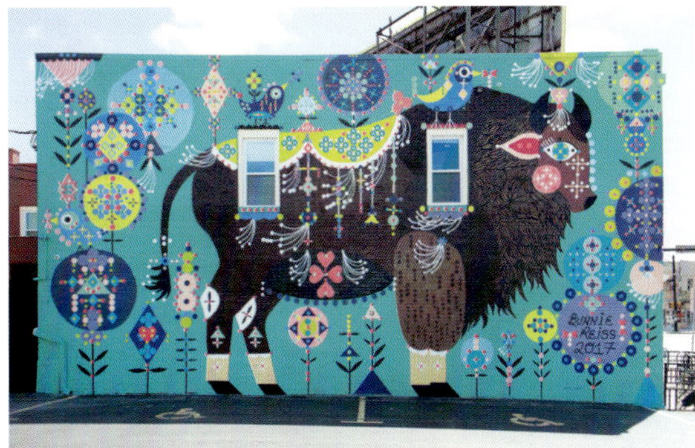

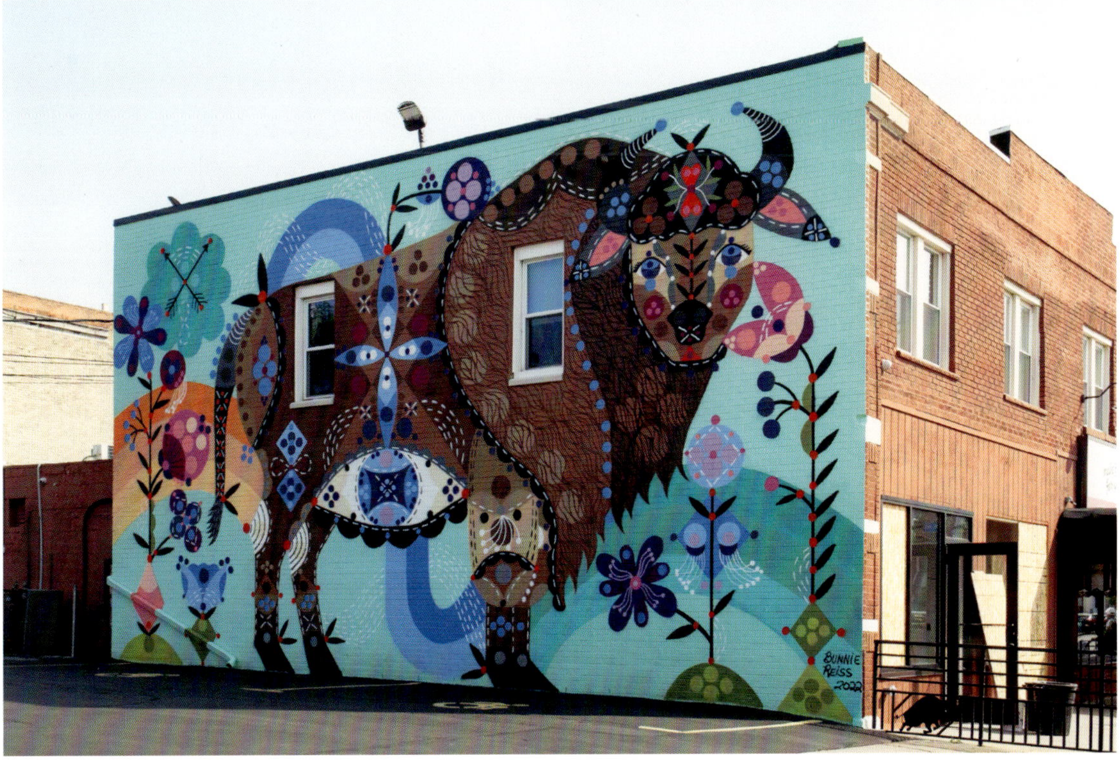

Buffalo is one of those places with hidden magic. My first mural was back in 2017, and the museum was just beginning to kick off a public art program. I had spent a lot of time in the Rust Belt area of the country, especially Detroit and Ohio, but I hadn't visited Buffalo. I was intrigued and upon arrival immediately fell in love with the city. Not only was the museum team amazing, but I slowly realized that there is a creative force that lives there and collectively makes up a wave of incredible talent.

The generous spirit, support, and appreciation feels so authentic and abundant in Buffalo. I have enjoyed all of my time painting, exploring, eating, laughing, connecting, and hope to get back there soon.

—BUNNIE REISS

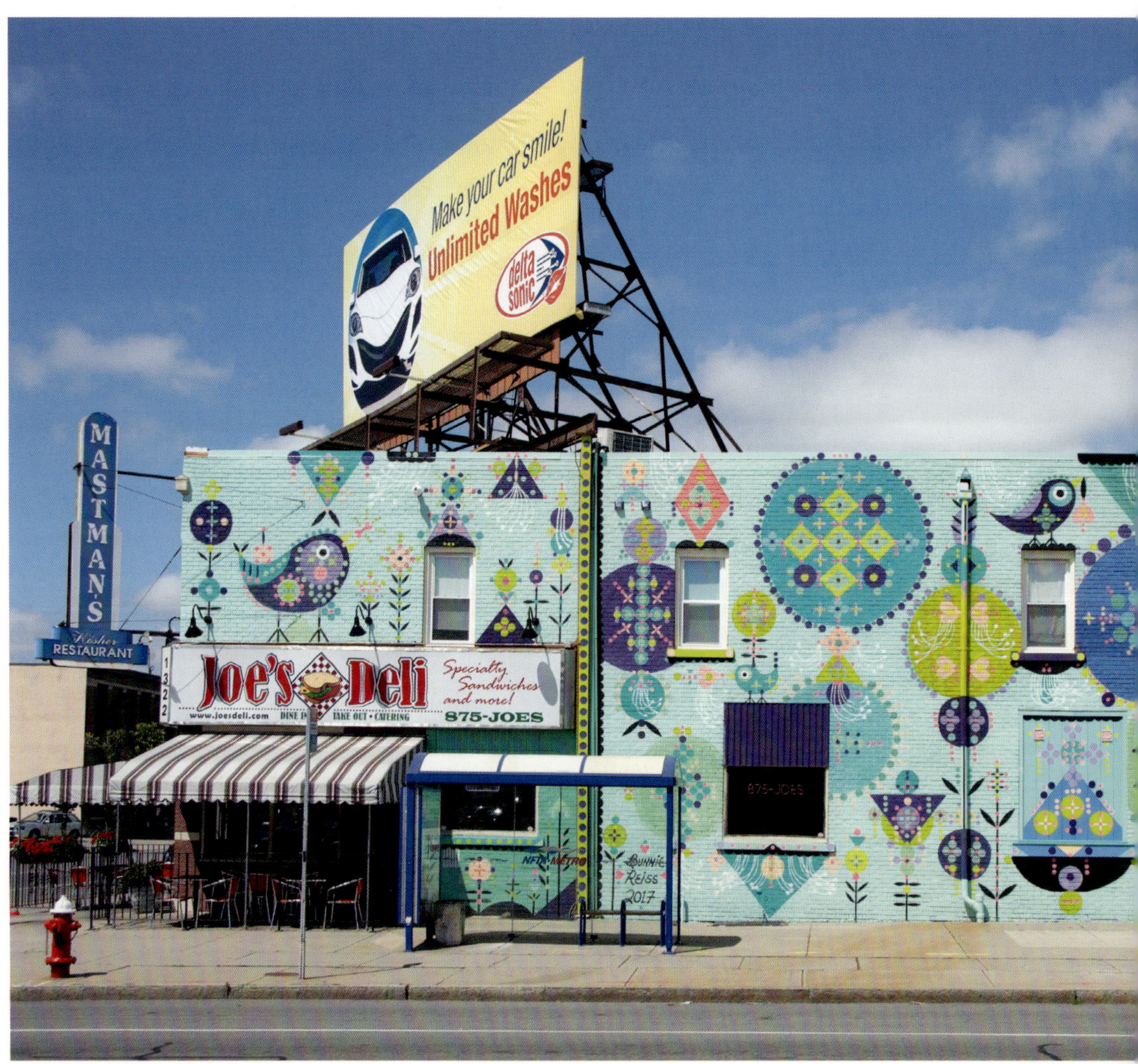

Reiss spoke to AKG Editor Matt Connolly in September 2022 about her experience creating and re-creating one of Buffalo's iconic murals.

MC: It's been a few weeks since you wrapped painting the mural. What did you think about that experience of coming back and being in Buffalo again?

BR: Being back now, it's just been such a treat to watch everything grow, to watch the museum grow, and the people grow. And, really, to grow together is sort of everything you want as an artist.

MC: It's unfortunate that because of the deterioration of the building the mural had to be repainted, but it does add opportunity to reimagine the mural or approach it differently. What, when you came back five years later, are you putting into it that wasn't there in 2017?

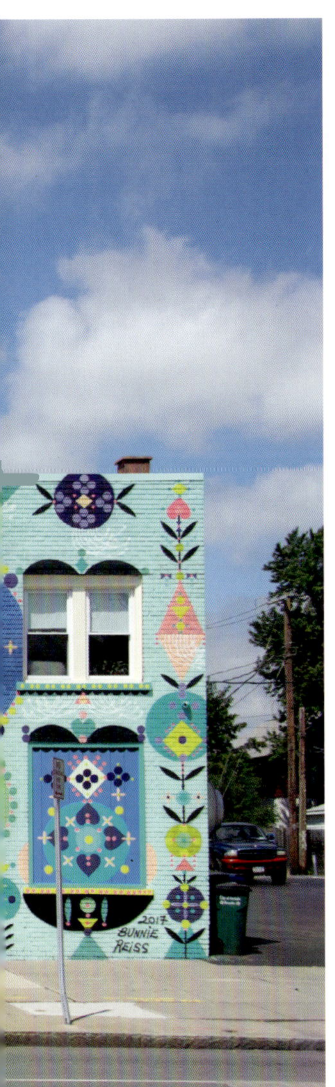

BR: Honestly, you never get an opportunity like this. To have something that large-scale needing to be redone completely, it was so interesting to see the growth of my work, just as an artist. And it was awesome for my own growth to see how much more proficient I am with spray paint, to see how much more proficient I am in my own narrative, with my own language that I've been developing for so many years. And how effortlessly it comes out of me now is really something.

It's five years later, but I mean it was a hell of a five years for all of us, so it's a loaded question. Because five years was like thirty years. So I'm definitely not the same person. I'm not the same artist. I think when I look at my work, the biggest takeaway for me is patience. I've developed a kind of patience with myself, with my thought process, that I didn't have before the pandemic. And it was very frustrating at first and it still is in some ways, because the world just moves slower. It's not as immediate, and I think we lived in a very immediate world for a long time.

MC: What drew you to Buffalo in the first place?

BR: When you're first putting public art up, your initial thought is, "I want to do all these big cities, I want to get these big, high-profile walls." And I think there's something to that, and it still feels really exciting to be awarded those, but, for my personal ethos, I think that inspiring people comes in a lot of different forms. When you go to areas that are a little bit smaller, a little bit different, or a little more tucked away, the impact of your art and the impact of the community on you is much stronger.

Shantell Martin: Someday We Can

Shantell Martin

Buffalo AKG Art Museum
March 11–June 25, 2017

Black ink on white
painted objects
Dimensions variable

Martin applied her signature style of black line on white surface to objects and walls inside and outside the museum—marking the first time an artist working with the Public Art Initiative had done so.

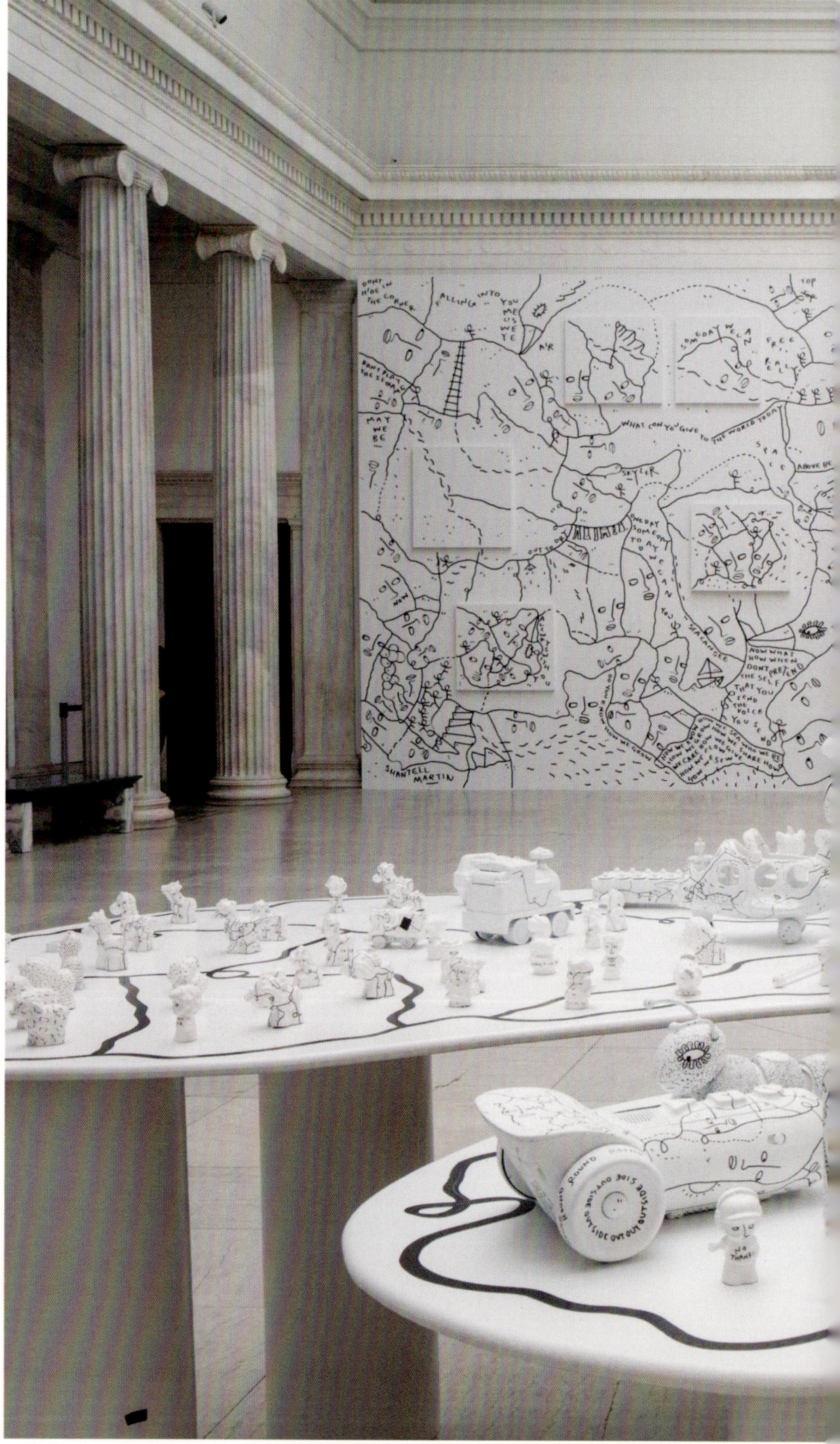

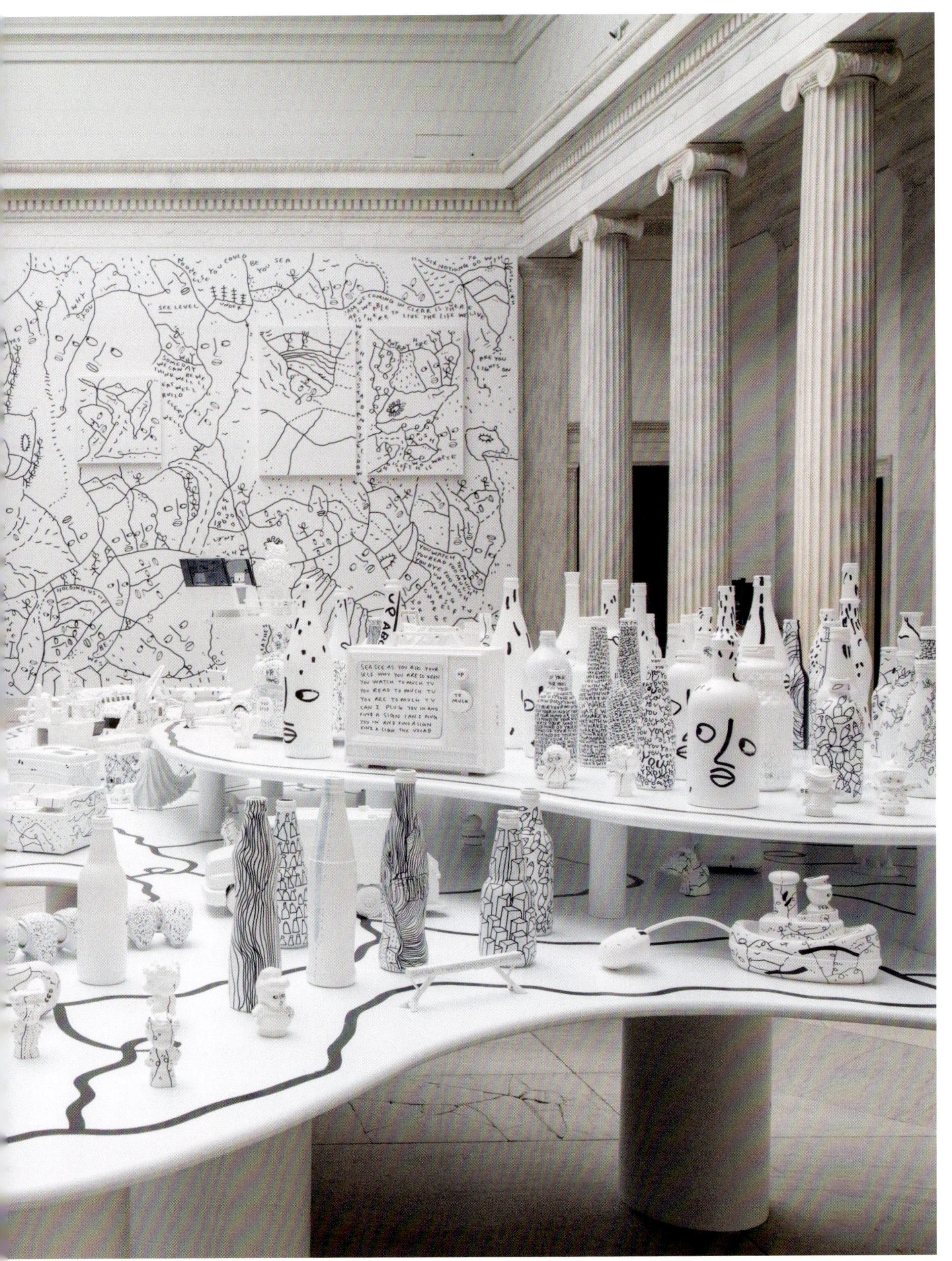

Dance Everyday

Shantell Martin

537 East Delavan Avenue,
Buffalo

Acrylic and spray paint
Approximately 22 × 200
feet (6.7 × 61 m)

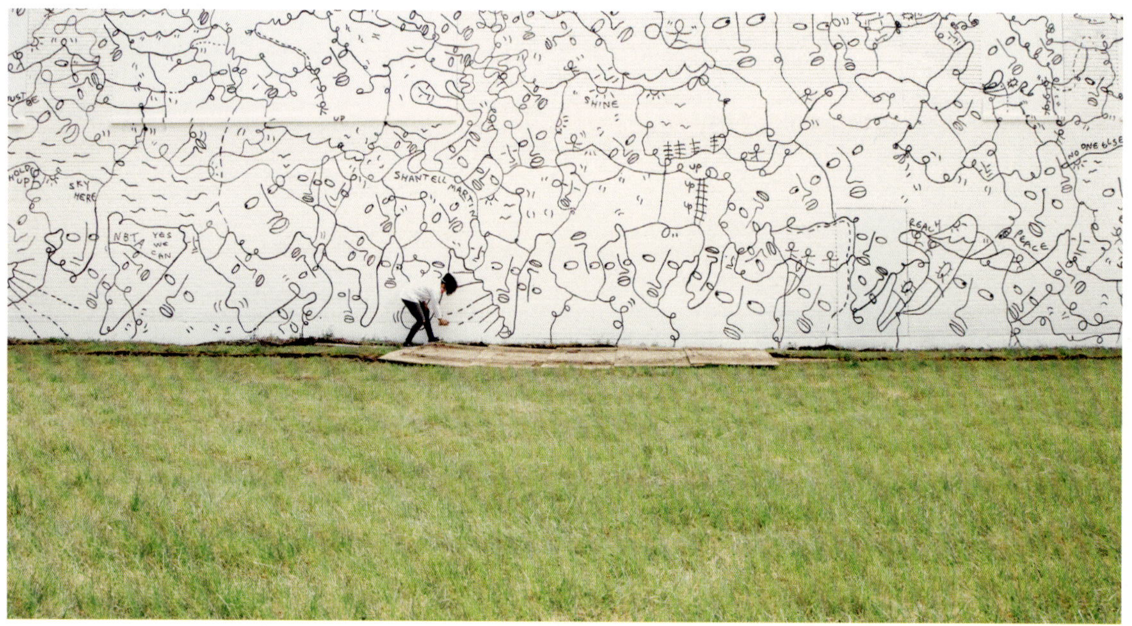

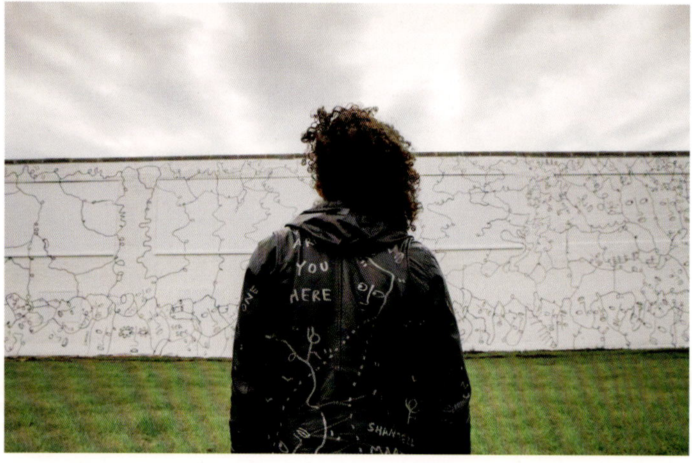

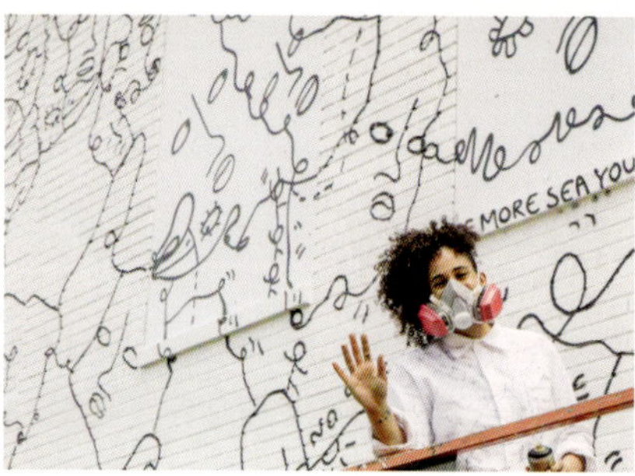

Welcome Wall

Keir Johnston and Ernel Martinez

751 Fillmore Avenue, Buffalo

Acrylic on Polytab
Approximately 27 × 42 feet
(8.2 × 12.8 m)

This mural features the word *Welcome* in thirteen languages, representing those spoken by the people of the surrounding neighborhood at the time it was made: Arabic, Bengali, Burmese, English, Farsi, French, German, Polish, Seneca, Spanish, Somali, Urdu, and Vietnamese.

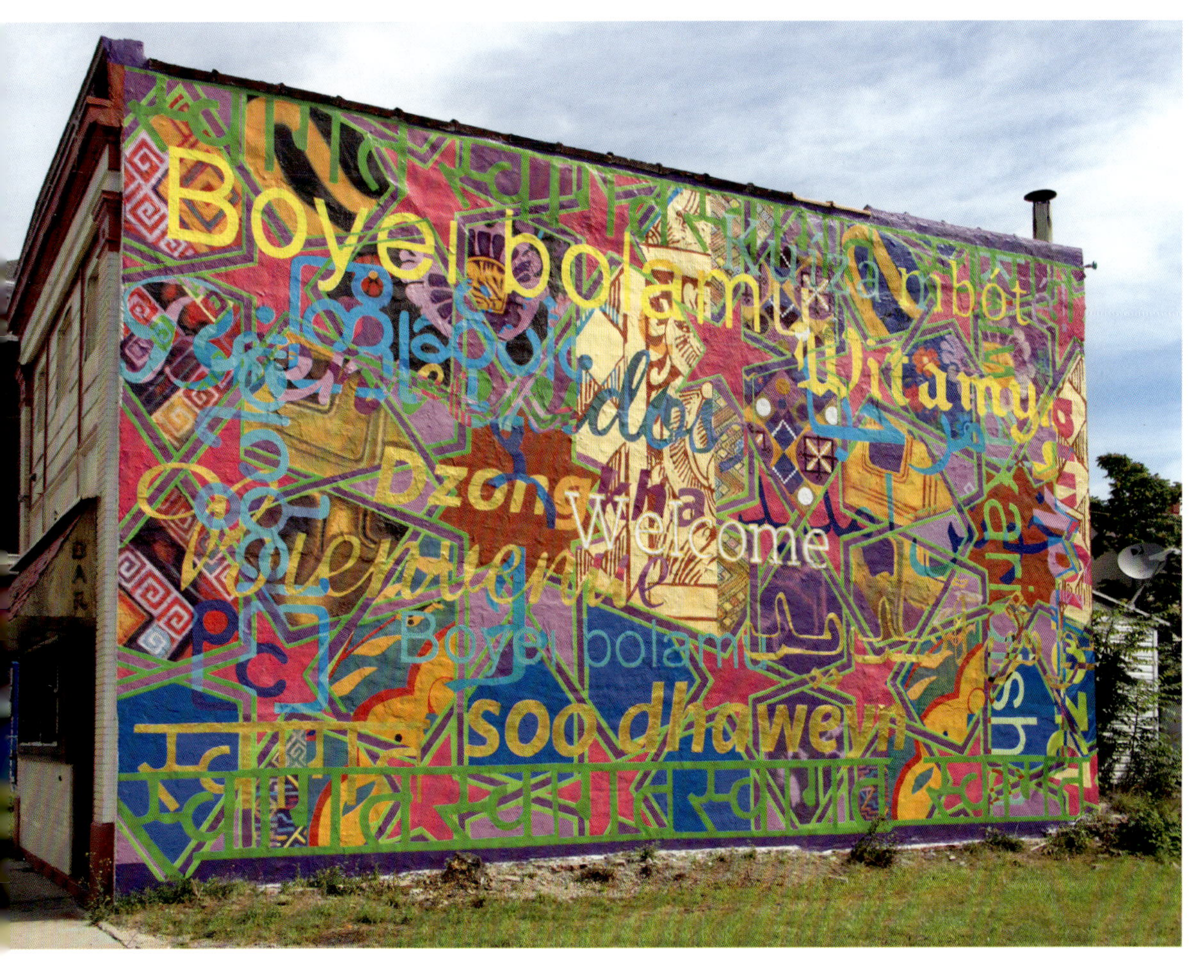

Gut Flora

Shasti O'Leary Soudant

NFTA Allen/Medical
Campus Station

Six powder-coated steel
structures
Each 11 feet (3.3 m) tall

On the Utility of Levity…

There's an oft-paraphrased quote attributed to Edmund Gwenn, the actor who played Kris Kringle in *Miracle on 34th Street*, as he expired: "Dying is easy. Comedy is hard." From it, one can infer a deathbed critique of those who plucked the low-hanging fruit of Gravitas, that moldering prime meridian of aesthetics. Gwenn understood levity to be a higher level of difficulty than drama, best attained through Mark Twain's wry equation:

Comedy = Tragedy + Time.

When you make a thing pretty, do you automatically forfeit its heft? To create buoyant art for public space is to, every so often, sip from a meniscus of joyless condescension, but the ironic tang of that caustic nectar can grow on you. At some point, it's tempting to deliberately invite derision just to taste it again. In contemporary art, beauty and mirth are rarely accorded merit or consequence. The perceived invalidity of "eye candy" as flimsy and intellectually undemanding gives short shrift to its function as a reliable vector of philosophic transmission, not to mention the degree to which that power is underestimated. Witness the hypodermic hilarity of the last line in Greta Gerwig's triumphant masterwork, *Barbie*: "I'm here to see my gynecologist," a mic-drop down a nine-mile-deep well.

The Inviting and the Intellectual are not mutually exclusive. Academe's resistance to popular culture has enfeebled the humanities. As we're watching vaunted institutions attempt to thwart irrelevance by offering popular courses that conscript Taylor Swift's earnest song catalogue to scholarly methodologies, we have no choice but to confront beauty's political undertow. Cultural connective tissue is an essential organ of the body politic, and that which imparts laughter, joy, and pleasure to so many is dismissed at our peril: beware the public's rebuke of those who would appoint themselves the arbiters of good taste. In the Attention Economy, they are routinely cannibalized.

The task of rigorously engaging a mass audience without exclusion, didacticism, gratuitous pandering, or ideological inculcation is akin to threading a needle with a minuscule eye. The endeavor demands considerable physical and emotional labor, copious restraint, and a genuine affection for humanity, but, even then, the proclivity of the particular to masquerade as the universal can curdle the best of intentions. I am ever mindful that a public artwork serves a multiplicity of agendas, not the least of which is my own desire to inject feminist vernacular into the public sphere by designing the most seductive objects I can conceive. Design is hegemonic if not deployed in tandem with community, and to pretend otherwise is hubris.

My sculptures resemble overgrown toys—but embody contradiction. Their materiality belies their warm, goofy veneer: rigidized stainless steel festooned in clownish color, bound up in bling, and gurgling with texture, entices

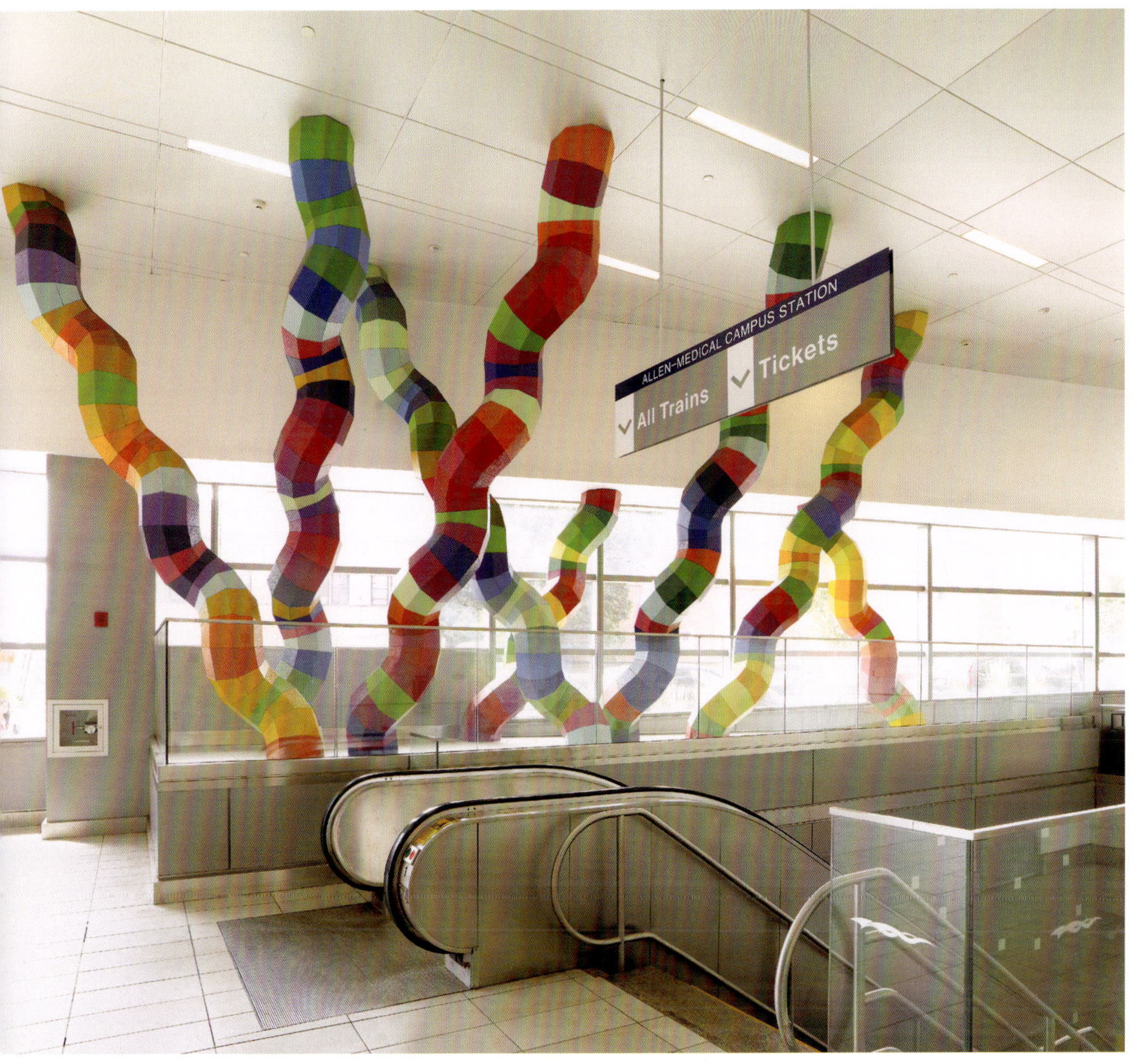

both the eye and the hand, an alluring magnet for the simple pleasure of touch for young and old. I can easily imagine a childlike giant impulsively stuffing one in its mouth, believing it sweet, then spitting it out after crunching into its salty core. I invoke the Power of Pretty fully cognizant of its disarming charm and revel in its capacity for cheerful subversion, but I'm also not looking for a fight. There's enough rancor in the world. I'm shamelessly striving for delight.

However, should a more cerebral viewer be itching for a phrenic grapple with the writhing deoxyribonucleic vermiculture of *Gut Flora* or the voluptuously corseted burlesque ballerinas of *Do Not Mistake Our Softness for Weakness* that pirouette outside of the Burchfield Penney Art Center, they'll encounter a gleaming twelve-foot-tall Can of Worms, well–equipped and fabulously dressed for battle.

— SHASTI O'LEARY SOUDANT

Patria, Será Porque Quisiera Que Vueles, Que Sigue Siendo Tuyo Mi Vuelo

(Homeland, Perhaps It Is Because I Wish to See You Fly, That My Flight Continues to Be Yours)

Betsy Casañas

585 Niagara Street, Buffalo

Acrylic on Polytab
Jersey Street side:
approximately 35 × 55 feet
(10.7 × 16.8 m); Niagara
Street side: approximately
35 × 45 feet (10.7 × 13.7 m)

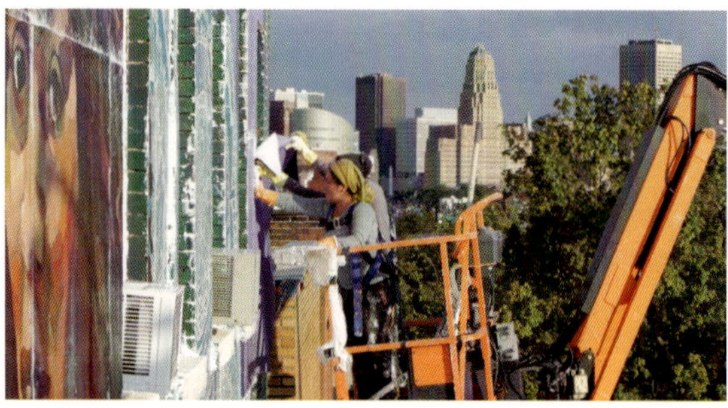

Imagery for this mural came out of conversations Casañas held with the local Latinx community. The artist then executed the mural on Polytab with help from the public on painting days at the Buffalo & Erie County Public Library and on site.

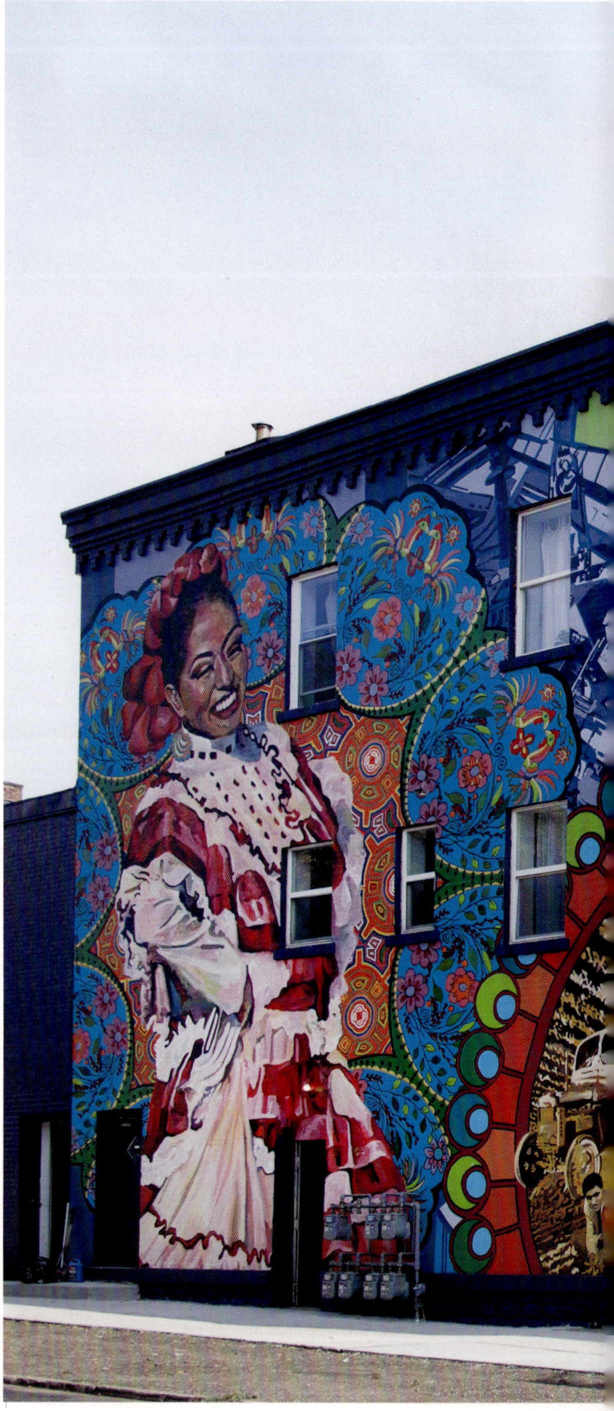

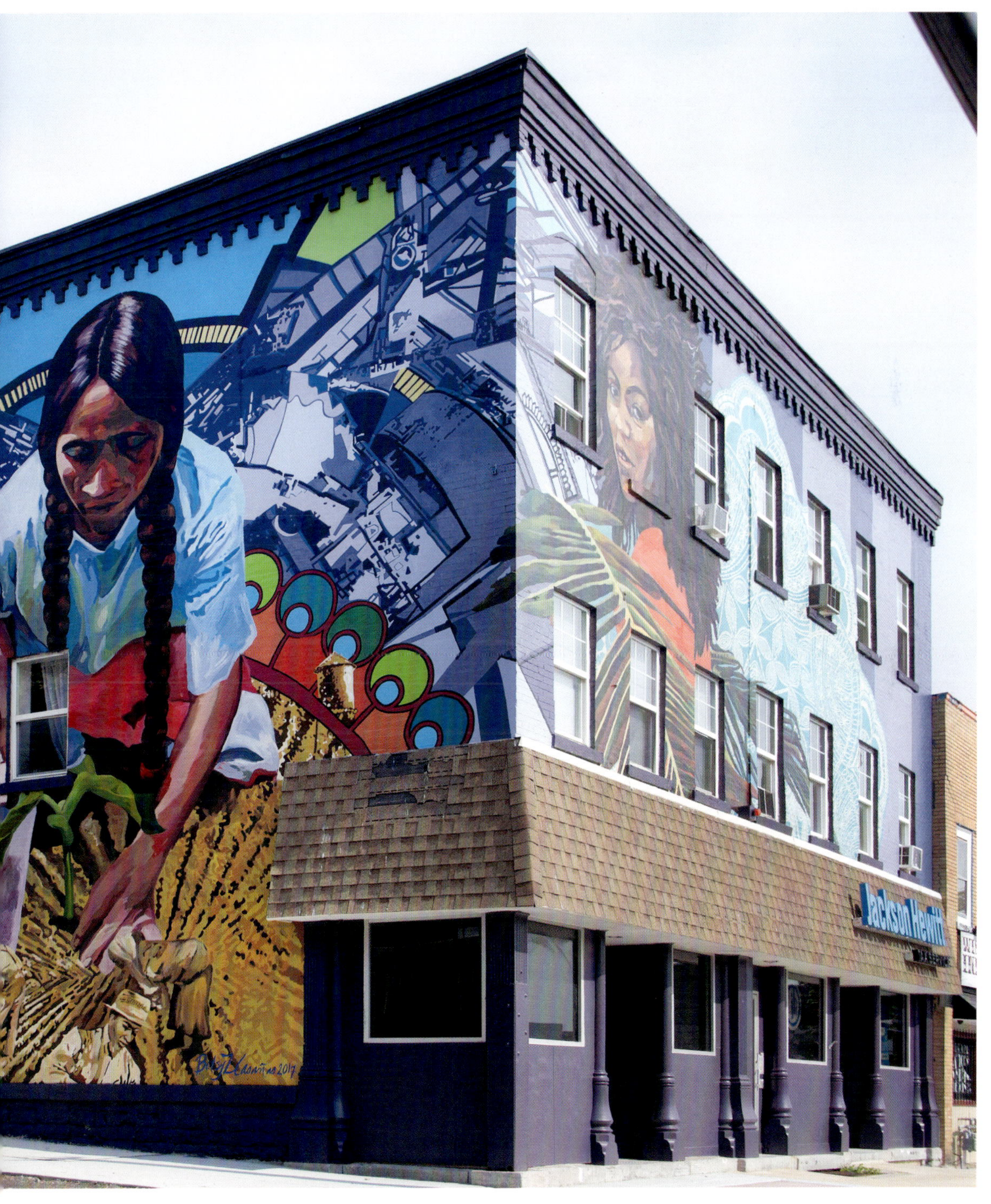

The Freedom Wall

John Baker
Julia Bottoms
Chuck Tingley
Edreys Wajed

Michigan Avenue and
East Ferry Street, Buffalo

Spray and acrylic paint
Approximately 12 × 300 feet
(3.7 × 91.4 m)

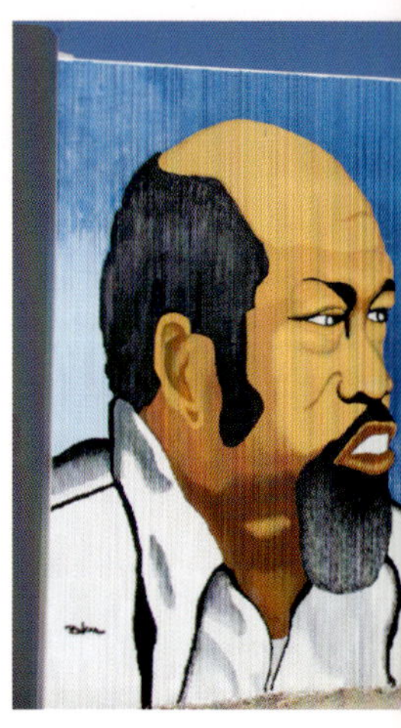

→ Bill Gaiter by
John Baker (left);
Malcolm X
by Edreys Wajed

→→ Rosa Parks
by Julia Bottoms
(left); Kwame
Ture, aka Stokely
Carmichael,
by Chuck Tingley

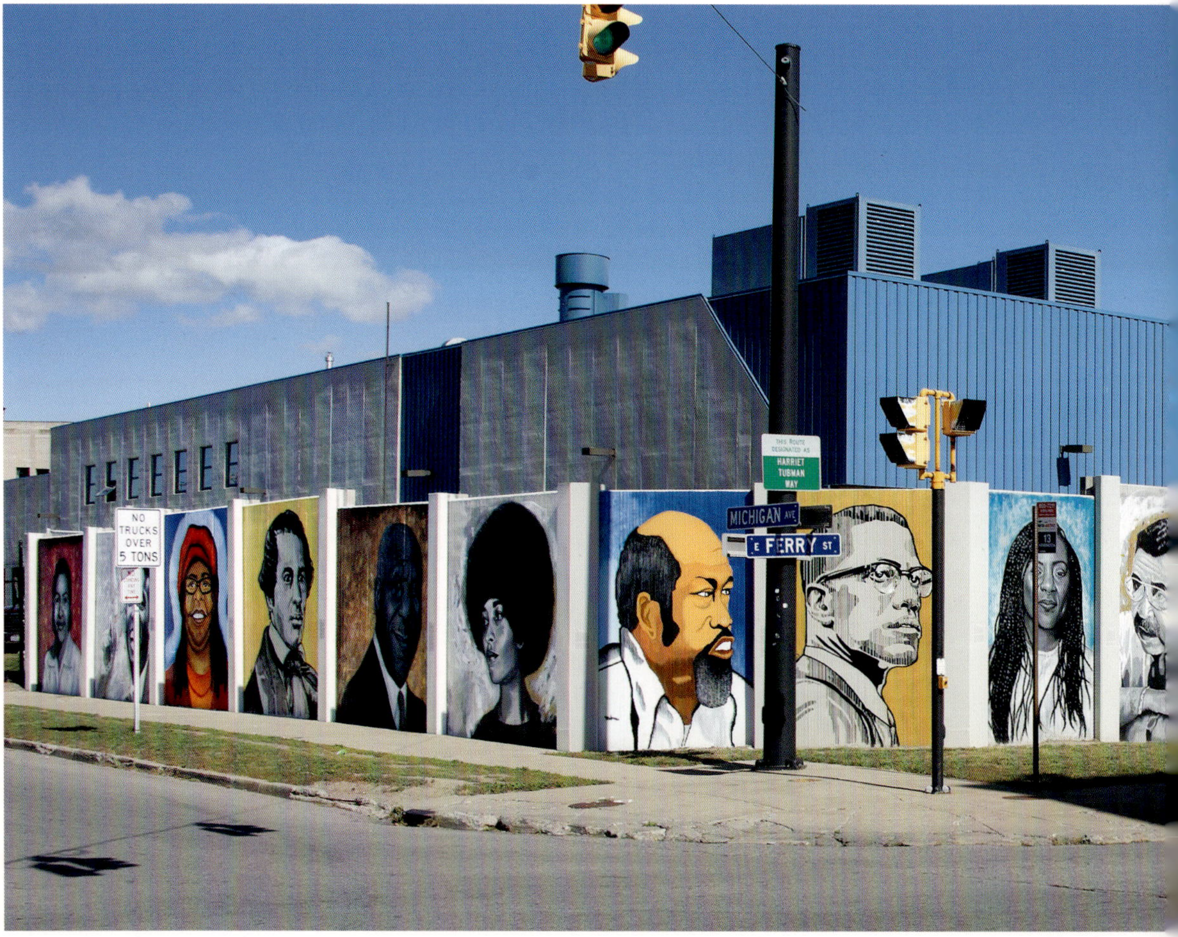

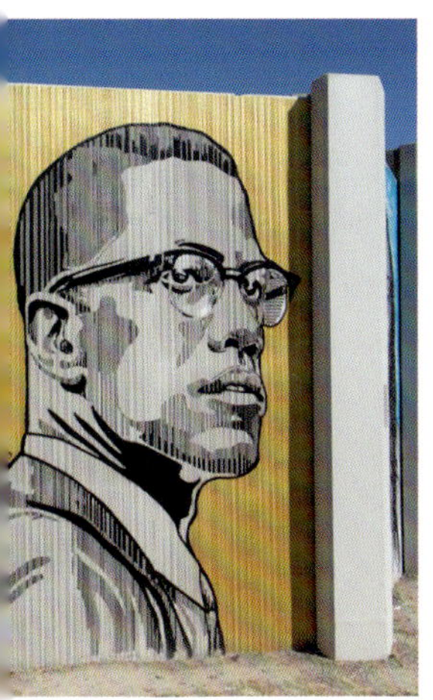

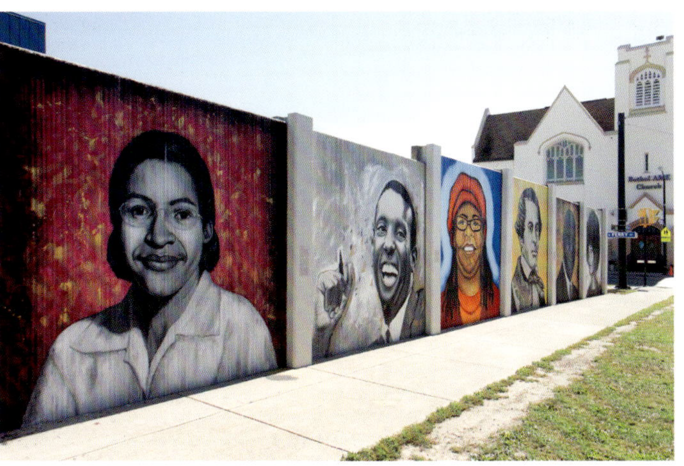

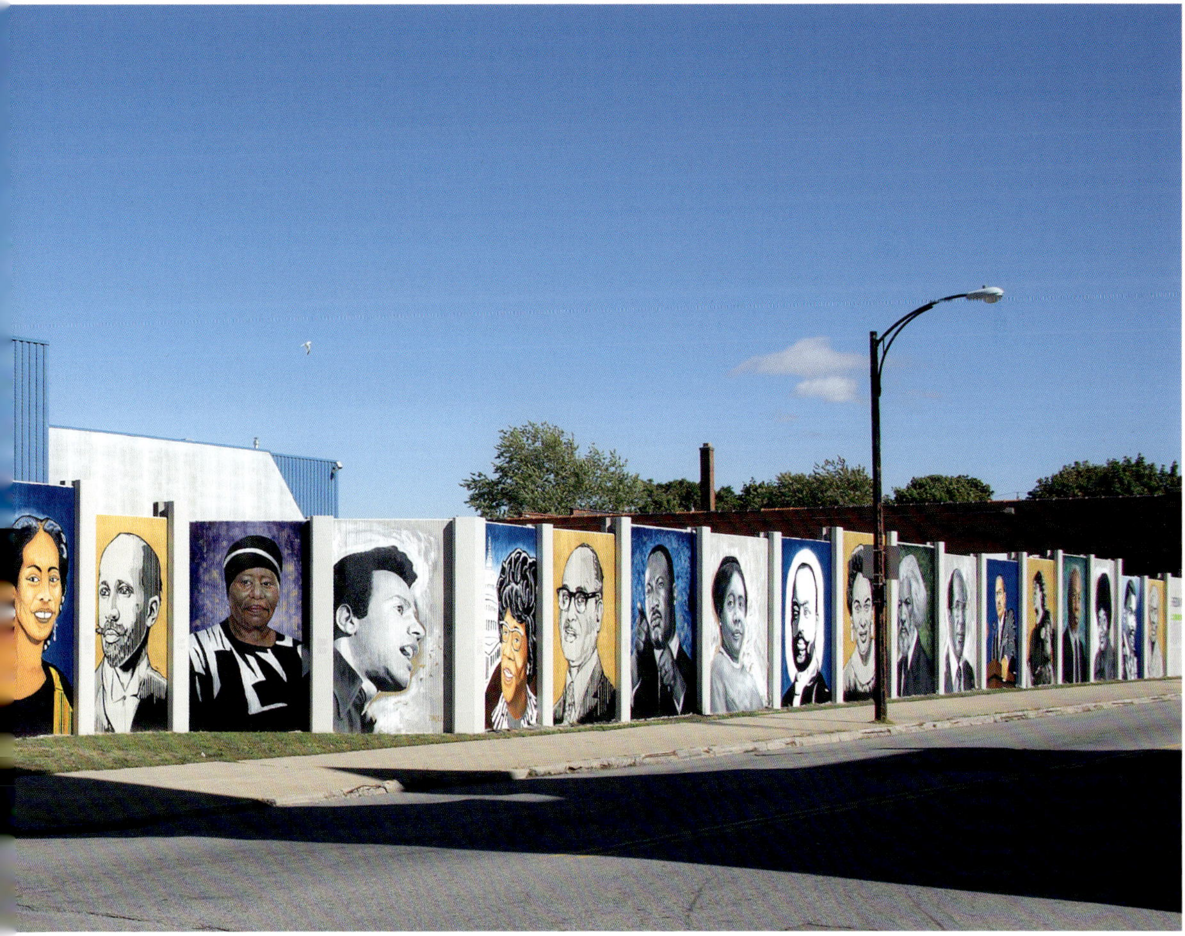

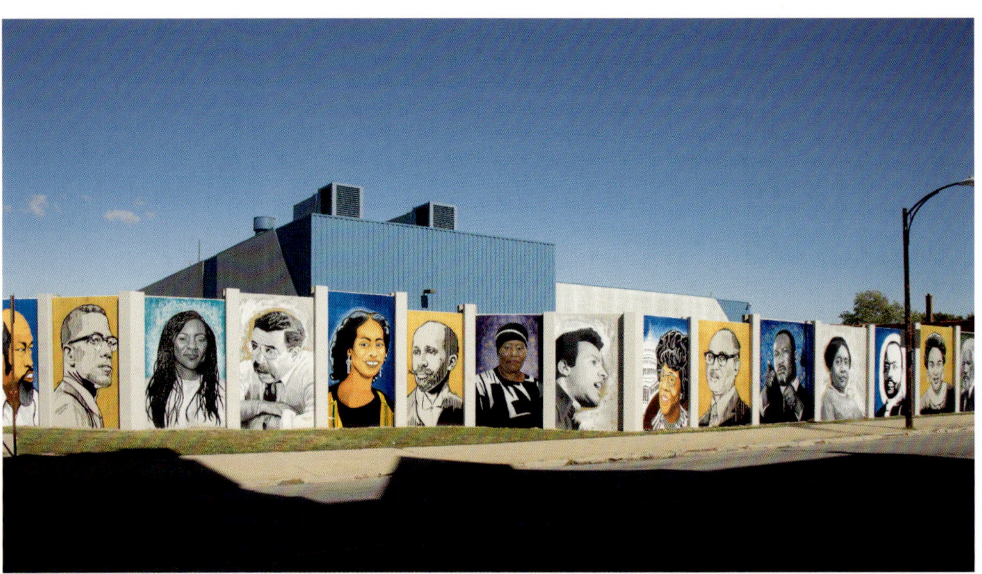

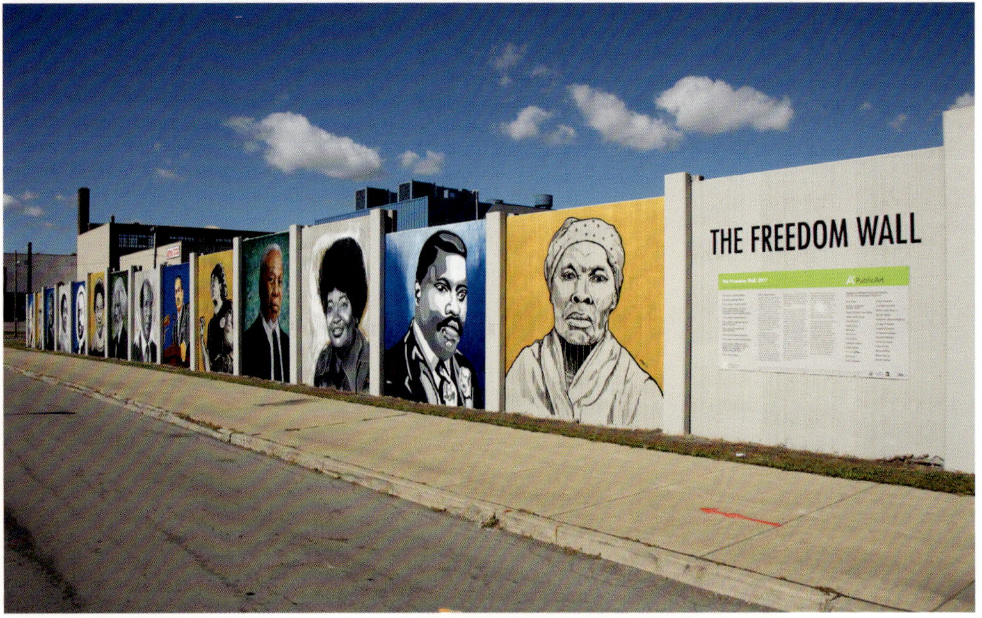
THE FREEDOM WALL

From my earliest recollection as a child, I've always imagined and entertained the idea of pursuing a professional career in the arts, particularly as a full-time working artist. After obediently fulfilling all the basic expectations of graduating high school, completing college, and finding full-time employment, I felt quite mediocre at best, wherever I landed. There were several moments throughout my adult life where I stepped off the paved and visible path and stepped into the dense forest of entrepreneurship as an artist. Although liberating, the excursions were brief, and I often returned to standard employment to more stably provide for my family. All along, I incessantly pondered precisely how I could make the transition into a full-time artist. It felt delusional and far out of my reach, yet intuitively logical, and to my surprise it was closer than I could have imagined.

Staring across the gorge of possibility and hope, with doubt personified as the narrator of my big wishful leap, the "how" emerged in the form of a phone call from Aaron Ott at the Buffalo AKG. He brought to my attention that he was curating and planning a remarkable and historic public mural project in the African American Heritage Corridor. He finished the conversation with a casual, "Is this something that you might be interested in?" Having not fully thought it all the way through, I replied, "Yes" and later fought and fended off frequent self-sabotages of second-guessings of my ability to deliver. That project was *The Freedom Wall*.

The summer of 2017 marked the transformation of a cement retaining wall at the corner of Michigan Avenue and East Ferry Street into a 300-foot-wide work of art, as well as a personal transformation and crucial pivot for my career. Self-discovery, community healing, deep restorative dialogue, and history-making were all happening simultaneously at this site. Art entered as a catalyst and bridge for steps towards mending a city divided racially and economically for decades and over generations. It was a masterclass in empathy, collaboration, and love, dipped in the sweetness of art. Since that moment, I can fortunately say I've continued contributing positively to our Buffalo community, using art as my love language, so to speak.

My gratitude to the Buffalo AKG is always at the ready, for what I have gained in access to resources, professional artmaking, and mural experience has served me with confidence and knowledge to walk in my purpose and practice as a full-time working artist. Thank you for supporting our ideas, amplifying our voices, and recognizing our value.

—EDREYS WAJED

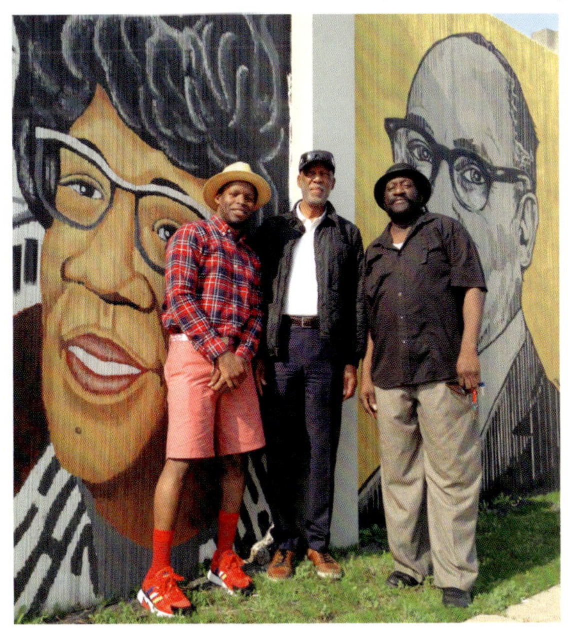

Artists Edreys Wajed (left) and John Baker (right) with Terrence Roberts, one of the Little Rock Nine, who visited the wall.

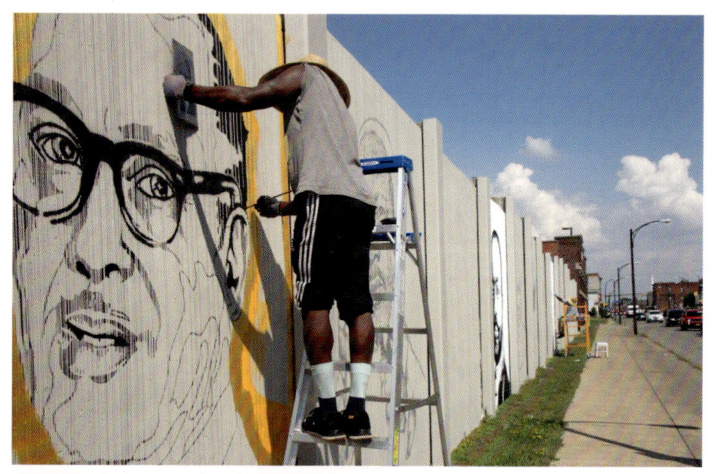

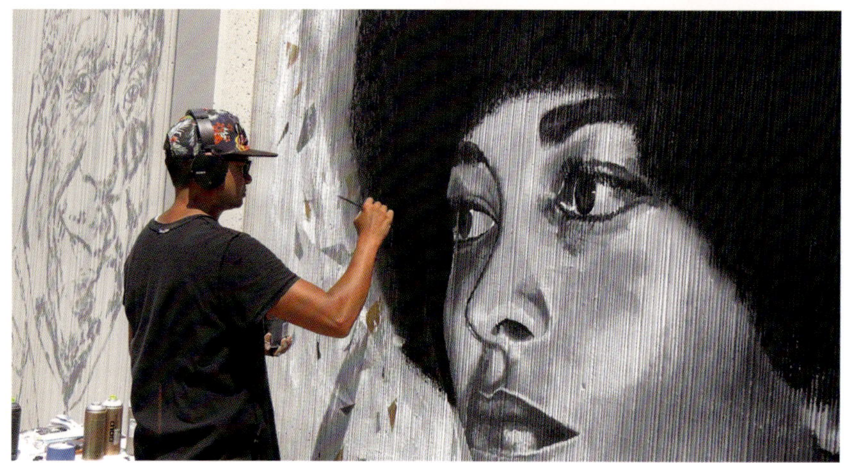

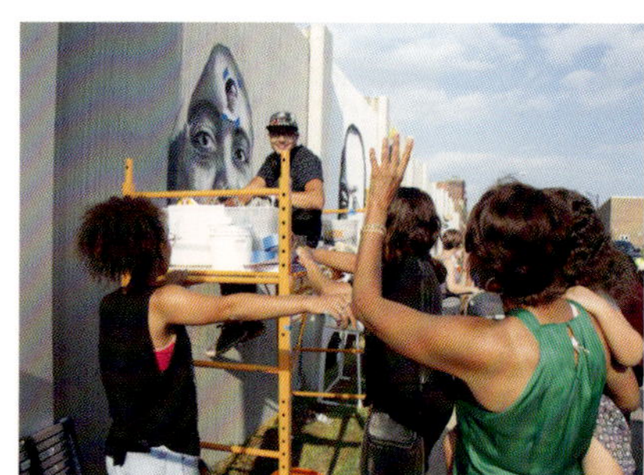

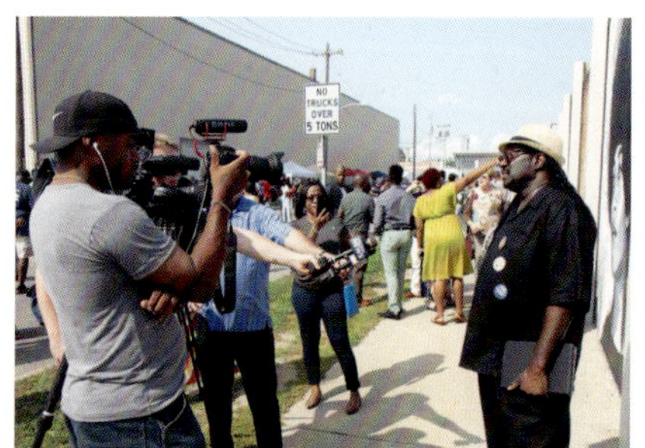

Public art is trial by fire. To create in the public eye means a number of things, most notably that it is of course…public. While this fact may seem obvious, its simplicity may obscure what that actually entails. Creating work in such a way often requires community feedback, increasing your scale, and, most nerve-wracking of all, laying your flaws bare for all to see. But that process is a crucible, and what's left after ego and fear are burned away may very well be what we all search for: our artistic voice.

My journey into public art was a whirlwind. I was brought on board by Aaron Ott and the Public Art team as the fourth and final artist who would help create *The Freedom Wall* alongside Edreys Wajed, Chuck Tingley, and John Baker. This project has become somewhat legendary and undeniably dear to the hearts of Buffalonians, but its origin was notably turbulent. The community was demanding a voice in the decision-making process and an institutional shift was needed. When I look back on this, I am grateful for that passion and the fact that the community was so resolute. I owe everything that has come since to that steadfastness.

So often in life when you are breaking new ground in uncharted territory, you find yourself unwelcome. But joining this project was different. I found that when I arrived, not only was there a seat at the table, there was support, encouragement, and genuine appreciation for my participation. The art world was not designed with the voices of Black women in mind, but creating public art has given me a megaphone. With *The Freedom Wall*, I suddenly found myself shouting with paint, speaking with brushes, and, even better, I found eyes attentive where ears had been unreceptive. There was something so validating, so encouraging about creating work that not only spoke to the truths in my heart but did so on a large scale. Creating public art gave me the ability to be authentic, to take risks, and to build a name for myself for those very things. My venture into public art allowed me the time and means to turn greater attention to my studio practice. The two branches of my work have been intertwined ever since, both in technique and concept. Because of my public art, people now listen to my studio voice as well.

As I am grateful to the community, I am also grateful to Aaron Ott and the Public Art team, not just for my story, but for the way in which the department has shifted the museum's accessibility. I grew up going to museums, but so many of us within the Black community did not. Many people have never felt comfortable enough to enter such a historically white institution. So often the message the world gives us is that there is "high art" and that it is almost exclusively "not for us." Public art has become a bridge of sorts, taking art out of the confines of the museum's walls. Additionally, there has been an institutional awakening to the reality that there is a wealth of talented Black artists here in Buffalo, and the scene is made richer for their inclusion.

—JULIA BOTTOMS

← Chuck Tingley works on his portrait of Angela Davis, one of the original portraits proposed for the project. ↓ Julia Bottoms works from a reference of the long-serving New York State Assembly Member Arthur O. Eve.

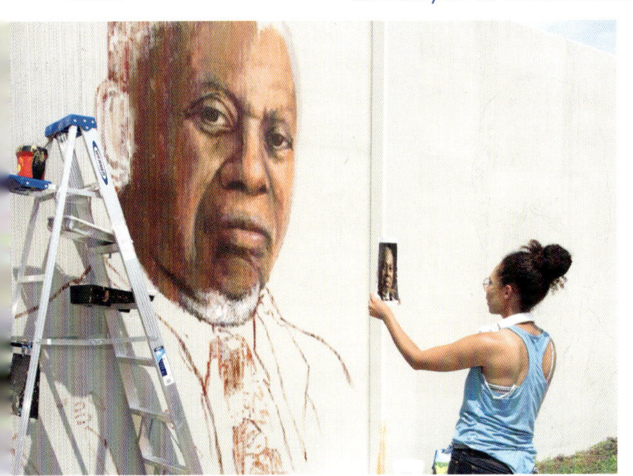

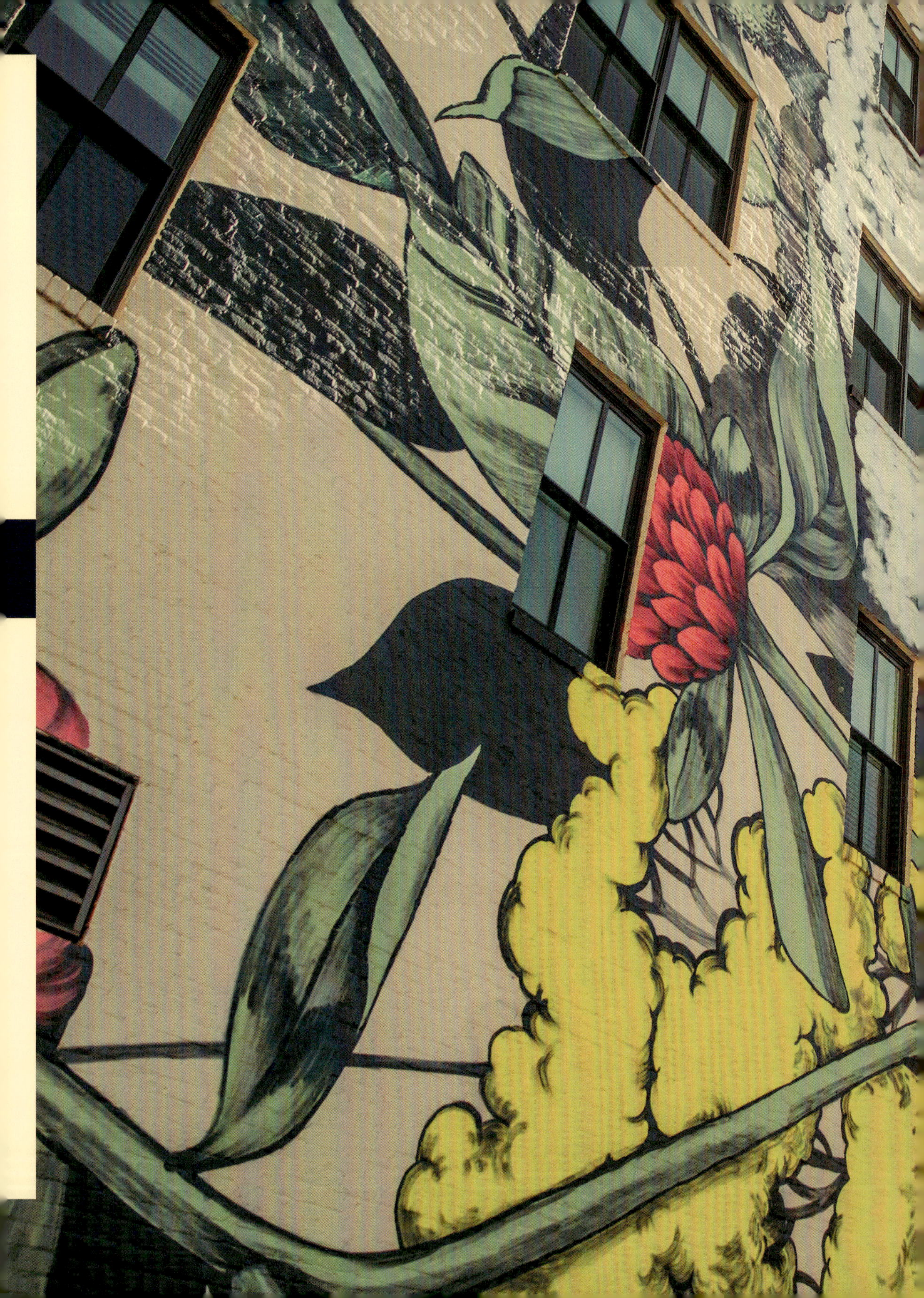

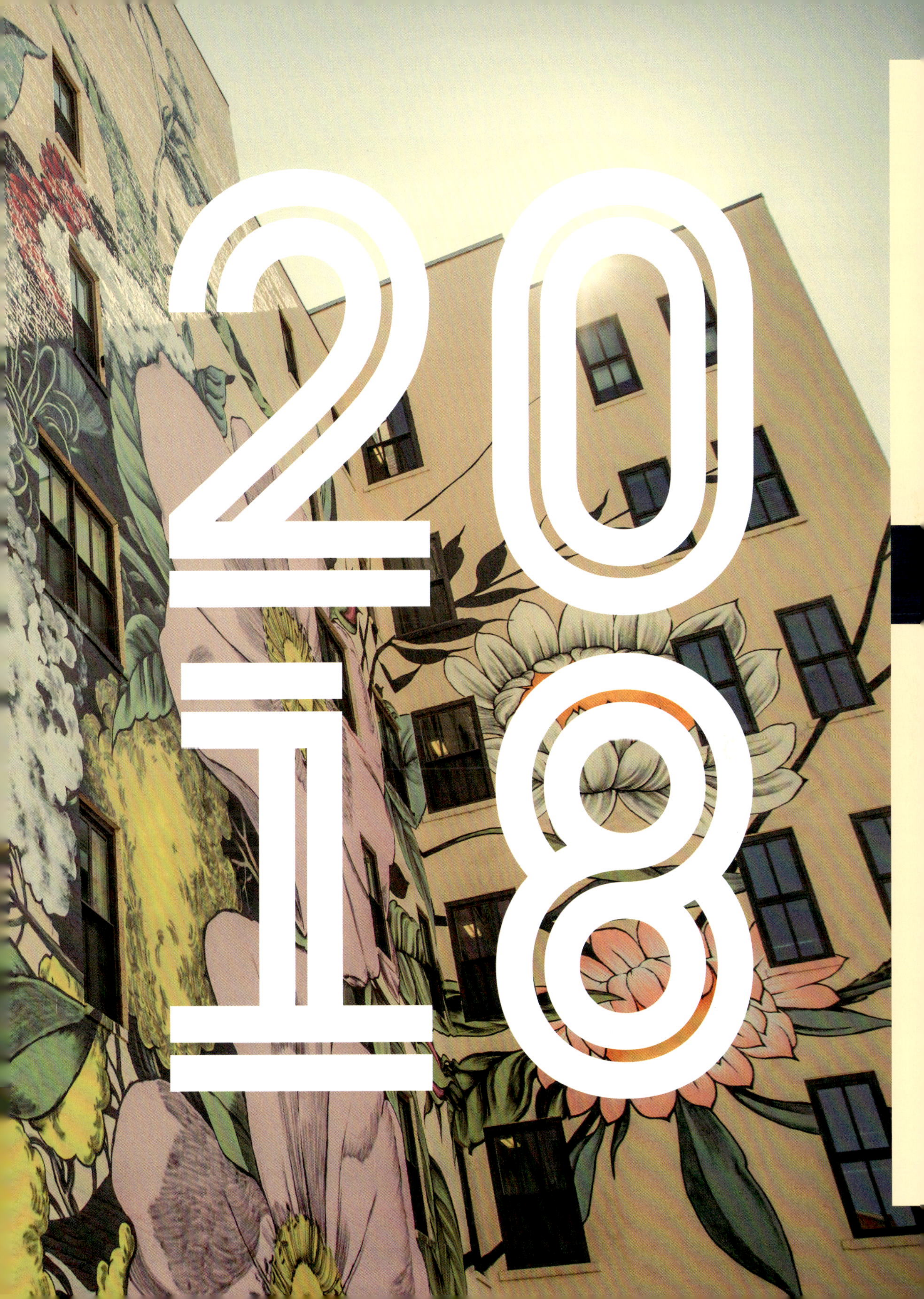

Emotional Wayfinding

Stephen Powers

Throughout Erie County

Fitz Books and Waffles,
431 Ellicott Street, Buffalo

Fifteen billboards;
reclaimed metal sign, neon
Dimensions variable

Over the summer of 2018, the museum distributed a tear-away postcard in various locations throughout the region, prompting Western New Yorkers to share their thoughts on what they like and dislike about Buffalo. The artist gathered these responses and used them to develop signage that was displayed throughout Erie County and the City of Buffalo.

The materials for one work in the series, *Running Home* (below left), was a sign that was originally designed and manufactured in Buffalo for a real estate company in Newark, New Jersey. Powers reclaimed and retrofit the sign with his own neon motif.

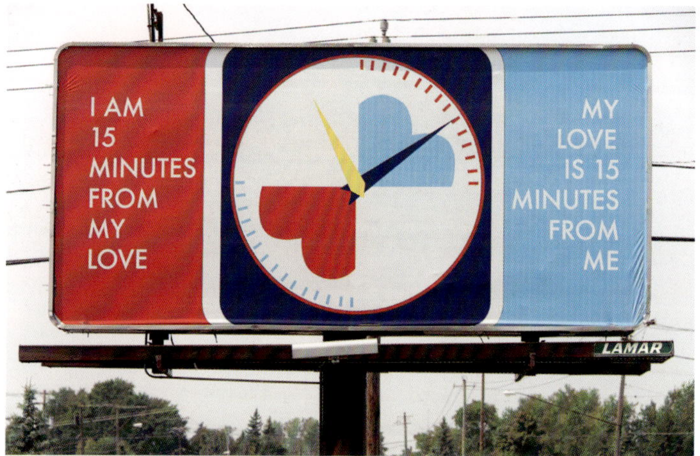

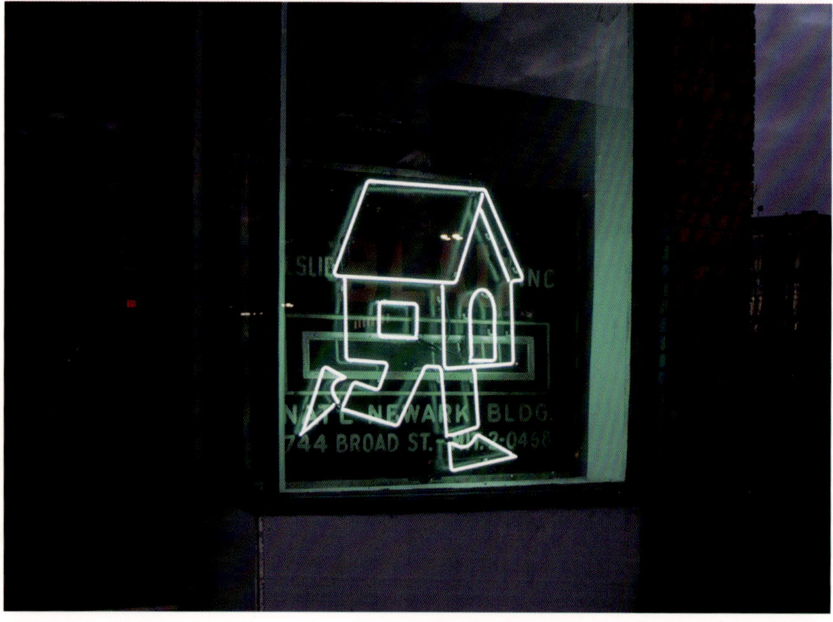

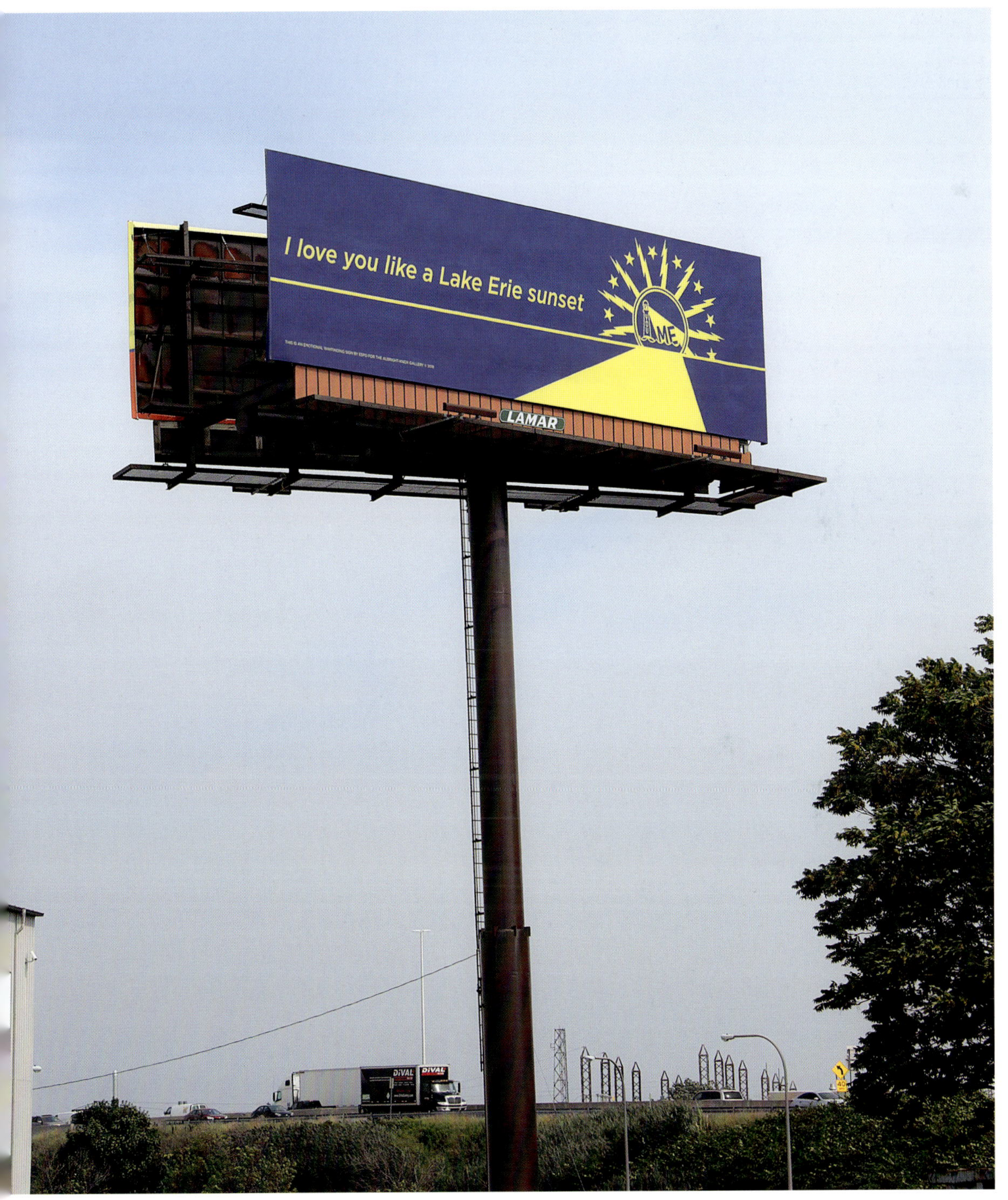

I love you like a Lake Erie sunset
THIS IS AN EMOTIONAL WAYFINDING SIGN BY ESPO FOR THE ALBRIGHT-KNOX GALLERY © 2018
ME
LAMAR

ONE through ZERO
(The Ten Numbers)

Robert Indiana

Wilkeson Pointe, Outer
Harbor

Ten Cor-Ten steel sculptures
Each overall: 96 × 96 ×
48 inches (243.8 × 243.8 ×
121.9 cm)

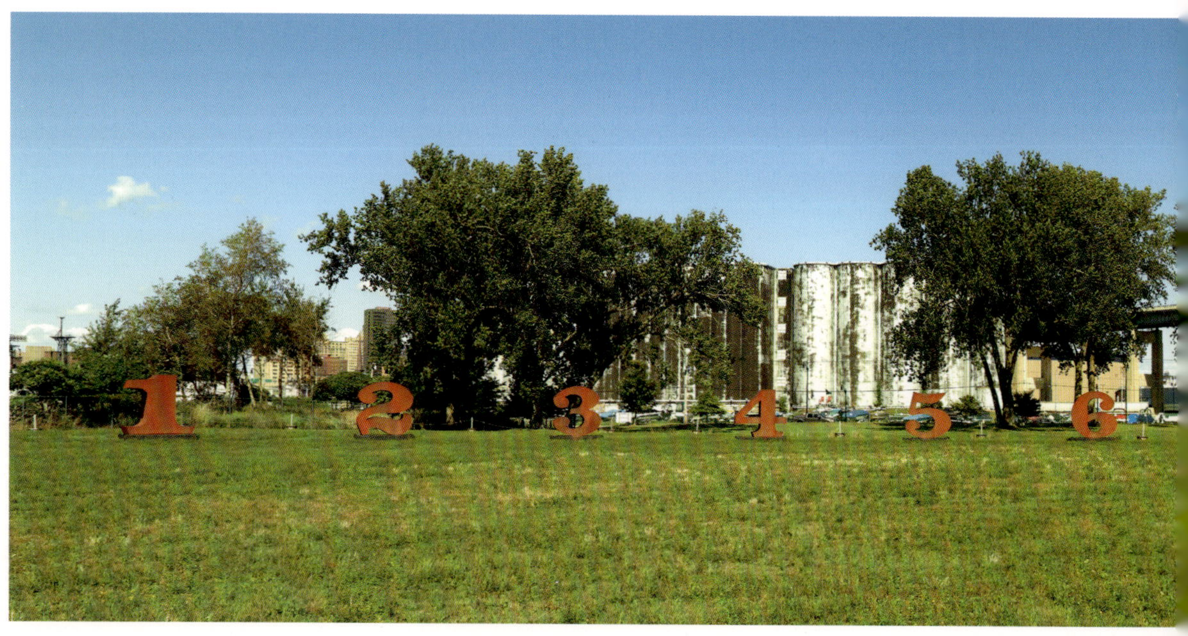

We Are Here

White Bicycle

1260 Hertel Avenue, Buffalo

Acrylic paint
12 × 30 feet (3.7 × 9.1 m)

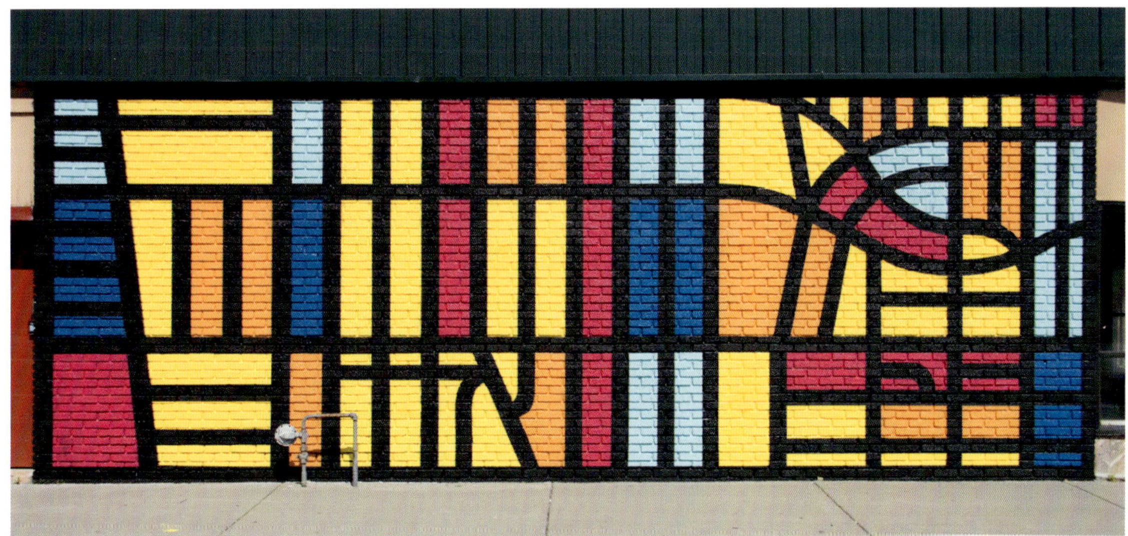

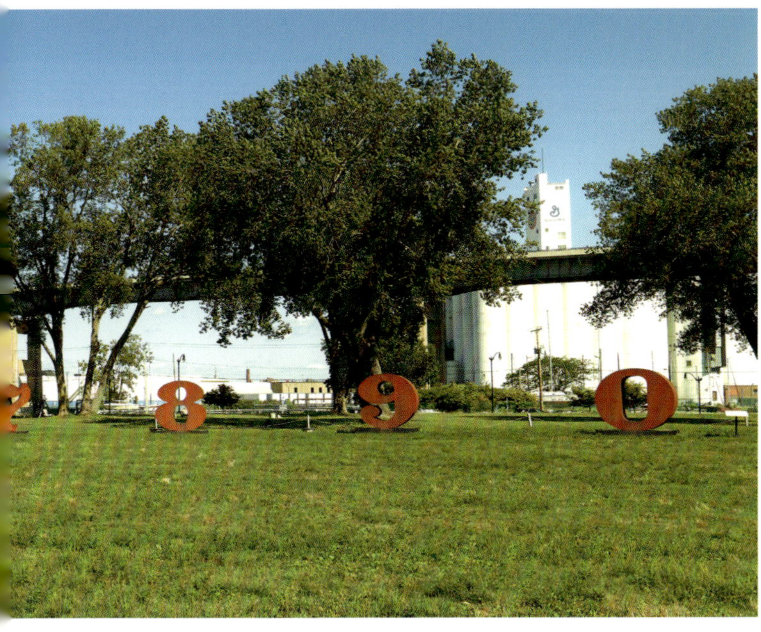

Wildflowers for Buffalo

Louise Jones

465 Washington Street, Buffalo

Acrylic paint
Approximately 80 ×
180 feet (24.4 × 54.9 m)

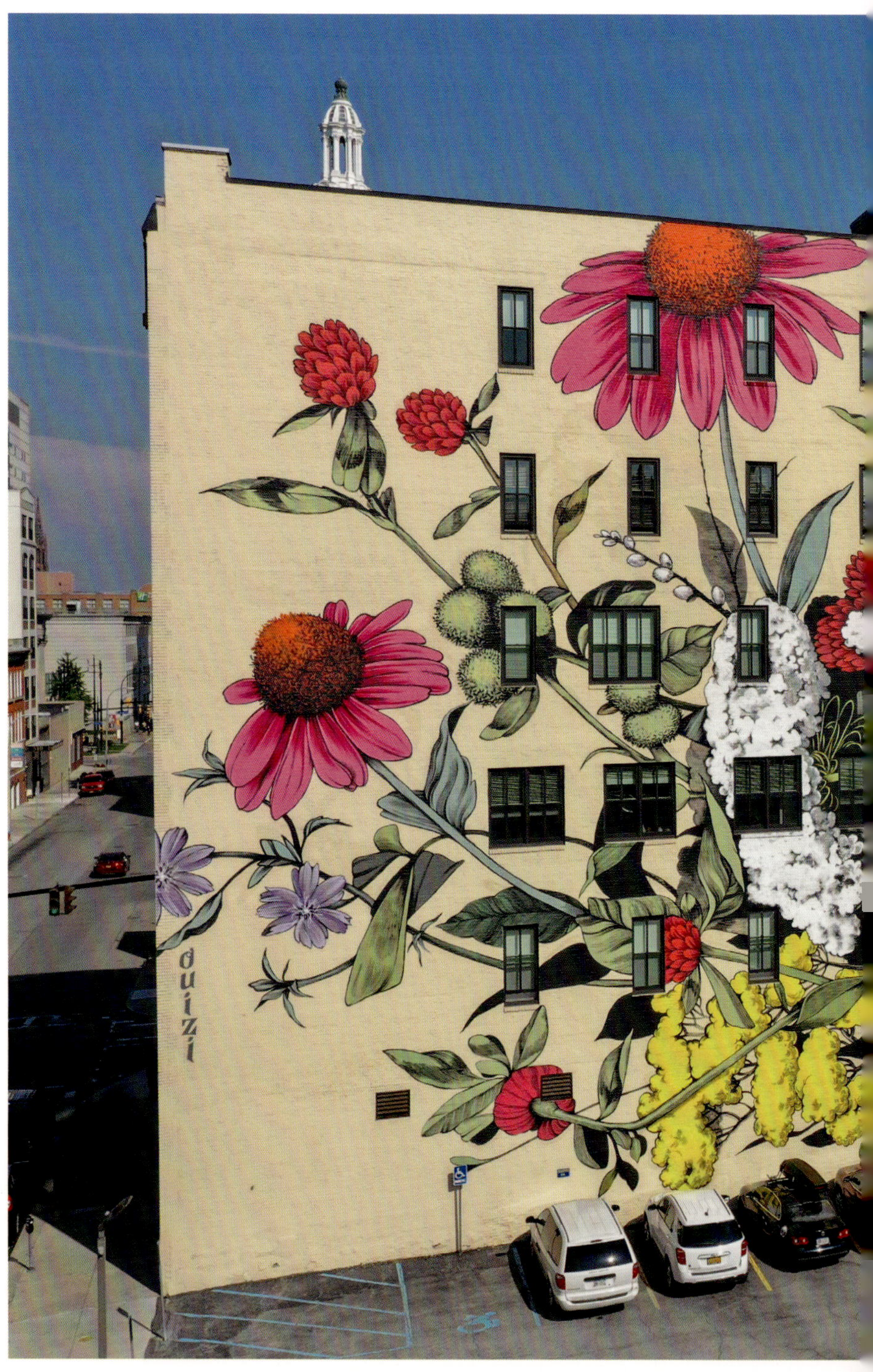

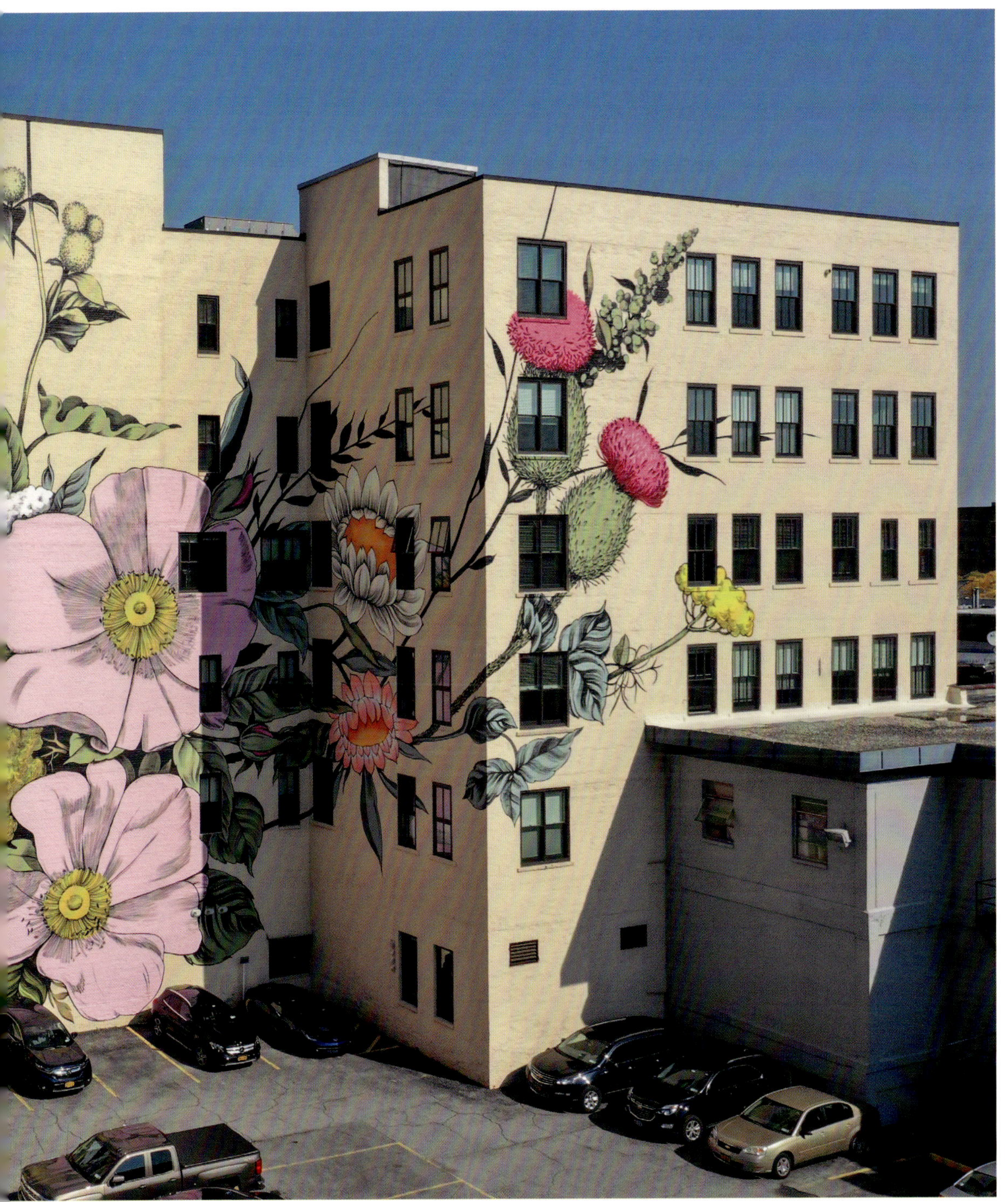

Our Colors Make Us Beautiful

Muhammad Zaman

1131 Broadway Avenue,
Buffalo

Acrylic paint
17 feet 6 inches × 42 feet
(5.3 × 12.8 m)

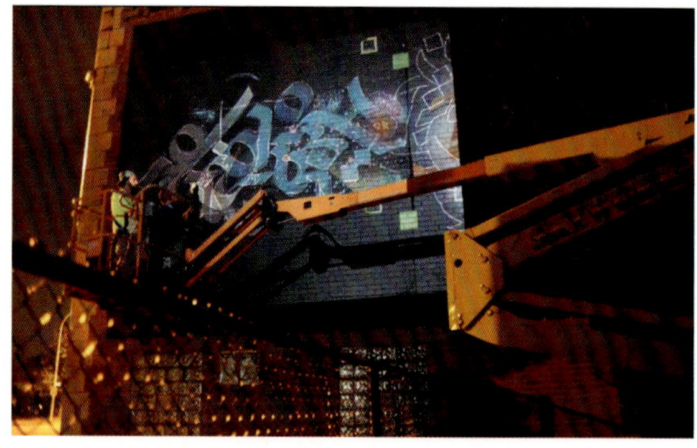

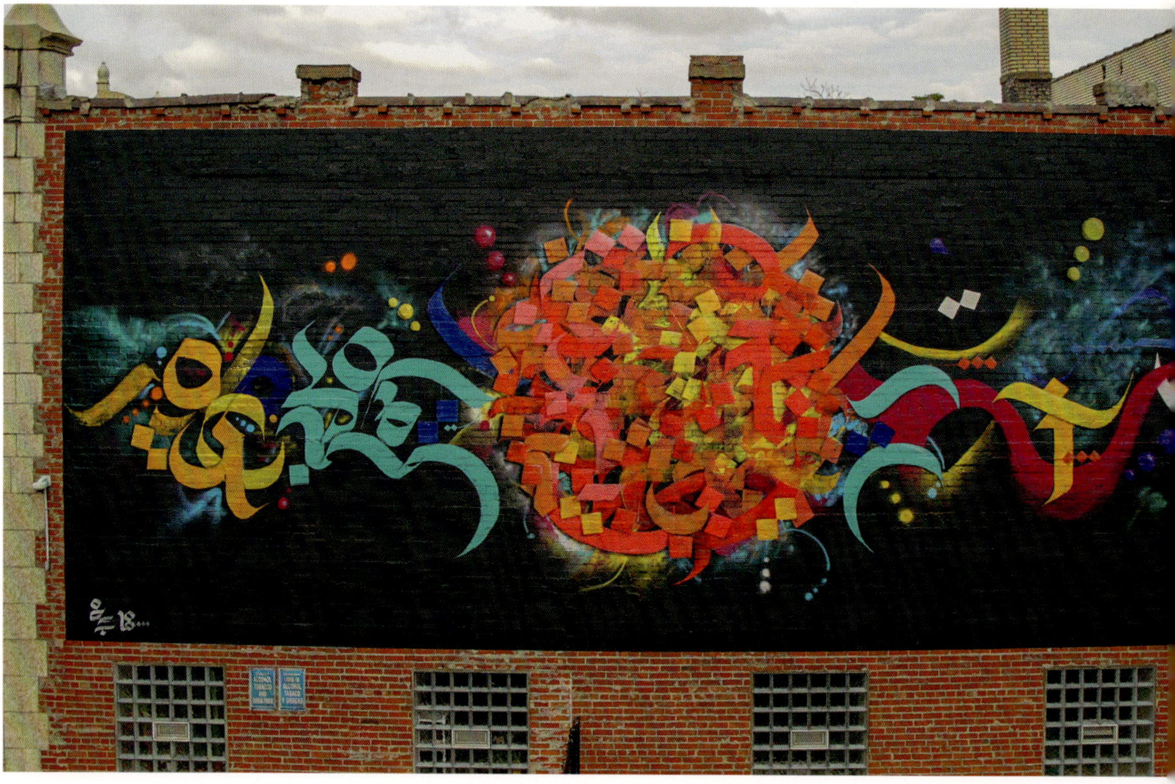

weego

Matt Grote and Chuck Tingley

1503 Hertel Avenue, Buffalo

Acrylic paint
25 × 60 feet (7.6 × 18.3 m)

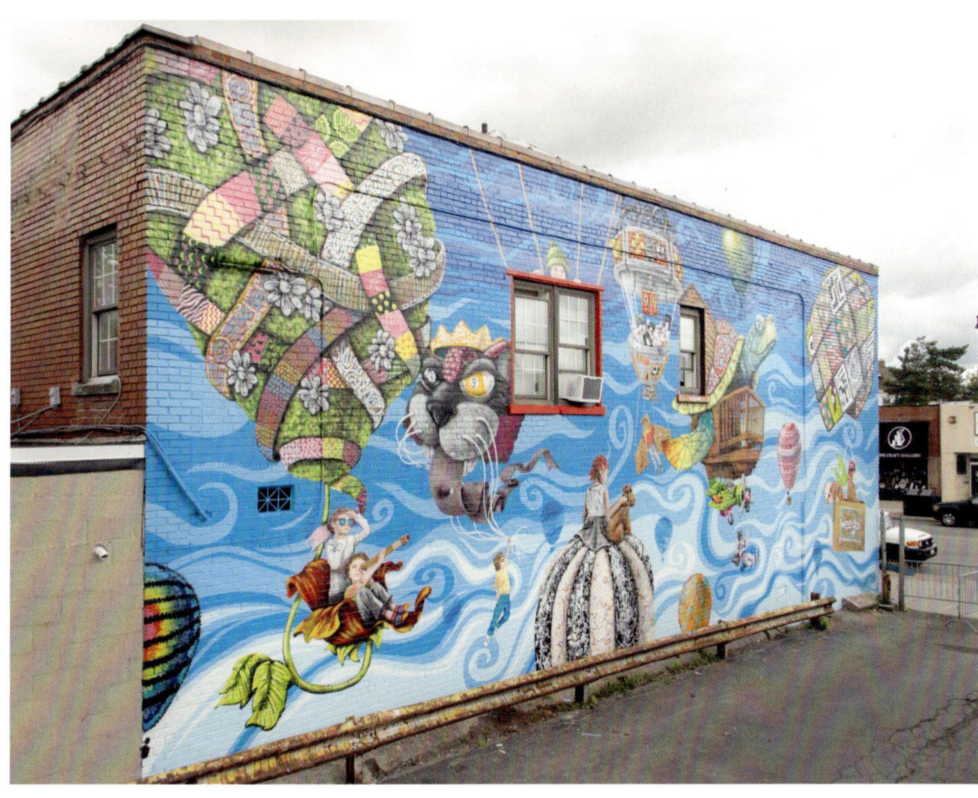

Work and Play

Otecki (Wojciech Kołacz)

617 Fillmore Avenue,
Buffalo

Acrylic paint
30 × 50 feet (9.1 × 15.2 m)

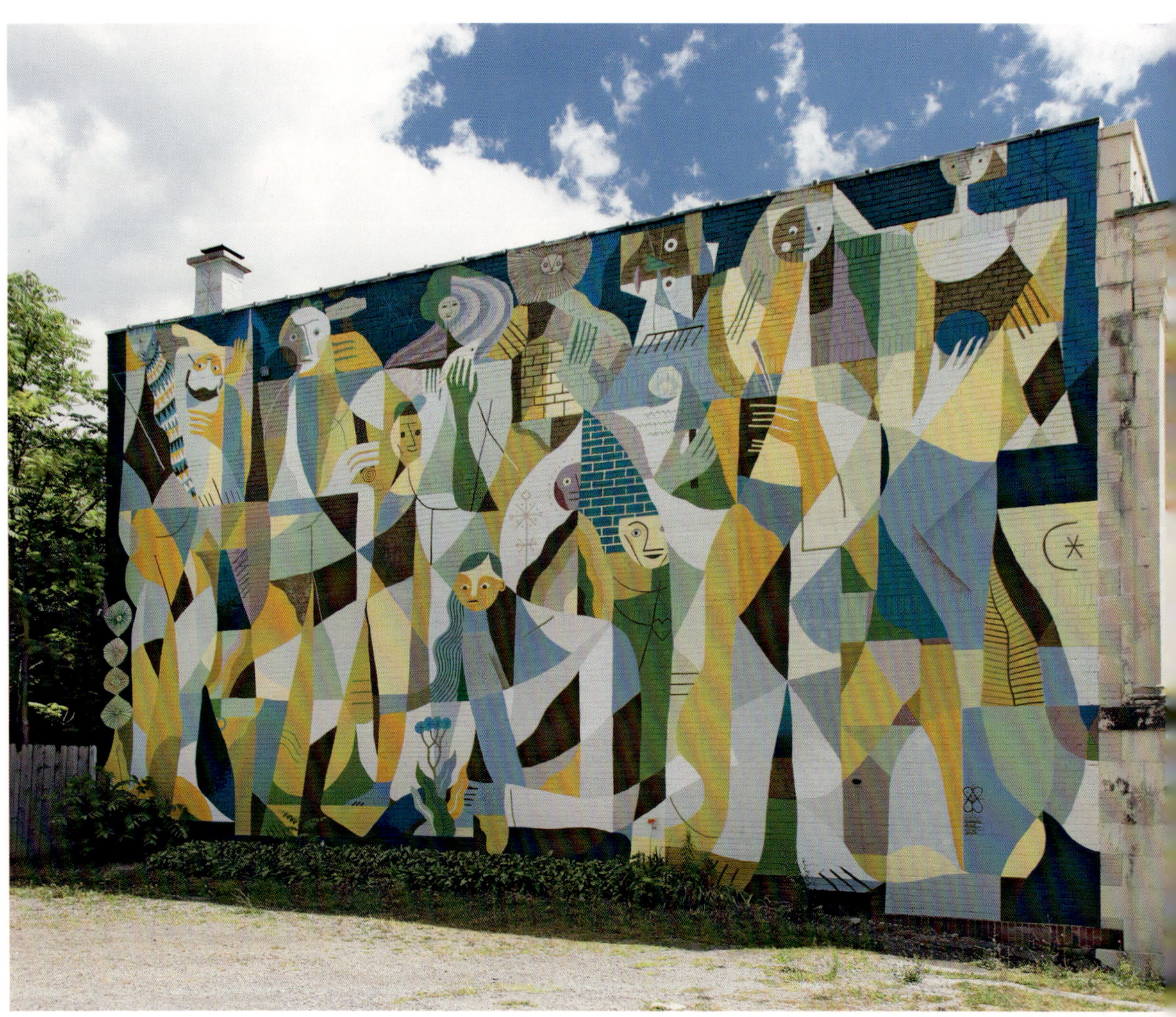

Balancing Act II

Aakash Nihalani

Five Points Bakery,
44 Brayton Street, Buffalo

Steel, aluminum,
and acrylic polyurethane
Overall: 108 × 96 ×
2 ½ inches (274.3 × 24.8 ×
6.4 cm)

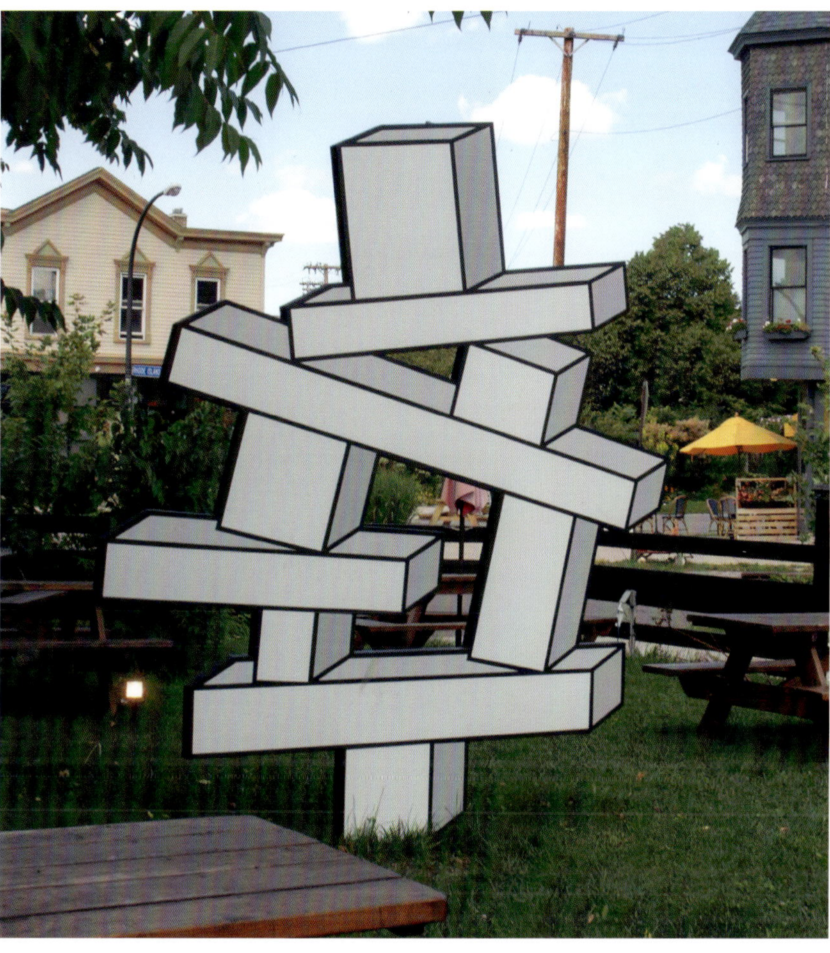

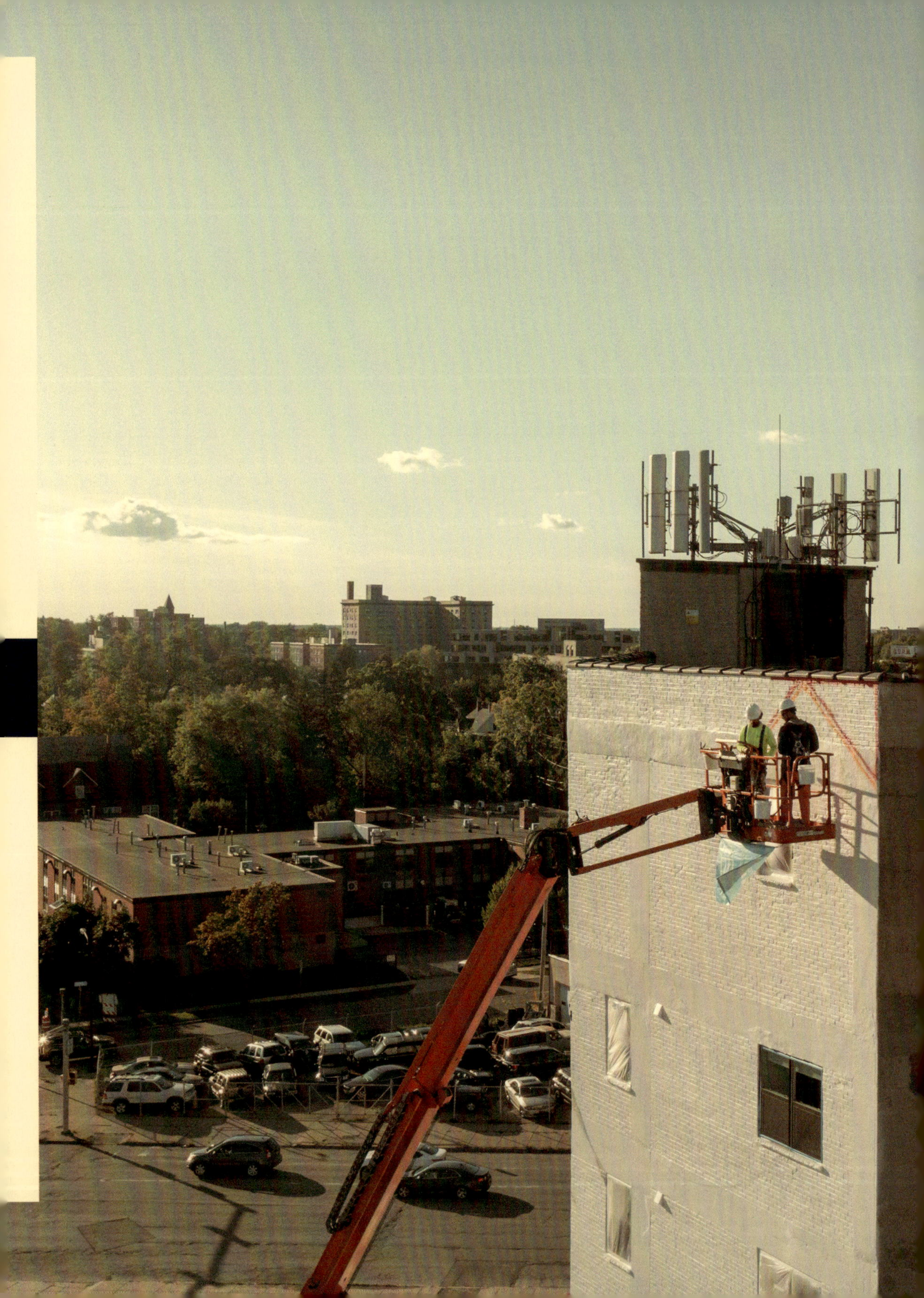

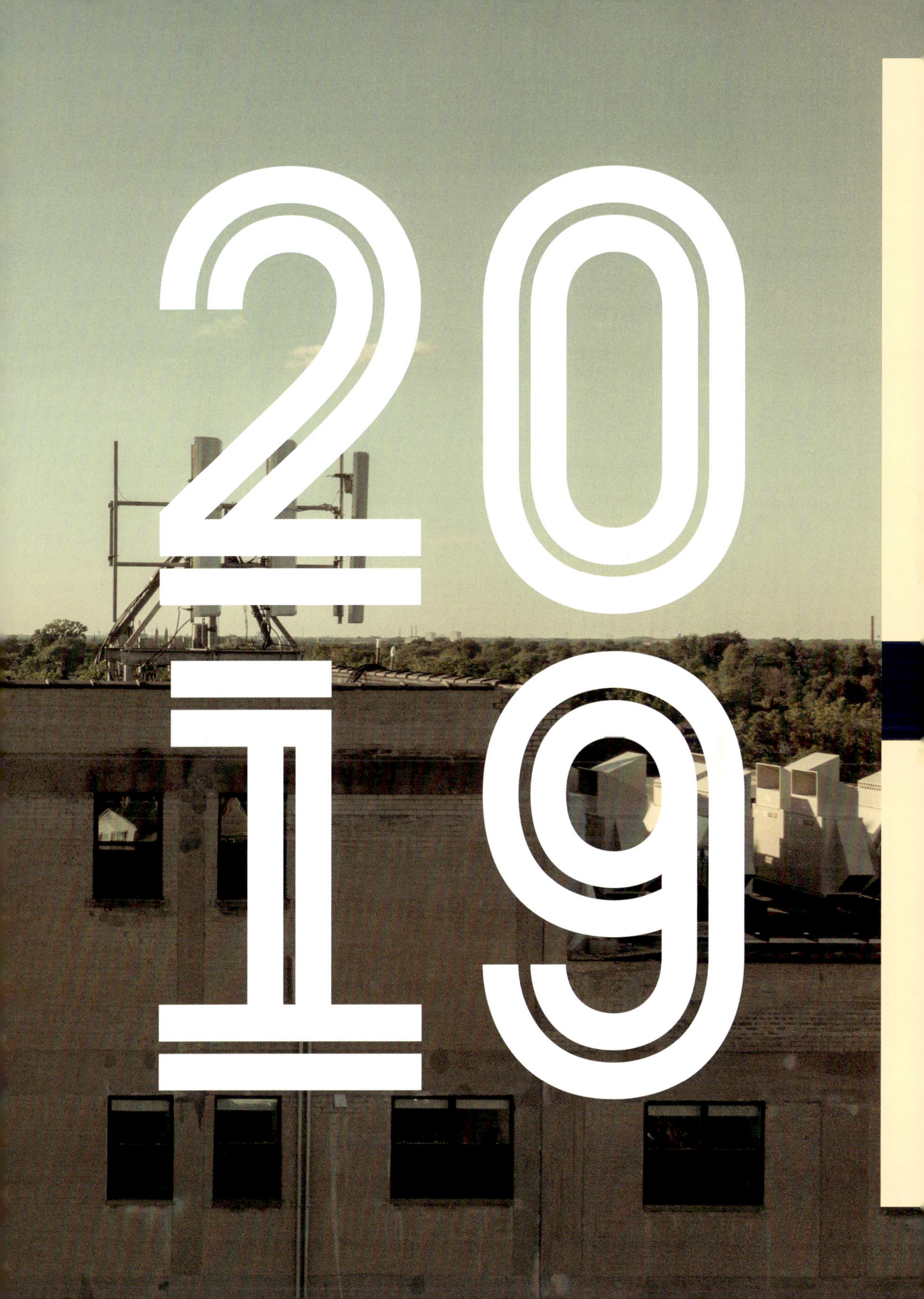
2019

Optichromie—BUF

Felipe Pantone

Back of Town Ballroom,
Washington Street, Buffalo

Spray and acrylic paint
44 × 90 feet (13.4 × 27.4 m)

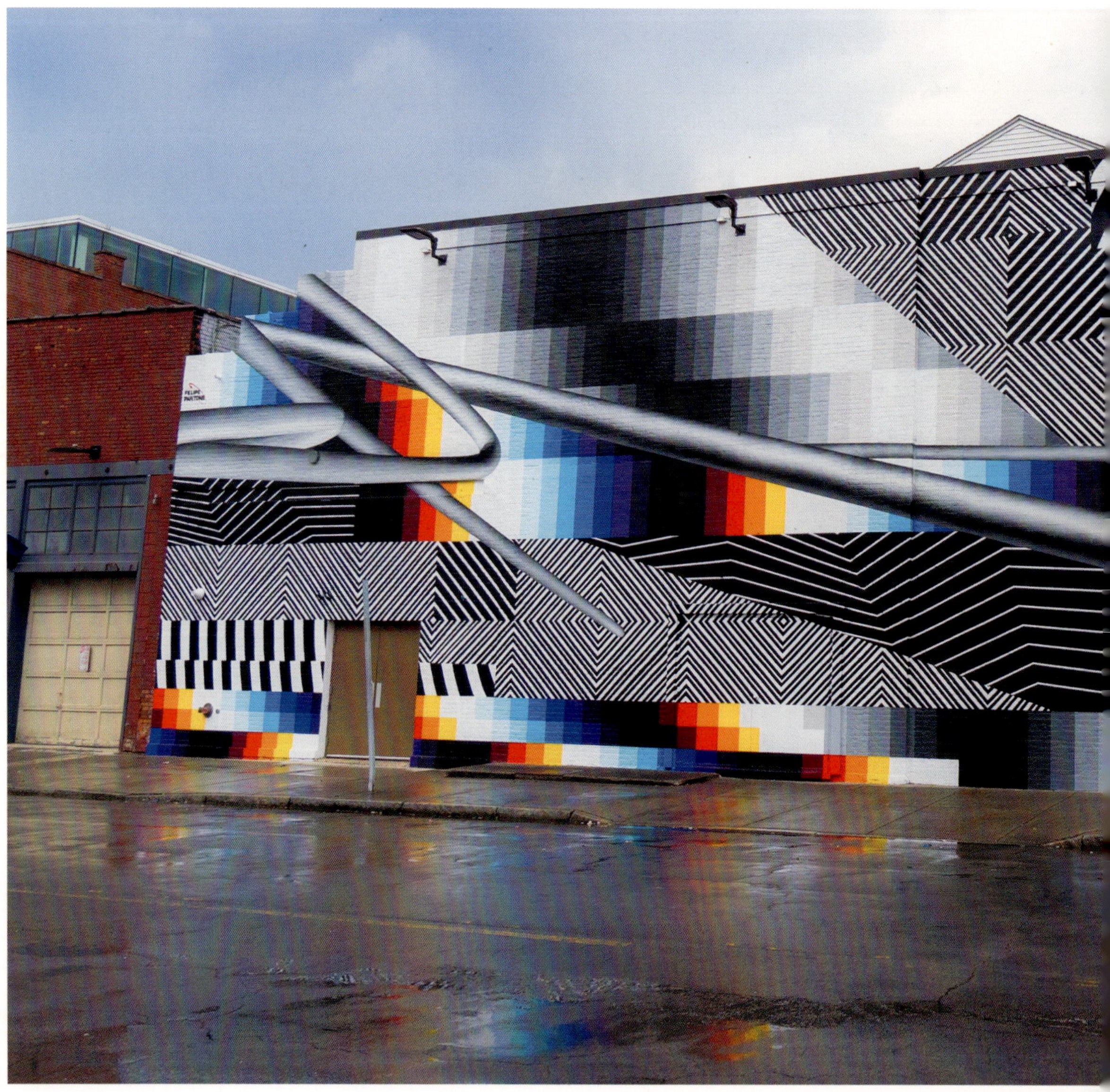

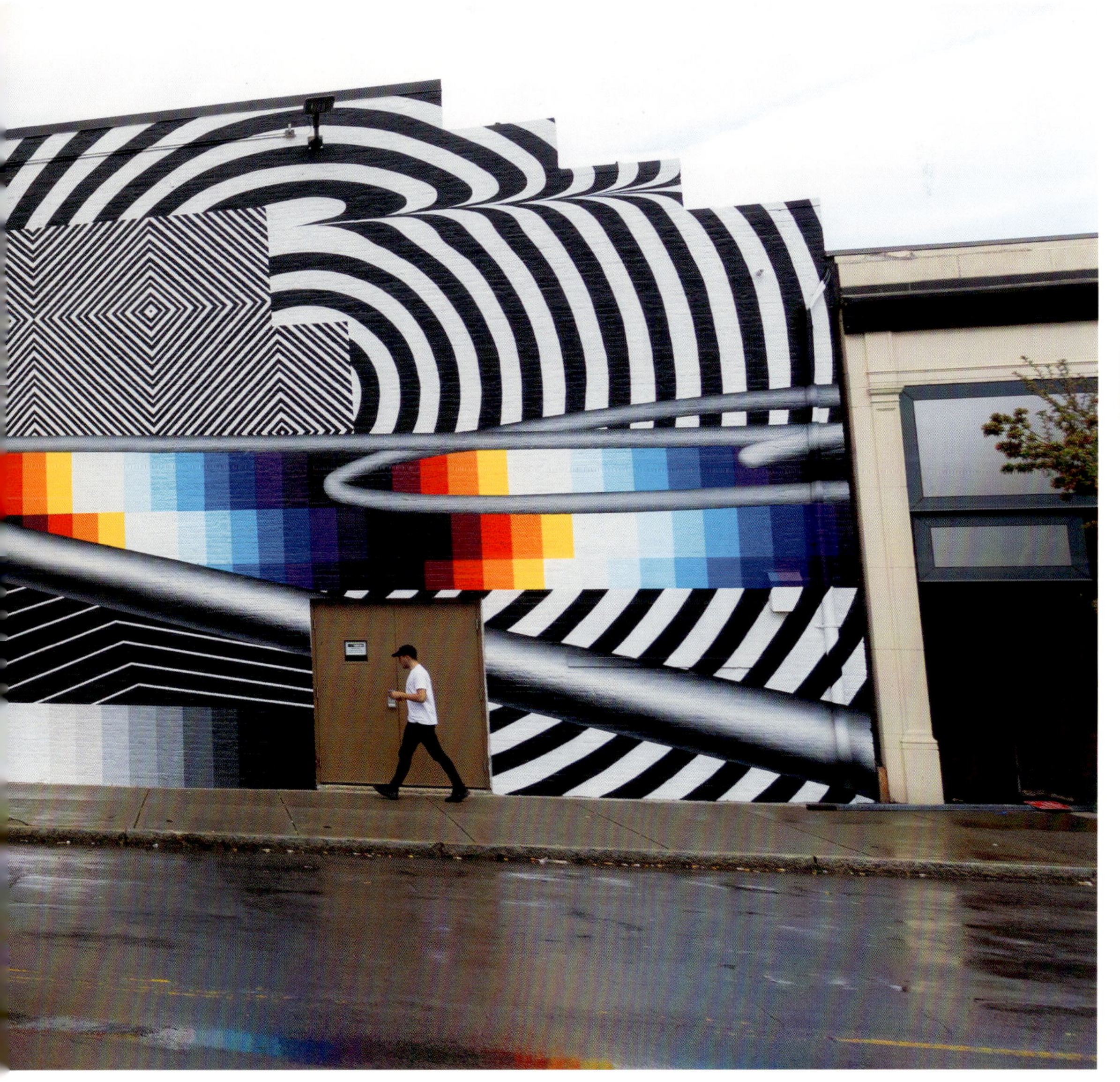

Botanical Blueprint

Hillary Waters Fayle

244 Dewitt Street, Buffalo

Acrylic paint
13 × 48 feet (4.3 × 14.6 m)

My background is in textiles, and the work I make is typically on a very small scale: tiny embroideries or more traditional work on cloth or paper. But I am almost always collaborating with botany in some way. I believe we all have profound and powerful connections to both cloth and plants, whether we're aware of it or not, and it's something I think about a lot. Aside from being integral to our survival, plants and textiles represent specific and symbolic connections to place, time, people, and memory. By bringing traditional textile processes into collaboration with botanical material, I want to express a hopeful interpretation of our complicated relationship to the land—an idea of what is possible when we move forward with gentleness and consideration.

When I was asked to consider this project, I wanted to do it because it felt like such an honor to make something beautiful and meaningful for the city that will always feel like my home, and because it was a chance to work at a scale I never thought possible for my work. I had no idea how to approach a project of this magnitude, and for a while I was intimidated by the idea of making something so huge—until I realized I could approach it as if I were making a quilt: pulling together many smaller pieces to create one large, unified whole.

There is a tradition in quilting where each person in a group embellishes a square of fabric and then all the squares are brought together and bound into a quilt. Each square embodies an essence of its maker and holds their presence through time, and that's an idea that I've always been enamored with. These "album" quilts were often celebratory, made by a group of friends or family to commemorate a special event or just their time together. I love the way these ideas are echoed in the mural: the collective who came together to make cyanotype prints forever celebrated, threaded together on the wall.

The knowledge that many hands make light work spurred the communal nature of quilting bees, and we approached making the source material for the mural with that in mind. Hundreds of people showed up to make prints of the plants surrounding them—each print uniquely capturing the botany, the moment, and a little, indescribable trace of the person making it. I wanted to pull all these prints, these moments, together as a version of an album quilt, seen through a botanical lens. I believe that the plants of a particular place hold the story not only of the land, but of the people who live there, and I wanted this piece to tell that story.

—HILLARY WATERS FAYLE

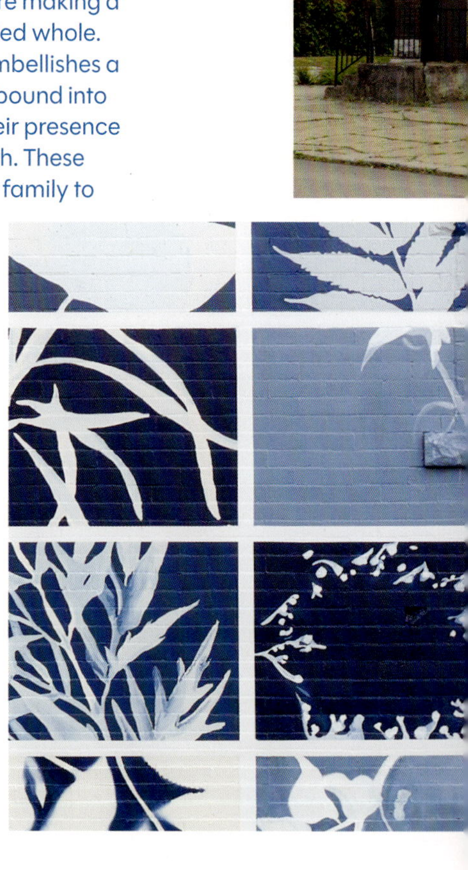

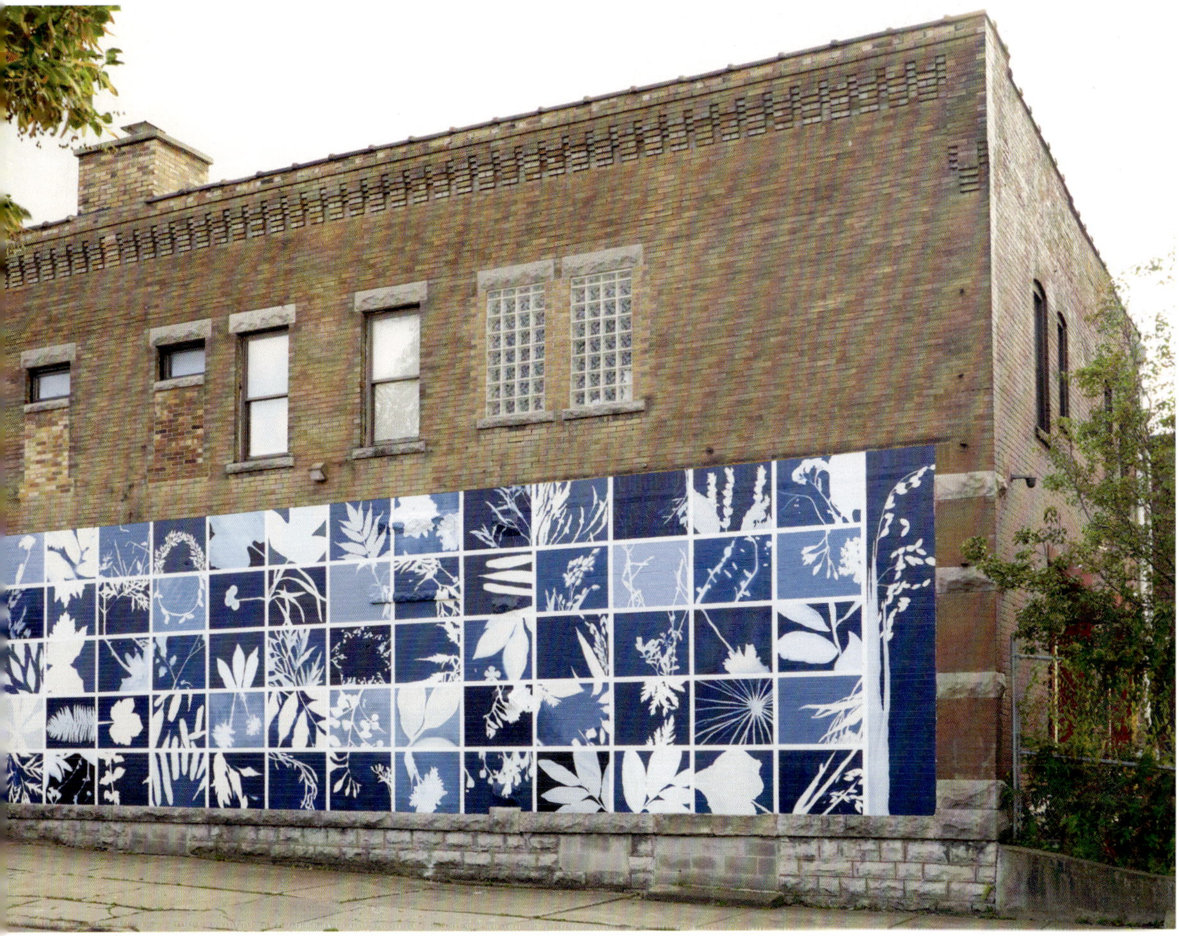

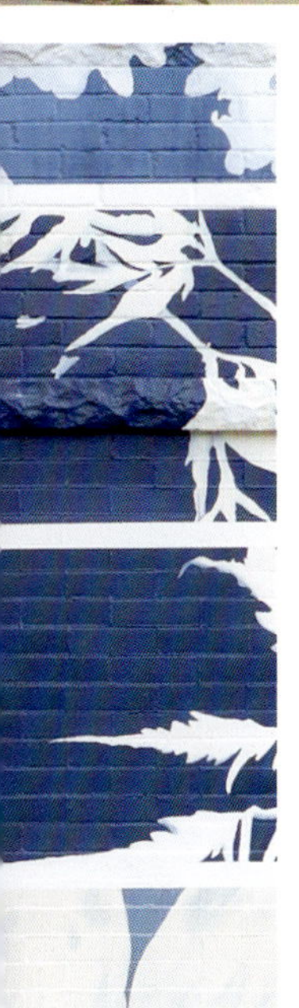

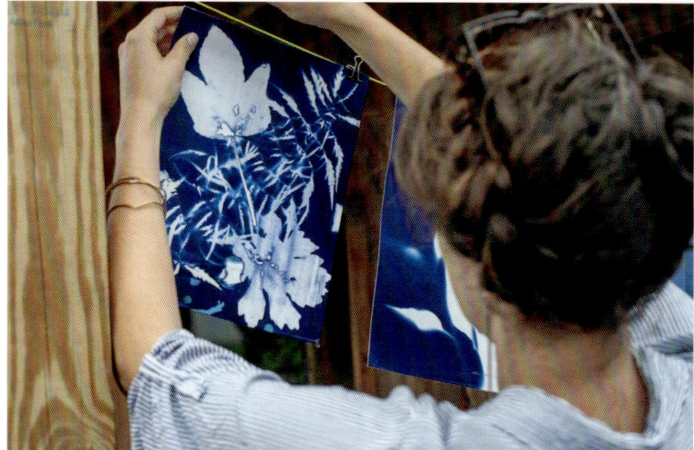

Fayle led cyanotype workshops to facilitate image-making that would inspire the design of the final mural.

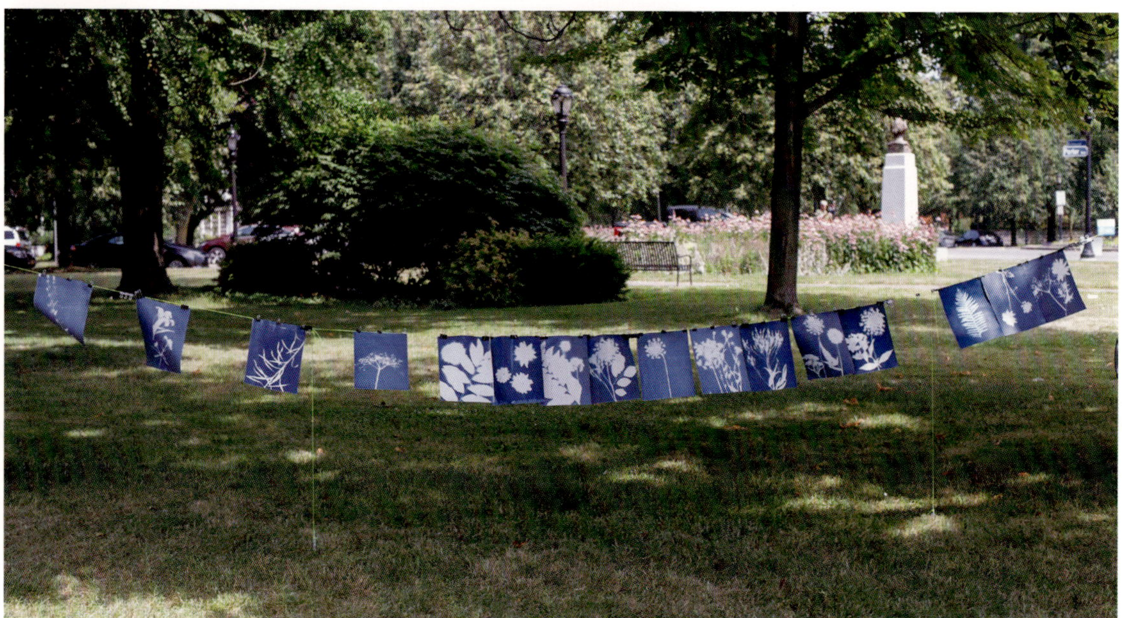

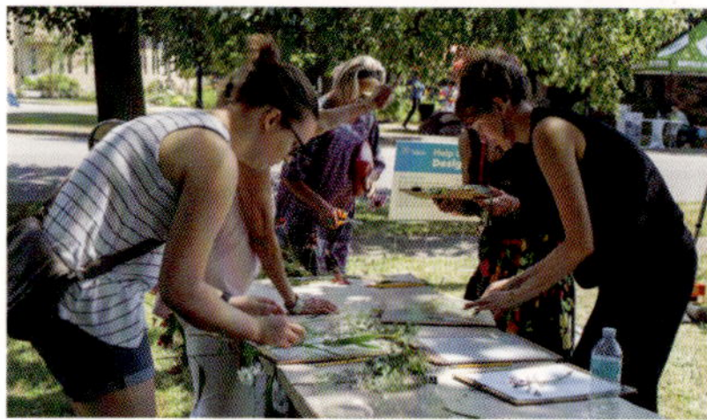

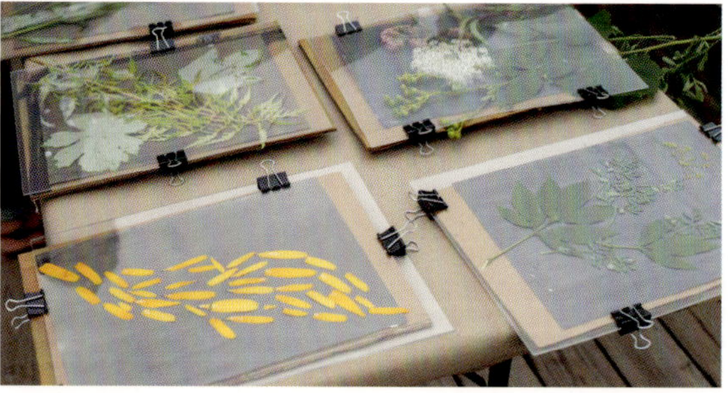

Untitled

Eduardo Kobra

1188 Hertel Avenue, Buffalo

Oil paint
38 × 53 feet (11.6 × 16.2 m)

To create this mural, Kobra drew on an episode in Western New York's history: the friendship between the nineteenth-century writer Samuel Clemens, also known as Mark Twain, and the less-well-known John T. Lewis, an African American man born in 1835, who saved the life of Clemens's sister-in-law and niece by stopping their runaway buggy.

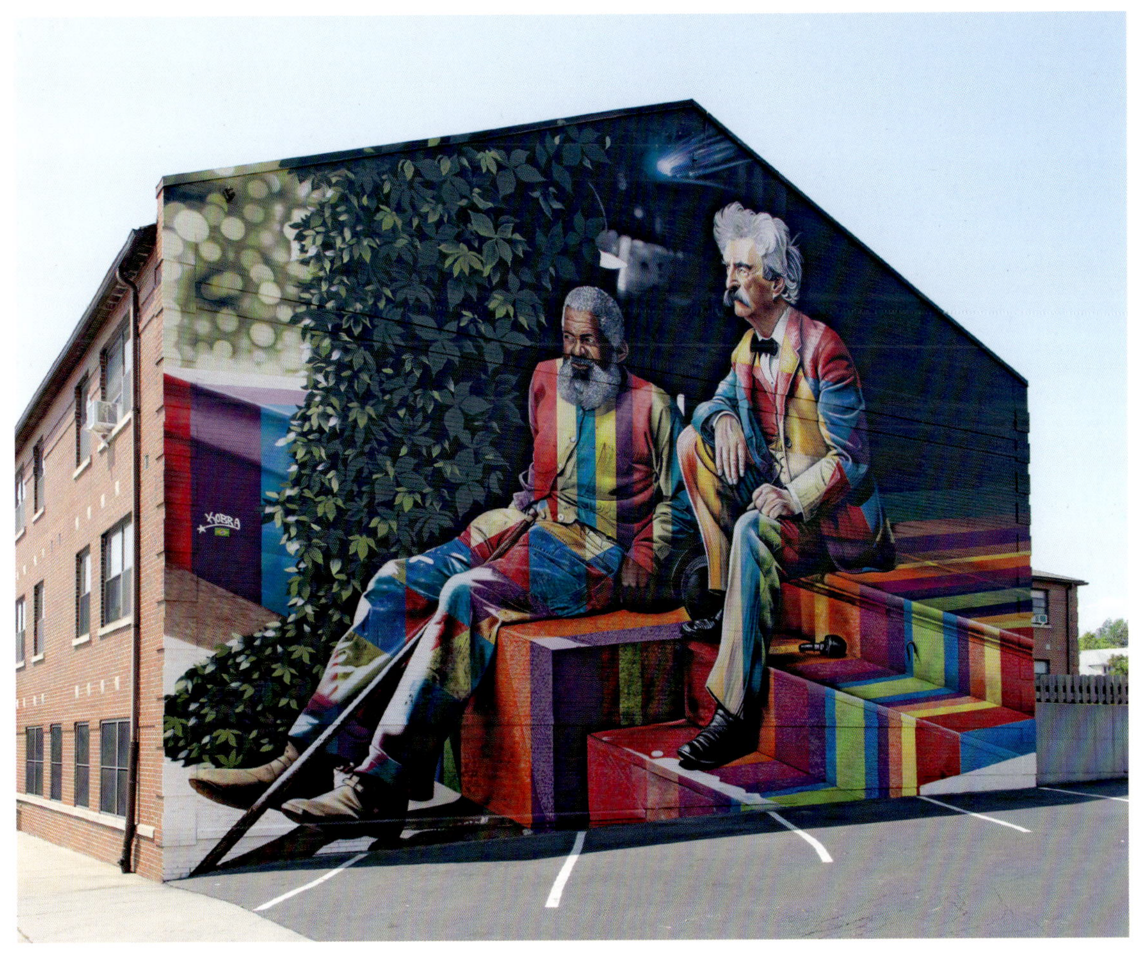

1800s Bikes in Vines

Nicole Cherry

1330 Niagara Street, Buffalo

Acrylic paint
26 × 86 feet (7.9 × 26.2 m)

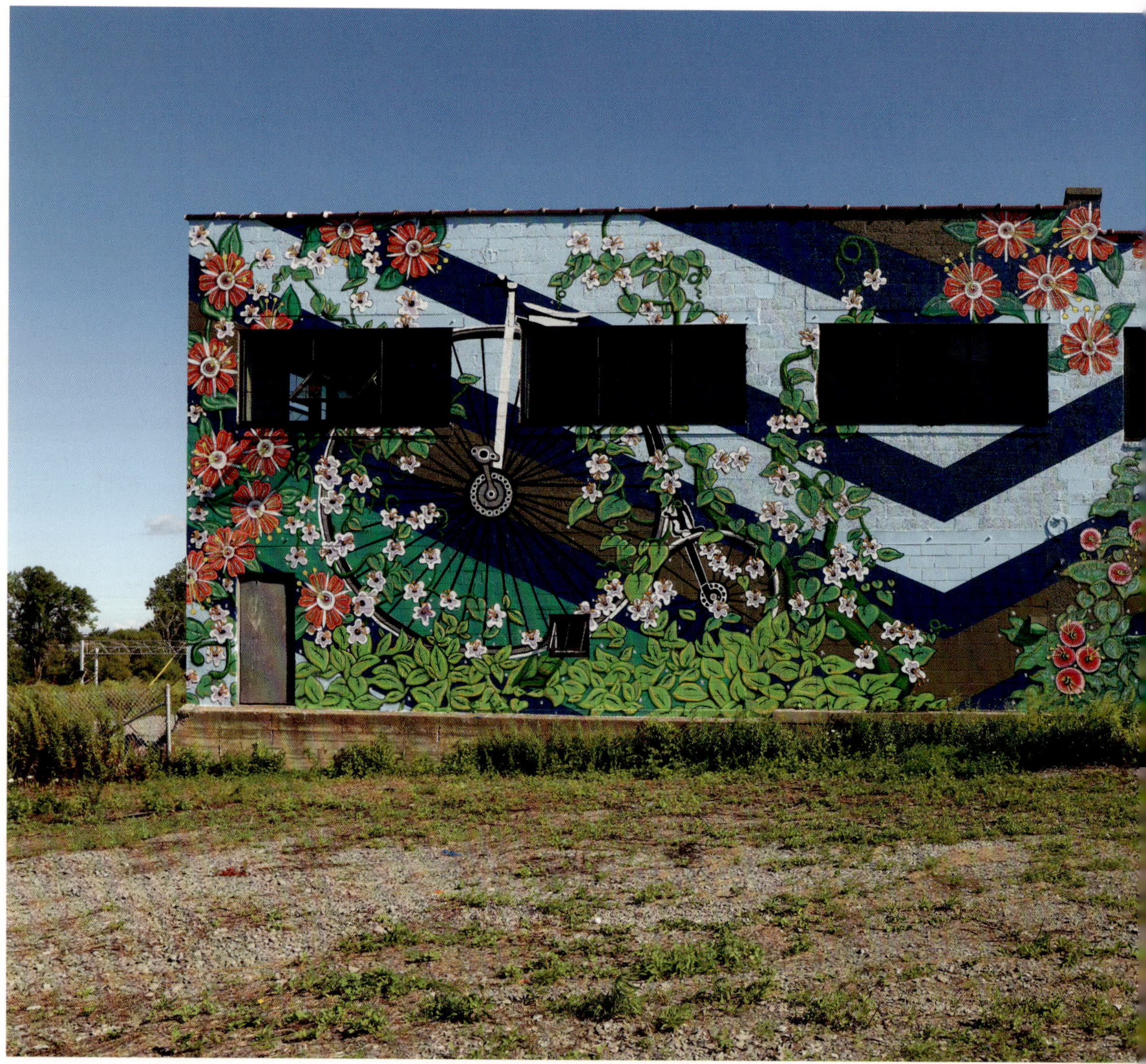

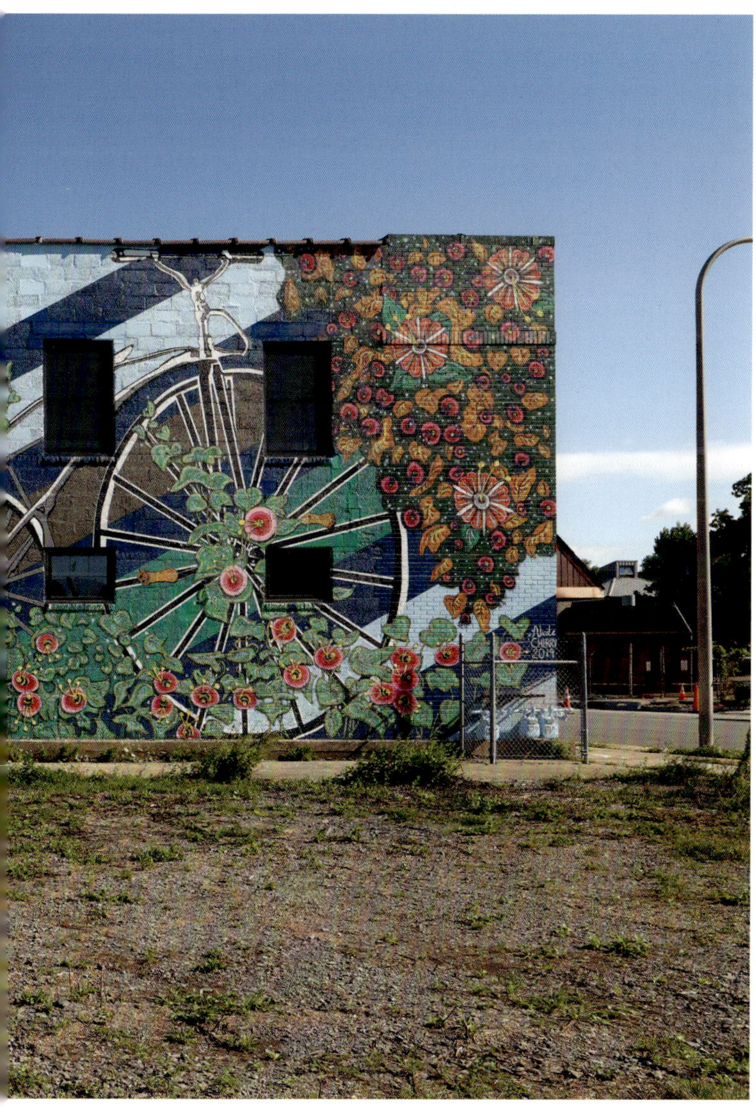

Meta-morphosis #5

Tavar Zawacki

1665 Main Street, Buffalo

Acrylic paint
90 × 160 feet (27.4 × 48.8 m)

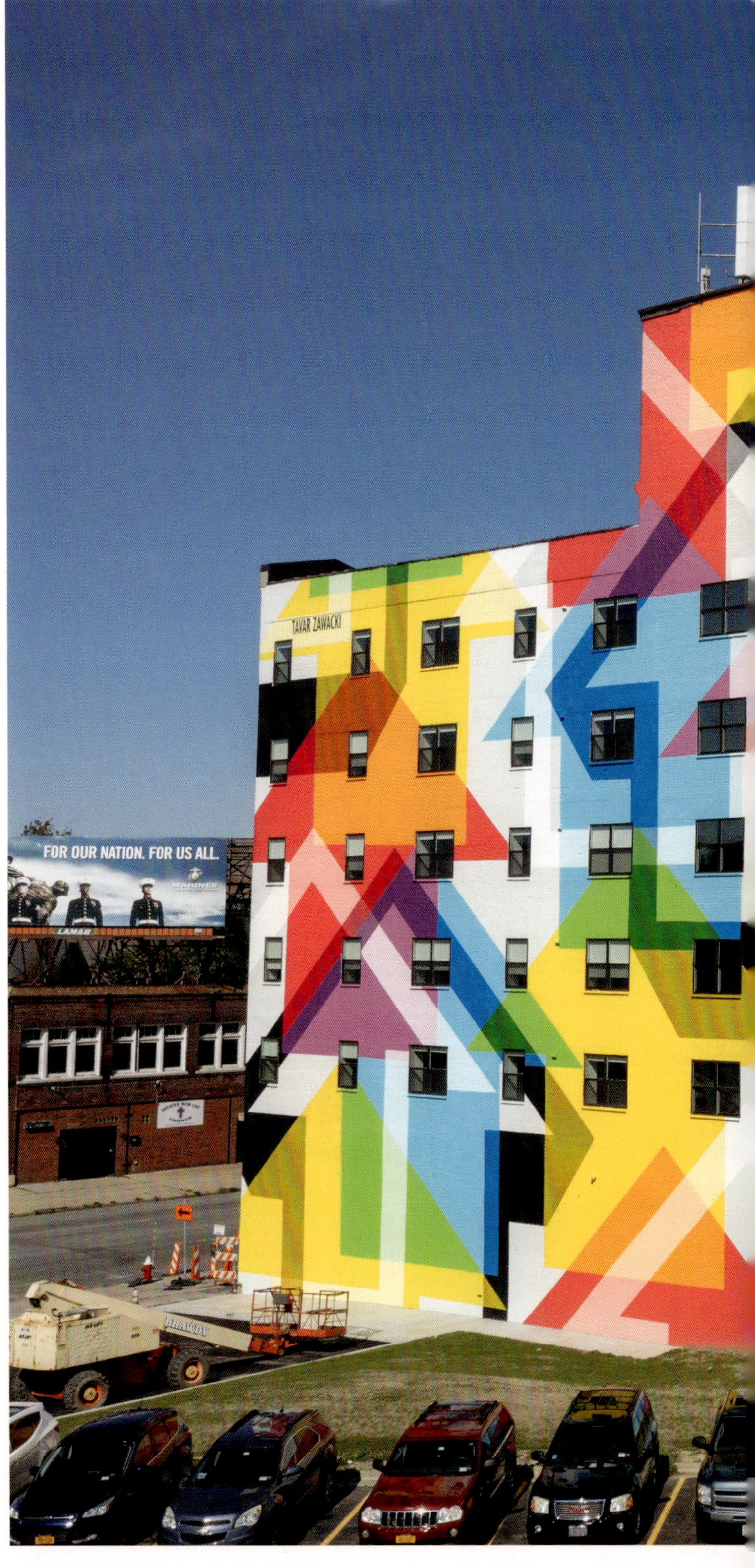

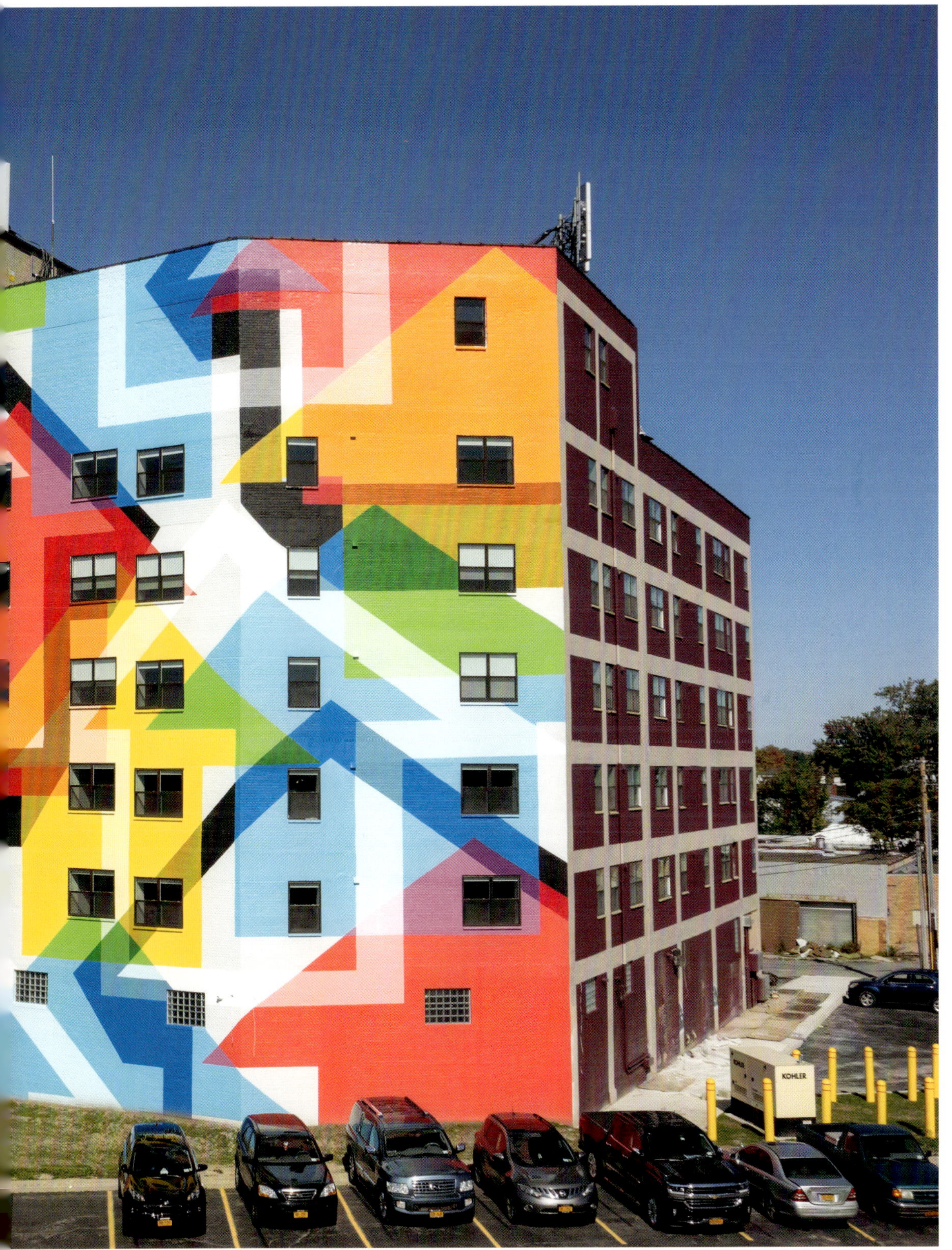

Green Kaleidoscope

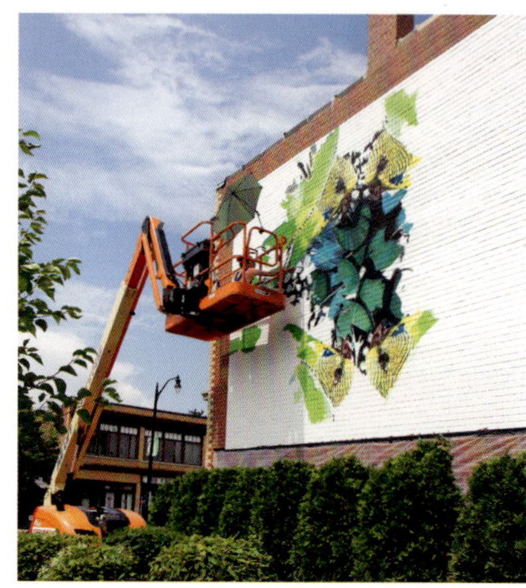

Augustina Droze

2302 Main Street, Buffalo

Acrylic paint
17 × 23 feet (5.2 × 7 m)

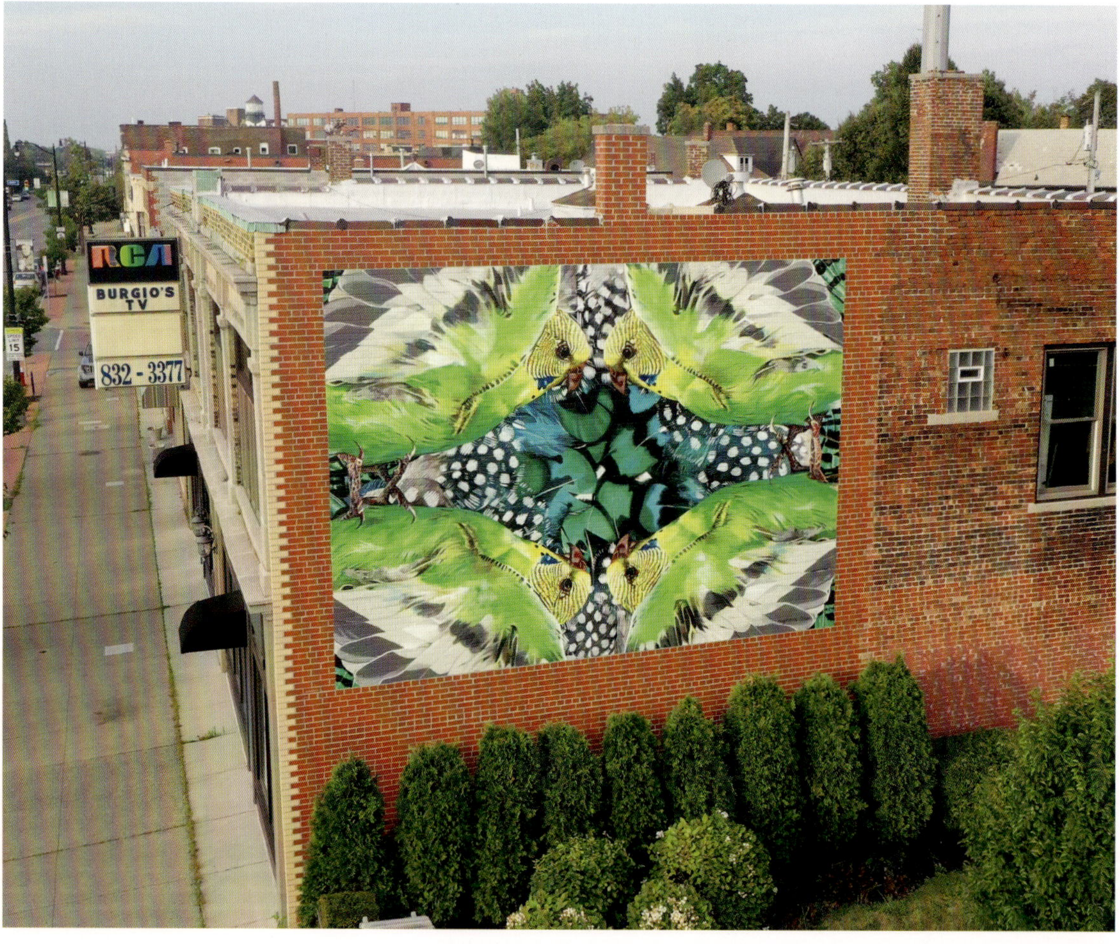

John Brent Mural

James Cooper III

Park Road at the
Buffalo Zoo

Acrylic on e-panel and steel
Overall: 11 × 24 feet
(3.4 × 7.3 m)

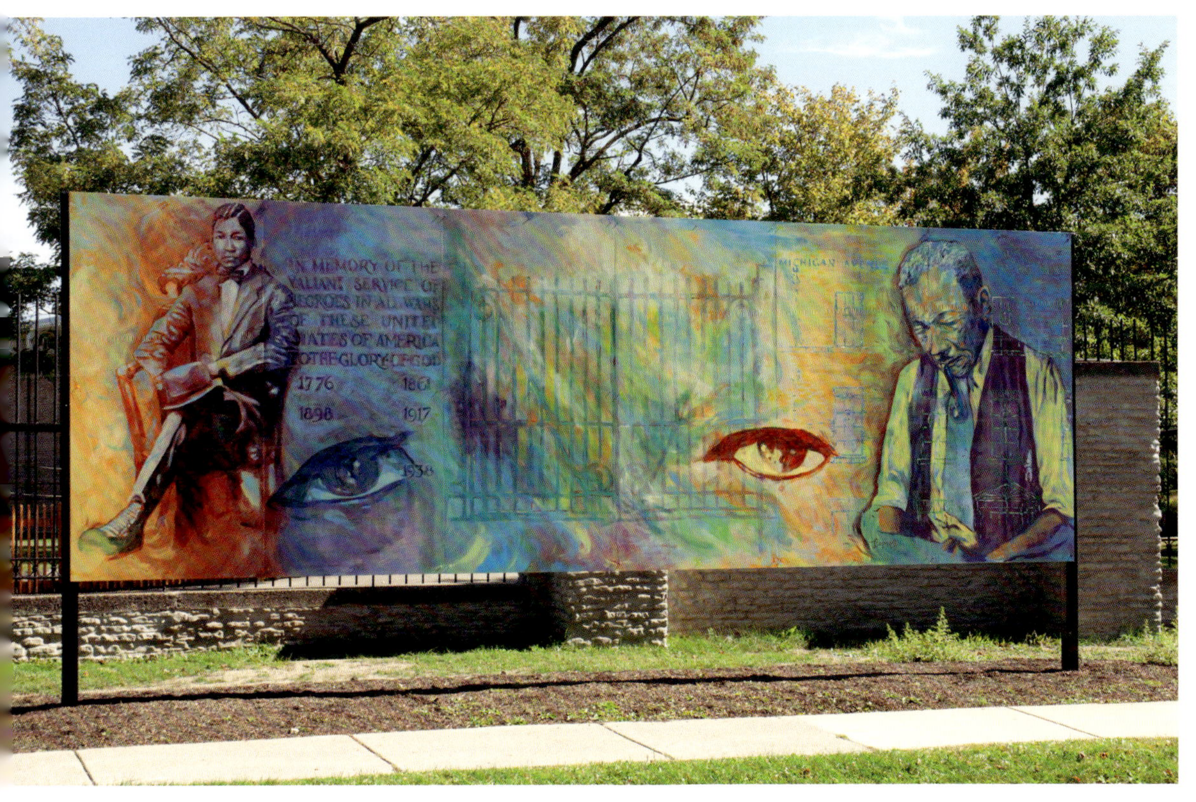

Walking Back Time

Logan Hicks

5 East Huron Street, Buffalo

Acrylic paint
25 × 50 feet (7.6 × 15.2 m)

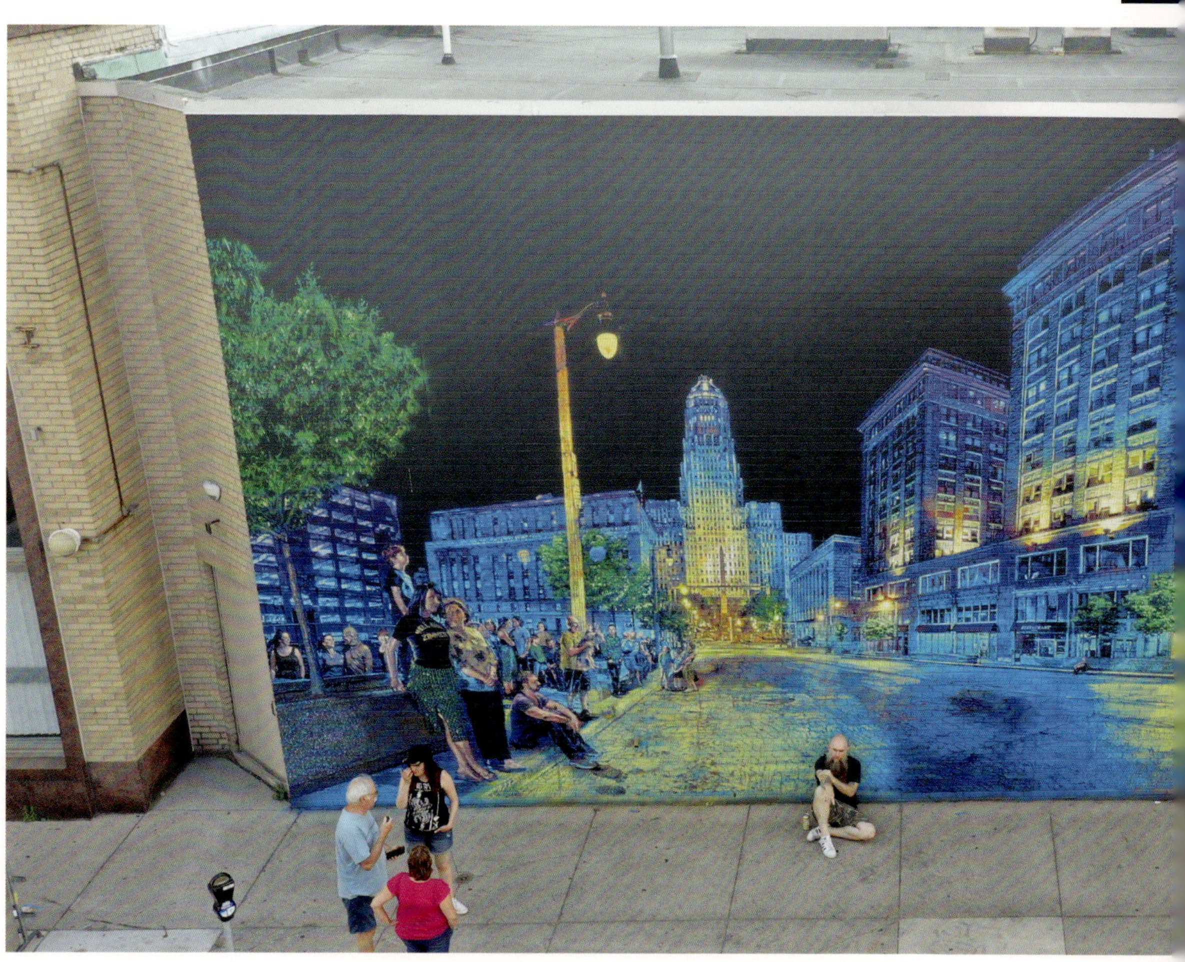

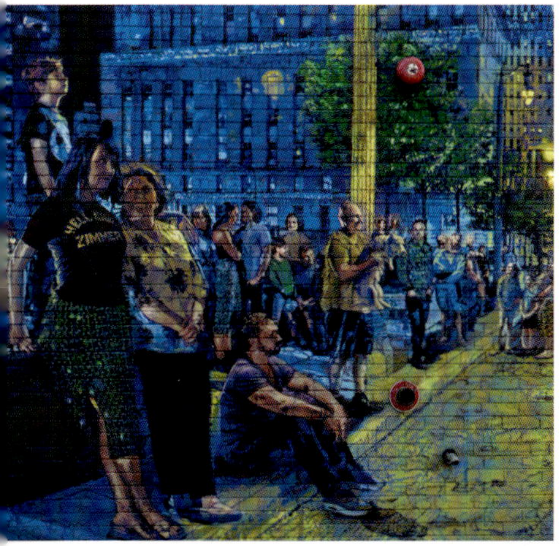

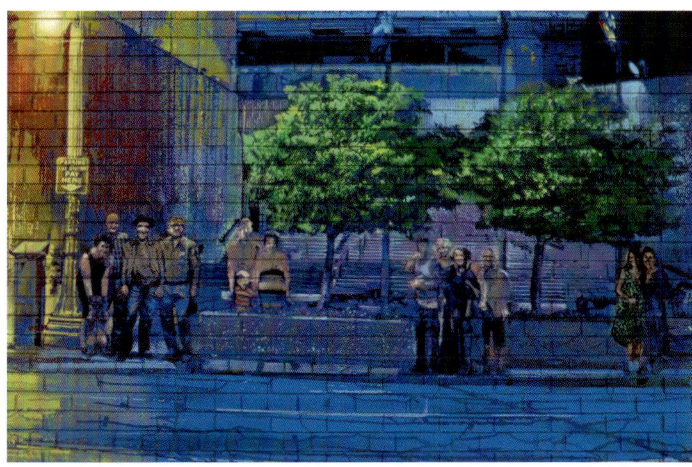

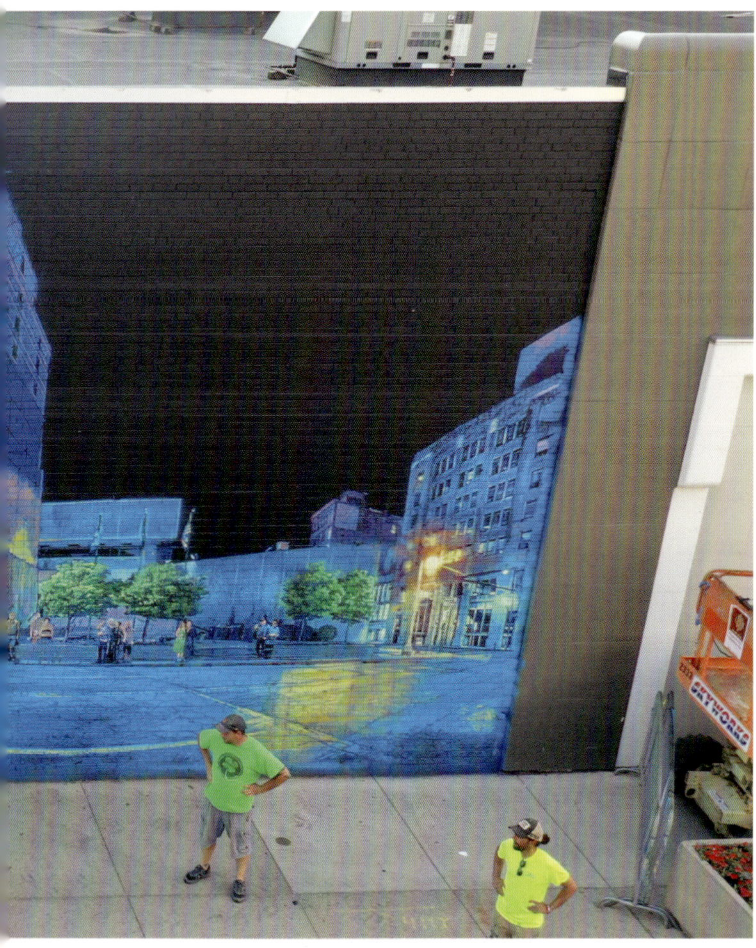

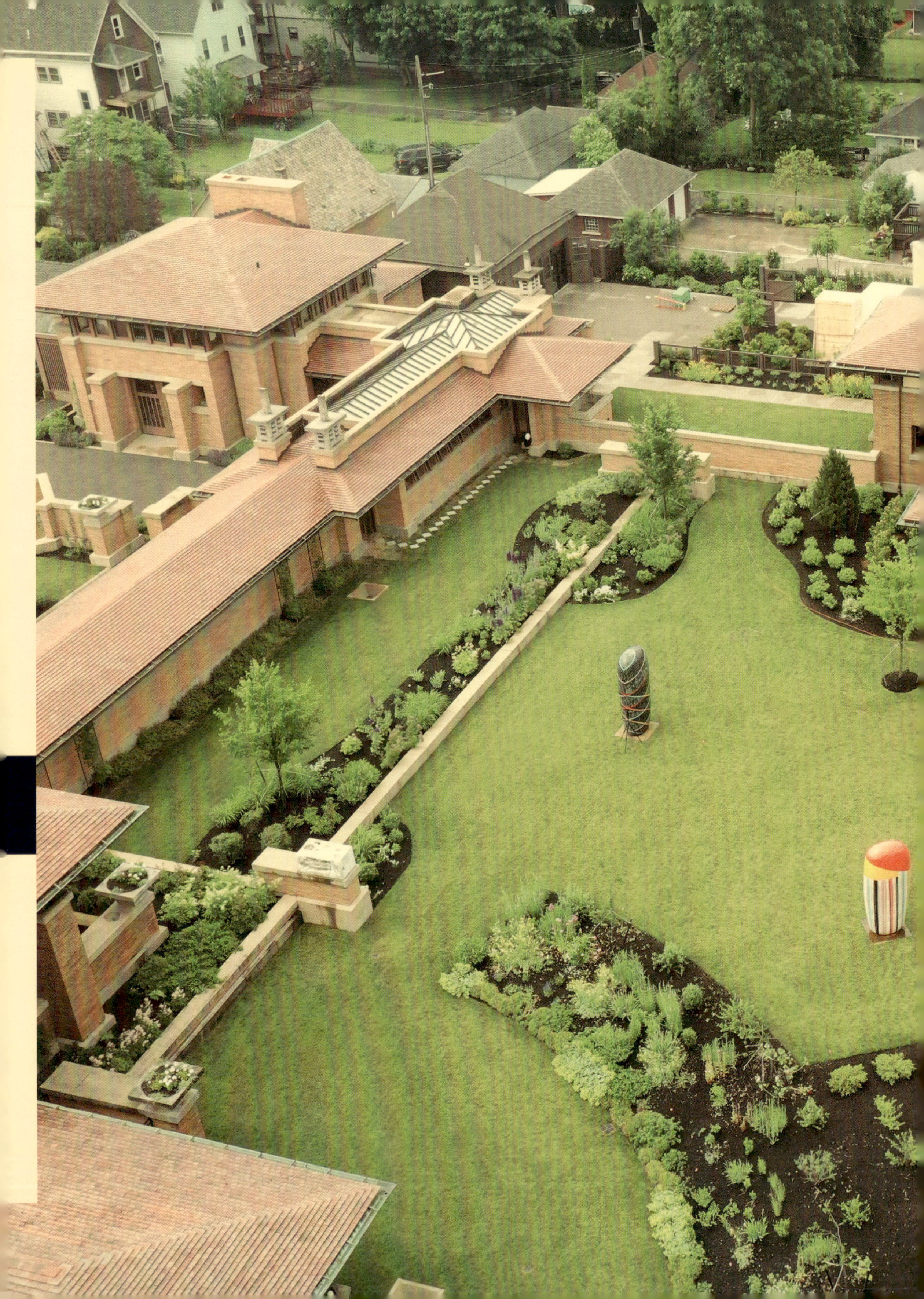

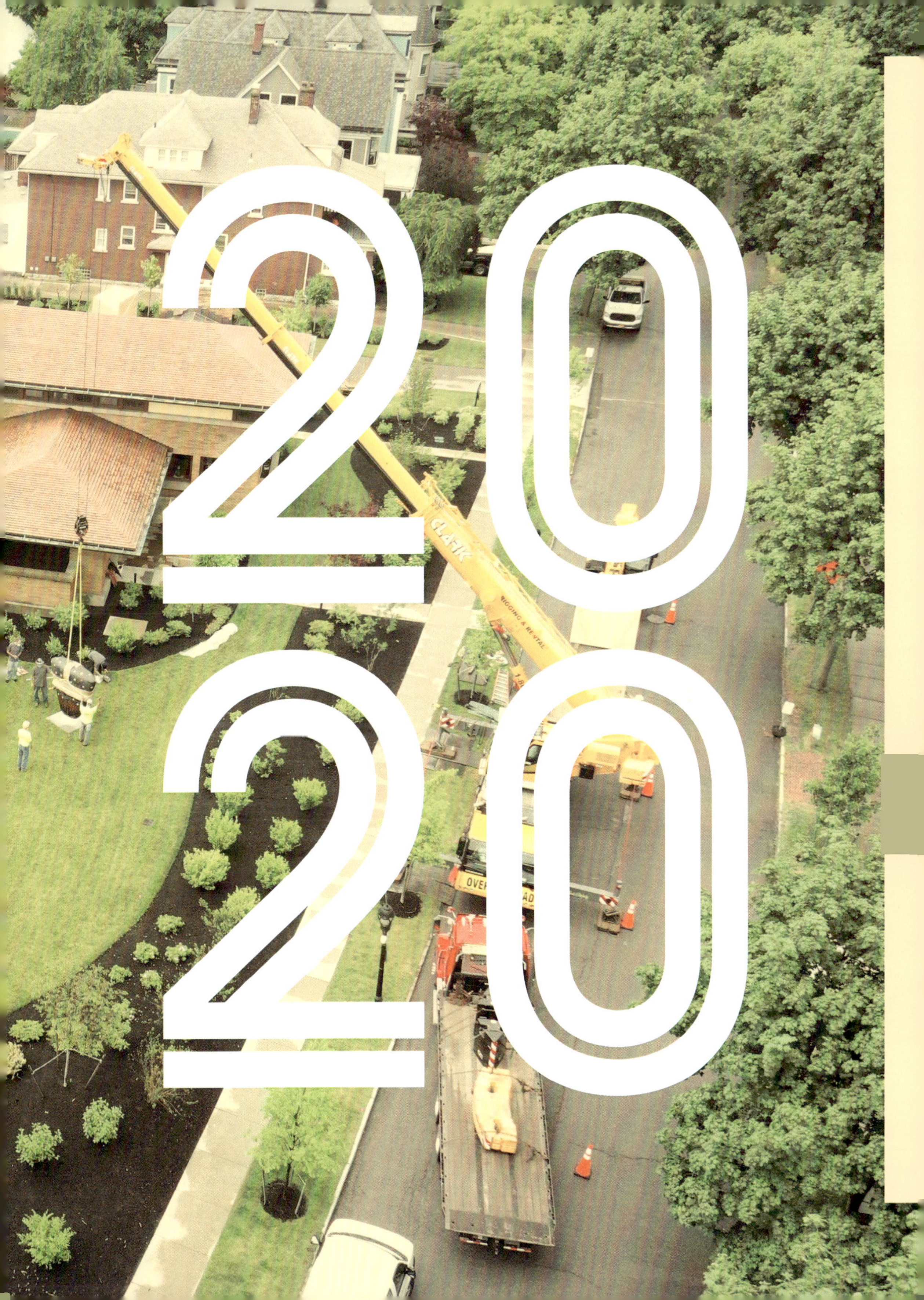

Before and Not Yet

Bryan Metzdorf

East Main and Mechanic
Streets, Springville

Acrylic paint
20 × 24 feet (6.1 × 7.3 m)

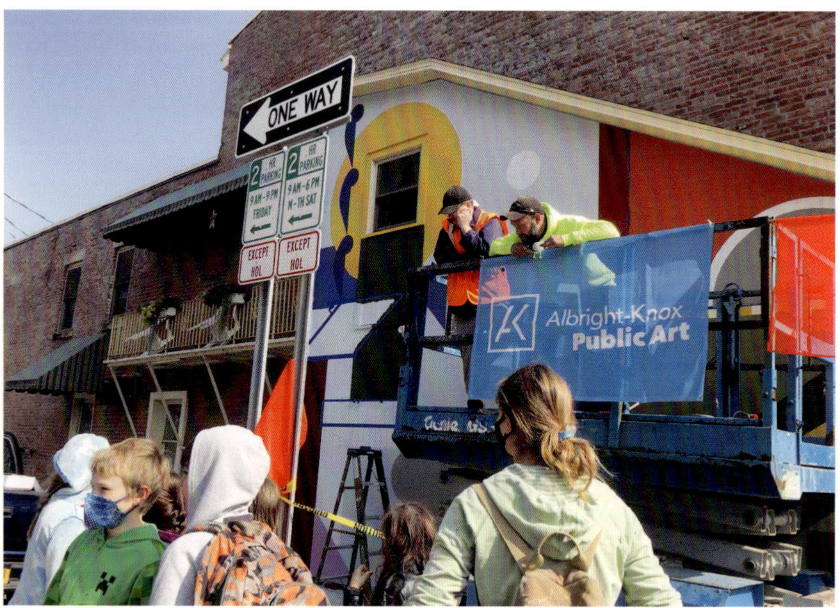

In September and October 2020, Metzdorf spent three weeks in residence at Springville Center for the Arts (SCA). During his residency, he worked with local K–12 students and created a public mural whose design borrowed from the architectural language and colors of Springville's Main Street.

Metzdorf (left) and project coordinator Zack Boehler address a crowd while working.

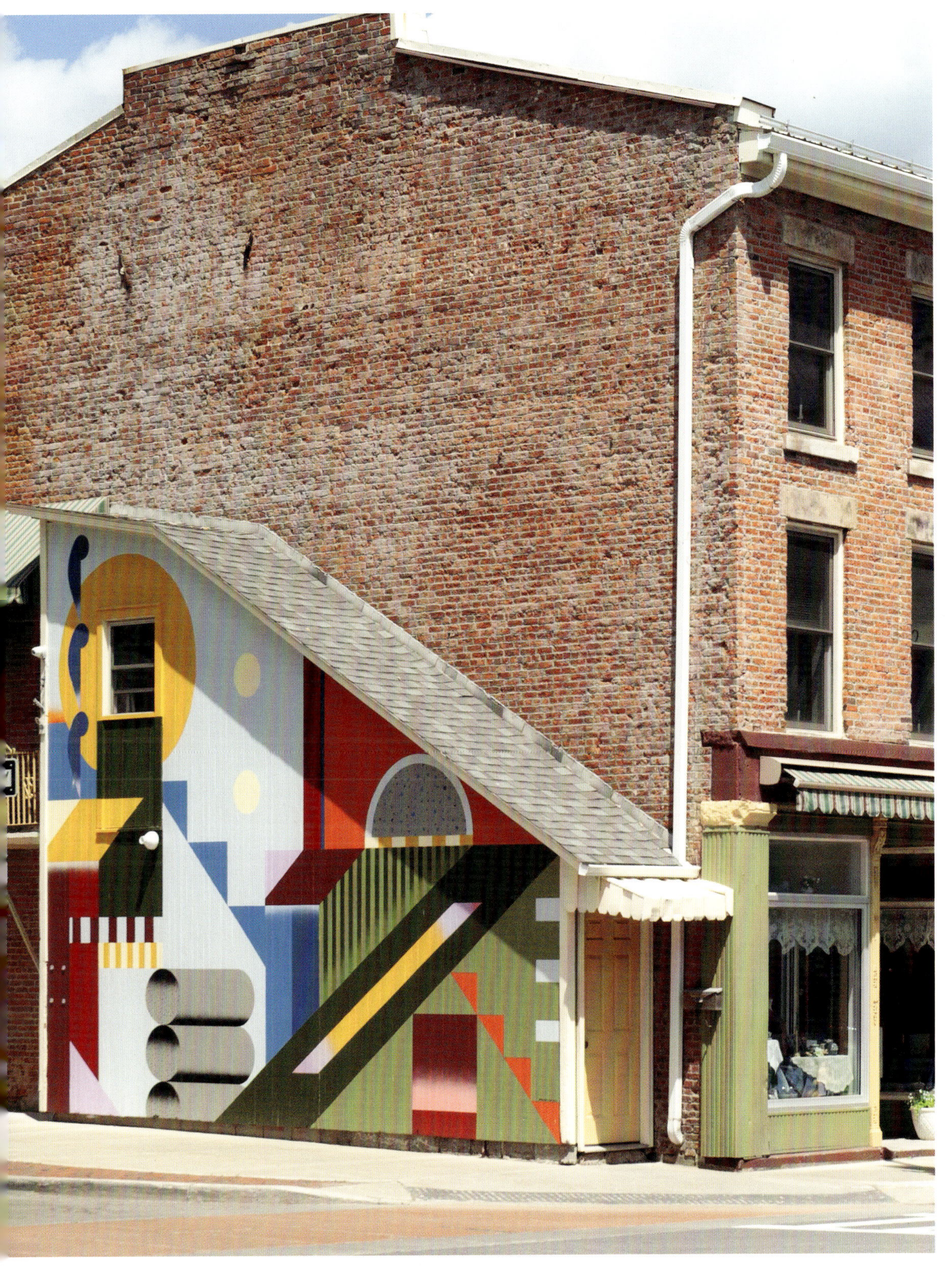

Cobblestone Commons

Monet Alyssa Kifner
Miriam Singer
Karle Norman
Morgan Blair
Cyrielle Tremblay
Thomas Evans, aka
Detour
Bradd Young, aka SALUT
James Moffitt, aka YAMES
Lauren Mckenzie-Pearce
Jason Brammer
Obsidian Bellis
Ellen Rutt

NFTA Yard (DL&W Terminal), Buffalo

Variable: acrylic, spray paint, and Polytab
Thirteen panels: 16 × 21 feet (4.9 × 6.4 m) each

Over the course of three summers (2020–22), twelve artists from Buffalo, Rochester, Toronto, Cincinnati, Philadelphia, New York City, Detroit, and Colorado painted twelve individual murals on the South Park Avenue facade of the NFTA Yard (DL&W Terminal) located in downtown Buffalo's Historic Cobblestone District.

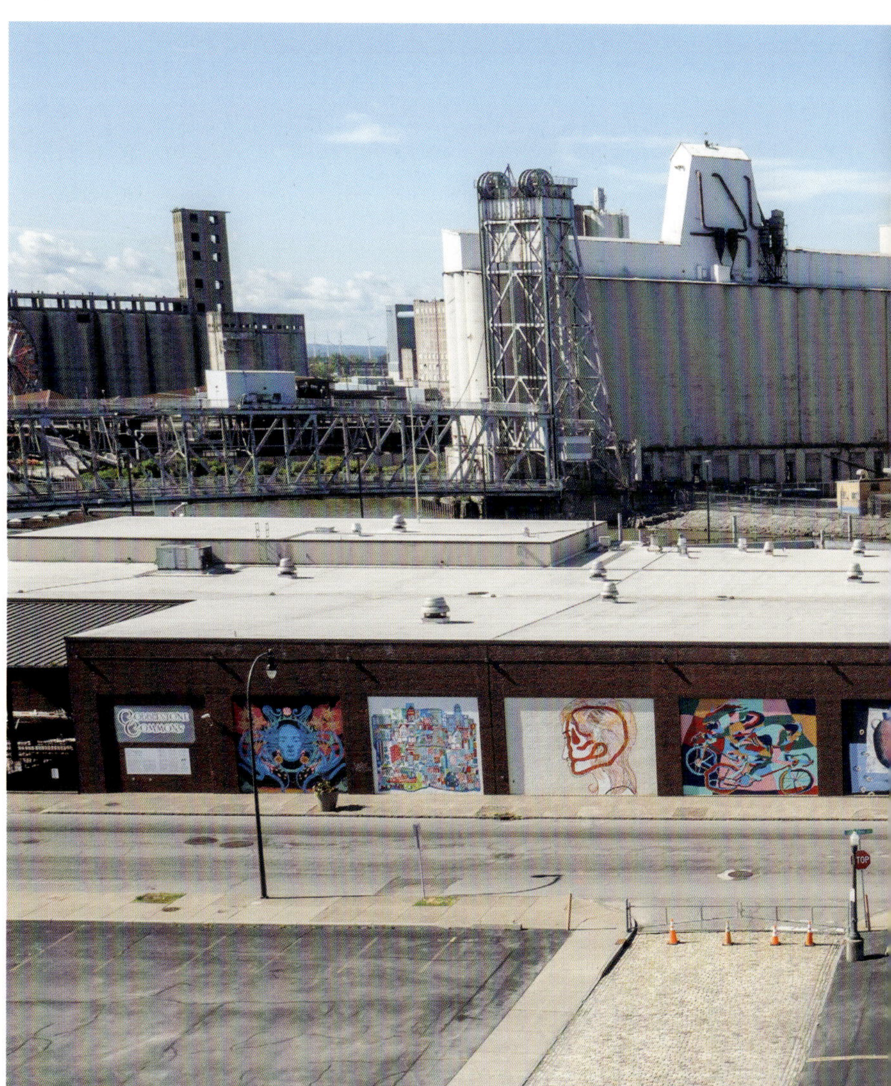

As an artist born and raised in Buffalo, working with the AKG is a dream come true for me. I grew up going to what was then the Albright-Knox Art Gallery. As a child, and later as a student at the Buffalo Academy for Visual and Performing Arts, I was always inspired by their collection. The AKG is one of the first things that come to mind when I think of home. At twenty-six years old, I still enjoy visiting the museum, especially since it reopened. It's even cooler for me now, in 2024, having created two murals in the city through the AKG Public Art Initiative.

After graduating with my BFA in Illustration from the Fashion Institute of Technology, I returned home to Buffalo. However, I felt isolated from my friends and community in New York City, and I was unaware of what was happening here in the visual art scene. Despite this, I focused on establishing myself as an illustrator, so I hunkered down in my studio and got to work.

Then, while getting my first big professional illustration job, working on portfolio pieces, and settling into life, I received an email from Aaron Ott.

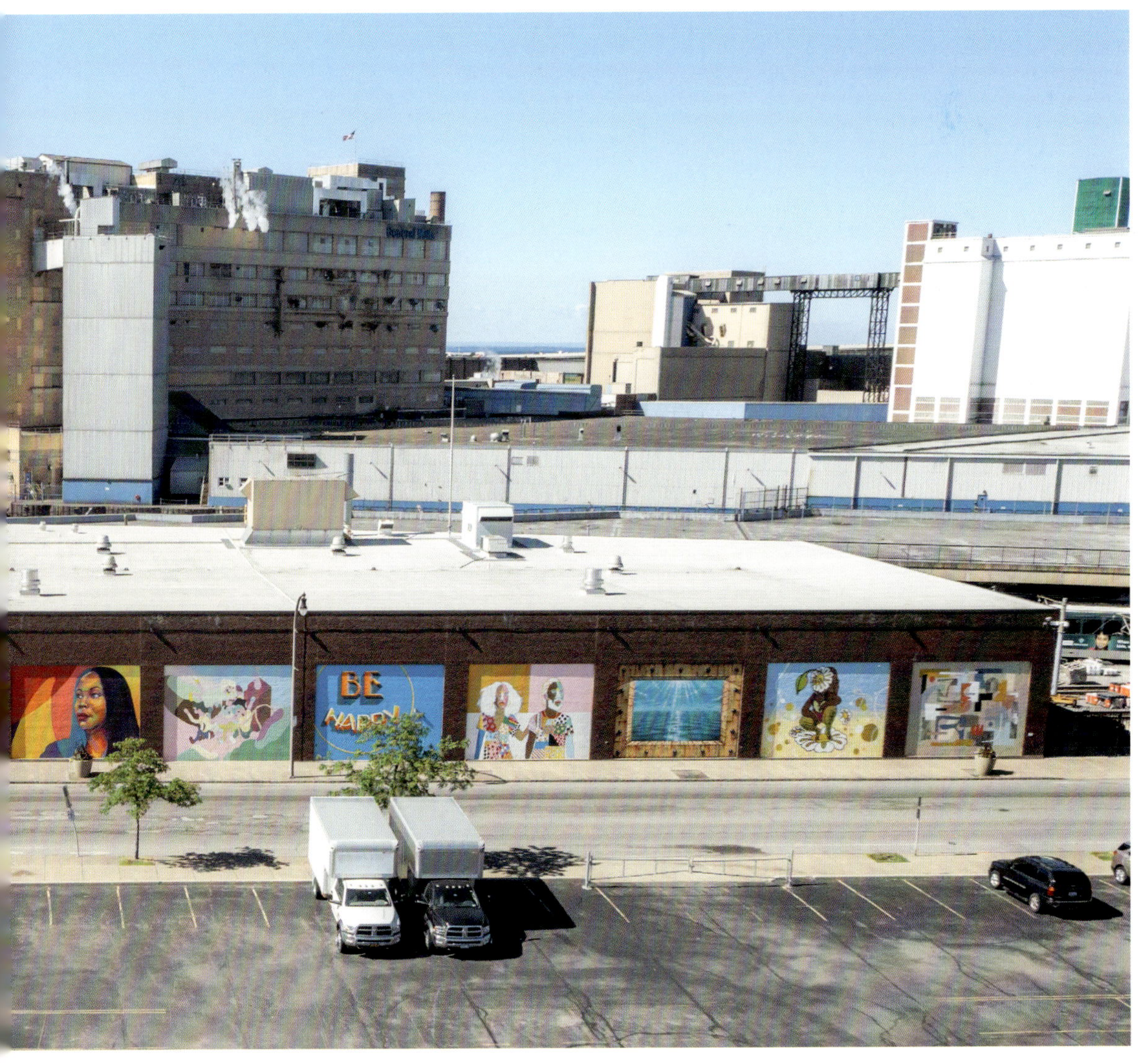

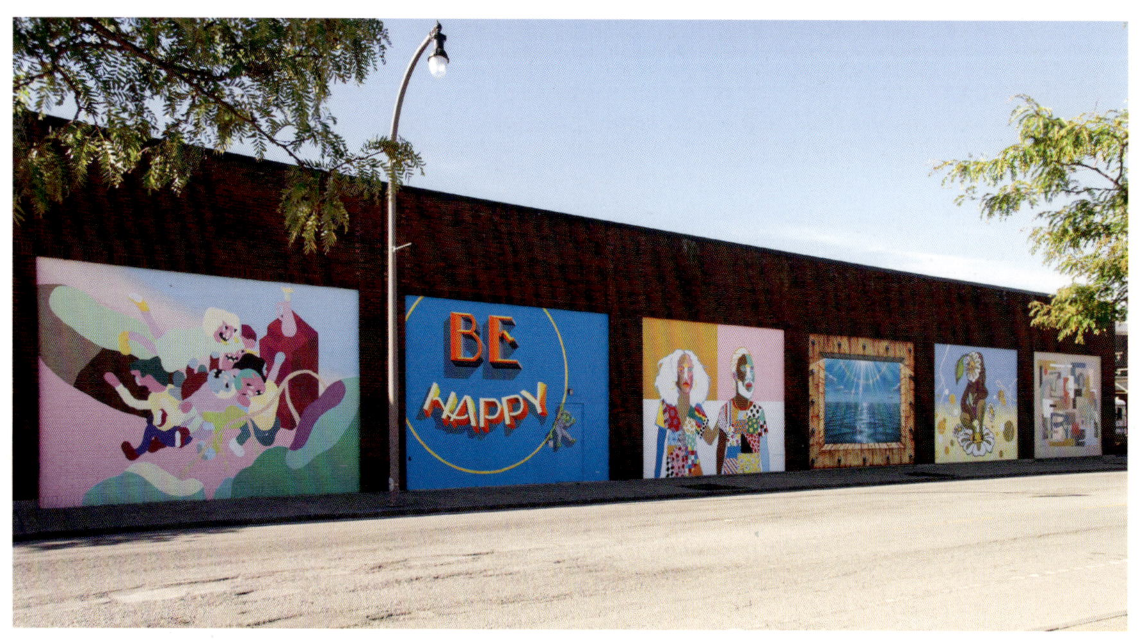

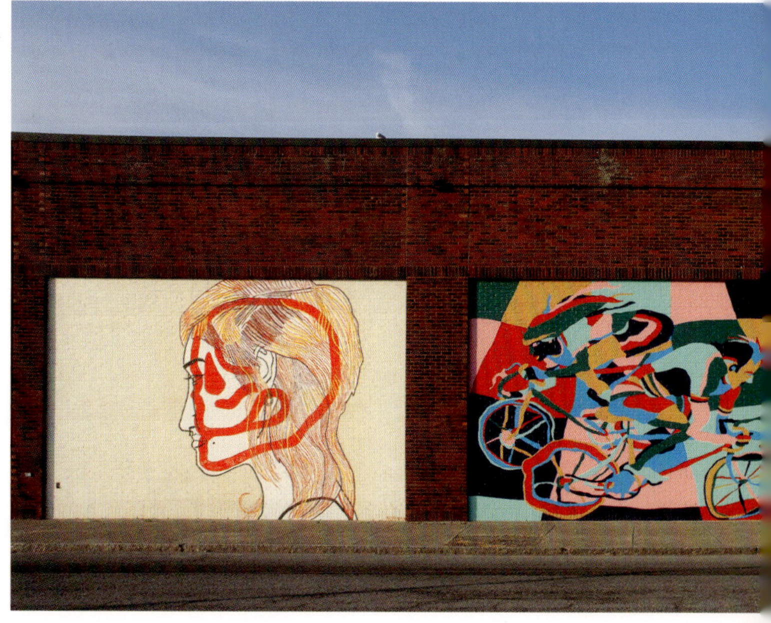

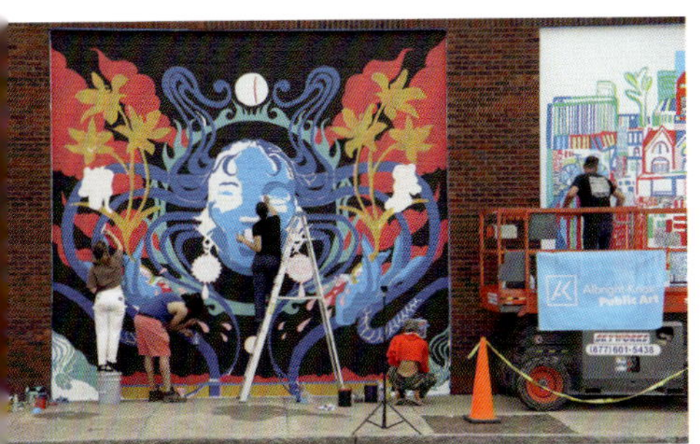

Kifner (center, on ladder) and assistants work on her mural for the project.

He offered me the opportunity to do one of the murals on South Park Avenue in the Cobblestone District in downtown Buffalo. I couldn't believe it!

As it turned out, he came across my name and work through an art raffle I participated in. One of the organizers saw my work and put it in front of Zack Boehler. He presented me to the team, and the rest was history!

Since then, I've done a second mural for the museum, in 2022. Working with the Public Art Initiative has introduced me to a new world of visual art that I had not considered. While I learned about mural work in school and got to do a small one in my graduating year at FIT, I never saw it as a viable option. However, after doing it, I loved the experience.

For both murals, I chose to depict women, as that is the main subject matter in much of my work. I wanted to honor femininity while also exploring the idea of the "divine feminine." Conceptualizing the murals allowed me to further explore my own visual language and world-building. The pieces have graphic elements in them that surround the figures, symbolizing the creative, feminine spirit.

Working with the AKG Public Art crew also exposed me to their knowledge and expertise. I am now aware of what goes into coordinating a mural job: putting together a proposal, materials needed, various techniques, physical expectations, and time management to meet a deadline.

While I expected to pick up skills and have some fun, I did not expect the social network that would come along with an opportunity such as this. In a time where we often communicate via a screen, I appreciated the physical exposure the AKG community gave me by introducing me to other artists in and outside Buffalo, some of whom are now my friends. They encouraged me to put myself out there and provided the environment where artists could meet one another.

Working on two good-sized murals gave me the confidence and motivation to challenge myself outside of my preferred media. In a personal sense, this is my key takeaway, because it showed me that challenging myself and being open to opportunities can lead you to unknown and exciting places.

The swaths of murals and three-dimensional work this team has executed are inspiring to see. Knowing what and who makes this possible instills within me much faith that the future of Buffalo will be something we have not seen before and that we all have a chance to make our mark on. I'm excited about the future and cannot believe I'm here.

—MONET ALYSSA KIFNER

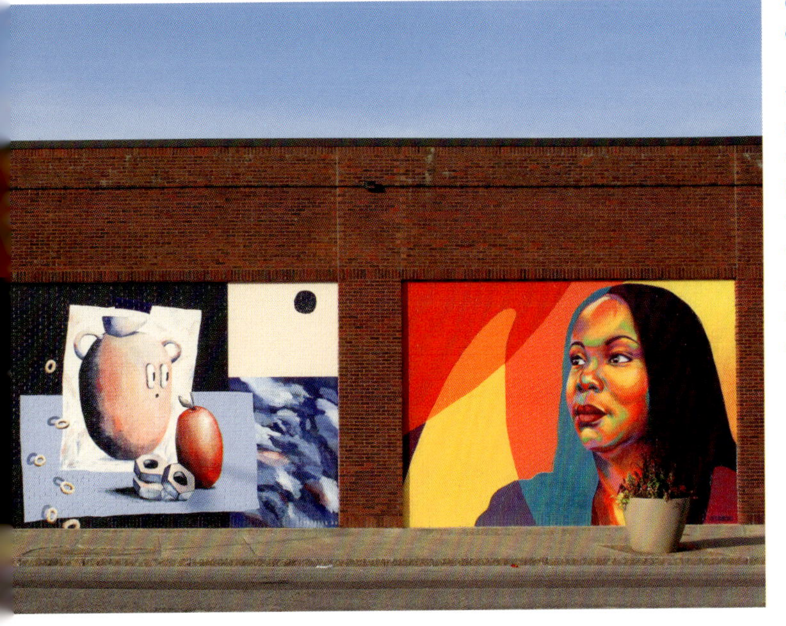

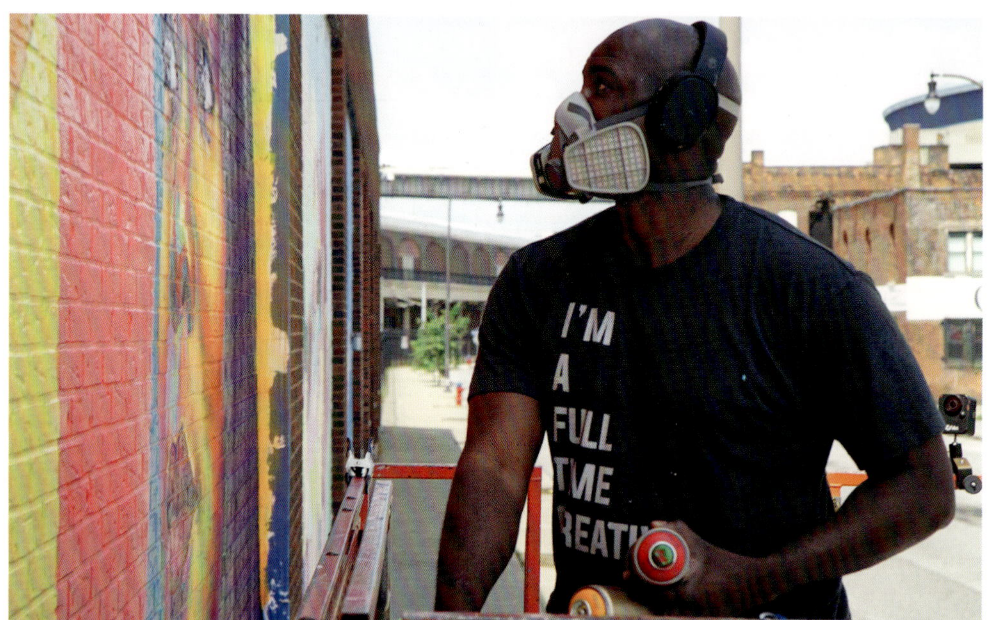
I'M
A
FULL
TIME
CREATIV

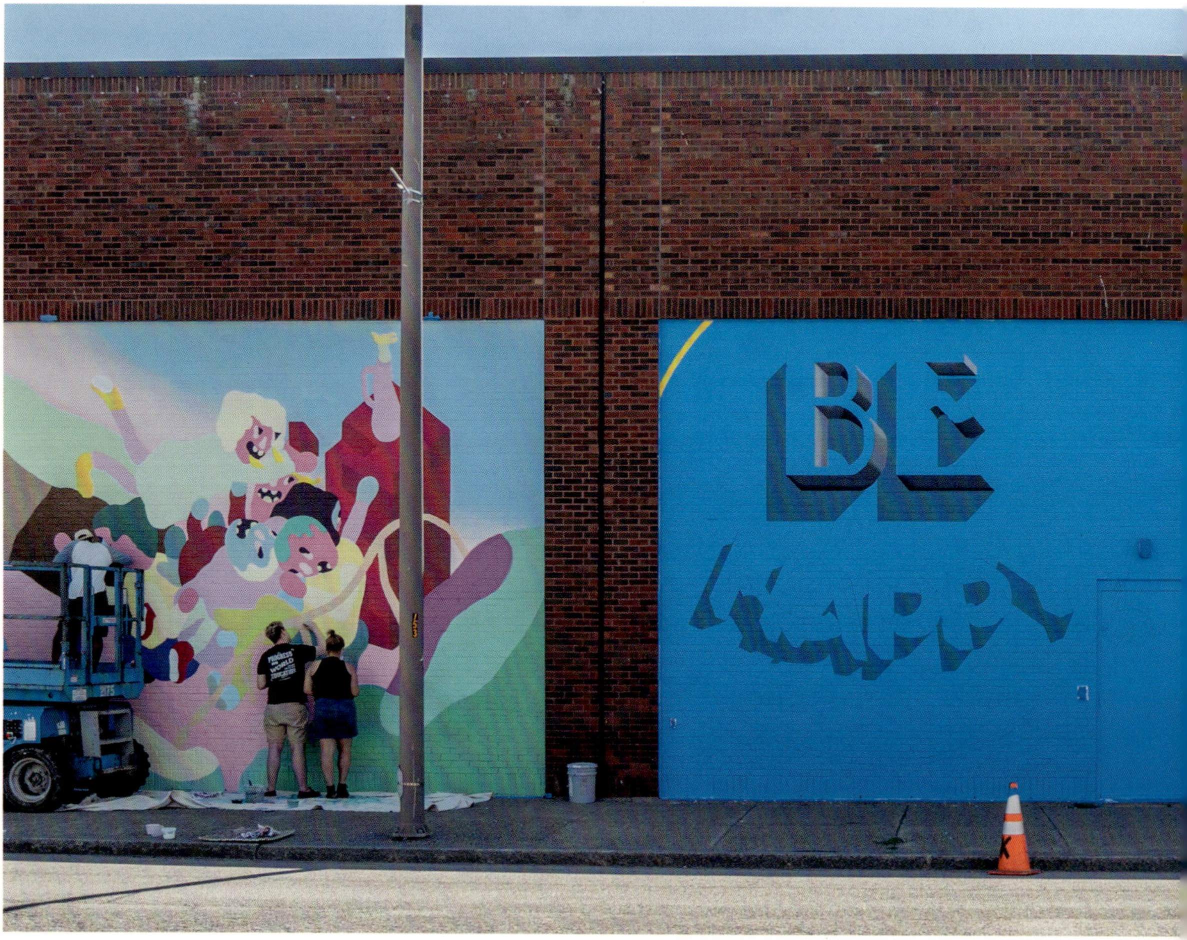

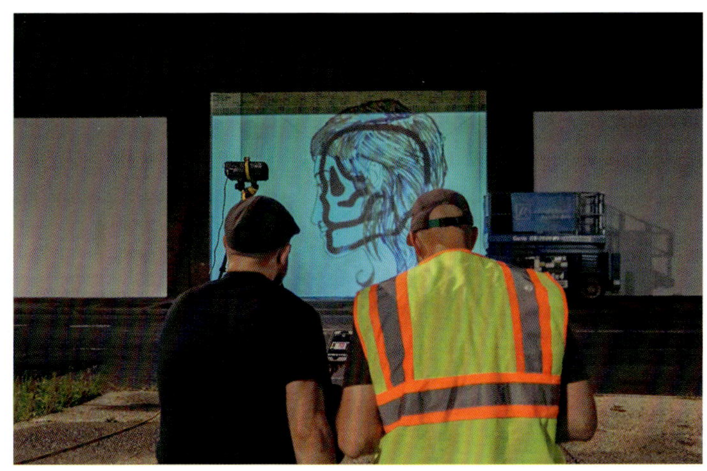

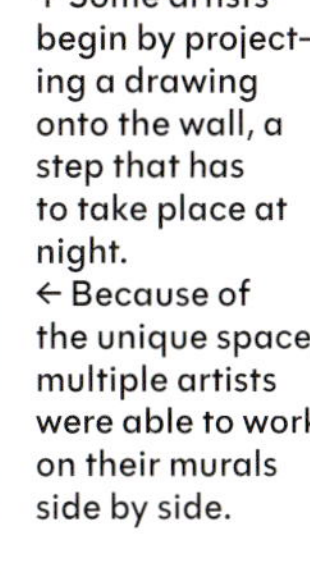

↑ Some artists
begin by project–
ing a drawing
onto the wall, a
step that has
to take place at
night.
← Because of
the unique space,
multiple artists
were able to work
on their murals
side by side.

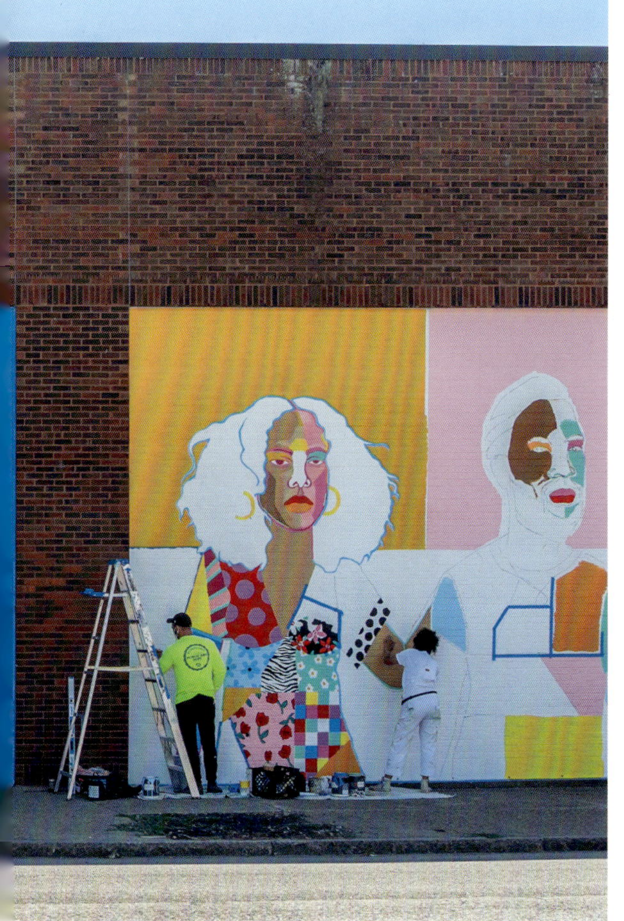

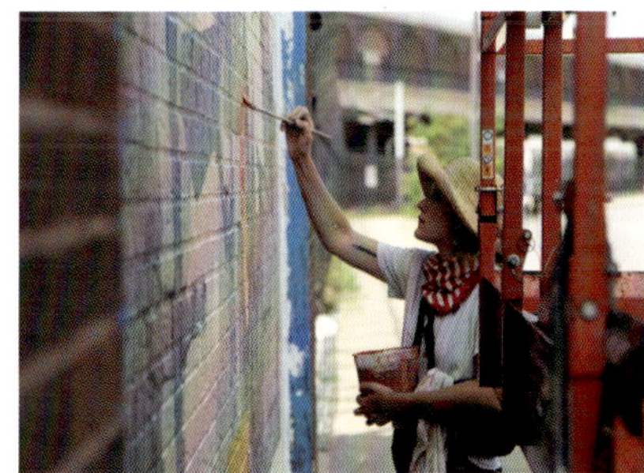

Love Black

**Edreys Wajed and
James "YAMES" Moffitt**

712 Main Street, Buffalo

Acrylic paint
29 × 45 feet 6 inches
(8.8 × 13.9 m)

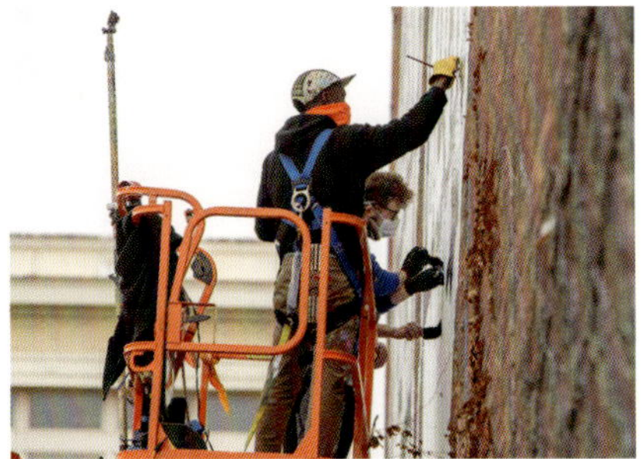

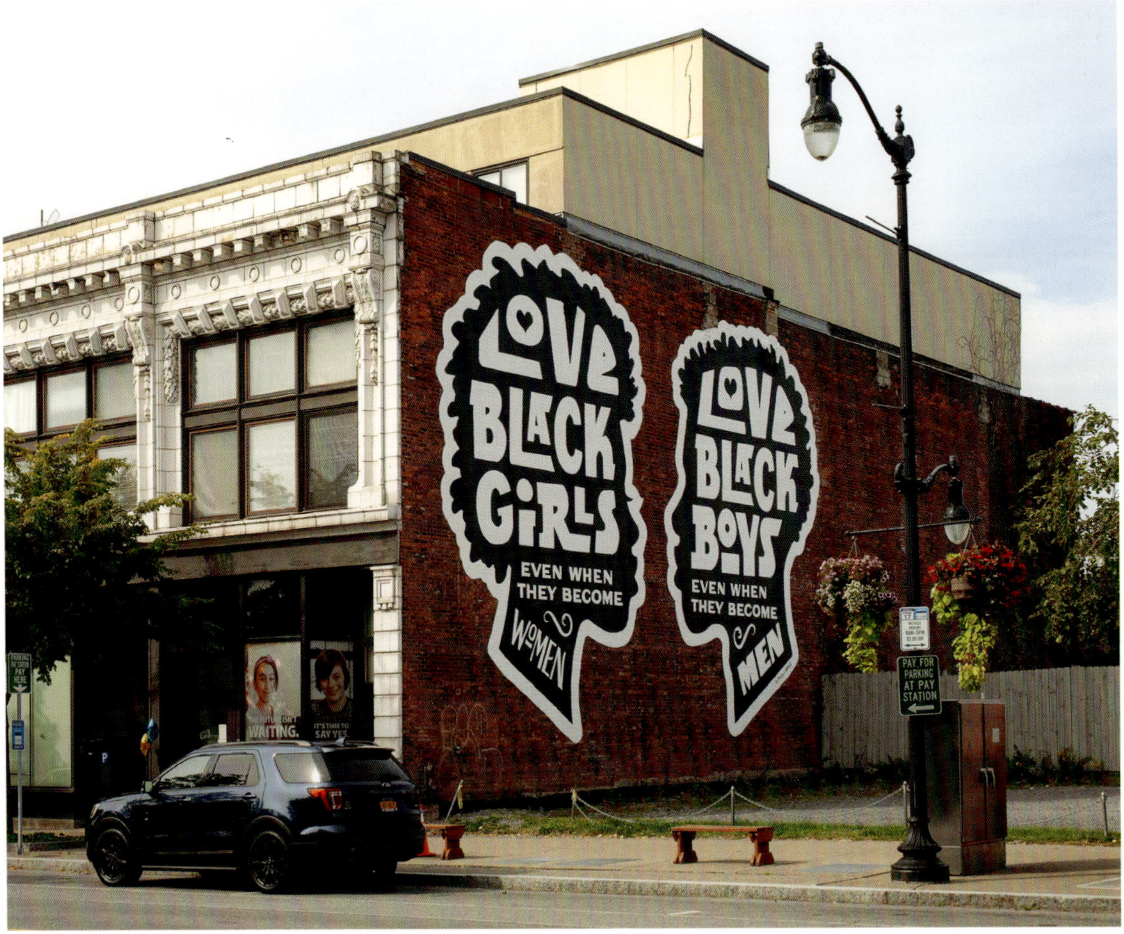

Stonewall Nation: WNY LGBT History Mural

Mickey Harmon and Ari Moore

Q Bar, 44 Allen Street,
Buffalo

Acrylic paint
20 × 40 feet (6.1 × 12.2 m)

Stonewall Nation is dedicated to the ongoing struggle of LGBTQIA+ activists and features the portraits of local and national figures that Moore selected based on her research and life in Buffalo's queer community.

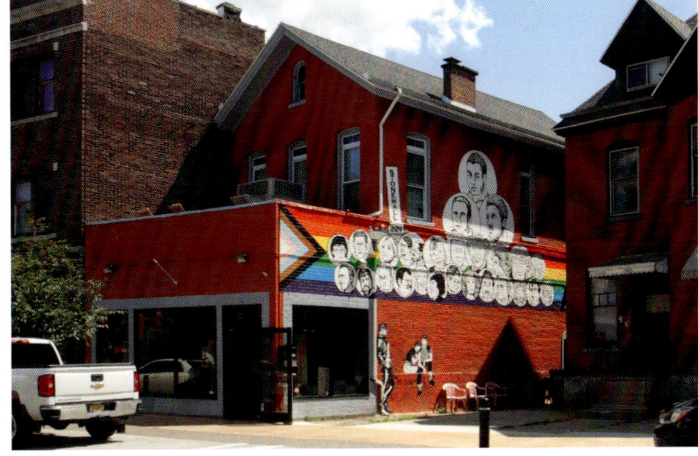

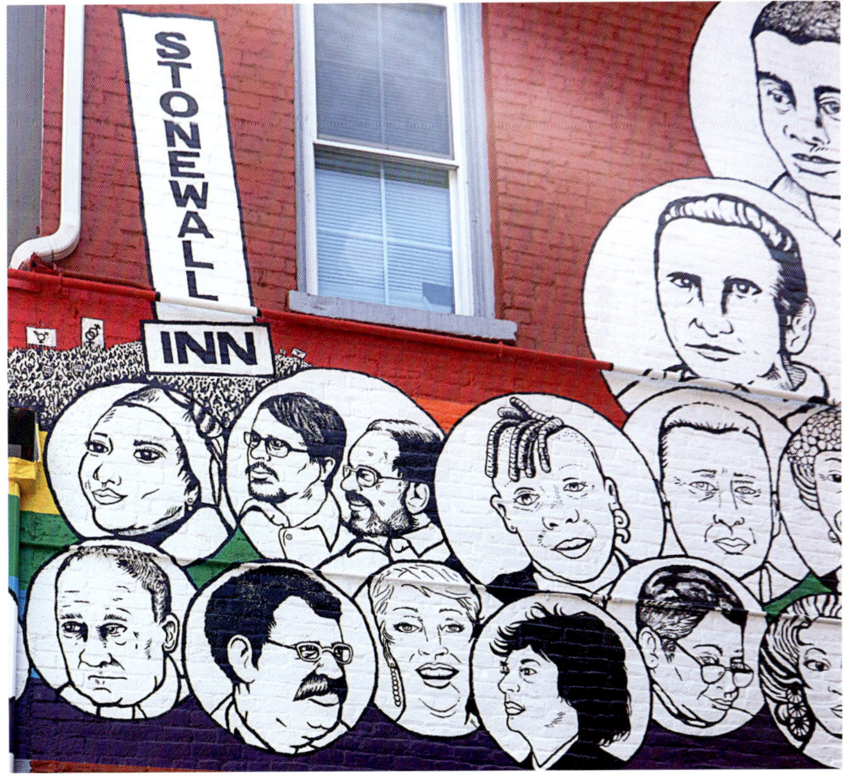

The Space Between: Frank Lloyd Wright | Jun Kaneko

Frank Lloyd Wright and Jun Kaneko

Frank Lloyd Wright's Martin House
June 26, 2020–October 24, 2021

Eleven ceramic sculptures
Dimensions variable

For this exhibition, staged at a time during the COVID-19 pandemic when only outdoor gatherings were deemed to be safe, seven massive ceramic sculptures by Kaneko were installed on the grounds of the historic Martin House, designed by Wright and built between 1903 and 1905. Several of Kaneko's smaller works were on display behind glass in the adjoining pavilion, creating in all a freely accessible outdoor exhibition.

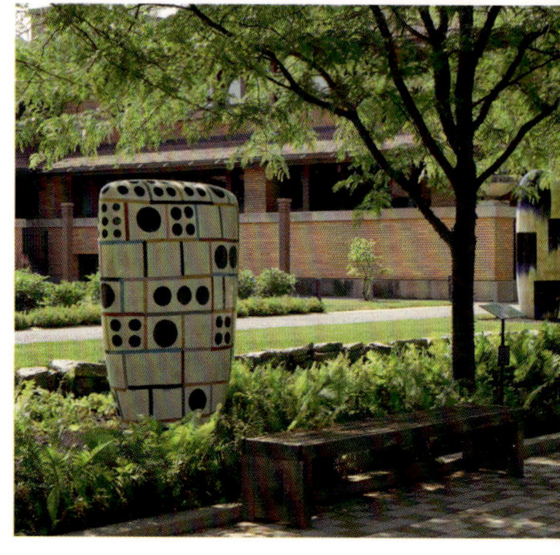

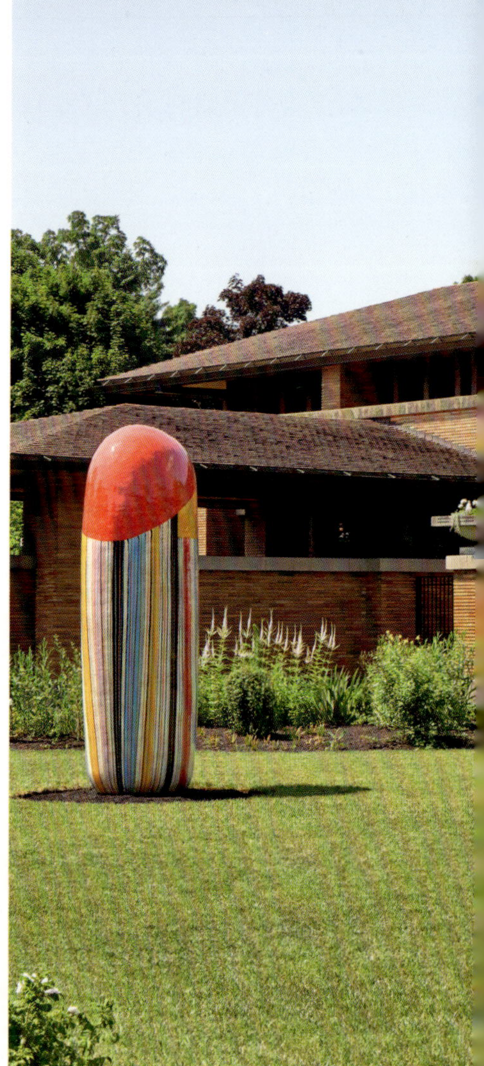

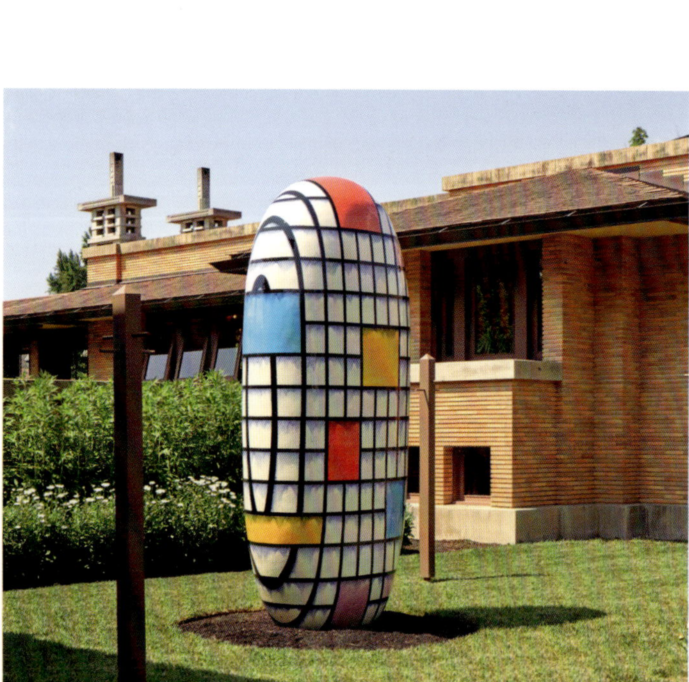

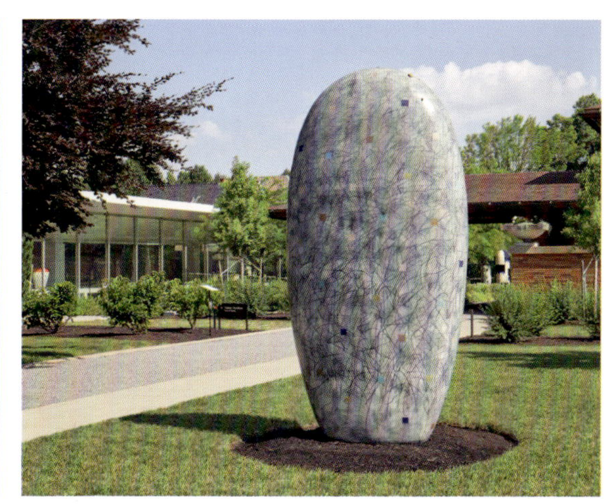

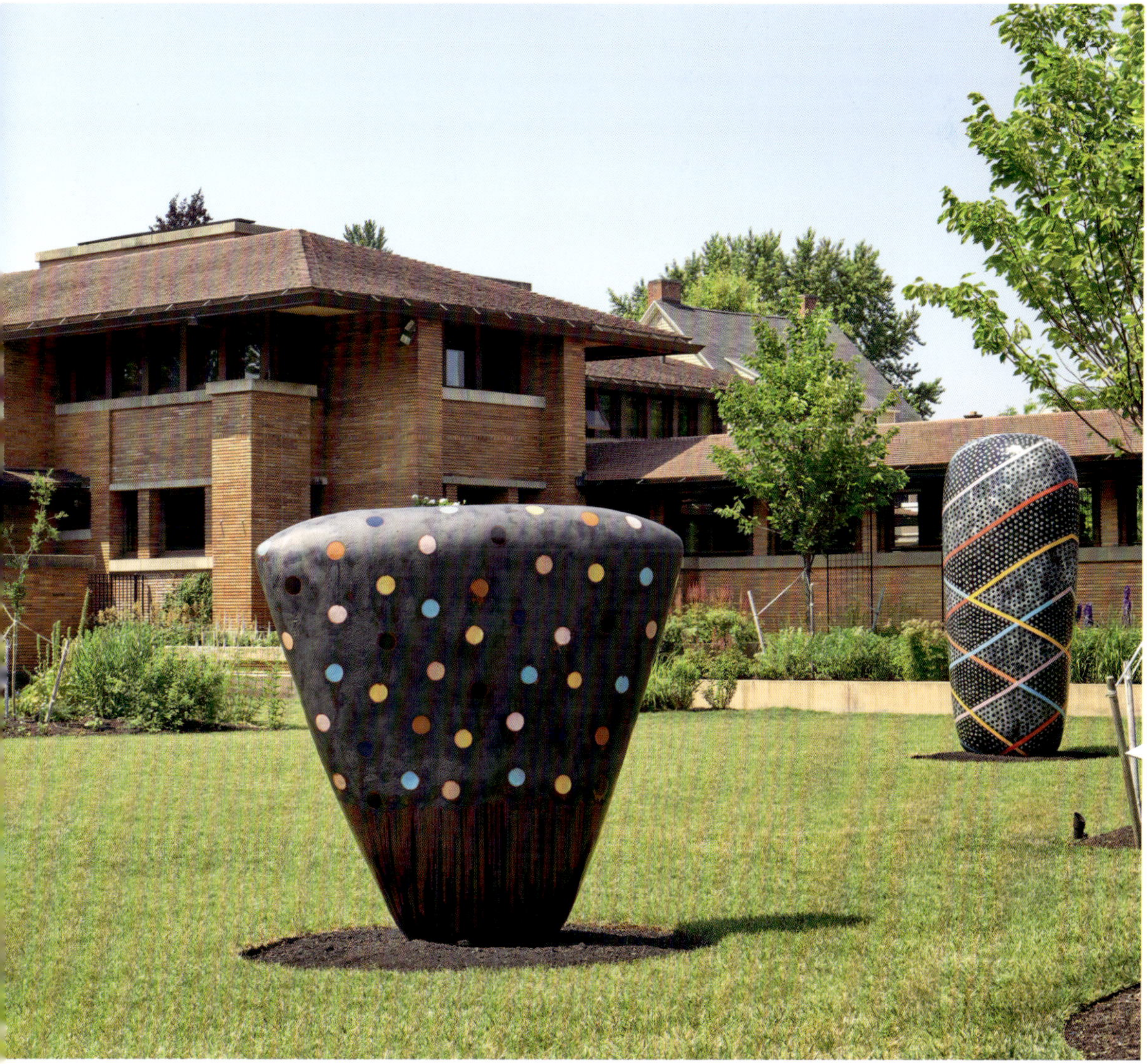

Works, from Home

Karle Norman
Jay P Hawkins, Sr.
Ashley Johnson
MJ Myers
Jason Seeley
Fotini Galanes
Adam Weekley
Sarah Myers
Chris Piontkowski
Obsidian Bellis
Rachel Shelton
Jon Mirro
Julia Bottoms
Tricia Butski
Jennifer Ryan
Omniprism

43 West Chippewa Street,
Buffalo

Acrylic on Polytab
Sixteen works, each 2 ×
3 feet (0.6 × 0.9 m)

In April 2020, the Public Art Initiative provided materials to sixteen local artists who, working from their homes, were asked to respond to the first weeks of lockdown in the COVID-19 pandemic.

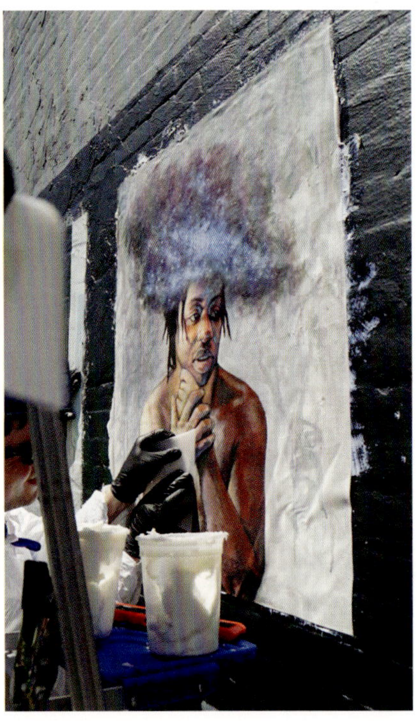

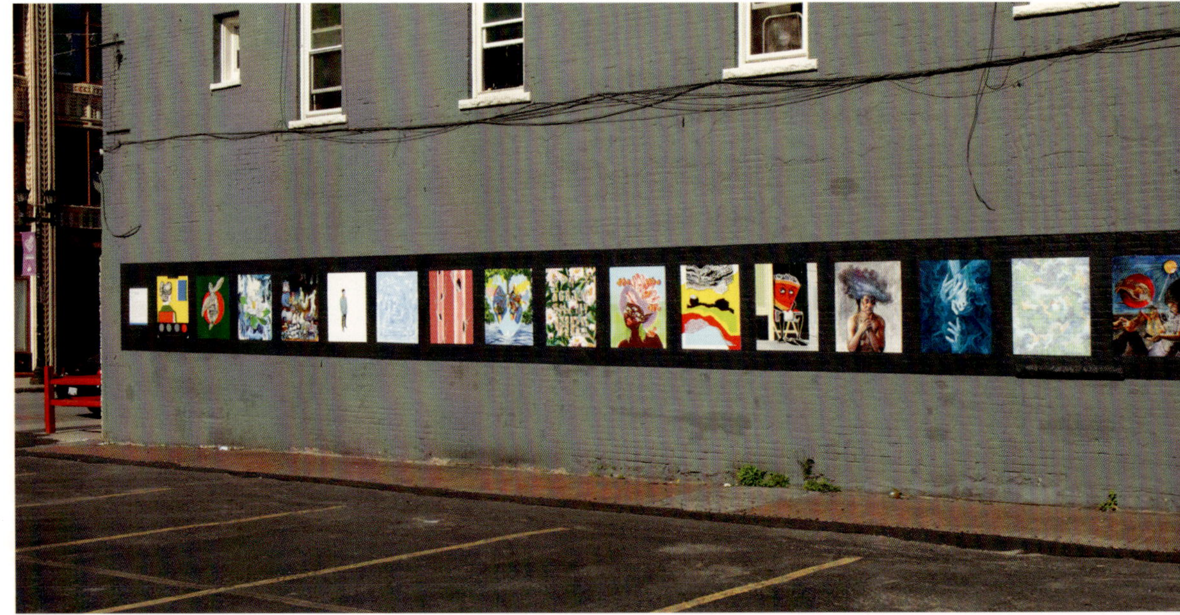

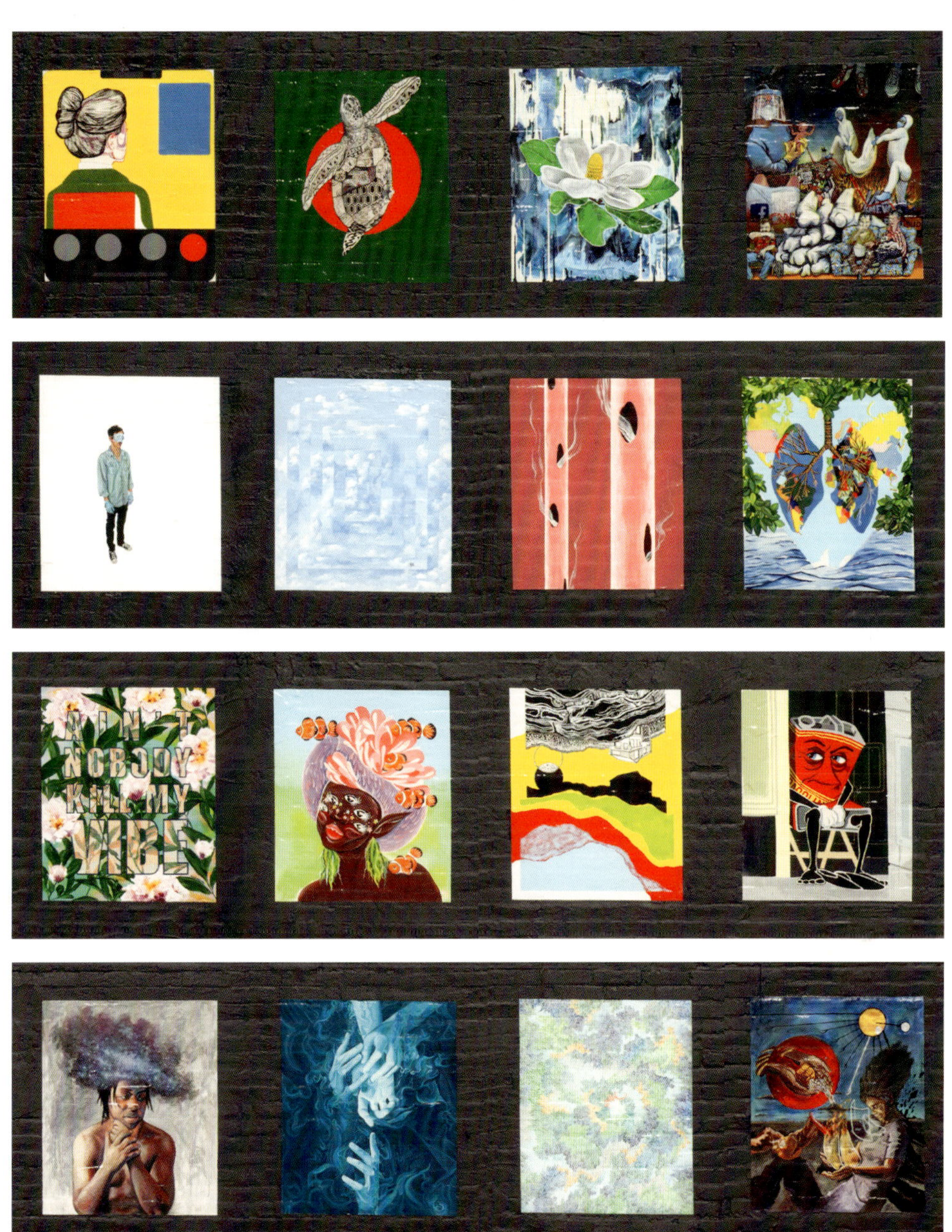

Becoming Centered: Public Art as a Community Conversation

ERIC JONES
Public Art Project Coordinator

Early in the summer of 2016, I received a cryptic voicemail from a woman named Julie. Her message indicated that she wanted to talk about a public art project we had recently launched with the fabric artist Amanda Browder. Browder, a quirky, brilliant craftsperson working at the inter-section of sewing and architecture, was planning a monumental installation of patchwork fabric covering three historic buildings in Buffalo (page 46). We had just put out a call to the community at large asking them to donate scraps of fabric in designated bins placed at locations like libraries and stores across Western New York. All of Browder's projects are community-centered and rely on donations, and, given our ambitions, we needed fabric—lots of it. Julie had answered the call. When we connected on the phone, we had a conversation that stays with me to this day. Julie's mother was a lifelong sewer, and appliqué was her craft of choice. She had spent decades perfecting advanced compositions of patterned fabrics—landscapes, animals, cityscapes—and she had reached a point in her journey through dementia when she was no longer able to sew. Julie was in the process of moving her mother into her own home and was at a loss for what to do with an entire room filled with beautiful fabrics her mom had collected for upwards of sixty years. Many pieces represented memories, such as the ones she procured at a friend's fabric store that had gone out of business, or the ones she bought to sew a barn scene for her new grandchild's nursery. Julie could not part with it, but she could not keep it all. She found our call for fabric an answer to her conundrum; her mother's treasure could contribute to something important.

We scheduled a time to pick up the collection, and then she told me, "You might need two trucks." I drove a box truck to her home the next week and pulled up to the garage, where she had lovingly packed up the overflowing materials. The boxes barely fit! Julie watched us drive away, seemingly relieved—the weight of the fabrics' abundance and significance had been offloaded, their ultimate utility serving a new and profound purpose. When we opened the boxes later that week, I witnessed for the first time the true mag-nitude of the gift. We didn't just receive scraps; we had years of half-completed appliqués in our possession. Small patchwork animals, plaid, and tartan figures on calico backgrounds. A lifetime's worth of creativity in fragments, waiting for a frame of reference. We used many of those mate-rials in Browder's installation (below), intention-ally positioning some of the appliqués front and center at the Richmond Avenue church.

At the end of the project, we had some leftover pieces, and one was an appliqué by Julie's mom.

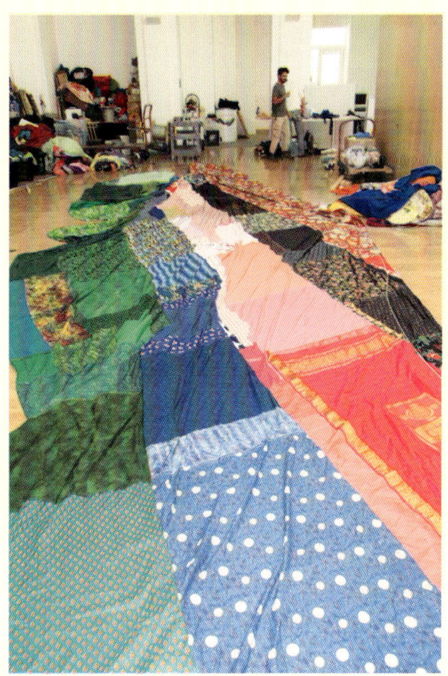

Amanda Browder's work involved soliciting cloth donations from the community, who deliv-ered in a big way.

I couldn't bear to discard it, so it hangs in my home—a duck of varying black and white calicos swimming on a blue-green pond dotted with reeds. It's not a masterpiece, or even a motif I would seek out, but it often reminds me of the power in connection, the reverberation of relevance, and the ripple effects of generosity.

The shape, line, color, and overall artistic merit of an artwork are often considered its defining features. But in our shared landscape, community involvement in public art projects becomes the defining element, often transforming an artwork from successful to phenomenal. By sharing their thoughts, personal insights, experiences, and even their sweat equity, local participants infuse public artworks with meaning and relevance in each unique community. Over a decade of projects, we have been honored by the patient partnership of cultural institutions, resident voices, community hands, and local artists, each one contributing to the refinement and evolution of the overall initiative. We have had missteps along the way, too. From dance parties in the street to contentious community meetings, the pendulum swings have been significant. But each oscillation has presented an important lesson, contributing to the evolution of our practices and, most notably, to our understanding of what is, truly, community.

Communities Are Dynamic

Undoubtedly, communities can vary widely from one side of the street to the other, from block to block, and from street to street; likewise, a definition of community will change depending on the person defining it and their daily experiences there. Communities are dynamic spaces, evolving iterations built upon memory and interaction with familiar places. They cannot entirely be defined by public art, people, or a specific moment, because they are always changing. A Polish neighborhood in 1950s Buffalo, for example, is now predominantly African American. As a result, even our best efforts to represent a community or group have inevitably become static or irrelevant. This is sometimes a bitter pill to swallow because a mural *feels* permanent. Producers, residents, and anyone engaged in its moment of becoming have real expectations about its longevity and relevance. We learned this lesson early on through a project called *Welcome Wall*, with Philadelphia-based muralists Ernel Martinez and Keir Johnston of Amber Arts Collective (page 73).

Martinez and Johnston were experts in the use of a new-to-us mural substrate called Polytab, or mural cloth. Unlike a wall that must be painted in place, mural cloth offers a substrate that can be painted anywhere, by anyone, in small sections. The process works like this: the design is scaled and transferred onto the mural cloth, which is segmented into five-by-five-foot squares in a large grid (right). The image is then color coded, which creates a giant paint-by-numbers exercise on each sheet of mural cloth. Anyone can paint it, as long as they can hold a brush and stay relatively inside the lines. The most attractive thing about mural cloth is that this process can unfold in the dead of winter and without lifts and ladders, democratizing the process and welcoming many people to produce it. A section of mural that would be well out of reach without scaffolding can be placed on a table for all to complete. Young hands are invited, too (perhaps with a little touching up at times).

Wanting to learn this process, we invited Johnston and Martinez to Buffalo. With a host wall secured by Broadway-Fillmore Neighborhood Housing Services, Inc., in the Broadway-Fillmore neighborhood, one rich with different refugee communities, the artists developed their concept based on the seventeen languages spoken within this small geographical area. After a few design reviews with our partners, the *Welcome Wall* design was approved: the word *Welcome* written in each of the represented languages set on a background of patterns from these cultures. The final design was then transferred to the corresponding squares of mural cloth, and we painted the mural over the course of dozens of community paint days at the historic Broadway Market and the central branch of the Buffalo & Erie County Public Library. There was skepticism in the familiar faces we encountered each day at the market, but the residents kept coming back to paint, and they brought others with them. Through discussion and a paintbrush, that skepticism turned to pride. Today, however, just eight years later, that neighborhood has continued to evolve. While several languages depicted in the mural still represent the local tongues, new refugees have settled in the area, and others have moved away. To some, the mural doesn't represent them, where they came from, or where they live now. To others, it represents the memory of neighbors they once knew. The lesson we learned was to let go of permanence and attachment and to focus more on the process and experience than the outcome.

For our second mural cloth project, we selected the Philadelphia-based Betsy Casañas in conjunction with our partners, the Rich Family Foundation, M&T Bank, and the Hispanic

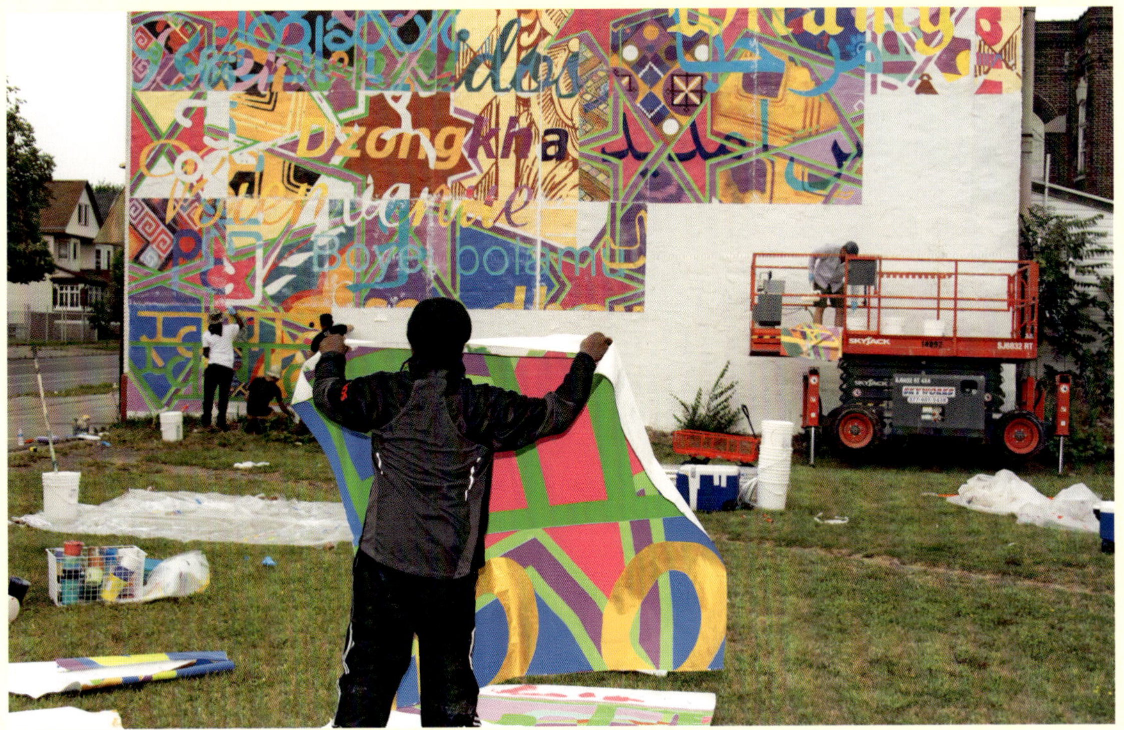

A volunteer lifts a painted section of Polytab to place it in the *Welcome Wall* mural.

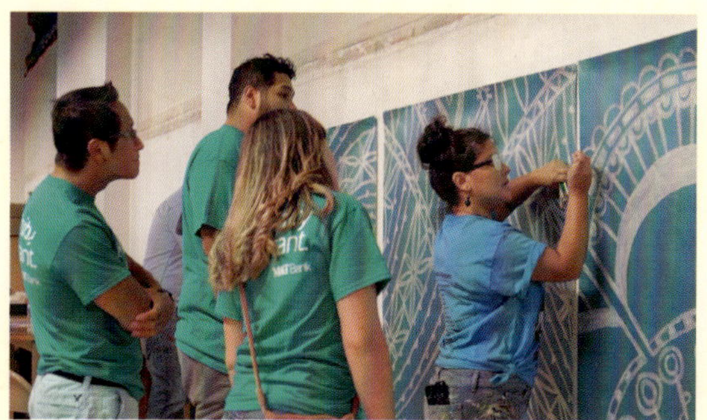

Heritage Council. In her previous work, Casañas had involved community voices and hands, from design through production, and here she developed a design derived from conversations with locals, which intertwined three women from Afro-Cuban, Indigenous, and Spanish cultures, each set on a background of motifs and mandalas from her cultural homeland (page 76). She also included imagery of industry and farmland—two pillars of Buffalo's historic landscape—to tell the story of what drew immigrants to the city.

With mural cloth as the substrate again, we could move the production of the artwork off the wall and into a more accessible public space. Once again, the central branch of the Buffalo & Erie County Public Library became our home base. Over the course of the mural's production, library patrons, youth organizations, school groups, corporate volunteers, and local artists made their mark during community paint days (left). The steady beat of music, conversation, laughter, and shared meals made the extremely ambitious timeline worth pushing toward. Admittedly, we missed our completion date by a few days,

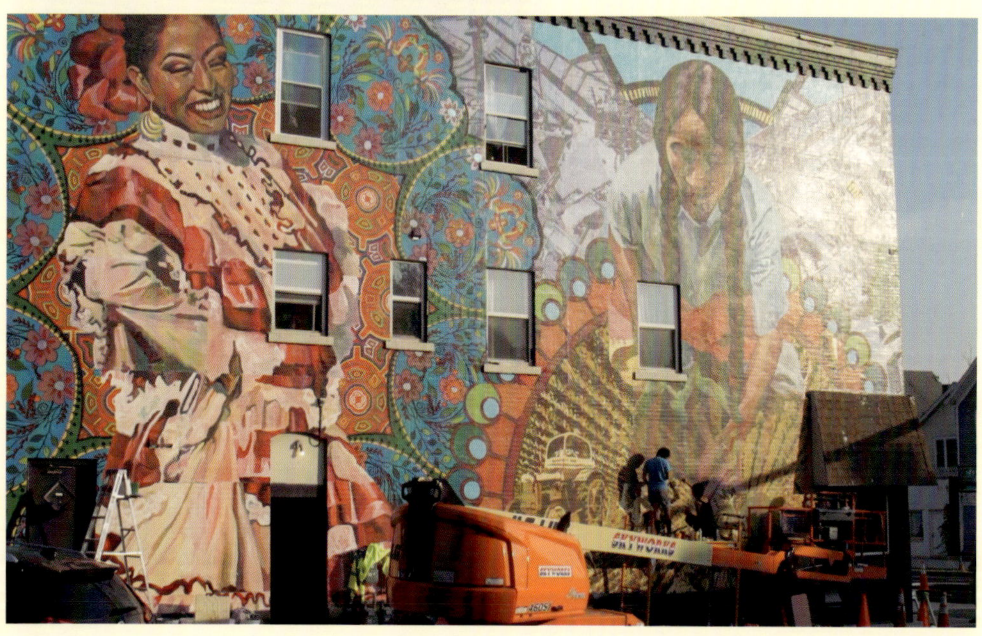

and, reflecting back, the enthusiasm of the participants encouraged an unexpected scaling-up in the level of detail and overall scope of the project. But in the end, more than five hundred people contributed to Casañas's work. On the very last day of installation, we threw a block party with the Hispanic Heritage Council. Politicians and representatives spoke, a Latino band played in the street, and Rich's provided a decadent spread. You would have thought a parade was on its way. Later, in the quiet of that night, we—the installation team and the artist's team—came back to complete finishing touches on her mural, *Patria, Será Porque Quisiera Que Vueles, Que Sigue Siendo Tuyo Mi Vuelo (Homeland, Perhaps It Is Because I Wish to See You Fly, That My Flight Continues to Be Yours)*. Looking at this new landmark in Buffalo's Avenida San Juan together, we agreed that each detail mattered.

Long after the dust had settled on this project, however, we heard from an employee at the museum who is part of and well connected to Buffalo's Latinx population that the mural did not represent his lived experience, and that he wasn't alone in this reaction. He was missing in the mural, as was the experience of other younger generations. This was difficult news to embrace at first, until we looked at it from this perspective: *of course*, a single image cannot sum up the plurality of identities, cultures, and voices of an entire group of people. Why should we ever have the audacity to expect it to?

Here's what we know from these projects: communities will change, and new eyes and hearts will have different perceptions of these artworks outside their window. Though our model for community engagements continues to evolve, projects integrating local hands as co-producers have been some of the most impactful, given the opportunity they present to take ownership of something produced alongside one's neighbor. Likewise, as our engagements evolve, so does the Public Art Initiative, as each project completed informs the next, and those thereafter.

Inspiring Engagement Doesn't Have to Be Complicated

Sometimes a simple, accessible, hands-on project is what the moment or the community calls for. Two precursor public art projects in 2014 harnessed community engagement early in the development of the program: Charles Clough's *Hamburg Arena Painting* and Tape Art collective's *Buffalo Caverns*. Each project served as an experiment for *how* to foster a connection between the museum and the community, but looking back, their success was more about offering the opportunity for hands-on work with a material than focusing on the final results. In these cases, the artist's job was to conduct the experience with participants and encourage experimentation, which both projects did, in vastly separate ways with different outcomes.

Buffalo native Charlie Clough invited participants to apply paint and push it across a mural-sized canvas using oversized brushes, creating a collective composition that would eventually be installed in the Hamburg Public Library (page 20). Similarly, the Tape Art collective used hundreds of rolls of green and blue painter's tape to transform an exterior wall of the Central Library with a temporary mural (page 21). Both projects were highly tactile, approachable, family-friendly, and scalable, and ultimately each engagement stripped away any trepidation about making mistakes, because everyone felt secure using the materials. Tape is safe, and what's not fun about using a giant paint applicator?

Engagements can also be about fulfilling a project concept simply through participation. Jenny Kendler's *Milkweed Dispersal Balloon*s and concurrent *ReWilding New York (Community Seed Stations)* (pages 36 and 37) sought to empower the public to help disperse native plant and wildflower seeds, with the goal of re-establishing diminished food sources for migrating pollinators, namely adult monarch butterflies. Performative in nature, Kendler's *Milkweed Dispersal Balloons* consisted of a modified hot-dog cart with a small helium tank, clear biodegradable balloons containing milkweed seeds, and associated accoutrements like hemp string and tags with information about habitat restoration. Through invitations from supportive partners, we attended farmers markets, food truck events, and Buffalo's renowned Garden Walk to find a curious and supportive audience excited about the project. Participants were not asked to release the balloons, but to pop them at home and distribute the seeds there. Comparatively, the community seed stations were stationary art interventions placed with partner locations across the county, thanks to a donation of ten newspaper "honor boxes" by the *Buffalo News*. Each box was wrapped in vinyl with a floral design created by the artist and repurposed to house free packets of native wildflower seeds (right).

Kendler's projects were valuable for their conceptual capacity—empowering public audiences to restore native habitats—and they were also early lessons about scaling and planning for a newly conceived public art program. We had amazing volunteers to assist in the seed packet filling and distribution (an incredibly tedious and detailed task), and the host sites helped keep the stations stocked, alleviating work for what was at that time a two-person team. Likewise, our partnerships with community organizations were crucial in the development and execution of the projects and would inspire similar partnerships for future projects. Without a doubt, we learned there was great interest from the public and community stakeholders who saw a benefit in the placement of public art and wanted to be further engaged in the planning and execution of our projects, which would become a useful approach for garnering increased public support moving forward.

Perhaps most important, these projects were accessible. No participant needed a special skill set or knowledge, to sign a waiver, or to give a major time commitment. Yet each public interaction—and there were hundreds, even thousands—felt profoundly impactful.

Many Hands

Perhaps representation can be found in other forms, not an obvious visual cue or clear-cut notion, but in the materiality of the work and in drawing people together through a shared experience. Two such projects, Kaarina Kaikkonen's *We Share a Dream* and Amanda Browder's *Spectral Locus*, discussed earlier, used textiles to convey collective representation by inviting fabric and clothing donations.

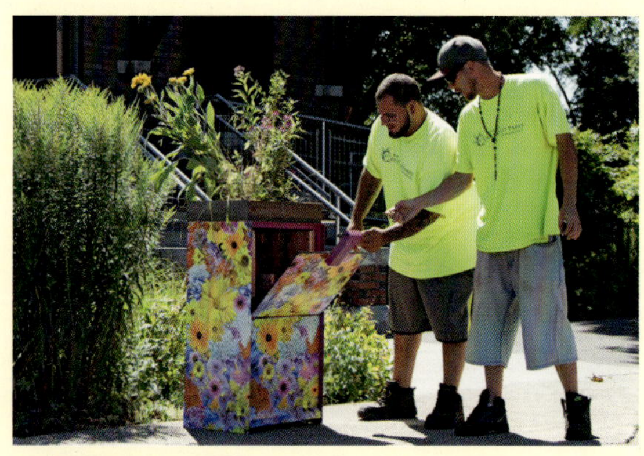

Jenny Kendler made use of repurposed newspaper boxes throughout the region to distribute seed packets.

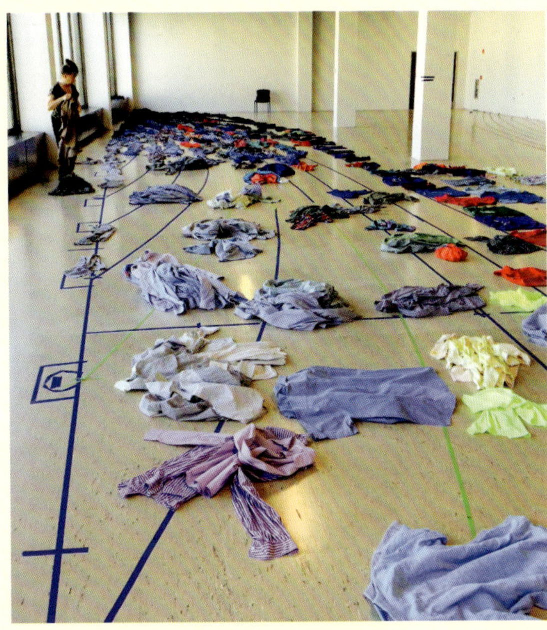

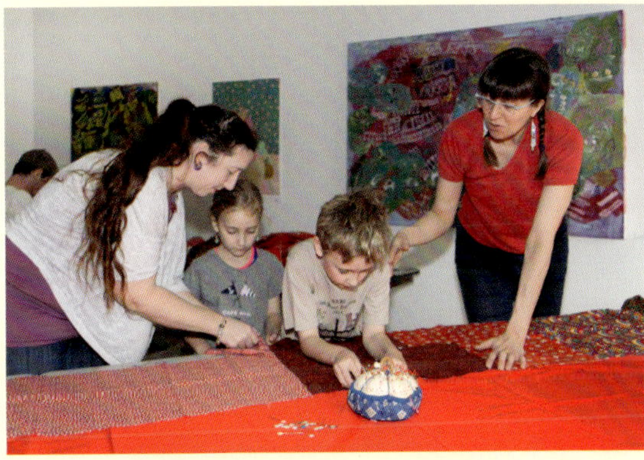

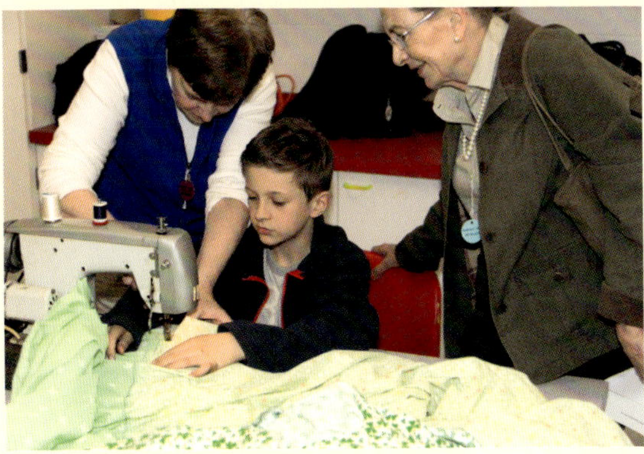

In 2015, Kaikkonen constructed her installation *We Share a Dream* (page 34) entirely from donated shirts. Clothing, she believes, holds the residual energy of a person, and when gathered it represents a community of people. In this work, thousands of shirts were strung together into a chromatic pennant-like installation evocative of prayer flags (above left). Exhibited above the ticketing counters at the Buffalo Niagara International Airport, it welcomed travelers to and from our region with a collective representation of our city and region holding hands. At the unveiling event, Kaikkonen said, "In every old shirt, there has been a warm, loving heart inside."

Alternately, Browder's practice exemplifies community inclusion through donated fabric, literally the fabric of our community, and the hands of the numerous volunteers who dedicated their time to assemble and sew the work. In *Spectral Locus* (page 46), ambitiously constructed fabric was installed on three buildings across Buffalo, most notably a church undergoing renovation. Browder exclaimed upon its completion, "It's standing!" But it was the engagements leading up to that moment that truly reflected a shared sense of community, as we worked with residents across the county to pin and stitch the work together.

Historically, community sewing circles are a common thread in most any society, the very means of assembling people to share and shape relationships with others. The richness of these circles came together after weeks of carefully planned pinning of fabric, each color panel placed in concert with the next to create a kaleidoscope of quilted sculpture (middle and below left). Our engagement events were an immense success, thanks in part to extremely supportive partnerships with the Buffalo & Erie County Public Library system, Starlight Studio and Art Gallery, Stitch Buffalo, the Olmsted Center for Sight, and Buffalo Arts Studio, all of which welcomed first-time and repeat participants into their spaces to joyfully assist with production. Many of these volunteers are still in touch eight years later.

Co-Production Builds Relevance

Our public was also invited to participate in the creation of Hillary Waters Fayle's mural *Botanical Blueprint* (page 100). Fayle's studio practice harnesses botanicals, cyanotypes, and crafts like embroidery and collage, utilizing unconventional materials such as leaves or flower petals to make aesthetically pleasing and widely accessible artworks. Her focus on flora opened the door to a partnership with Garden Walk Buffalo, a long-established and beloved festival that welcomes people into private yards to enjoy the surprise and delight of blooming gardens. We set up a station for spontaneous artmaking with Garden Walk attendees, who were invited to arrange compositions of local plants and flowers on light-sensitive paper, which was then exposed to sunlight before a dip in a water bath, producing

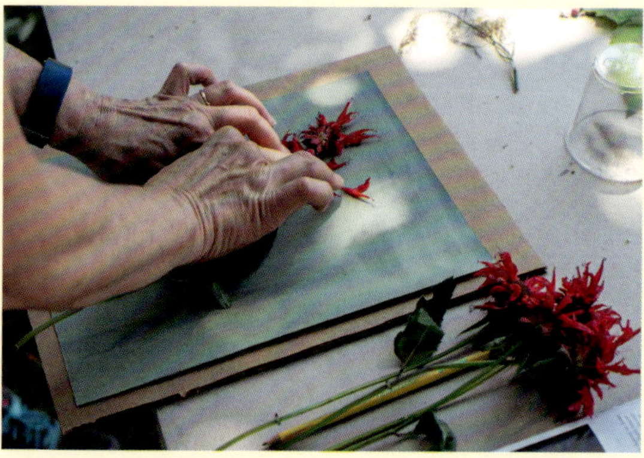

To arrive at the design of her mural, Hillary Waters Fayle led a cyanotype workshop, where participants created prints of local flora.

a print they took home and another they donated to the project (below). From the hundreds of submissions, Fayle designed a mural, which was painted on her behalf by the Public Art team.

But the project also had a secondary goal. A decade earlier, a talented artist had painted the host wall. As well-meaning as the endeavor had been, the content of the mural wasn't well received by the neighborhood. It had been defaced and tagged repeatedly, each tag resulting in another strip of covering paint along the bottom of the wall. The result was a long-standing eyesore in a residential neighborhood. We were thankful for the outpouring of locals who came by during the installation of Fayle's mural to support its production, and I will never forget their words of support. Even though the mural could have landed almost anywhere else, these residents felt seen and represented because someone had initiated a much-needed visual change, uplifting the neighborhood.

One of our most informed murals in recent years was a collaboration with the Buffalo Municipal Housing Authority, which reached out to the museum with a prominent wall in mind, hoping to breathe new life into an aging building. Of consequence was the location: a major intersection of a freeway and Main Street, just on the fringe of a university and opposite a hospital. Many eyes know and see this ten-story wall every day. We knew this wall well; it was among the smoothest in the city! And it formed the exterior of a housing project for adults and seniors. Over the span of about two years, we worked alongside the residential commission to glean the residents' ideas about artists, content, and styles, ultimately deciding that they—namely, their portraits—would serve as the primary subject.

With their guidance, we selected Aaron Li-Hill for the project. Li-Hill's practice principally

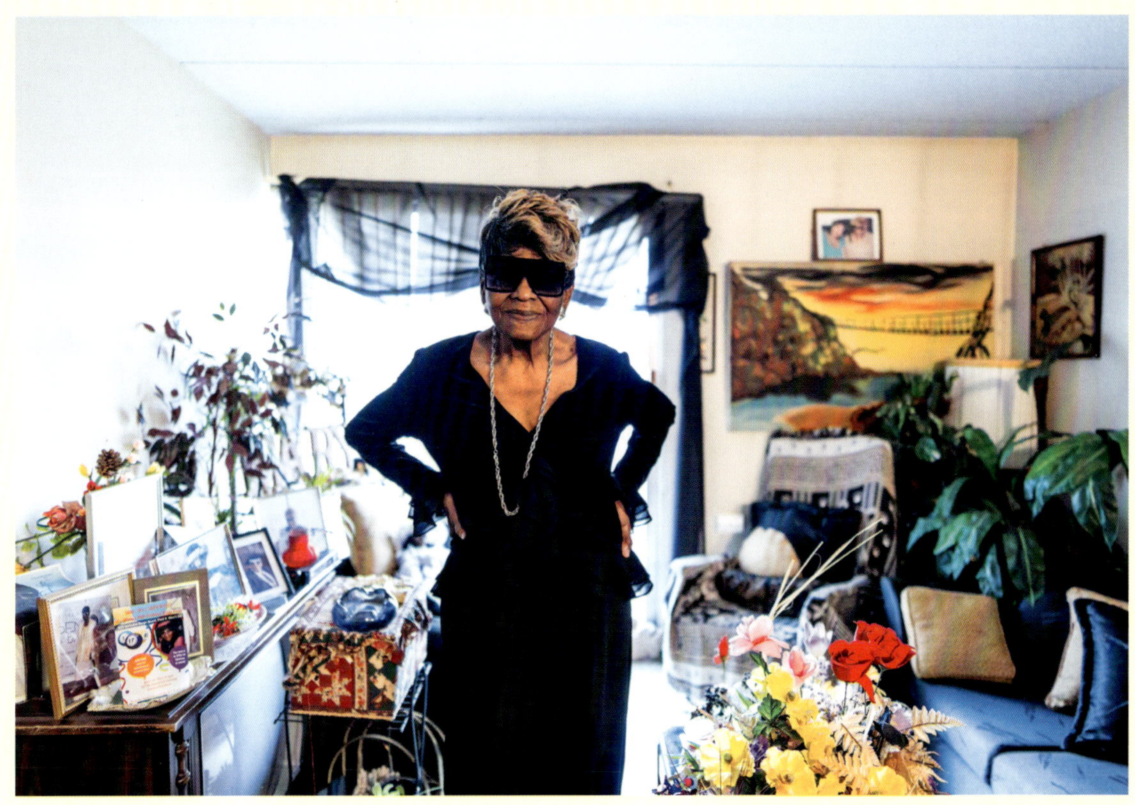

explores figures and movement, and his gorgeous portraits have an uncanny way of capturing the depth of a person's character. Upon agreeing to the project, we flew him to Buffalo to meet with residents. He teamed up with local photographer Patrick Cray to shoot photos of the residents and learn personal information that would inform his work (above). Li-Hill selected seven community members for his composition. Little did we know the impact this would have on the residents, who often felt they weren't seen and had been forgotten, or that they didn't matter, but they told us every day of the mural production.

Upon our daily arrival to the wall, we were usually welcomed by groups of residents and guests checking in on our progress and looking for known faces on the wall while walking their dogs and running errands. None of the residents knew if they had been included in the mural design or not, so as each face appeared, it became a cause for celebration, even if there was another who was disappointed that they hadn't been selected. But when it came to Ms. Mary, who at ninety-one years old was the resident who had lived longest in the building, the most stylish lady on the block, and always wearing a pair of sunglasses, no one could argue with her inclusion. Residents cheered when they saw her on the wall, larger than life. Also celebrated was the central figure of the mural, a Haudenosaunee and Navajo (Diné) resident named Bow and Arrow, who represents the original inhabitants of the land on which the building stands, and their continued strength and resilience today. Each person

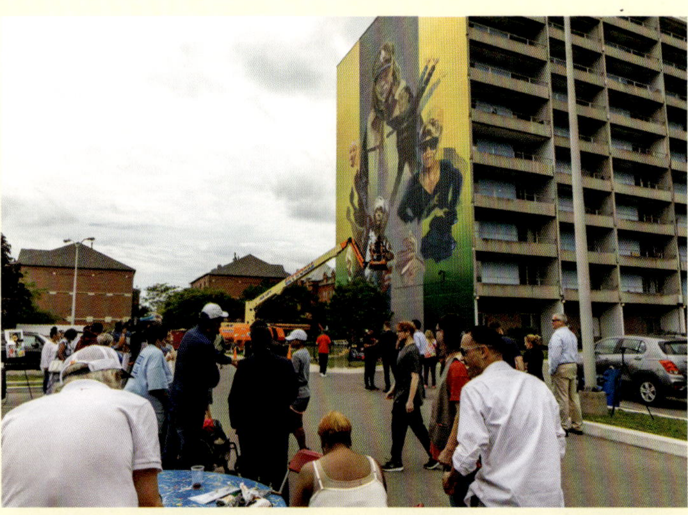

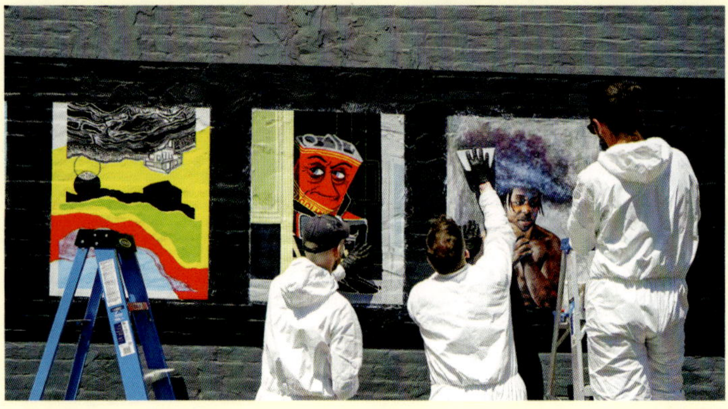

included in the mural had a story about the community to contribute, one that had brought them to this moment and place over decades of becoming.

However, it was the unveiling ceremony that truly celebrated the residents and recognized every-one involved for their contributions (left). We consider them as co-producers, even if they didn't have to pick up a paintbrush, because they fully informed the work, not only for the mural content and artist selec-tion but in capturing the essence of the people on the wall and the space itself. The conversations, smiles, and visits from our resident friends pro-vided important insight about the positive impact this project was having for them—they felt seen. In turn, their words energized our days and kept us inspired to finish the mural in a remarkable sixteen days, the last of which was the day Li-Hill returned to London. He simply couldn't leave without making every effort to produce his best work for them, and of course, he arrived that morning to find the residents welcoming him back one last time.

Adaptation and Innovation

There are memorable moments during projects in our past, but the years and obstacles around the COVID-19 pandemic were an excep-tional disruption. Gathering people was an essen-tial part of our practice, and now gatherings had become jeopardous, for who knows how long? As the world flocked outside, so did we, and the

Public Art Initiative became one of the museum's most active arms. We felt an obligation to provide the public with some normalcy and inspiration, but further, to provide work for our community of artists in need of work and income.

Works, from Home (page 126) became a new project model for us. As it responded to the critical need for distance during the pandemic, it also unlocked a new level of potential for the mural cloth substrate. We'd preached many times that mural cloth could democratize the mural process by pulling the mural off the wall and onto the tables of community participants, but what if we went a step further and fully removed ourselves from production? What if we put the mural entirely in the hands of local artists? This embodied the very idea of what we were tasked with, so we assembled boxes of mural paints and cloth and dropped them off on the doorsteps of sixteen local artists known for their artistic merit who had agreed to the project. With a flexible timeline and the freedom for each artist to develop their own concept, the resulting sixteen-piece collaborative mural speaks to individual and collective experiences over the initial pandemic lockdown (opposite, below).

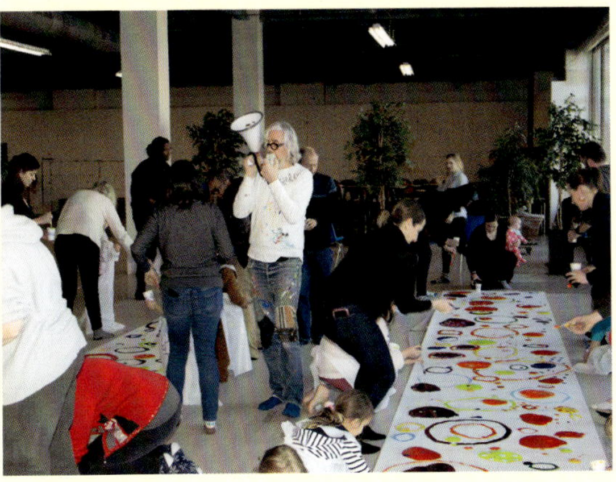

Months before, Aaron Ott and I had begun working on a co-curated exhibition of work by the acclaimed French children's book author and multidisciplinary artist Hervé Tullet. *Hervé Tullet: Shape and Color* was on view June 26 to September 12, 2021, in our satellite space on Buffalo's East Side, Albright-Knox Northland, which served as a gallery, classroom, and public forum during our campus expansion project. We wanted to activate AK Northland during Tullet's exhibition to empower our guests as artists and creators, in the vein of the painting engagements Tullet had conducted with worldwide audiences. Likewise, his public painting productions were much akin to mural cloth engagements, so we decided to incorporate a public art component to further engage our audiences. This would ultimately serve us better than we expected.

Originally, Tullet's exhibition was based on his *Ideal Exhibition*, an earlier project that produced a wealth of creative content along with online supplemental videos to guide viewers through a series of his studio practices. Tullet understands that an exhibition can exist anywhere, be any size, and last any duration. He also knows the impact children and adults can make when given the autonomy to make creative decisions within a few parameters. He demonstrated this sort of engagement for us in Buffalo, directing hundreds of individuals to create large paintings for inclusion in his exhibition (left). Tullet arrived at each workshop with a contagious smile and a huge "Bonjour!" readying himself and his audience for a buoyant reading of some of his most popular titles. He has mastered the art of participation using simple directives in his books, and he familiarizes everyone with his prompts before handing them a brush and paint. Tullet then moved the group around a long roll of paper in a choreographed flower-painting production

using circles, dots, and lines, with each participant finishing another's work until the paper was
filled. It belonged to all of them as co-producers
of the exhibition.

It was an exciting start that would distract
us from increasingly loud whispers of the looming
pandemic. We had planned to see Tullet again in
the coming weeks for additional painting workshops, but travel restrictions curtailed our plans,
and he would unexpectedly need to go back to
France to manage familial responsibilities. His
return to the States became impossible, and
we would end up shipping work to Buffalo from
his studio in Paris for the exhibition. This
took extra time to produce and gave us a valuable
opportunity to reorient ourselves. We didn't feel
this way at the time and had no idea from day to
day how things would unfold, but I can't imagine
these rich engagements being any different today.

Undoubtedly, the core of Tullet's writing and
art practice is an explorative process that gen-
erates more excitement for discovery than fear
of mistakes. This was a time for exploration and
discovery, and we were fearful for long enough.
Because we had already planned a cloth mural for
Tullet's engagements, we reorganized the show
with a simultaneous residency program inside
AK Northland over the run of the exhibition. The
participating artists would take up the mural
cloth process in the gallery space itself, providing
the public a sneak peek into each artist's creative
process, while co-creating Tullet's mural work for
the exhibition.

After thoughtful consideration, local artists
Julia Bottoms, Tricia Butski, Max Collins, Fotini
Galanes, Rachel Shelton, and Phyllis Thompson
were selected, and each would produce a ten-
by-fifteen-foot mural to be installed just a couple
of blocks down the street from AK Northland
(page 149). A group of painters and printmakers

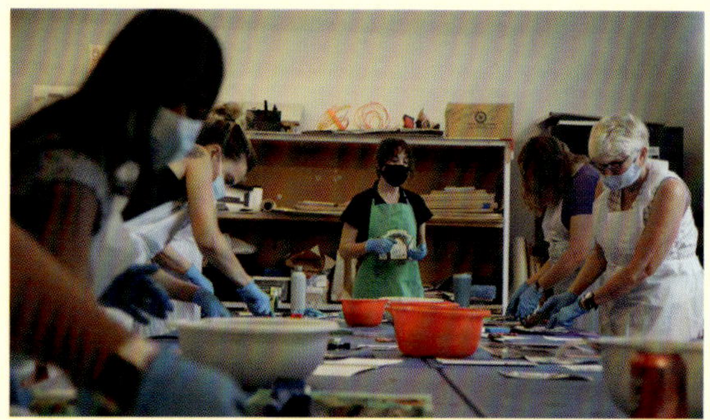

Rachel Shelton, a resident artist during the Tullet exhibition, leads a workshop on do-it-yourself printmaking using crayon and Coca-Cola.

with strong studio practices, they were invited to include
public spaces if they wished. The artists, representing
a wide range of personalities and identities with strong
backgrounds in education and otherwise engaging
audiences, were selected because we wanted
artists who could interact and connect with our
guests meaningfully. They wouldn't disappoint.

Granted, this was the first time that most
of these artists had worked with Polytab, or had
even considered working in a public capacity,
and whether they did or didn't after this was up
to them, but they were there to learn and interact
with a curious audience looking behind the scenes
of creative minds. Split into two groups, the residents staggered their production over the summer,
most assuredly lending a fresh look to return
visitors in the days leading up to the week of
installation. The residency was important for several reasons, but giving our audience, especially
young people, the opportunity to see and talk
with working artists was priceless—all the while
having a creative space just steps away (above).

Remarkably, Tullet's exhibition opened
in accordance with social distancing measures,
and we welcomed more than 5,100 people to AK
Northland in the thirty-four days the residencies

were operating. Here, we learned to reunite while
looking at, making, and talking about art.
While artmaking was a signature element of our
intended programs, we didn't even know how
to share art supplies months earlier, but we would
thankfully include these gallery offerings again.
Additionally, we completed the cloth mural
and distributed 3,200 customized art packets to
schools and county library branches, each containing a selection of art supplies and access
to online videos of Tullet leading viewers through
a variety of creative exercises. The richness of
these engagements surpassed anything we expected
at the time, short of Tullet himself arriving.

Undoubtedly, public art has been an
impactful program that has transformed our
collective aesthetic landscape, while inspiring
municipalities, city representatives, community
organizations, and residents to champion
their own public art initiatives. We've strived
to deliver the best outcome, realizing our mission
of empowering artists and inspiring viewers
while strengthening an appreciation of our
shared landscape with artworks that reflect the
communities they reside within. In ten years,
we have learned the map is not the territory
and definitions of community will evolve,
as will the uniqueness of each community and
our projects.

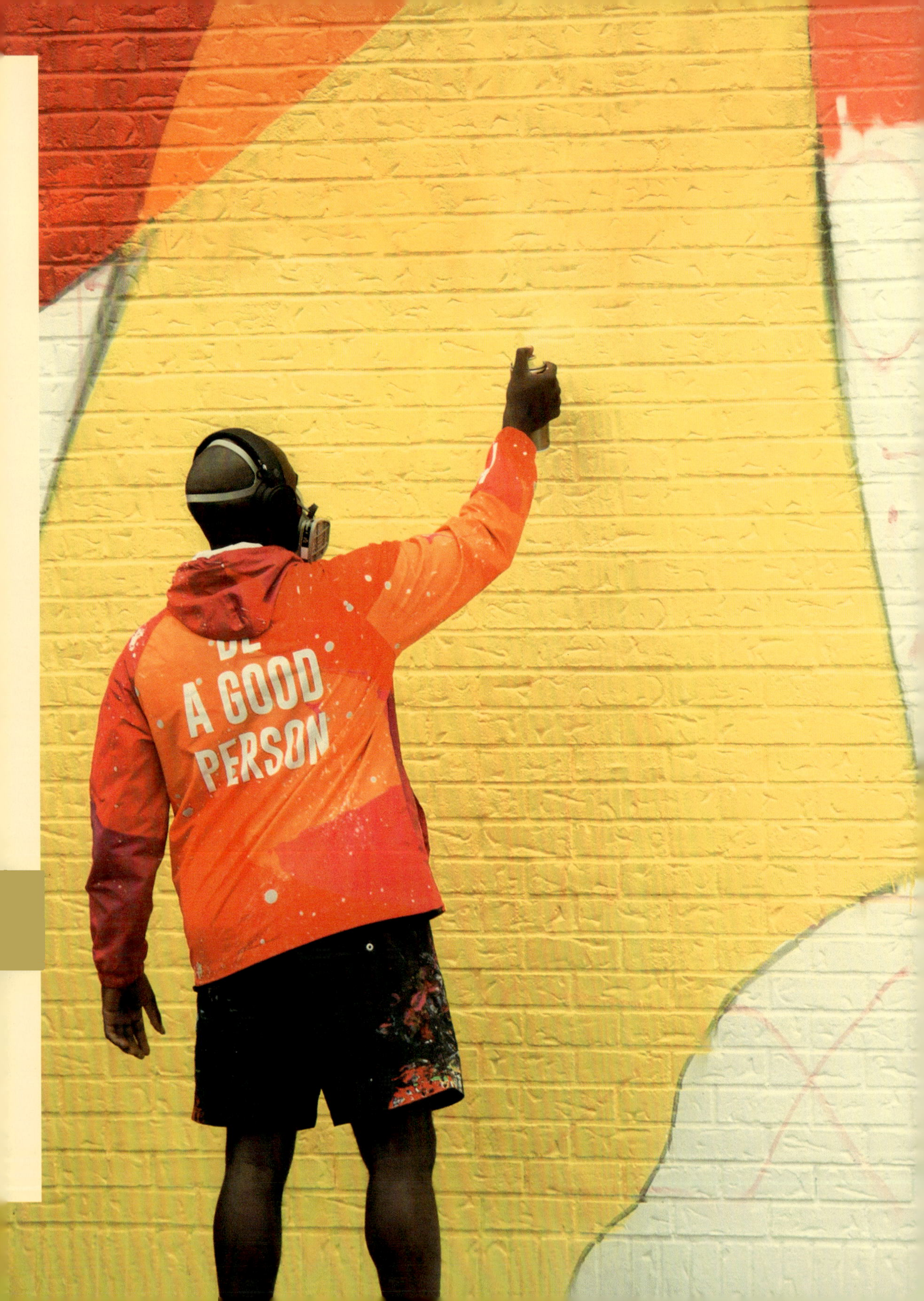
A GOOD
PERSON

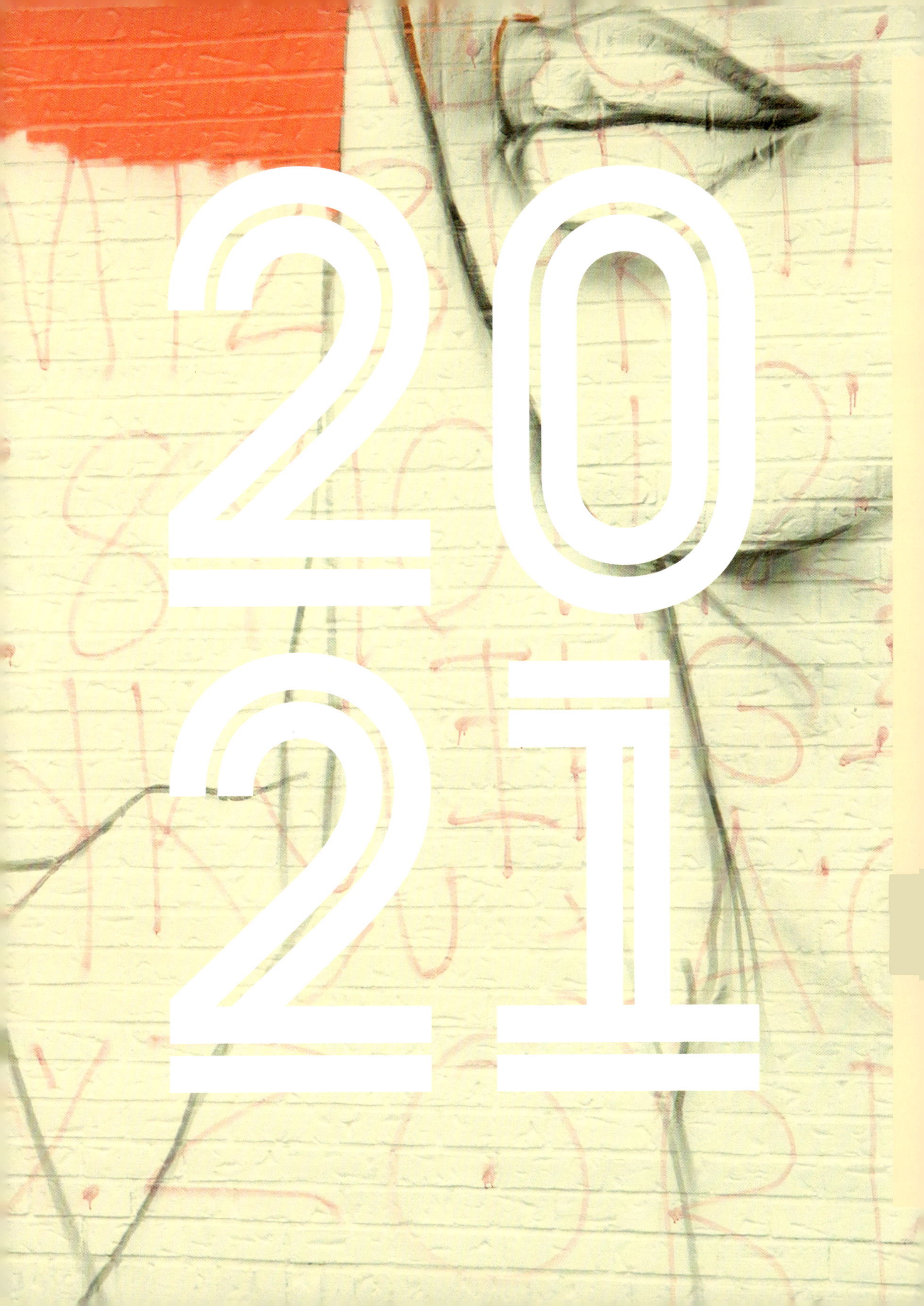

Buffalo Soldier Wing Stance (The Tree of Y)

Maya Hayuk

D'Youville University
Health Professions Hub

Mineral paint on
compressed concrete panels
60 × 96 feet (18.3 × 29.3 m)

After years of painting massive exterior artworks all over the world, I have developed a few credos on my work practice. For years, I refused the help of assistants, not only because I needed the freedom to totally improvise my murals creatively, but in a way because I felt like I needed to prove myself to the skeptics of women working in this field. But eventually I did start learning ways to make the process that much more efficient with the assistance of others, which has only yielded more enjoyable and better outcomes. The goal to make something I could feel incredibly proud of that also would speak to the community only improved. And nothing in the root of my philosophy became compromised once I farmed out the job of, say, carrying buckets.

So, I came up with a catch phrase: "The Art Is Only As Good As the Producer." Rather than taking my DIY philosophy to the point of self-harm (literally), I started finding people who I trust—who believe in me. The first thing I had to get over was a kind of self-imposed fear that I would be somehow annoying in my creative process to those who were helping me out. My pace, my rhythms, my way of working out the puzzles at hand—I felt awkward that anyone would have to be standing around while I worked through the making of a painting. I had to get over that quickly—there's no shame in my process or what it takes.

But still, over the years I kept finding myself up against this bizarre challenge I call the "believability factor." Once I had completely dialed in my production process and knew how to properly do things down to the minutia, I was still (and am still) often questioned. The last thing I want to do is waste anyone's time or money—and the last thing I want to feel is that I am in any way "asking too much." I take great pride in the precision of my productions. I know my craft.

So, every once in a while, I am blessed with a production crew like the one from the Buffalo AKG Art Museum. We took on a project together—something incredibly monumental to be painted on the sunny side of a huge facade at the hottest time of the year—no big deal. From the first email to the last drop of paint, they took care of every detail, and that freed me up to be only thinking about the creative process with my amazing team. When I say that this mural is one of the best I've ever made, please remember that it's only as good as the production crew. And in this case, you can believe it by seeing the stellar results. Thanks, all.
—MAYA HAYUK

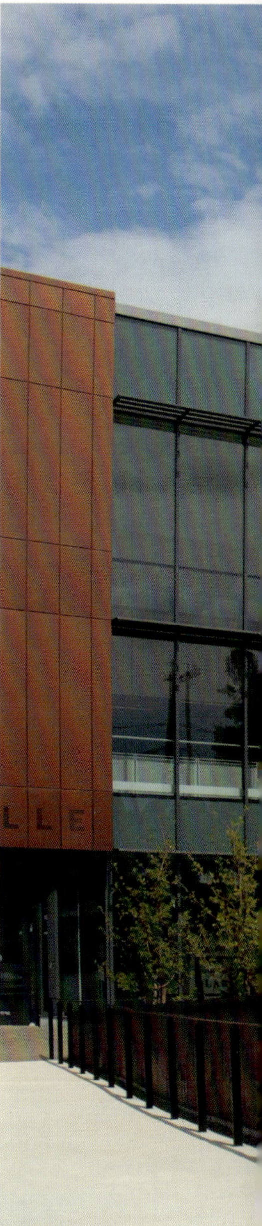

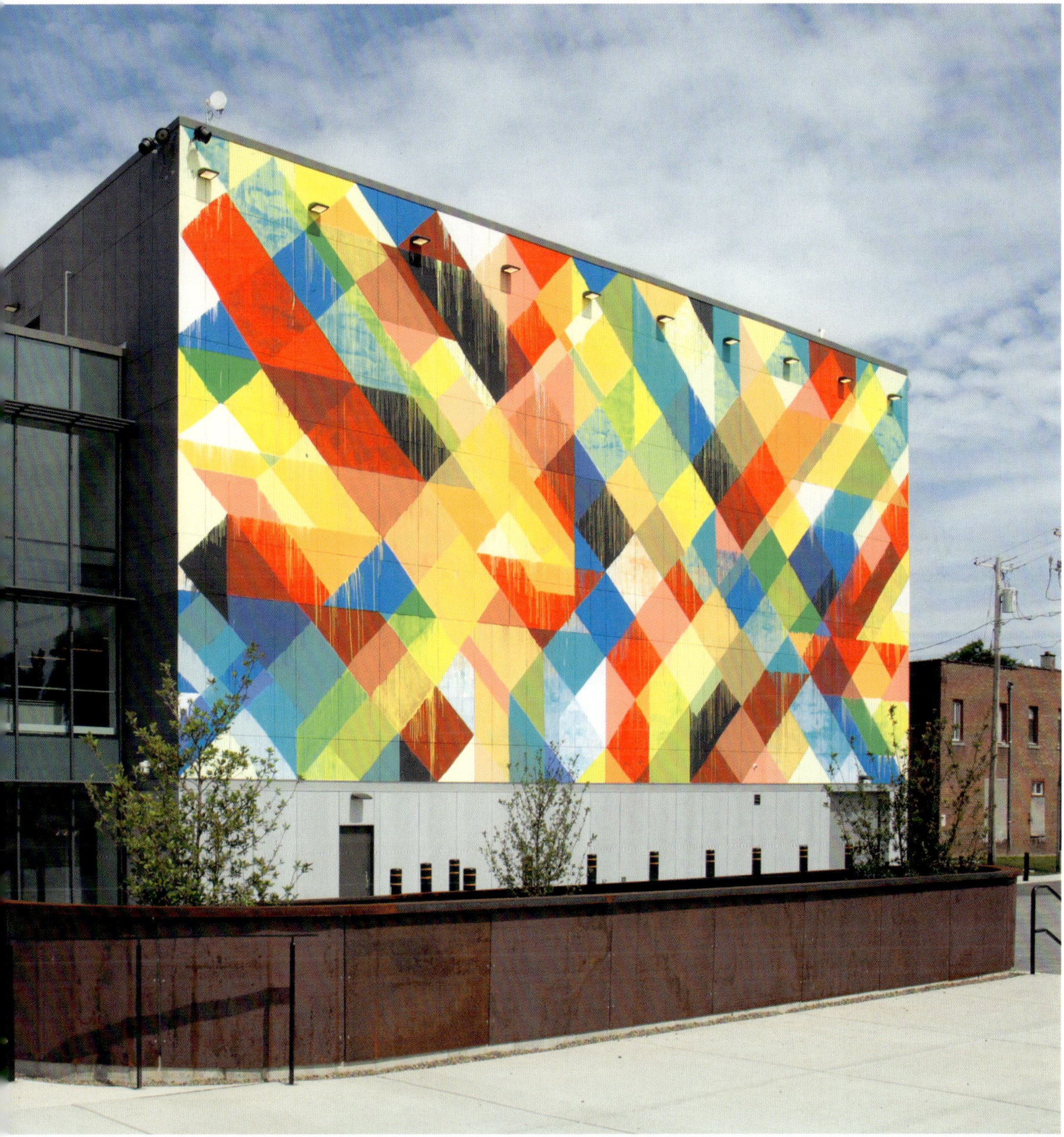

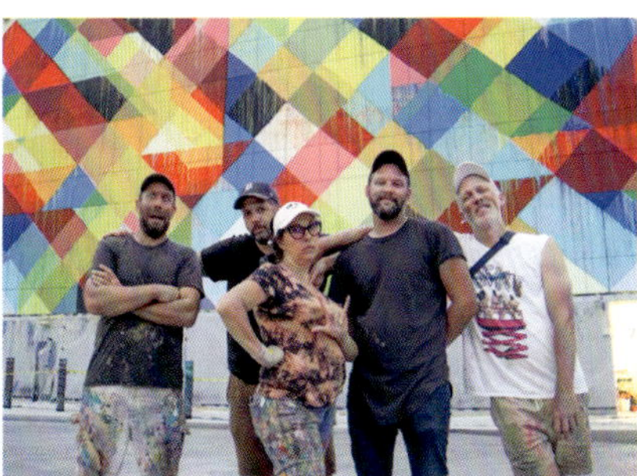

Hayuk poses with
members of
her team and the
Public Art crew.

Golden Hour

Josef Kristofoletti

201 Ellicott Street, Buffalo

Mineral paint on
Minerit panels
East panel: 69 × 62 feet
(21 × 18.9 m); West panel:
47 × 57 feet (14.3 × 17.4 m)

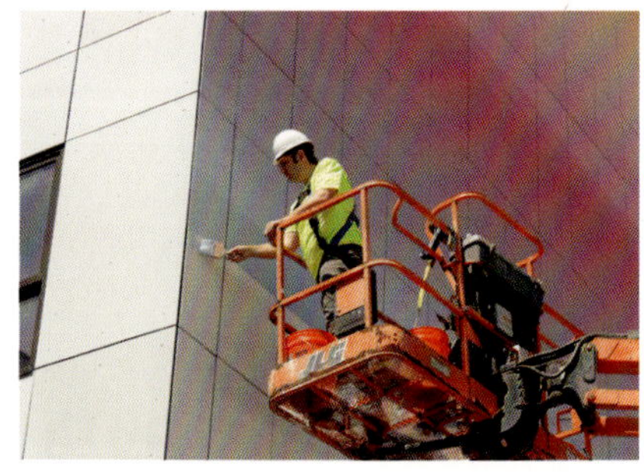

Kristofoletti
paints his entire
mural with a
four-inch brush.

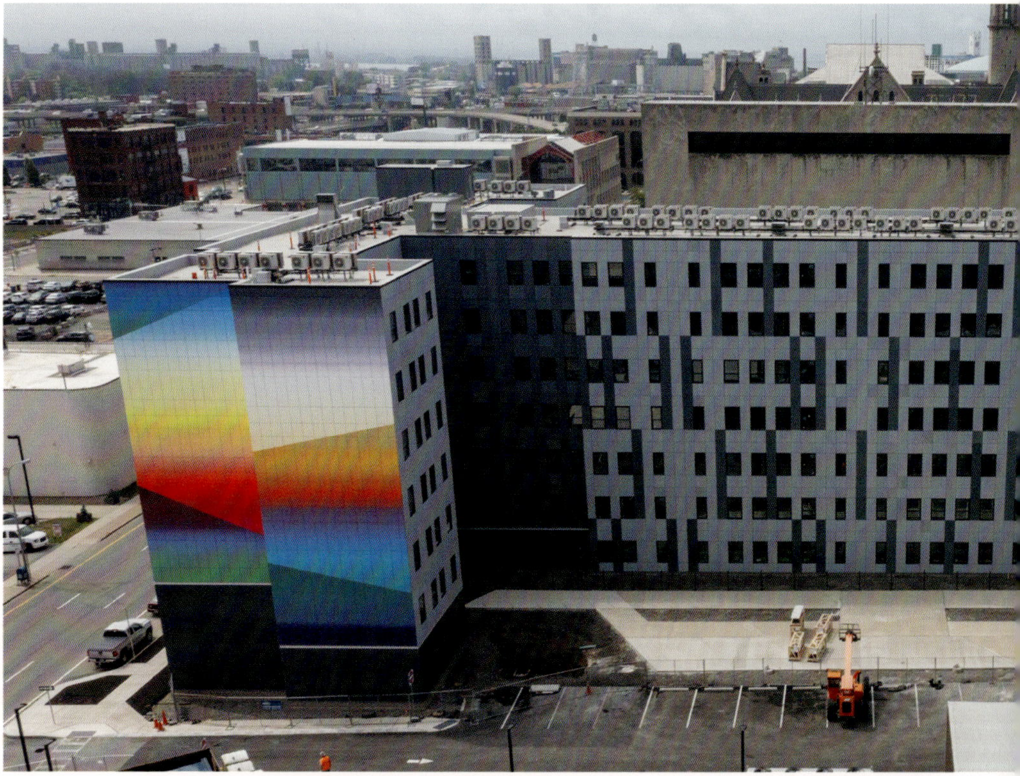

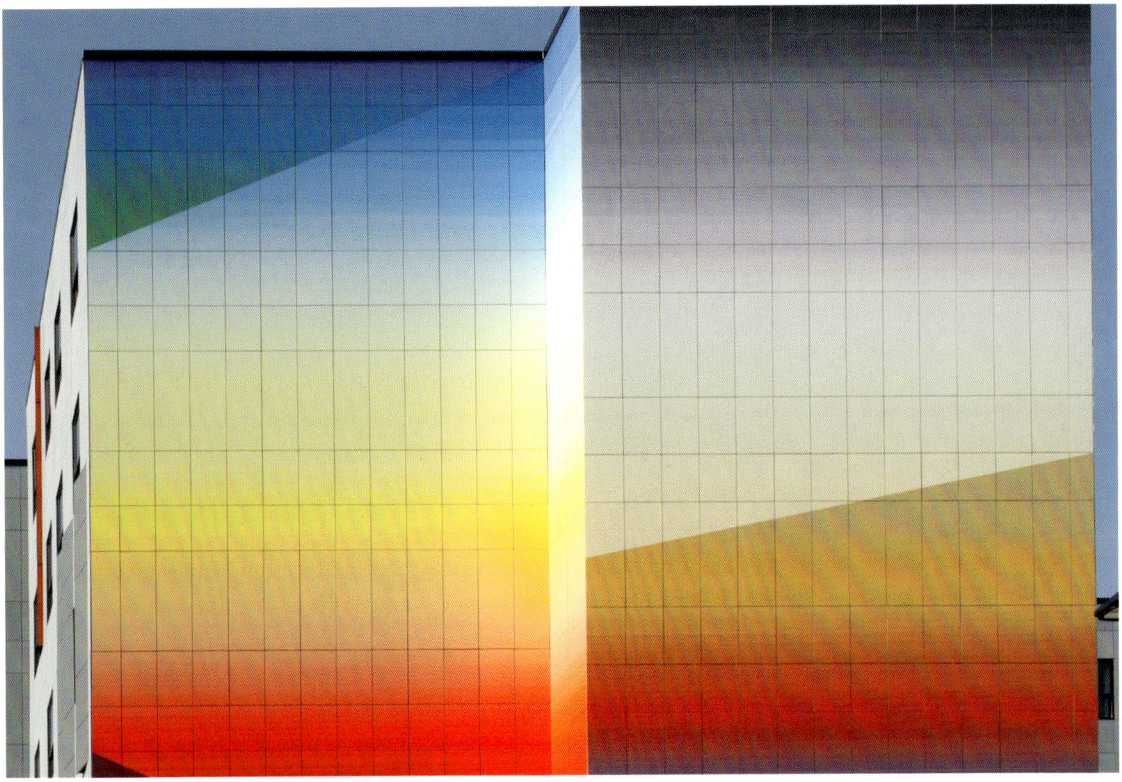

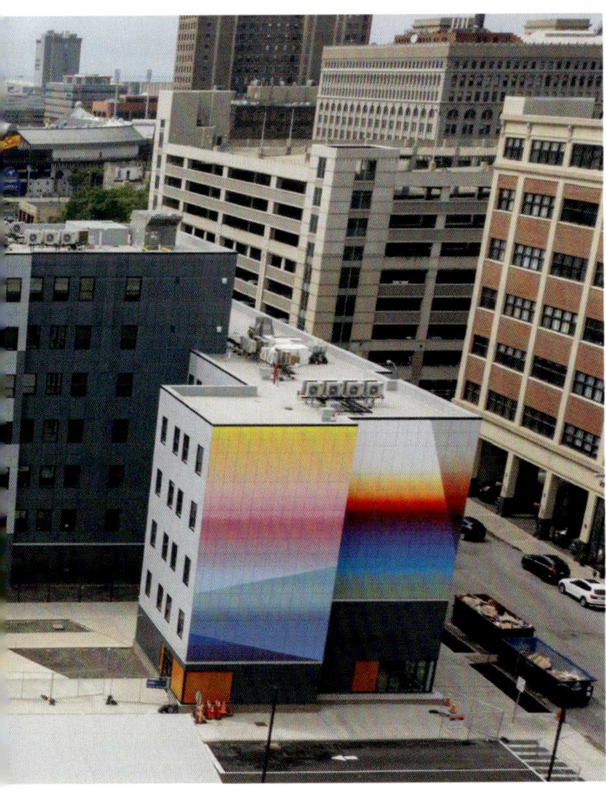

Traits points
taches gribouillage
(Lines dots stains scribbles)

Hervé Tullet

847 Main Street, Buffalo

Acrylic on Polytab
25 × 85 feet (7.6 × 25.9 m)

From his studio in France, Tullet collaged together photographs of work made in the exhibition at Albright-Knox Northland—*Hervé Tullet: Shape and Color*—to design a mural that integrates some of the central components of his wide-ranging artworks.

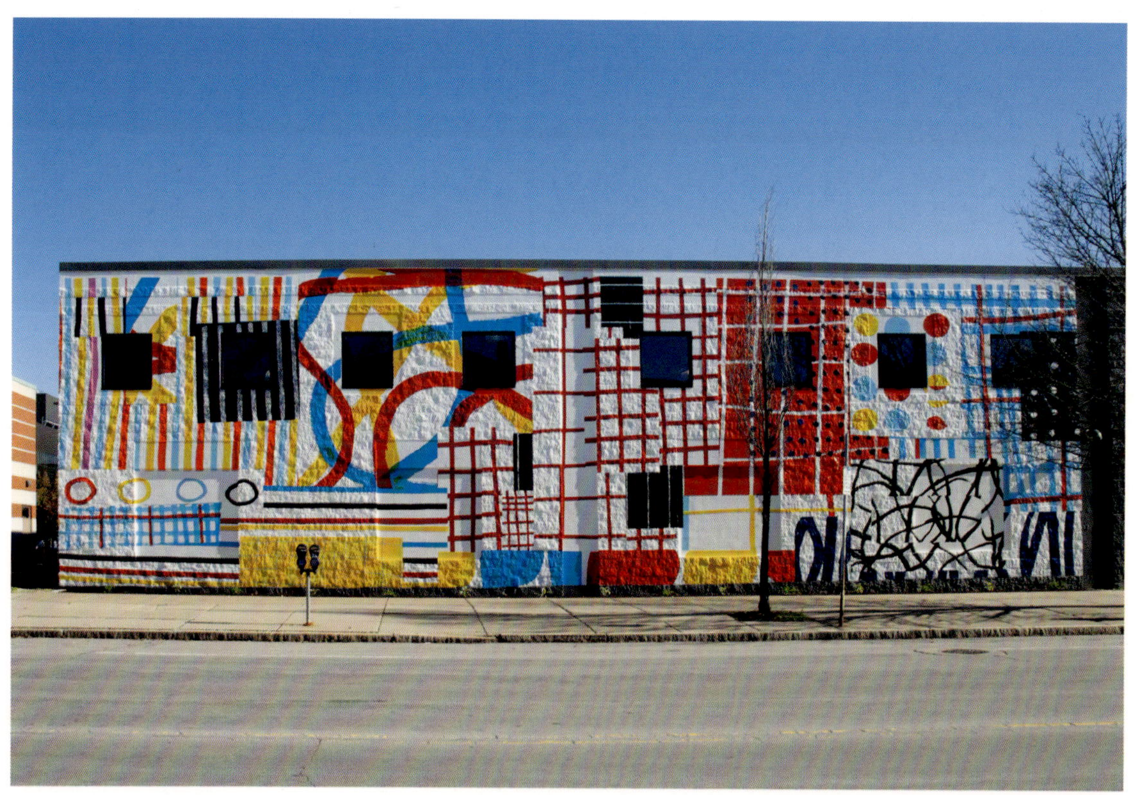

Hervé Tullet: Artist-in-Residence Program

714 Northland Avenue,
Buffalo

Acrylic on Polytab
Five murals: 10 × 15 feet
(3 × 4.6 m); one mural:
15 × 10 feet (4.6 × 3 m)

Prior to 2020, artist and children's book author Hervé Tullet was scheduled to conduct a series of workshops in Buffalo with plans to create a mural as well as site-specific work for the museum's temporary offsite location, Albright-Knox Northland. Those plans were suspended indefinitely by the COVID-19 pandemic, and the museum instead brought in local artists who would occupy Albright-Knox Northland amid Tullet's installations. The artists, Julia Bottoms, Tricia Butski, Max Collins, Fotini Galanes, Rachel Shelton, and Phyllis Thompson, created murals while museum visitors looked on. Working on Polytab allowed the artists to work within Northland's walls, while Tullet-designed art activities helped activate the exhibition space. The residencies generated an atmosphere of dialogue; visitors learned insights into artistic practice, and, if they were inspired, could sit down and create their own art.

Once completed, the Polytab murals were installed down the street on Northland Avenue.

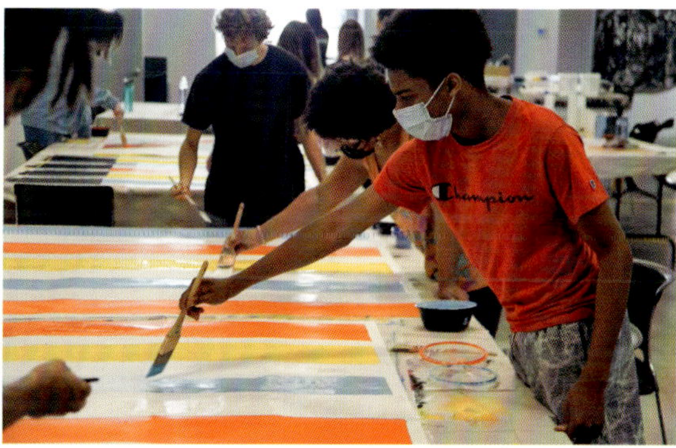

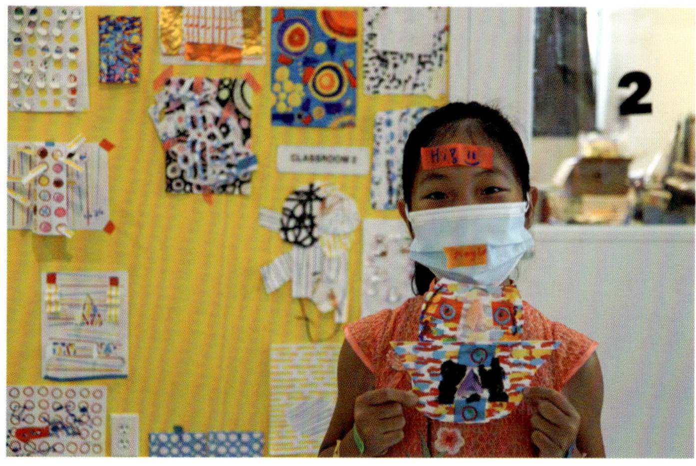

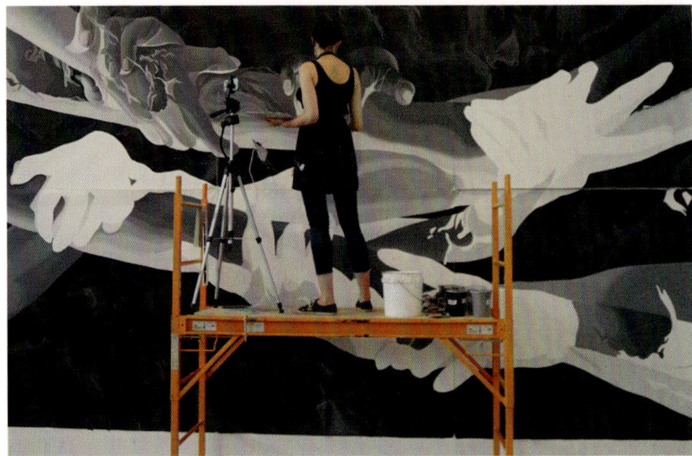

Artists worked live during the exhibition and shared their process with visitors.
← Tricia Butski.
↙ Julia Bottoms.
↓ Bottoms's guide for building up skin tones.
→ Rachel Shelton adds a layer of white spray paint.

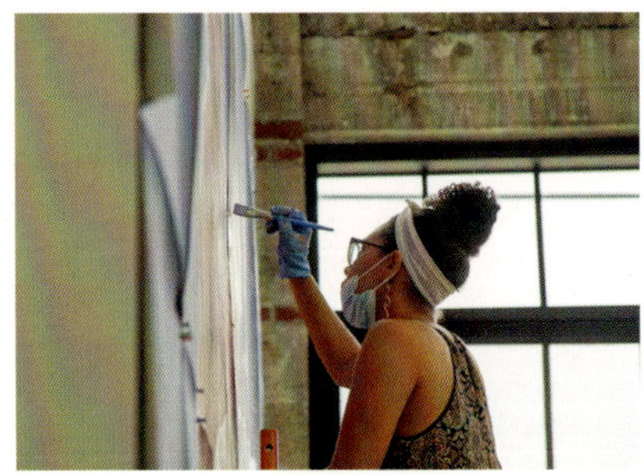

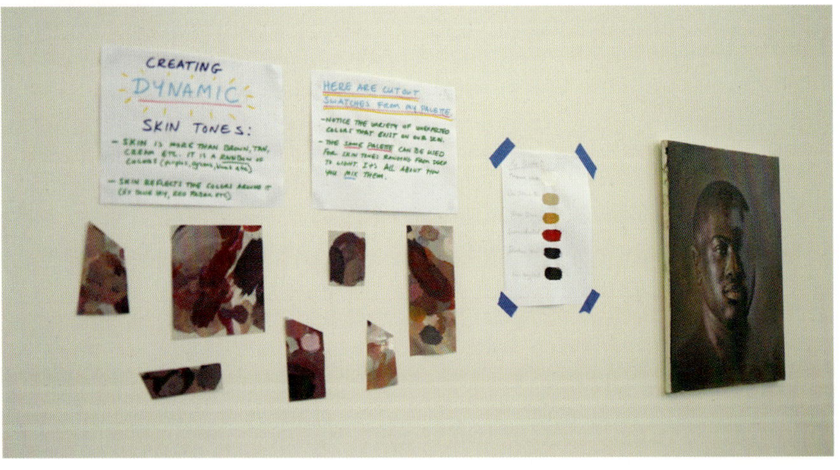

A Less Than Usual Amount of Despair

There's a version of the art world where the artist sits alone in their studio, and they think and they read and they write and they sketch, and they try some stuff, and once in a while they make a piece of work that feels finished and ready to be seen by the public. In this scenario, you, the artist, get to be completely in your own headspace, you don't have to consider anyone else's opinion, and you can be unswayed, which sometimes is exactly what we need as artists—to be unswayed. As someone who came firmly from the camp of believing that this is the essence of being an artist, I've learned that there might be a better way.

There is another version of the art world that the AKG Public Art team facilitated beautifully during *Hervé Tullet: Shape and Color*. Alongside the exhibition, inside of it, they hosted artist residencies. In this version of the art world, there's a big space full of art, activated by artists working on murals while engaging with museum visitors. In this version, there's communication.

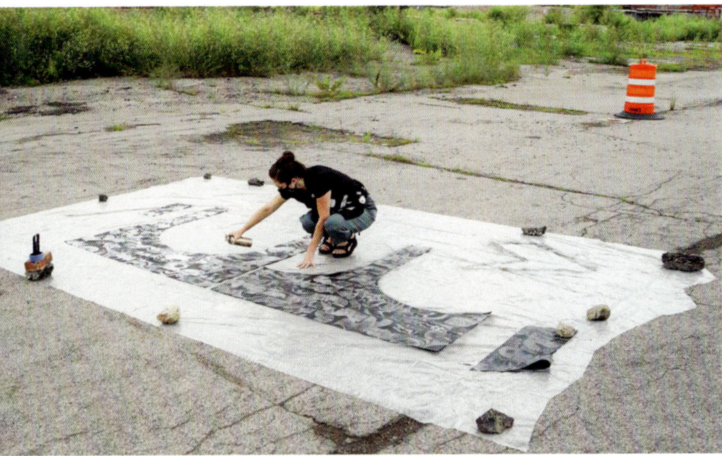

There's hearing how people read the work while you're making it and discussing any number of things. There's experimenting and sometimes failing in front of people, allowing them to see the process. There's the warmth of conversation and the undeniable motivation that comes with somebody being interested in what you're doing.

This model served both the artists and the people who came to experience the art. Visitors were offered a better understanding of the labor and decision-making that goes on behind studio doors and might view the role of the museum differently as well, watching it support living artists and adding to the texture of local neighborhoods. The next time these visitors saw artwork elsewhere in the world, they would have a little more insight into what went into the making of it.

There is a place for each of these scenarios, but what the latter did for me was to actually change the art I wanted to make. When I started developing my idea for the mural, I was concerned about bringing more negativity into people's lives as they commuted to work and school, but my work is what it is, I told myself—or so I thought. Luckily for me, the Public Art team was massively supportive of experimentation and growth and gave me the latitude to let the piece evolve over the course of the residency.

By interrupting the thought and production processes with conversations about art and life and history with folks from all walks, I began to feel more hopeful about what humanity is capable of. Until then, my work had often come from a despairing perspective. I'm not saying that has completely changed, but I'm not saying that it hasn't. The many genuinely engaged people I interacted with shifted my plans for that mural. Removing the barrier between the studio and people who experience the art prompted a desire to share some of that hope.

—RACHEL SHELTON

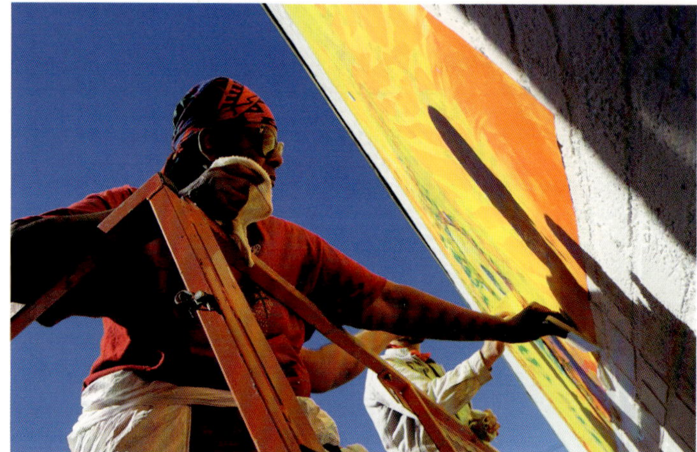

Resident artists installed their finished murals down the street from the museum.
← Phyllis Thompson.

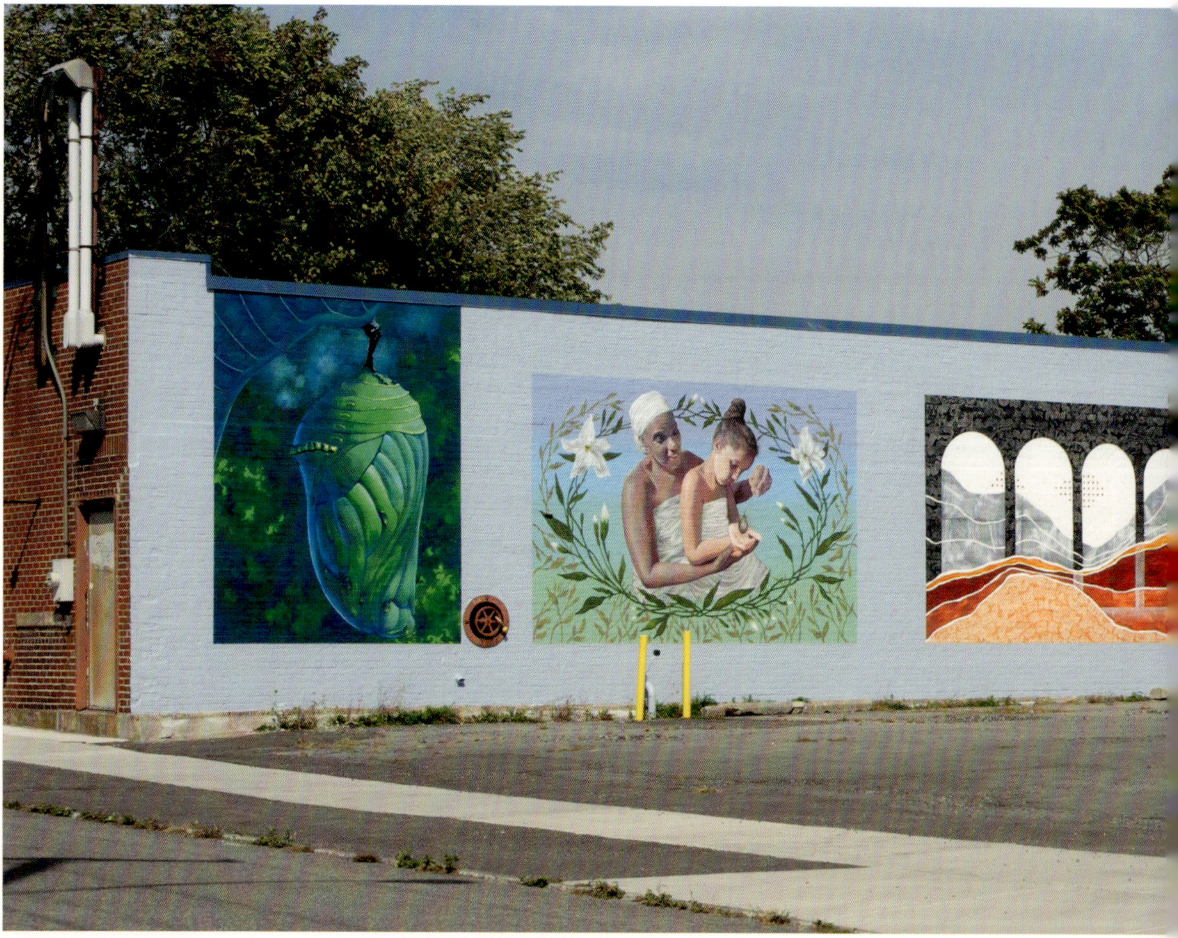

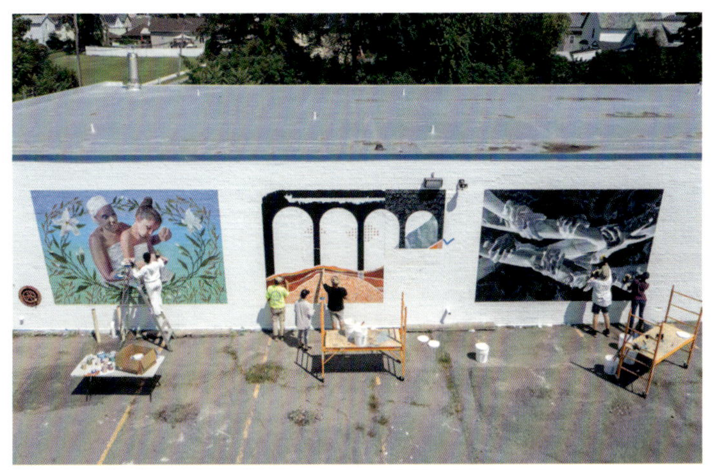

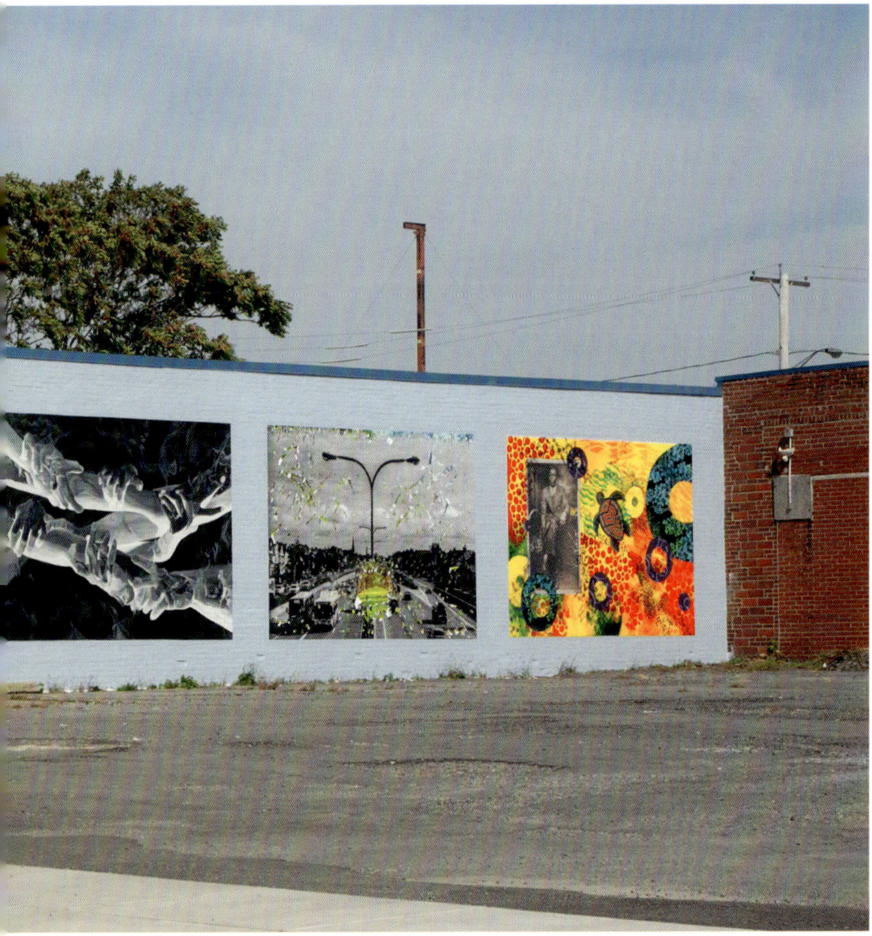

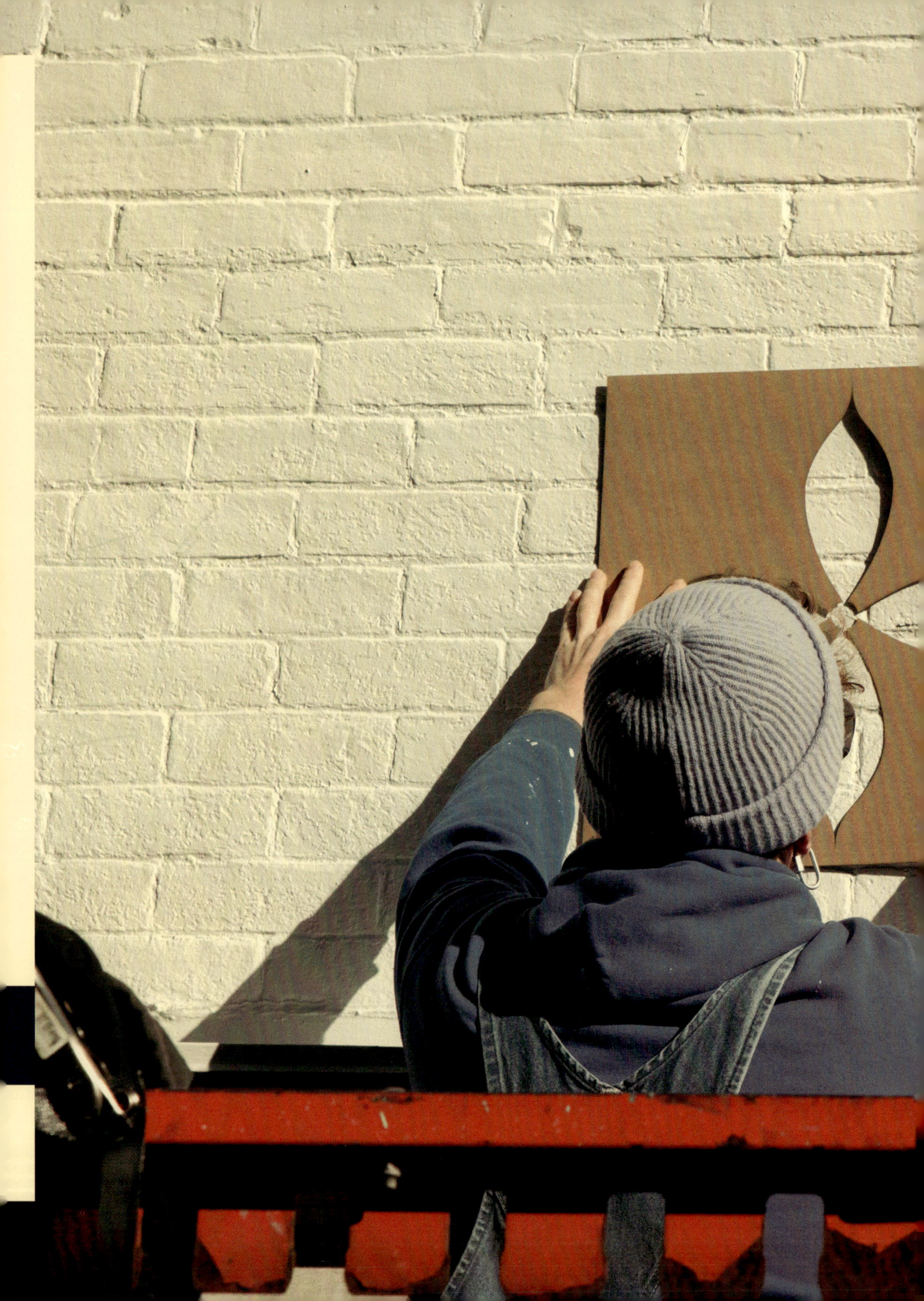

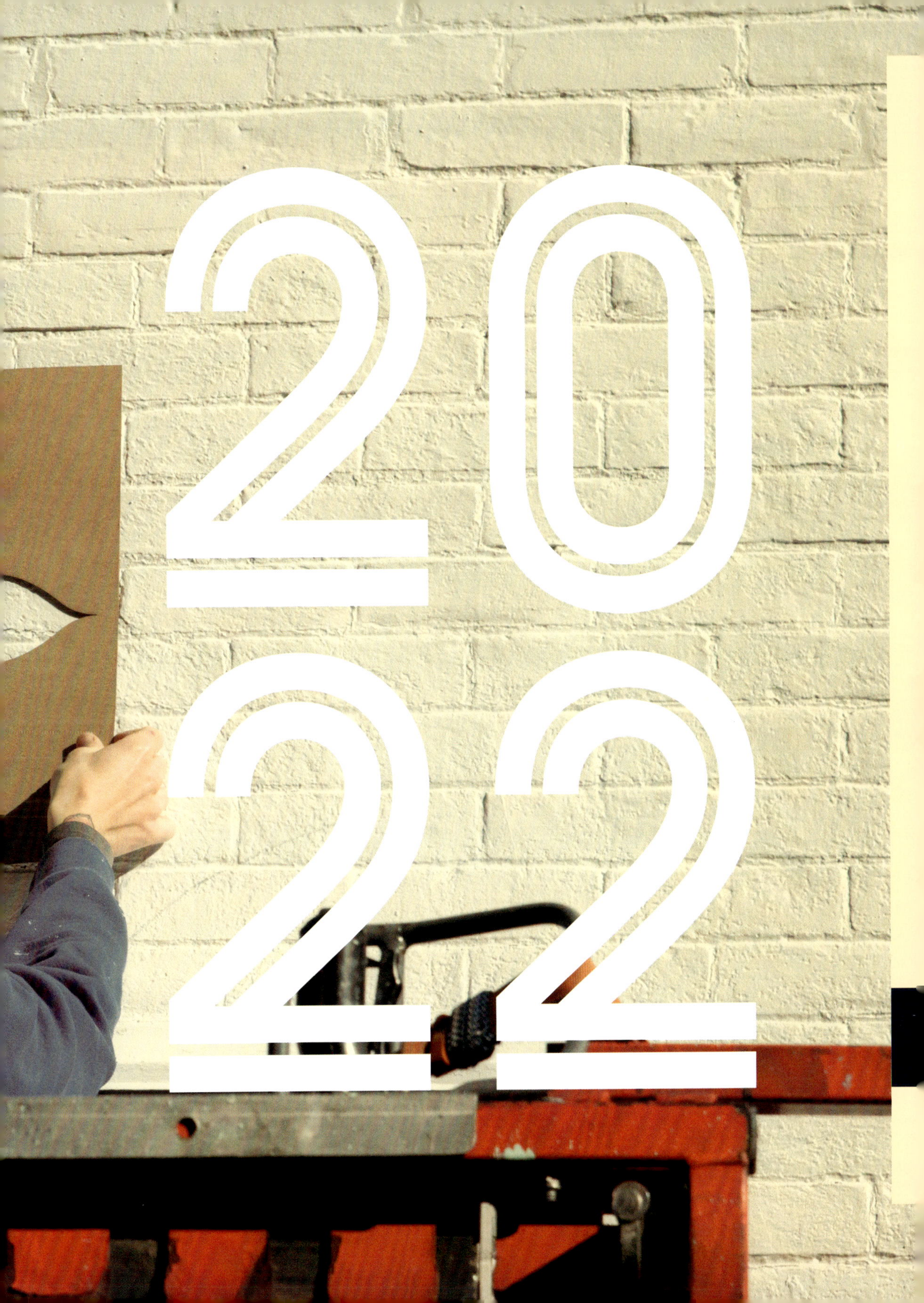
2022

Verdant Vessel

Beau Stanton

Delaware Avenue &
Allen Street, Buffalo

Acrylic paint
37 × 25 feet (11.3 × 7.6 m)

In creating this mural, Stanton incorporated some of Buffalo's iconic architectural and sculptural elements, including the stained-glass ceiling from the council chambers at City Hall and one of the eight caryatid sculptures adorning the Buffalo AKG Art Museum's exterior, sculpted by Augustus Saint-Gaudens (right).

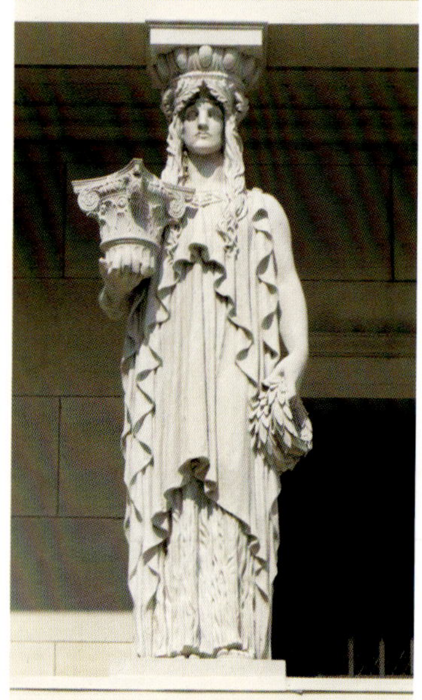

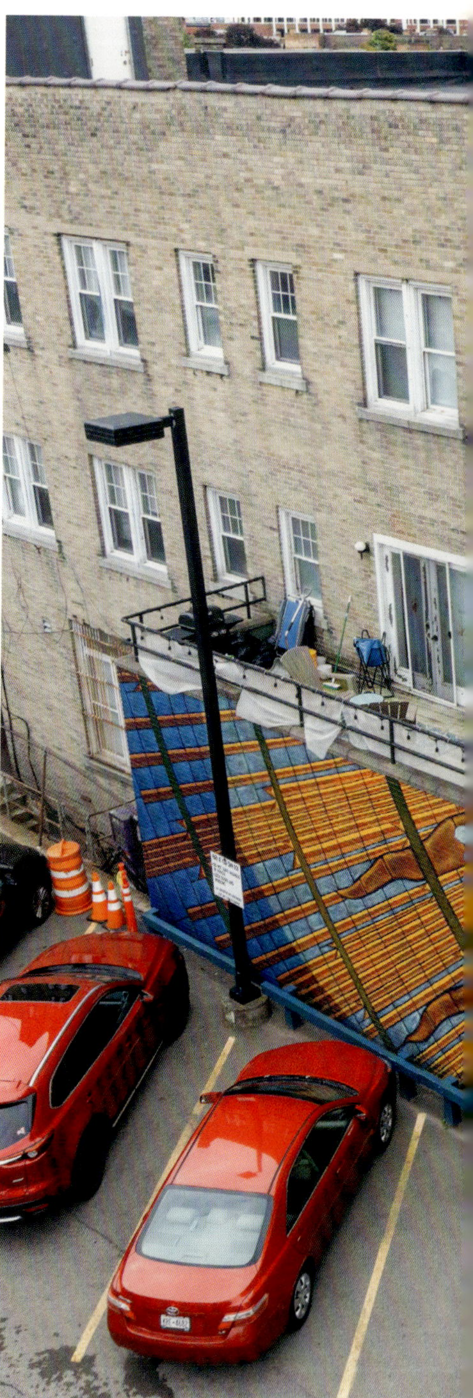

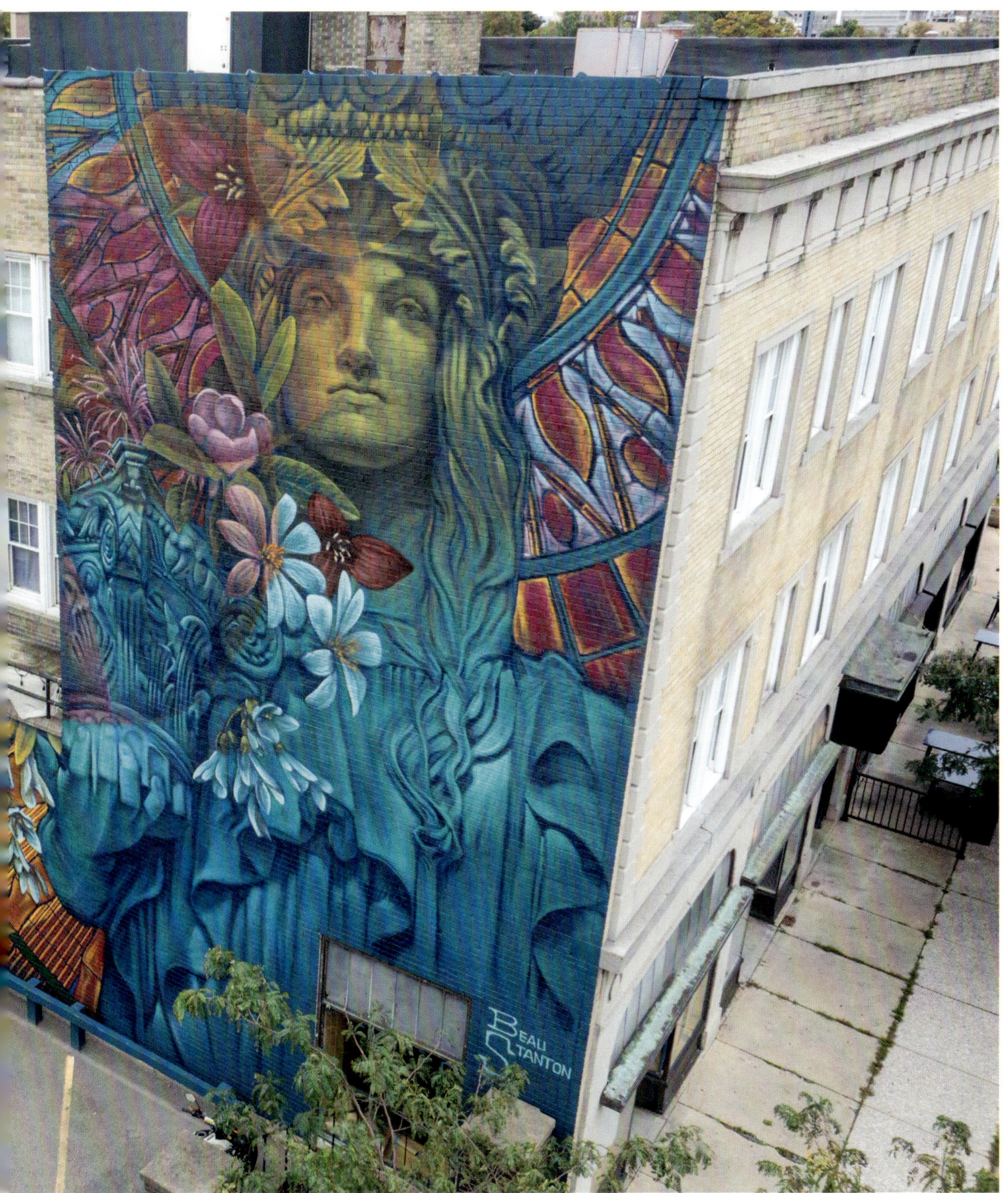

Sarah Braman: Finding Room

Frank Lloyd Wright's
Graycliff, Derby
July 30, 2022–March 19, 2023

Various media
Dimensions variable

Organized by Associate
Curator Andrea Alvarez
and Public Art Project
Coordinator Zack Boehler,
Finding Room placed
Braman's outdoor and
indoor sculpture on
the grounds of the historic
Wright home on the
shore of Lake Erie.

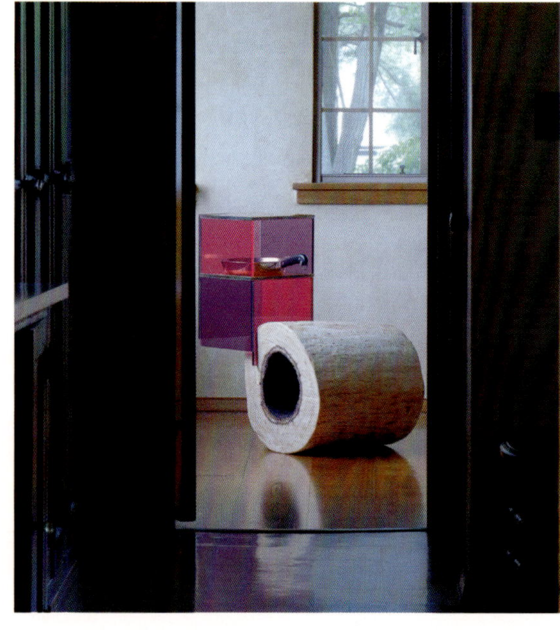

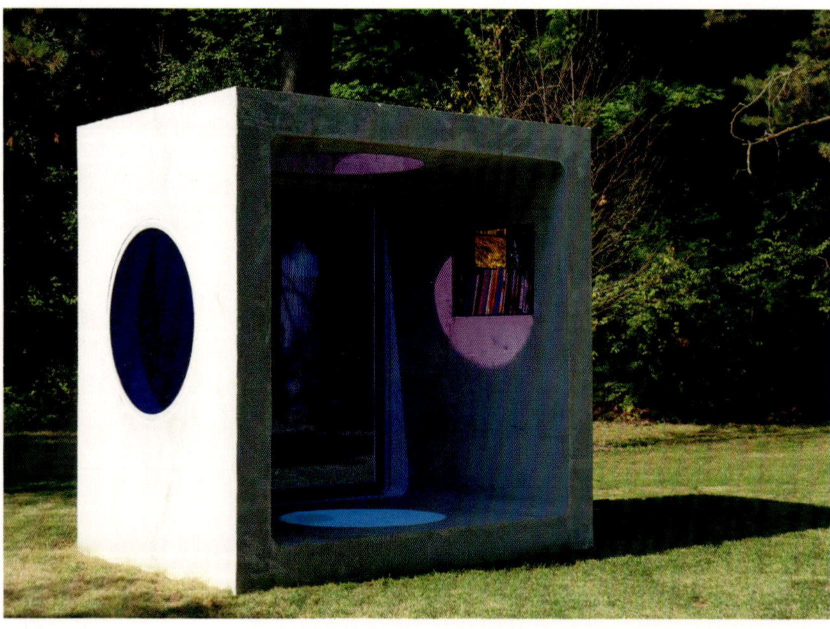

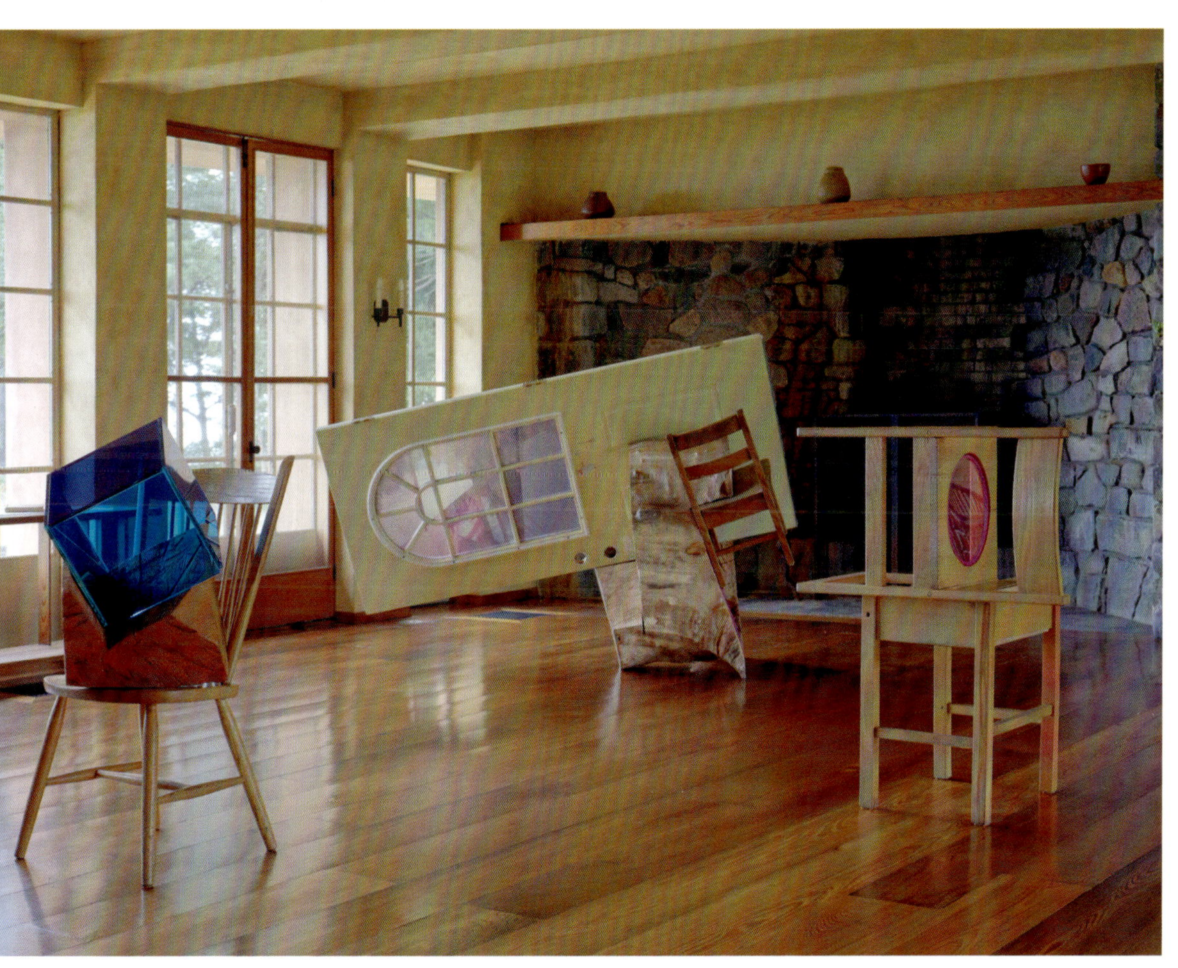

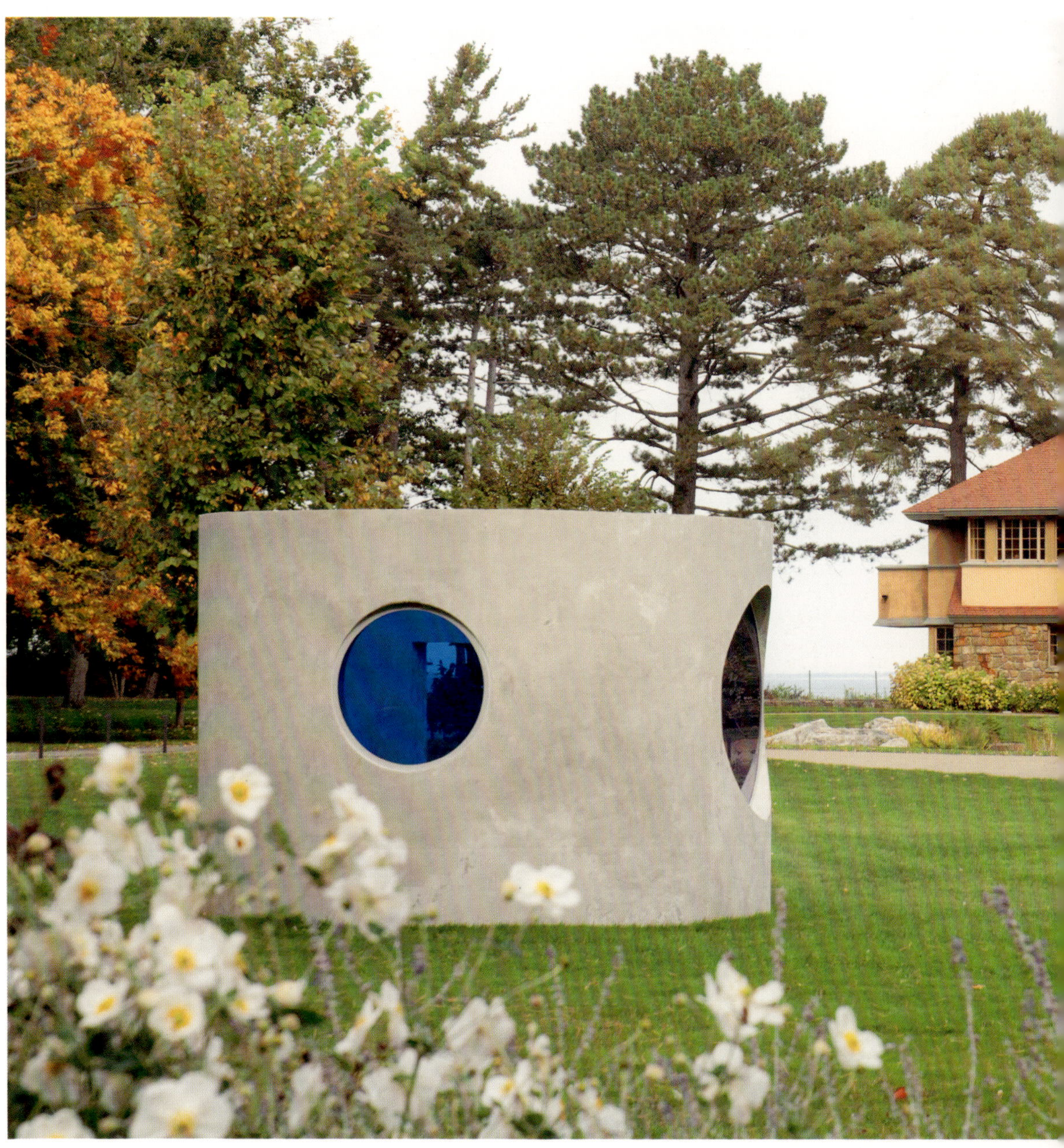

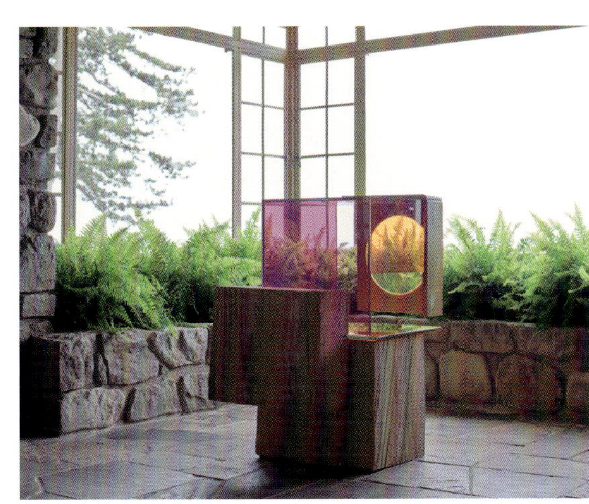

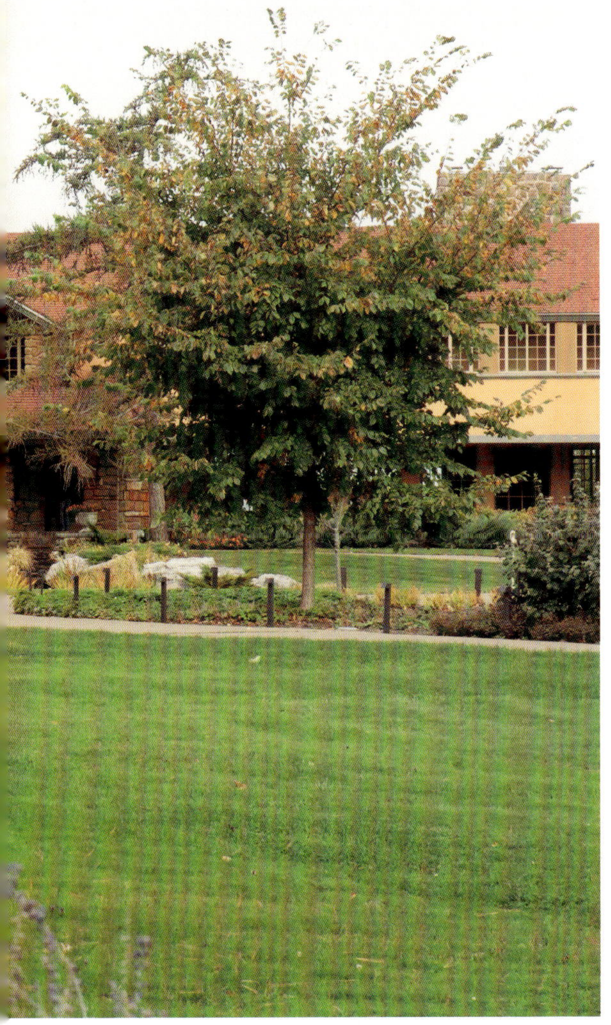

Queen City

Adeyemi Adegbesan, aka Yung Yemi

1410 Main Street, Buffalo

Digital print and acrylic paint on Polytab
25 × 15 feet (7.6 × 4.6 m)

In early June 2022, Adegbesan visited Buffalo to interview and photograph an array of local creators in the fields of poetry, literature, music, and the visual arts. From these meetings, he selected Annette Daniels Taylor, Jillian Hanesworth, and Curtis Lovell as subjects for the mural.

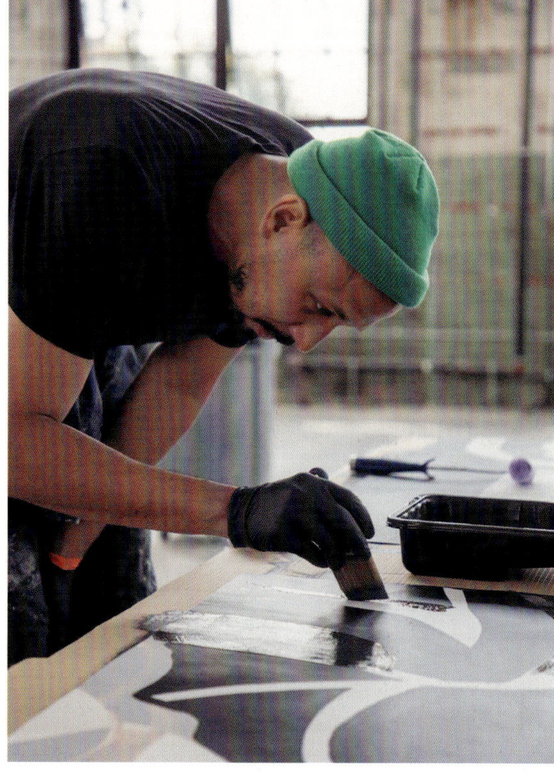

Adegbesan created his imagery on Polytab at the museum's Northland Avenue location before applying it to his mural wall.

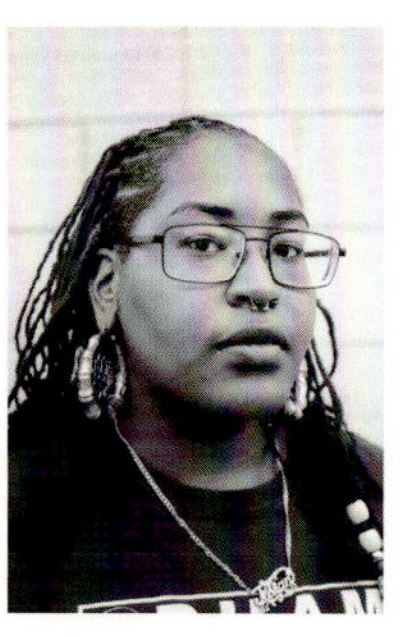

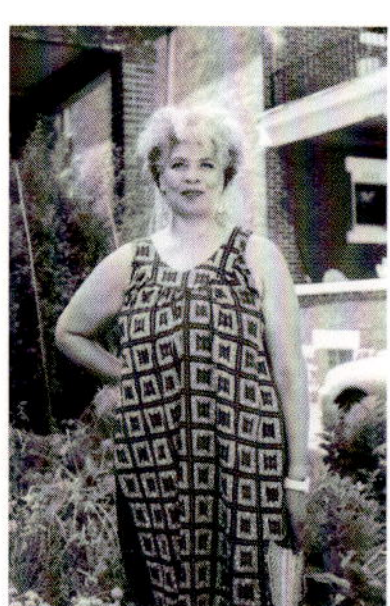

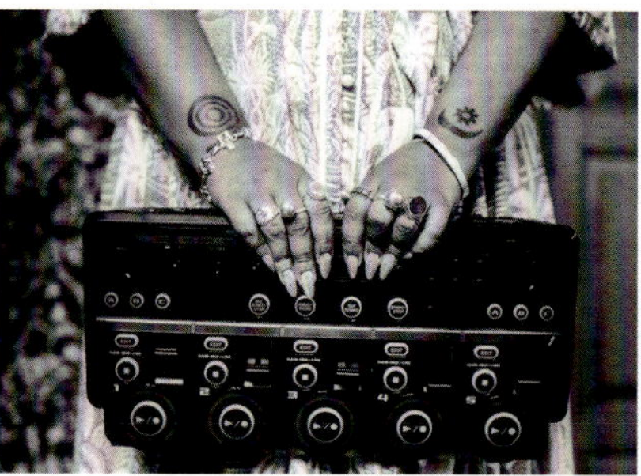

Portraits that Adegbesan took of ←← Jillian Hanesworth, ← Annette Daniels Taylor, → and Curtis Lovell created the raw material for his mural.

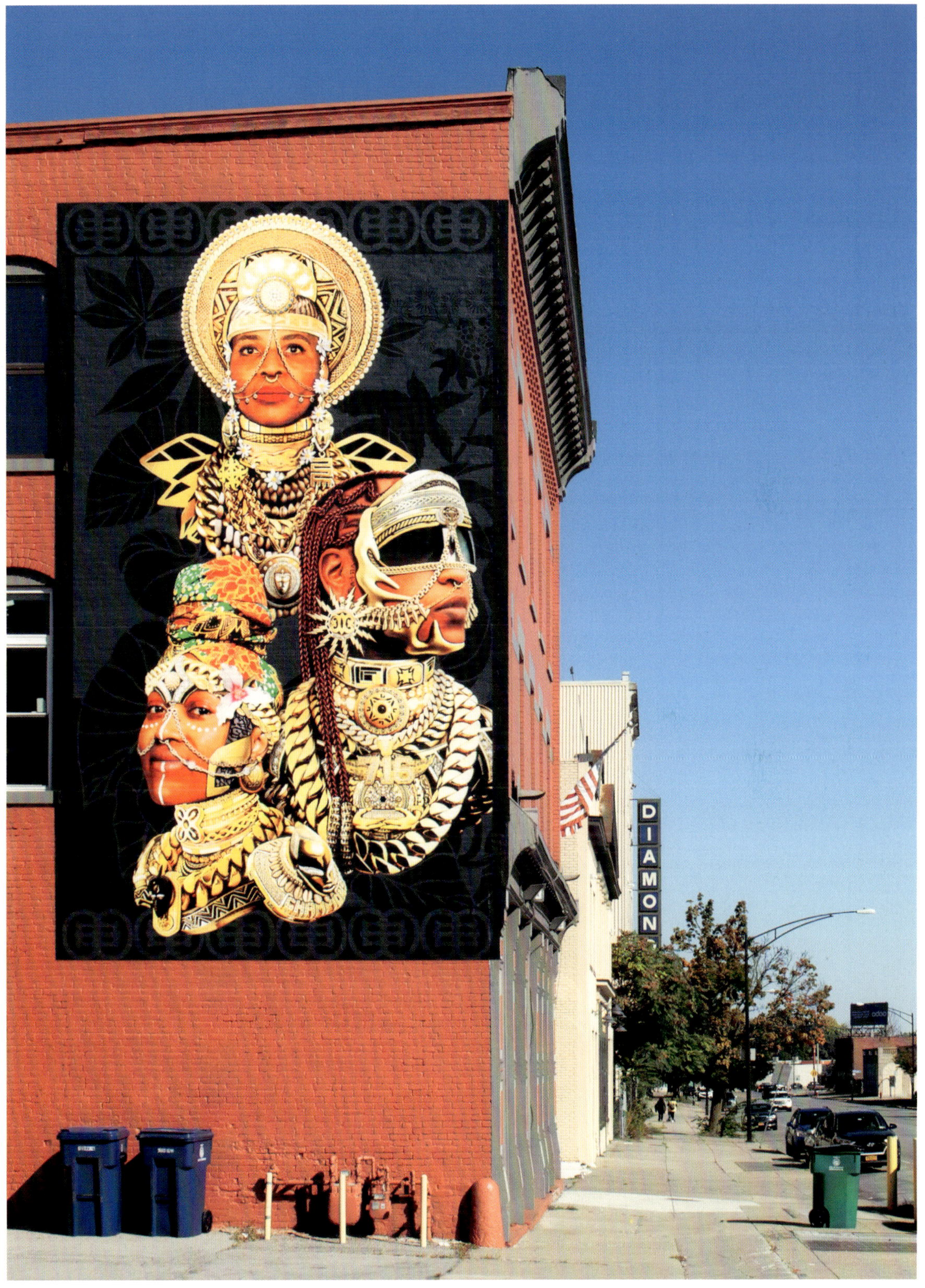

Woven Together

**Julia Jamrozik and
Coryn Kempster**

D'Youville University
Health Professions Hub,
Buffalo

Handwoven pillows
Dimensions variable

The vibrant colors of these pillows evolved from a series of workshops held with high school students from the neighboring International Preparatory School at Grover. With fabric handwoven in traditional patterns on backstrap looms, artisans from Stitch Buffalo, an organization that provides space for refugee and immigrant women to create handcrafted goods and find economic empowerment, then sewed pillows in sets of two, three, four, and five.

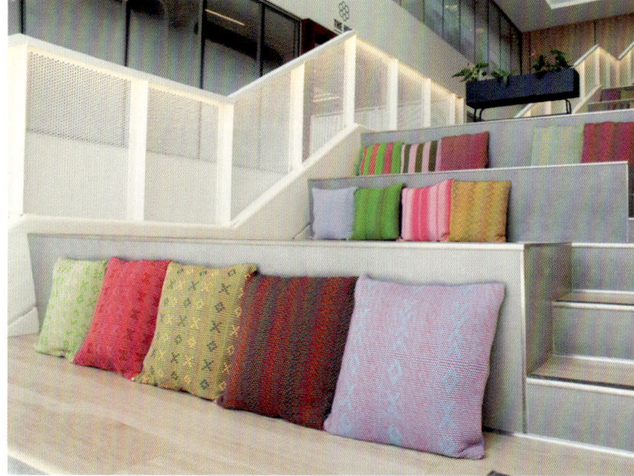

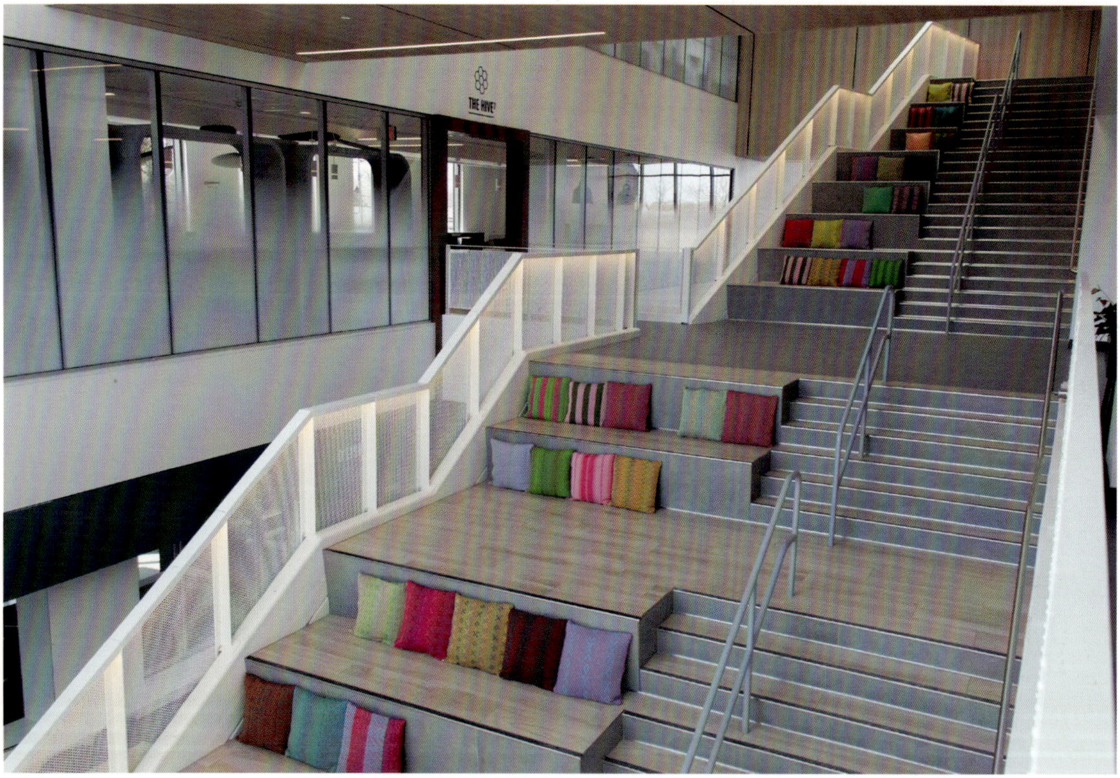

The Divine Feminine

Monet Alyssa Kifner

Lace & Day, 445 Franklin
Street, Buffalo

Acrylic paint
22 × 27 feet 6 inches
(6.7 × 8.4 m)

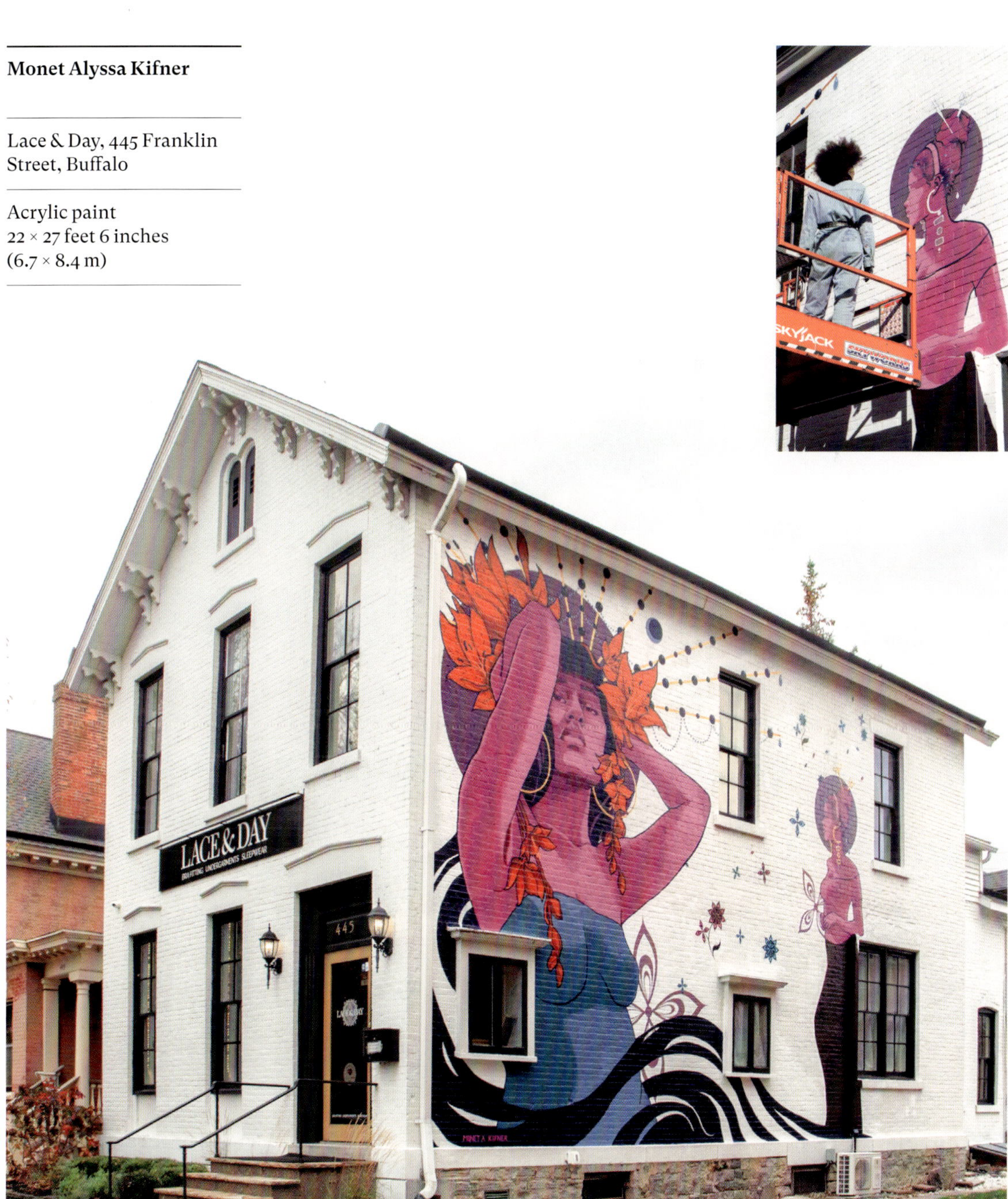

Moments in Making: Finding Room for the Artist in Public Art

ZACK BOEHLER
Public Art Project Coordinator

In almost every public art project there is a *moment*, usually near the completion point, right before those involved need to shift gears and go back to their regular jobs or catch a flight back home, when an immense feeling of satisfaction pours over everyone. In this moment, all of the months of work leading up to the installation and execution of a new work of public art drift away and the magnitude of that experience lives solely in a place of celebration, a place where all the relevant participants—individuals and communities, passing audiences, property owners, producers, and especially the artist—feel synchronicity and pride in a brand new work of art.

Most industries have these palpable moments, when collective work leads to a true sense of satisfaction. Even if it is as simple as completing a monumental task before cutting out for the weekend, we share an experience when creating work together. For me, this moment is often revelatory and always unique. I have a strong memory of working with the renowned stencil artist Logan Hicks on his mural *Walking Back Time* on Washington Street in downtown Buffalo (page 110). A major corridor in the center of the city, Washington is always bustling. Hicks, his partner and sometimes assistant Lori Zimmer, and I had been fighting a tight timeline disrupted even more by unfavorable weather, and we were down to the wire. Hicks's process includes meticulously arranging large-scale stencils, painting over them, removing them, affixing the next layer of stencils, painting, and so on, through many layers to create an almost hyperrealistic image based on his own photography (right). On a wall roughly twenty-five-feet high and fifty feet wide, the task was daunting. The circumstances forced our hand into painting on the Fourth of July, and, using every ounce of daylight we had, we finished one of the last major layers of his mural as the sun set.

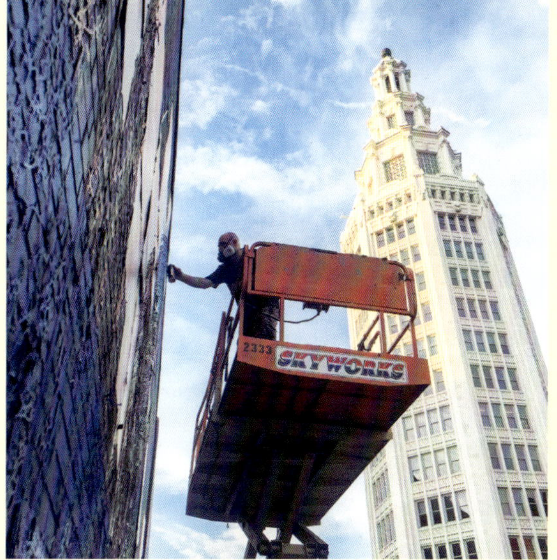

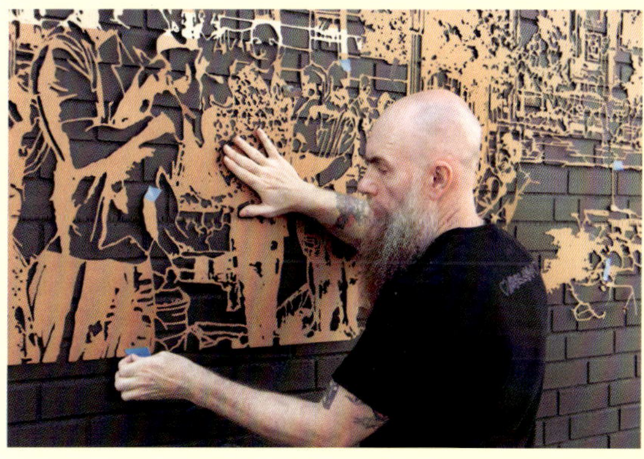

↑↑ Logan Hicks works as the clock ticks down to Fourth of July fireworks.

↑ Hicks works up his imagery with spray paint from a series of layered stencils.

We basked in the nearly finished wall, delirious from the nonstop day of work we had just completed, and waved at the approving honks from drivers passing by. Without enough time to make it somewhere for Fourth of July fireworks, we took the scissor lift back up past the top of the wall and watched the fireworks over the city of Buffalo, on a quiet island of our own above that busy thoroughfare, in our moment.

I believe that many visitors to the Buffalo AKG Art Museum are hoping to have their own moment with an artwork, or with art in general. As the sixth oldest art museum in the United States, and the oldest dedicated to collecting art of the present era, the Buffalo AKG, with its vast and renowned collection, provides a likely place to feel such a moment with modern or contemporary art.

When producing works of art in a public setting, the discourse of the museum is not implicit. There is no understanding of an expected experience in spaces usually thought of as open, and, in such situations, the entire audience—makers, producers, community members, property owners, and visitors—has claim to the space and, by relation, to the art. Whereas inside the museum the audience may expect to have a conversation with a work of art, in public the audience is conversing simultaneously with a hundred different variables. Sometimes that dialogue is parallel to the art, sometimes it is part of the art, and sometimes it may be in opposition to the art, but it is nonetheless simultaneous to the artwork, because art in public is not fixed—it is a component of a larger, active, real-time space.

The critic Sheila Regan discusses public art curators as a new type of arts administrator: "Not only do they have to talk a good game about their projects, they have to negotiate the conflicting demands of multiple stakeholders: artists, community groups, government entities, private-sector players like developers and building owners, and anybody else who has a say in how the work is planned, made, and displayed."[1] Managing these types of intricacies among so many involved parties arguably requires a public art curator to be much more sensitive and strategic than their in-gallery counterparts. Joe Hart, the former senior editor of *Public Art Review*, proposes that a curator working in public art is less of a curator and more of an acting producer, reminding us that a public art curator is not just asking an artist to add artwork to a space, they must understand the complexities in creating a space.[2] A curator working in public art has a responsibility to understand the area where an artwork is placed before taking any action and must make the effort to understand how the community around a work may interpret the location once altered.

The goals laid out by Buffalo AKG Curator of Public Art Aaron Ott in the Public Art Initiative's founding documents are to enhance the museum's mission of putting artists first and to exhibit contemporary works of art in the public realm. We often describe this as "making the walls of the museum porous." To the Public Art team, this means that we try to make all of the communities of Western New York feel welcome inside the museum by producing artwork situated in their neighborhoods. We want to dispel the notion that museums are only for some elite portion of the population. Our program aims to extend the experience you might have in a gallery, where you are confronted by art that gives you pause, to anywhere in Western New York.

The premise seems straightforward—using the expertise and legacy of a world-class art museum to bring a suite of public art to its immediate community—but the reality is more complex. The work that happens inside a museum's galleries is the result of the collaboration between an artist and a curator. It is a space that allows an artist to create, exhibit, and speak freely. Similarly, audiences come to a museum hoping to find works that they relate to, that reflect them or their feelings, or that challenge them. No matter the specifics, they come to the museum with the understanding that they are coming for an experience, a conversation with art.

As it turns out, when producing work in public spaces, the hardest work lies in seemingly the simplest thing: letting the artist make art. The Buffalo AKG is, at its core, an artist-first organization. Throughout its long history, the museum has been active in its support of working artists, its defense of work that is challenging, and, more than anything, its role in providing space for an artist to be an artist. This is not to say that museums do not have agendas, stances, or ideologies; rather, inside a museum or gallery space an artist can be afforded the opportunity to present their work with no implications other than what they intend.

It is not our role as art-world professionals to force an artwork into a space. It can be tempting, through an understanding of a particular artwork and a belief in an artist, to act unilaterally in placing a work. Worse, it is easy to lean on the perceived authority of an arts institution in justifying those decisions. This is a process I struggled with in developing an exhibition of Sarah Braman's work, eventually titled *Finding Room*, in collaboration with my Buffalo AKG colleague Associate Curator Andrea Alvarez (page 158). We needed to find a public space where we could simultaneously show the artist's monumental outdoor sculptures and her far more delicate indoor works. Braman

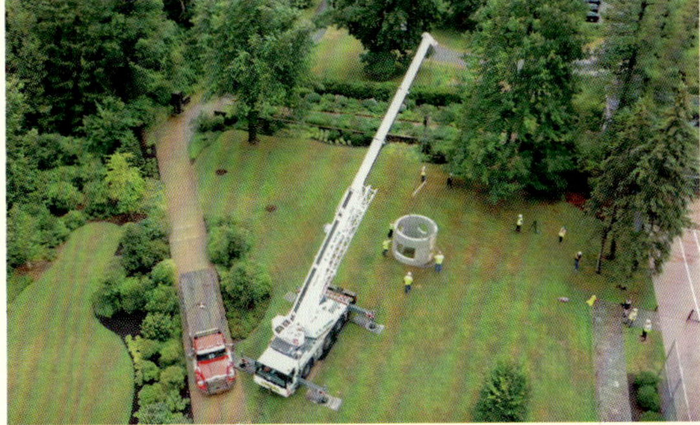

uses wood, colored glass, concrete, and found objects to create meditative spaces that ask the viewer to contemplate the repetitive mundanity of daily experiences in a more reverent light. The work is minimal and modern while also radiating a warm sense of familiarity. Andrea and I toured several sites in Western New York looking for a location that could meet our needs for indoor and outdoor space while also promising an audience for the work.

Because I believe strongly in Braman and her work, I wanted to place the exhibition somewhere I felt it would make a big splash. But merely identifying a location that seems like a cool place for a work is a disservice to the value of art in public places. The temptation to do so comes from the desire to have a successful opening or initial response from viewers, but this only serves the notion that art is to be participated in for cultural cachet. Placing an artwork in a public environment that helps the audience delve into the meaning of the work not only allows the work to be considered for its meaning—the meaning of the work in relation to the viewer in this space—it also often allows for a new interpretation of its environment. Considering with Andrea where this work really made sense in a larger holistic way led us off the beaten path, to a Frank Lloyd Wright–designed estate in the region, Graycliff.

We found this incredible lakeside location thanks in large part to a supportive partner in Anna Kaplan, Graycliff's Executive Director. There, Braman's work was able to resonate in concert with a great architect's work. Domestic space is a key exploration in both Braman and Wright's work, and, while their aesthetics are very different, the material comparisons of wood, cast concrete, and colored glass are immediate and rich. Braman was able to show her indoor and outdoor works together for the first time, and visitors viewing both the Wright property and Braman's work were able to make cross-generational connections about space and our relationship to it. Placing Braman's contemporary work in the context of Wright's legendary space was key to the success of the project for the artist, the site, and the museum team.

Producing public art often requires the curator to look beyond finding the right setting for the work. For the Braman project, the Graycliff setting offered what could be viewed almost as an extension of the museum. When producing in an even more public space, such as a subway station or an intersection, the dynamics of the people in that space and the collective shared history of their many experiences create a discourse that successful public art cannot ignore. There are many theorists

working in public pedagogy, a framework based on the notion that the majority of our education comes from the public sphere: we learn more about our society and ourselves from what happens around us than we will from formal classroom experiences. This notion that constant education takes place in "public" in the broadest sense—on the internet, in pop culture, or in politics, for instance—highlights public space as an overlooked cornerstone of our shared educational experience.

With this understanding, it becomes impossible for a public art project not to be considered an intervention in a public space. As the producers of this work, it is our role to determine how to make that a positive intervention, one that reflects the people, history, or discourse of that space. This is not to say that the work cannot be challenging to an audience, but, if public space belongs to the public, then public art should reflect rather than confront members of the public. This is a dynamic curators engage with, perhaps even more than an artist does. The artist's role is to create work they find meaningful, and, while some artists' practices revolve around this type of public engagement, it would be unfair to ask an artist to produce more than art. It is our role as public art curators to do the work that allows the artist to make art, while also making place.

Another *moment*, albeit a much less private one than the Fourth of July I spent with Hicks, occurred at the completion of *The Freedom Wall* (page 78). This is one of the most complex and rewarding projects I have ever been a part of and was one of my first in my role at the Buffalo AKG. For me, in light of the celebratory block party that saw hundreds of people come out to Michigan Avenue on Buffalo's East Side (right), amid the music, the charcoal grills, and the sea of smiles, it could have been easy to forget how the project began.

Completion of *The Freedom Wall* was capped by a community block party.

Some months earlier, on a cold winter evening, a public meeting was held in a library a few blocks away from *The Freedom Wall* location. The intention of the meeting was originally to gather names of potential subjects to be painted on a massive stretch of concrete wall that bordered the north end of Buffalo's African American Heritage Corridor. Based on the location and the physical design of the wall, Aaron wanted to produce twenty-eight portraits of local and national figures, past and present, from the fight for civil rights. The one piece of advice he repeatedly heard from the community members he was working with was to choose an artist who could faithfully depict these key figures.

While the community meeting in the Frank E. Merriweather, Jr. Branch Library was planned as a discussion of people to be depicted in the mural, what the meeting became was an open forum—or referendum, really—on the choice of artist. The dialogue that night was challenging, but so important to the development of our public art program. By being too directly focused on the specifics of the artwork, we had inadvertently ignored the much larger history and conversation happening in the public space the location was situated within. That misstep made the project feel confrontational to the community members, no matter how well-intentioned the curatorial aim.

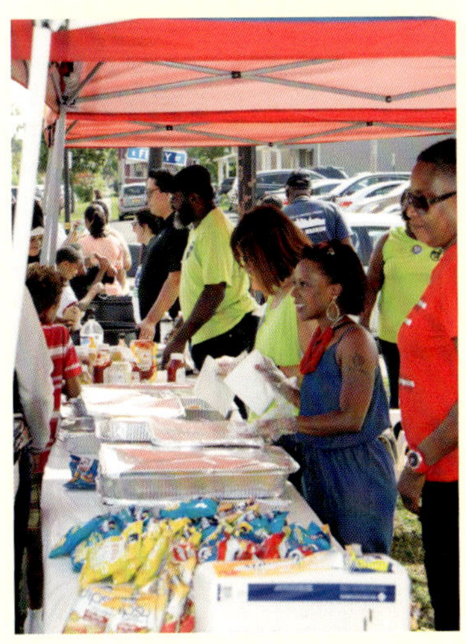

After many conversations, the scope of the project was expanded to include three local artists. Adding these artists to the project alleviated what was at the center of the anger felt by the community: issues of representation and opportunity. Expanding the pool of artists undoubtedly made *The Freedom Wall* a more successful project. The community members who were outraged at the library were the same community members celebrating at the block party. This project honors a deep history of local contributors to the Civil Rights movement and places them next to recognizable national luminaries. The educational contexts are rich for those who know that history and for those who need to learn it. It was also an educational experience for us at the Buffalo AKG. We learned what a true commitment to making meaningful public art looks like, and, even though we took a few lumps along the way, the process has absolutely informed the many projects that have come since.

We needed this same spirit of fostering dialogue and questioning not only ourselves as curators but also the status quo in the development of our first residency program. Springville, New York, a rural community of just over 4,000, is the southernmost place of major population in Erie County. Given its location forty-five minutes south of Buffalo, executing public art in Springville is a vastly different experience than producing a project in the city. Through a great, and now lasting, partnership with Springville Center for the Arts and their enigmatic director Seth Wochensky, we were able to establish a home base studio and housing for a residency program. The intention was to bring an artist to Springville for an extended period and have them maintain a studio practice, really get to know the community, host some workshops with young people, and create a small mural

as a lasting public art legacy of the artist's
time there.

Thinking carefully about who would be a good
fit for such a project, I landed on a Grand Rapids,
Michigan, artist named Bryan Metzdorf (right).
His work is abstract, but, when contextualized, it
emerges as rearranged maps of distinct geographical or architectural elements of a place. Having
known him for some years, I felt he and his
process would be well suited to the particulars
of this residency.

The surprise came when Wochensky got
pushback about the mural component from government officials. Springville Center for the Arts
had already executed several small murals around
town, but the inclusion of an abstract work
prominently featured on Main Street drew extra
discerning eyes. Springville is a fairly conserva-
tive town steeped in tradition, and its Main Street
has that quintessential small-town look. In this
case, discussions between the curatorial team and
community stakeholders exposed how thoroughly
we had considered the location and the artist.
We needed to confront the status quo and through
conversation explore the intention behind making the artwork. The turning point in the conversation came when Springville Center for the Arts
found a turn-of-the-century image of the building
we were proposing for the mural (center right).
That was my moment for this project. To all of our
surprise, the building had originally been painted
in a geometric pattern to encourage passing travelers to stop.

That research moved the project forward.
Metzdorf lived in Springville, created many studio
pieces, and executed a mural of rearranged architectural elements from the rest of Main Street
(page 114). There may still be some residents who
do not celebrate this abstract modernist artwork,
but I can attest that once the community began

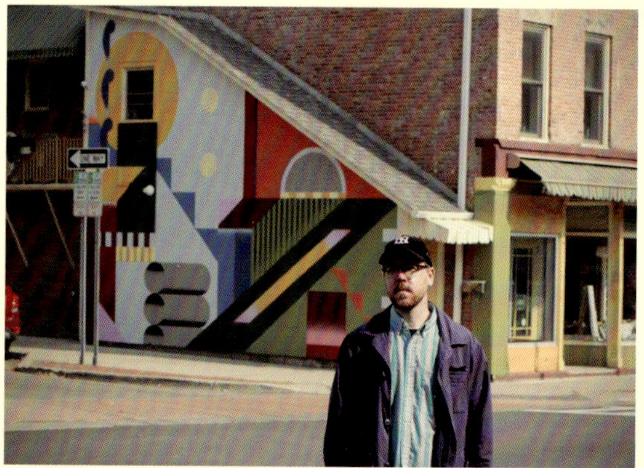

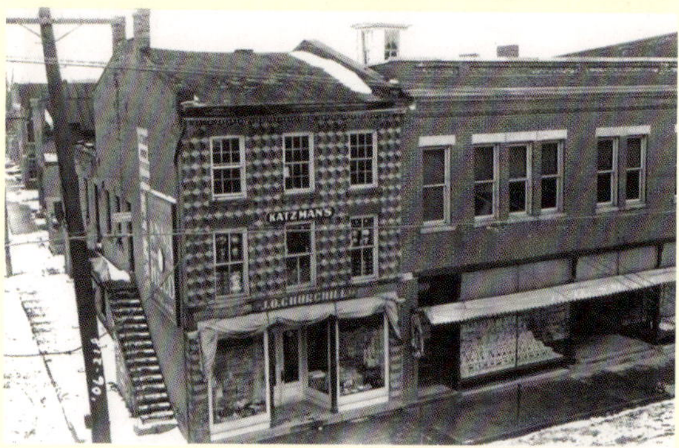

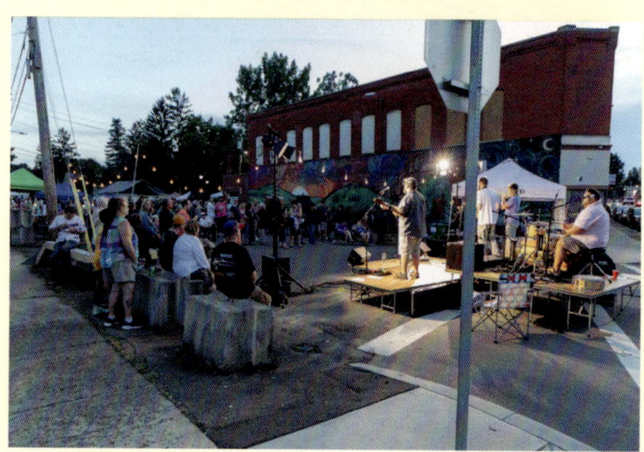

to understand Metzdorf's approach to his mural, their support followed. We have since finished a second residency in Springville with the artist Mandi Caskey, aka Miss Birdie, whose mural was unveiled to a vibrant block party of hundreds of people not too different from *The Freedom Wall* celebration (below, opposite). That type of response is not something I would have expected a few years earlier, but, in truly being a partner to the community, engaging in dialogue, and working to build meaningful content into artwork, we found a great success.

As exemplified in *The Freedom Wall* and the Springville residency, it is crucial to a project's success to determine all of the unique active and passive collaborators in a space and to solicit their view of what that space means. This includes the artist, the property owner, the immediate community, the wider community or general audience, and the museum. Each project is distinct in these categories, and they are certainly not interchangeable. A property owner may envision something on their property, while the tenants inside the space may want something radically different. In some cases, a property owner and those active in the space may desire something that doesn't respond to or reflect the surrounding community members who will interact with the work the most.

Usually, a project asks the community to respond to one artist, but, in the case of *Cobblestone Commons*, we were able to offer work to twelve artists (page 116). Just around the corner from KeyBank Center and next to Buffalo's waterfront park, Canalside, sits a transit authority–owned complex used as the repair depot for the city's

subway trains. The building is long, well more than a normal city block, and relatively low. There were thirteen distinct inset spaces along the wall, each about twenty feet wide by sixteen feet tall. The features of the wall told us that this was *not* the space for a single artist; rather, a cohort of artists could be brought in, each given one architectural inset to work on. To further this notion, the community we worked with was unique, in that it wasn't residential. For the most part, the area hosts establishments that cater to the arena crowds and office spaces. Our partners and the community voices were the business owners' association, and, because their businesses rely on having a diverse audience that comes to the neighborhood for events, it was in their interest to also have public art that appealed to a wide range of audiences.

Cobblestone Commons also exemplifies something very special that is core to the public art program: our ability to work with local artists. As a globally minded collecting institution, the Buffalo AKG can often feel separate from the local arts community. Until the development of the Public Art Initiative, there was not a direct avenue for local artists to exhibit at the museum or have their work enter its collection. Public art conversely looks for diverse voices, including those from the local scene. Every season we have several projects focused on a local artist, but never was that strength as apparent as when art by local, national, and international artists was intermixed across twelve panels.

Rarely is the curatorial directive so open in public art. It was truly the opposite of the norm; it asked, how can we show the widest range of styles and disciplines? We split the project over two years, partially to divide the workload per season but also to extend the longevity of the project. We had planned to execute the murals in the lead-up to a yearly festival that happens in parking lots across the street from the wall, but the COVID-19 pandemic halted those plans. Fortunately, we were able to execute the artwork safely, with some special considerations. The final roster of artists was Ellen Rutt (Detroit), Obsidian Bellis (Buffalo), Jason Brammer (Chicago), Lauren Mckenzie-Pearce (Cleveland), James Moffitt, aka YAMES (Buffalo), and Bradd Young, aka SALUT (Rochester) in 2020; Thomas Evans, aka Detour (Denver), Morgan Blair (Brooklyn), Karle Norman (Buffalo), Miriam Singer (Philadelphia), and Monet Alyssa Kifner (Buffalo) in 2021; and, due to pandemic-related border restrictions, Cyrielle Tremblay (Montreal/Mexico City) in 2022.

In no other public art project is such a broad range of styles and diversity of viewpoints represented. From the abstract work of the Detroit-based Ellen Rutt to the Afrofuturist-inspired first mural from Buffalo local Monet Alyssa Kifner, there is something for every taste. And while we are very happy with the responses from the tens of thousands of people who pass by on

their way to and from the arena, the real community on this project became the artists. Never have we had the space to have so many artists working at the same time, side by side, on their own walls but together. Our local artists, some new to mural painting, worked next to seasoned veterans whose work appears all over the world. The exchange of knowledge and ideas, coupled with the high energy of shared production, made *Cobblestone Commons* a unique experience. By creating a space for the artists to be artists, we answered the public desire for the space as well.

Balancing the interests of all stakeholders on a public art project can force the interest of the artist to become secondary, if that balance is not managed with clear intent. Worse, public art can be co-opted by parties whose interests don't align with the principles or intention of the artist. When not managed carefully, art can be used as a means to an end, and that end can be performative, when a partner is only doing something to make themselves look good, or capitalistic, when someone is attempting to profit from or increase the value of their property from a project, rather than offering a platform for the voice of an artist and the community.

The overarching question becomes how to extend the Buffalo AKG's commitment to being an artist-centric organization when public art, by its nature, cannot solely be artist focused. It is a problem we have wrestled with many times, and sometimes we have not succeeded in answering it completely. It becomes our role, as the producers of a public art project, to put an artist and project together in a situation where the artist is not hampered by the added components of working in public, but instead is supported by the community in executing their art. As an extension of

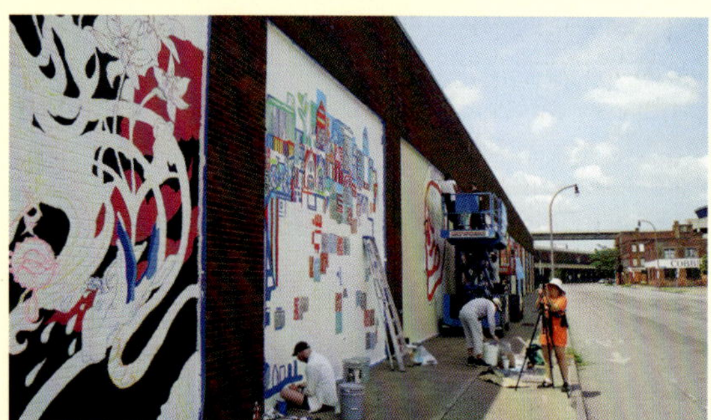

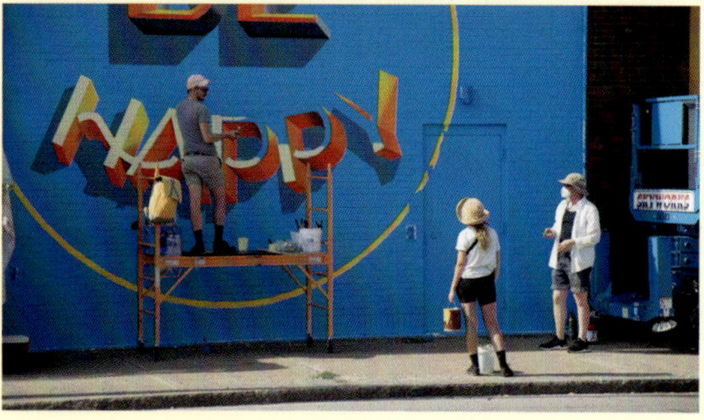

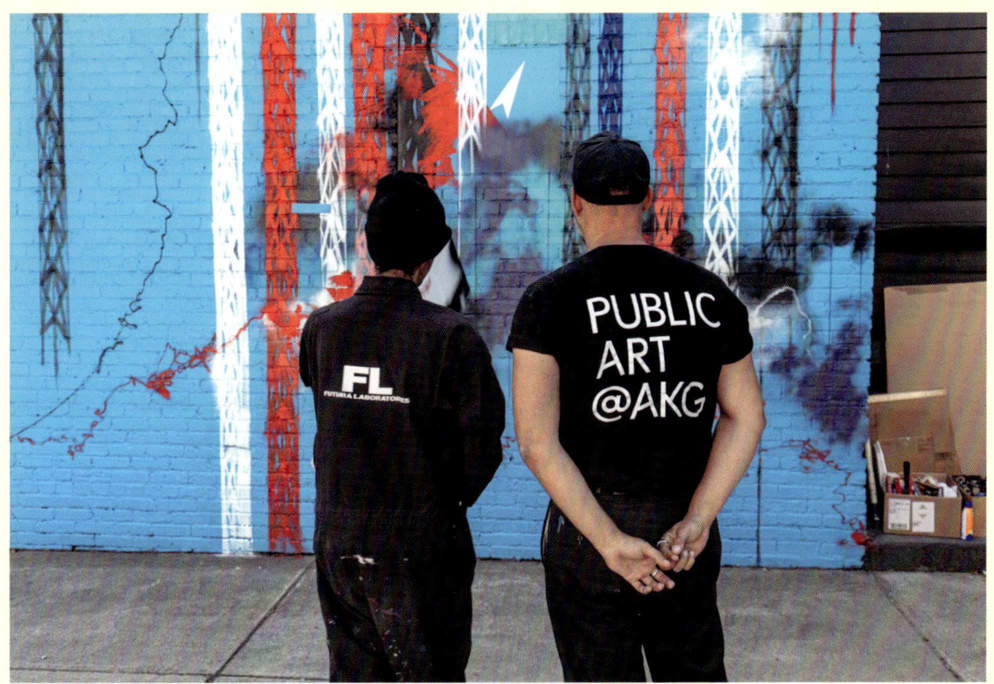

the project itself, we act as the intermediary to hear all of the voices and their goals for the work and disseminate them in the best ways possible, making sure we are truly supporting the community, the audience, and the project partners, while also supporting the artist's right to make their best work. It takes a genuinely revolutionary action as a producer not to dictate a project but instead to cohesively hear and lift simultaneous voices to the forefront. If a highlight of the process is those moments of satisfaction, then the roadmap to getting there is through many hundreds of prior moments spent carefully constructing an environment that allows participation and ownership in a process that results in the creation of an artwork authored by the artist, but part of us all.

For me, and I hope for so many others, there have been a lot of *moments* in my time with the Buffalo AKG Art Museum's Public Art Initiative: West Coast–based artist Bunnie Reiss returning to Buffalo to paint a new mural after her first was decommissioned because of building repair. Local artist Karle Norman completing his mural and seeing his work for the first time anywhere near that scale. Felipe Pantone, from Valencia, Spain, warming up to Buffalo's cold temperatures in May. Futura 2000 (above) painting a trademark atom to finish a mural in Buffalo's Elmwood Village. And on and on. But one moment that I will always hold dear was with celebrated artist Maya Hayuk. Upon completing a very large signature mural, she thanked me and the program. She said it was rare that she felt so supported and cared for when executing a project, something she has done all over the world. For me, the task is to create meaningful public art, but at the core of public art is the artists, and creating the space for an artist to make an artwork—well, that is always a *moment*.

1   Sheila Regan, "Hard Work in a Hybrid Space," *Public Art Review* 28, no. 2, issue 56 (Spring/Summer 2017): 82.

2   Joe Hart, "Co-Creationists," *Public Art Review* 26, no. 1, issue 51 (Fall/Winter 2014): 27–28.

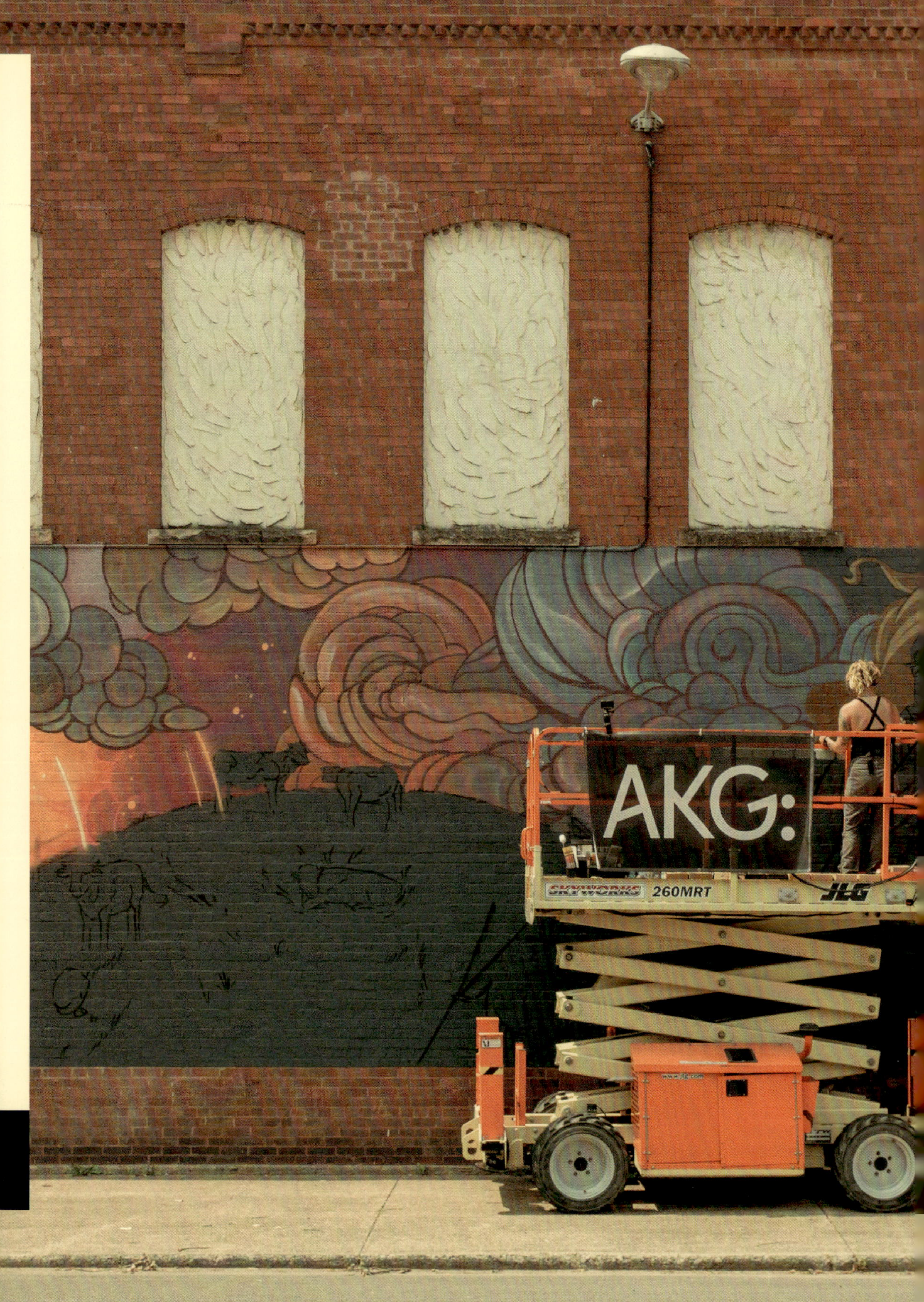
AKG:
260MRT
JLG
SKYWORKS
www.jlg.com

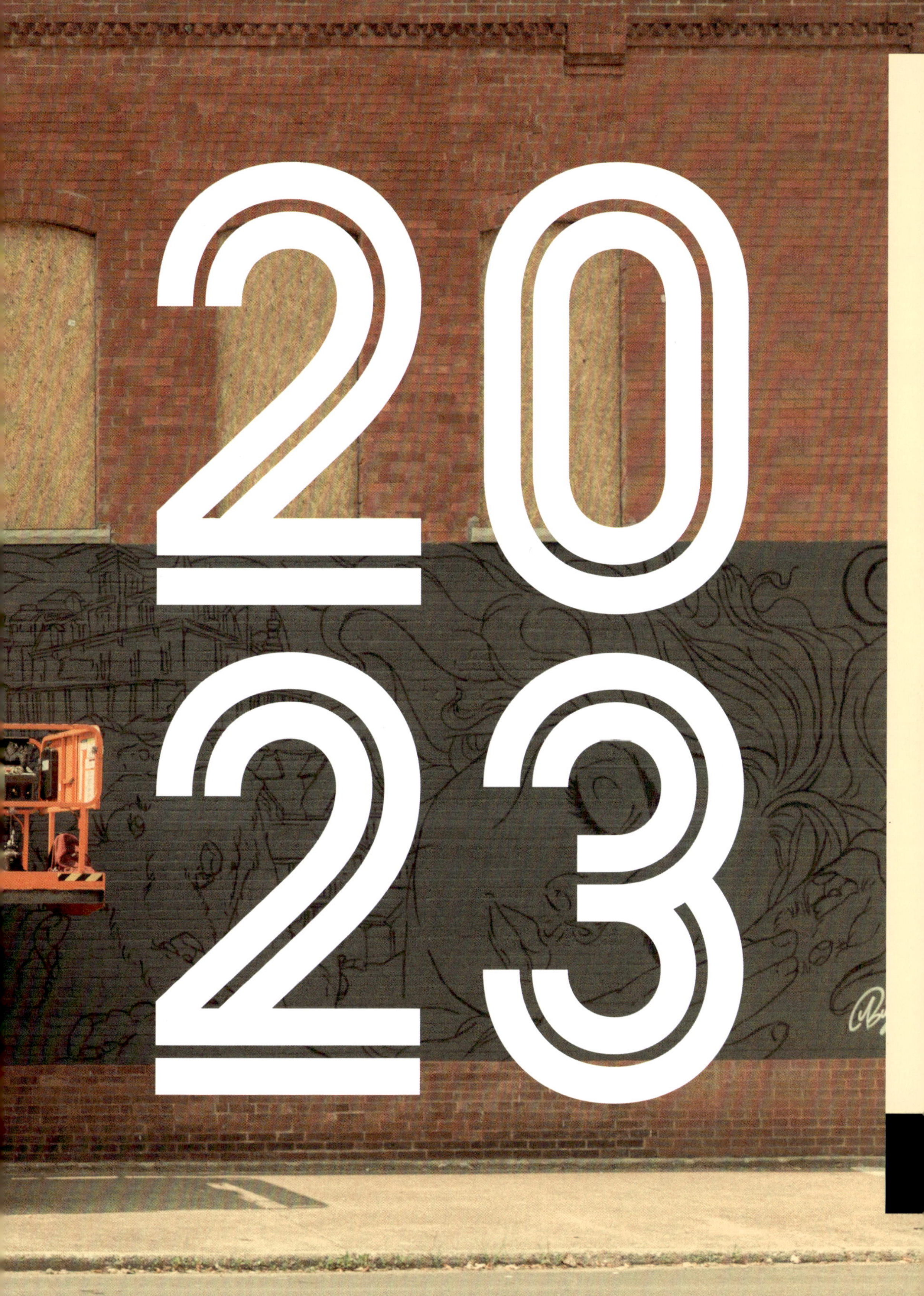

Bradford Reds

Futura 2000

712 Elmwood Avenue,
Buffalo

Acrylic and spray paint
15 × 35 feet (4.6 × 10.7 m)

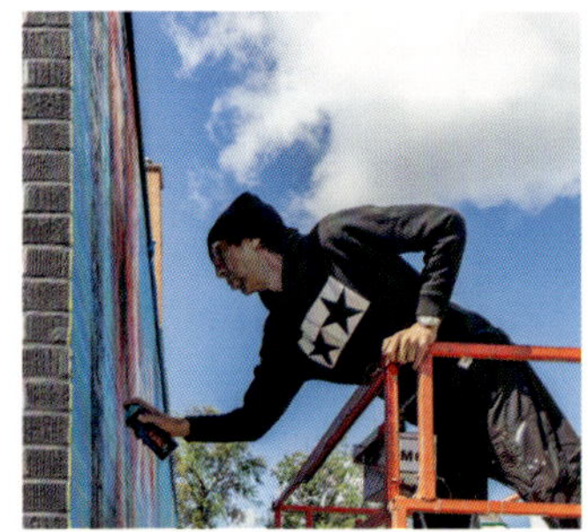

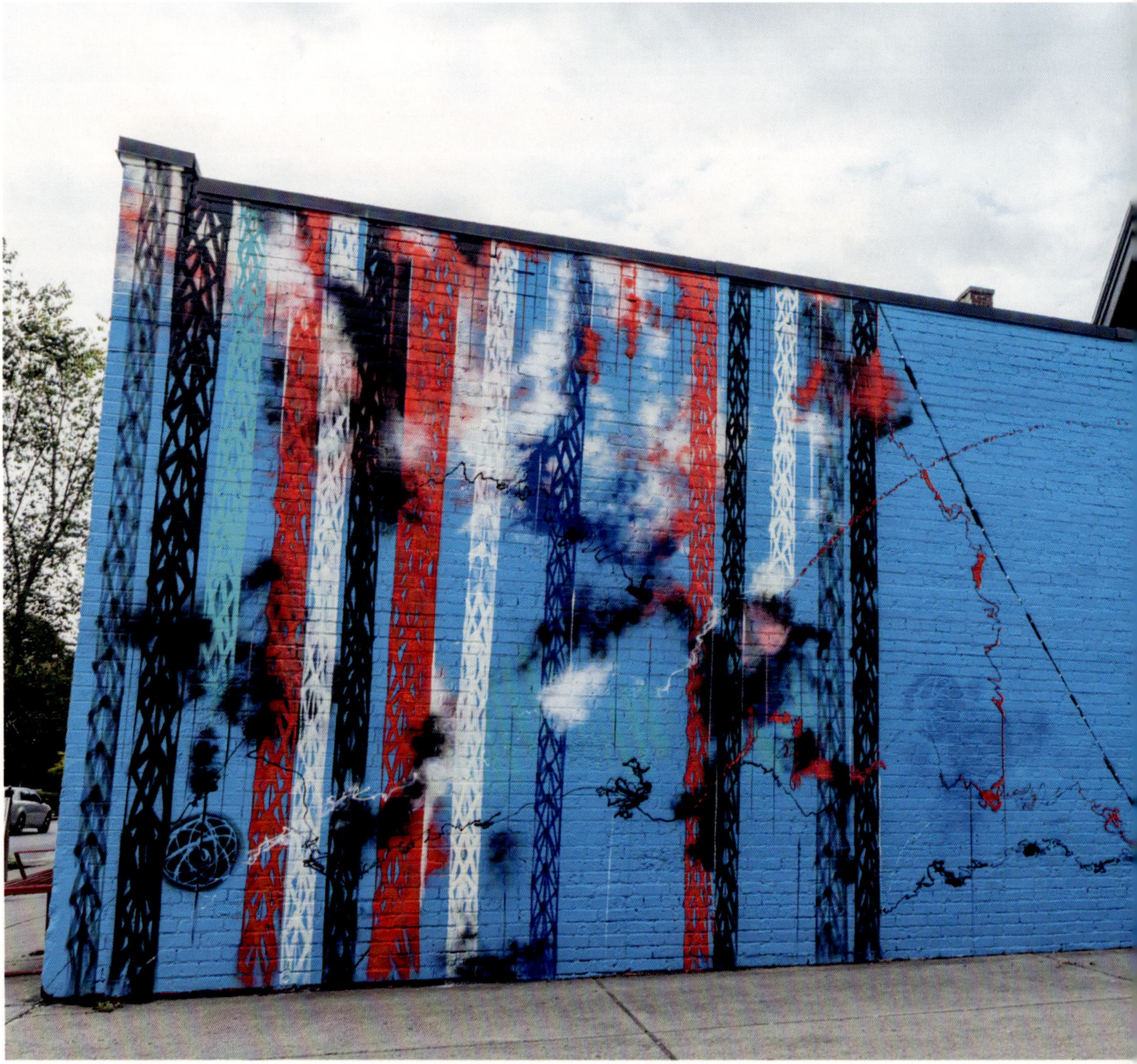

in the tradition of the master muralists, the fresco futurists and the stereotypical street artists, it is with great pleasure that I've been able to make my contributions. thank you.

GEODATA: BUFFALO, NEW YORK 2023
712 ELMWOOD AVENUE

the writing on the wall started as ancient hieroglyphics, I've always seen it as: communication in various visual forms. the telling of stories, with illustrated subjects. in modern metro society with public spaces, it is most likely advertising, political messaging and/or personal self expression. I prefer the latter, but would argue it could also be a form of advertisement.

the dawn of the post graffiti era, my evolution as a spray painter has been one of the most advantageous aspects of my story. practice makes imperfect, but it's nice to try to do the impossible. I think you simply learn from your own mistakes and make adjustments and modifications.

my participation in the BUFFALO AKG ART MUSEUM funded and curated PUBLIC ART INITIATIVE coincided with two exhibitions which were ongoing at the UB CFA and the ANDERSON GALLERY, which will conclude in february 2024.

my wall on ELMWOOD was a continuation of recent works on canvas, which were on exhibition at the UB CFA. specifically a series of paintings, which were actually named after neighborhoods in BUFFALO. the abstract nature of my work can often contribute to the technical subject matter, which in this case, is the crane like structures, what I see as metaphors for growth, change, and progress.

in the last decade, amongst the walls I have painted/created, BRADFORD REDS is certainly the most recent. but if I may add, the strongest. all the pre-arrangements, the organization and the support was extremely helpful and totally on point. thank you, ZACK and JEFF for all your time and patience.

in closing, it's the words PUBLIC ART that attract me. works in the PUBLIC SPACES that can be viewed by an unknown number of individuals. the communication of ideas and the experience of creating the actual ARTWORK is the greatest honor.

—FUTURA 2000

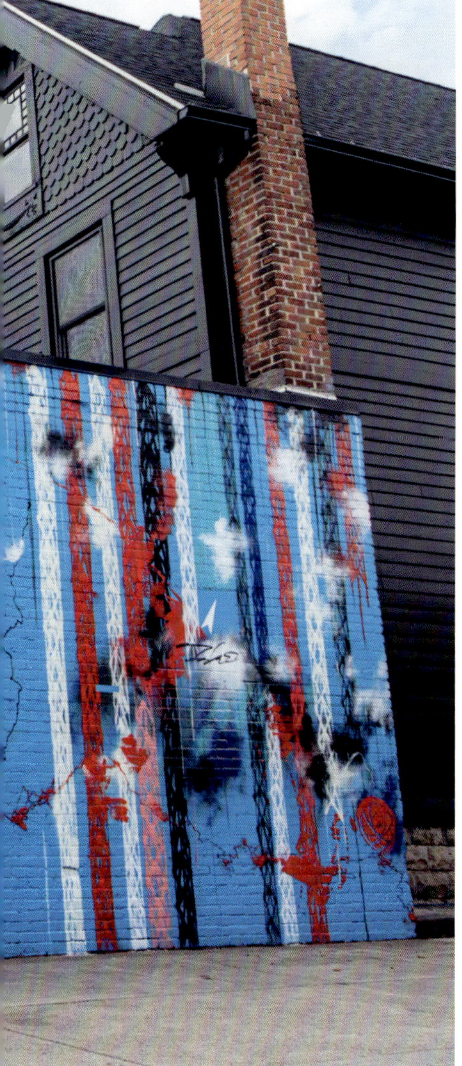

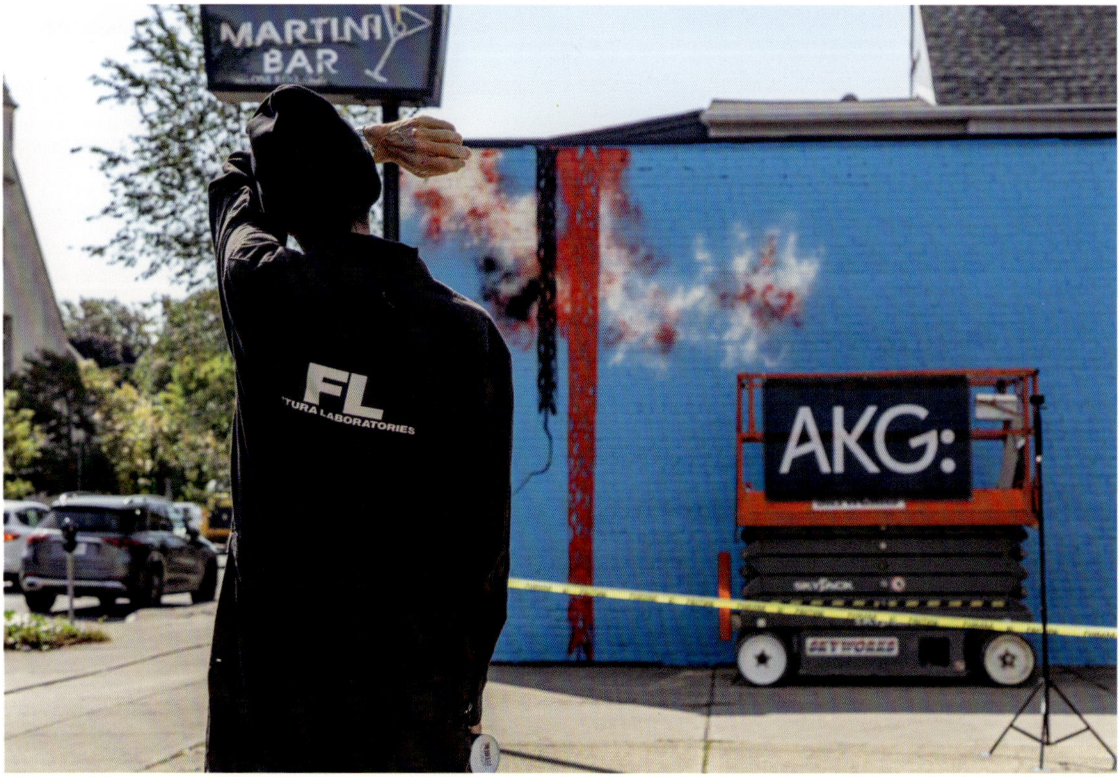

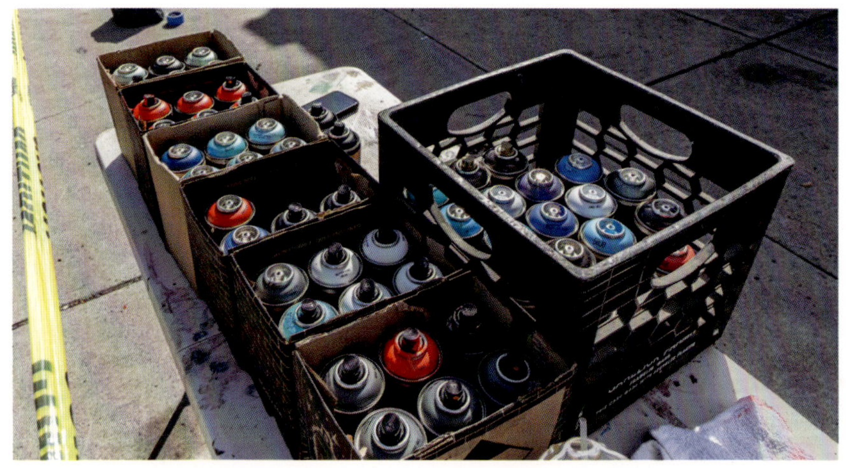

JM: You could say you've been making "public art" for years, to use a new term. You've been thinking about the idea of making art for people to observe in a public setting for longer than most people, so you have a particular insight into it.

FUTURA 2000: To me, for one, I appreciate the space available, right? Because maybe prior to this generation, a lot of what I remember were individuals that weren't getting permission, per se, but they also weren't asking for permission. They were just sort of taking that space.

Now, fortunately, such a culture and creative movement has been established that many people around the world embrace the idea of having young artists come and decorate their wall, paint a mural, deliver some message, perhaps, depending on what the artist is doing and the meaning behind his or her or their work.

I mean, for me, it goes back to the graffiti ethos at the core, which is "getting up," getting up, as in putting your name there, putting your name on a public wall—some people on a private wall, you know, they weren't very particular about who owns said wall. But I also come from a school, I believe that we had a kind of a code: you don't need to write on a tree, you don't need to write on a monument. From a New York City point of view, there's so much gray and diminished space, let's try to beautify it.

But it's the same thing, too, now. I put my work up on a wall, I don't know who's going to happen upon that. It's all to be determined. Someone might come and be like, "Wow, that's amazing." Another individual might come with a can of paint and spray all over it. But it's like the beauty of knowing that you're kind of—not a public service—but you are giving, in a sense, your work to the community, and I really like that.

JM: What's your take on Buffalo?

FUTURA 2000: I'm old enough to have experiences around the country and the world, and I know when I'm in a spot where there are really wonderful people, where there's a genuine kind of reality. It's

not pretentious, it's not people putting on airs. No, it's just folks being folks. I'm still quite old school, and you know what I miss?

JM: What?

FUTURA 2000: Hospitality, kindness, cool people. I mean, yeah, they had me in a hotel that was previously a mental institution, but that was cool….And you know what, I got to know your city a lot better. I was driving around like, "Oh, I know where I am." I know how to get downtown. "Oh, I gotta go to the Anderson [gallery]. I have to get on Humboldt, hang a left at Main Street and Englewood." Like, I'm a newbie, but I'm also a quick study, and I really love this place. Probably by the time the show comes down you'll be like, "Damn, he's back."

JM: To quote you, "I'm a local now."

FUTURA 2000: Well, I kind of am. I need to, no pun intended due to the history and location, but I gotta get with the indigenous community, right? I gotta come in and get with the locals. Figure out what we're doing and let's do it together.

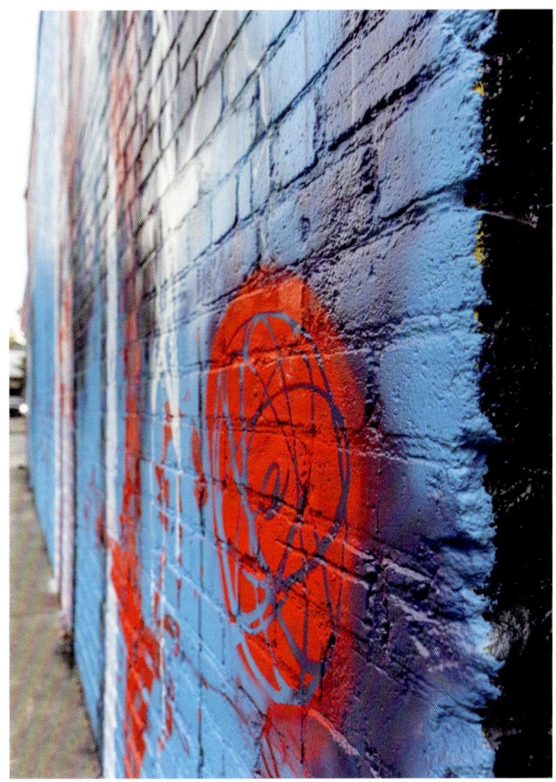

THE STARS PULLED DOWN FOR REAL

Robert Montgomery

502 Washington Street,
Buffalo

Steel and LED lights
6 × 24 × ½ feet (1.8 × 7.3 ×
0.2 m)

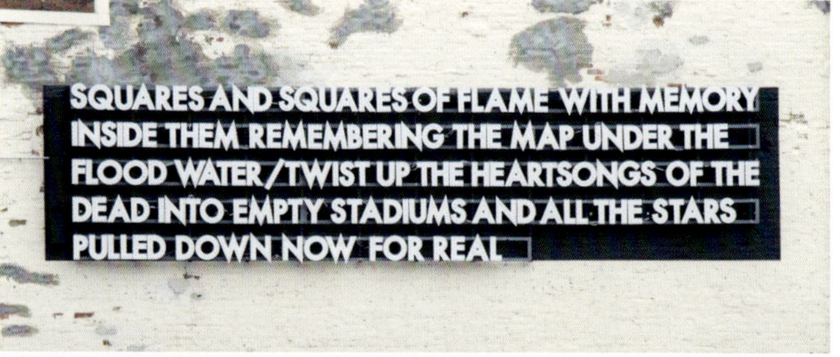

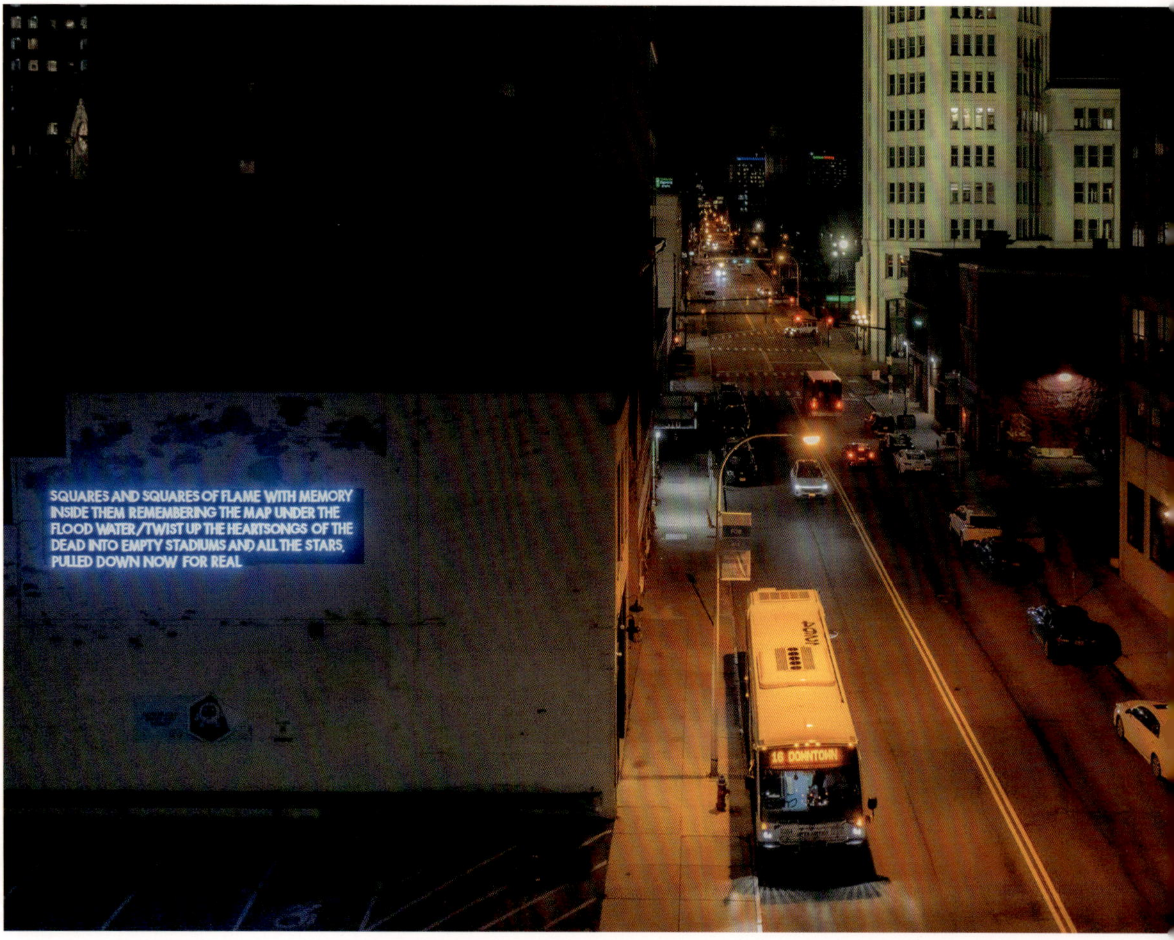

Leap

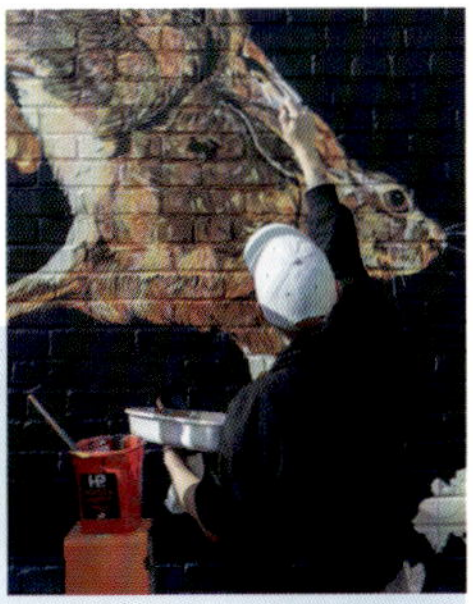

Alyssa Capri

3124 Main Street, Buffalo

Acrylic paint
26 × 15 feet (7.9 × 4.6 m)

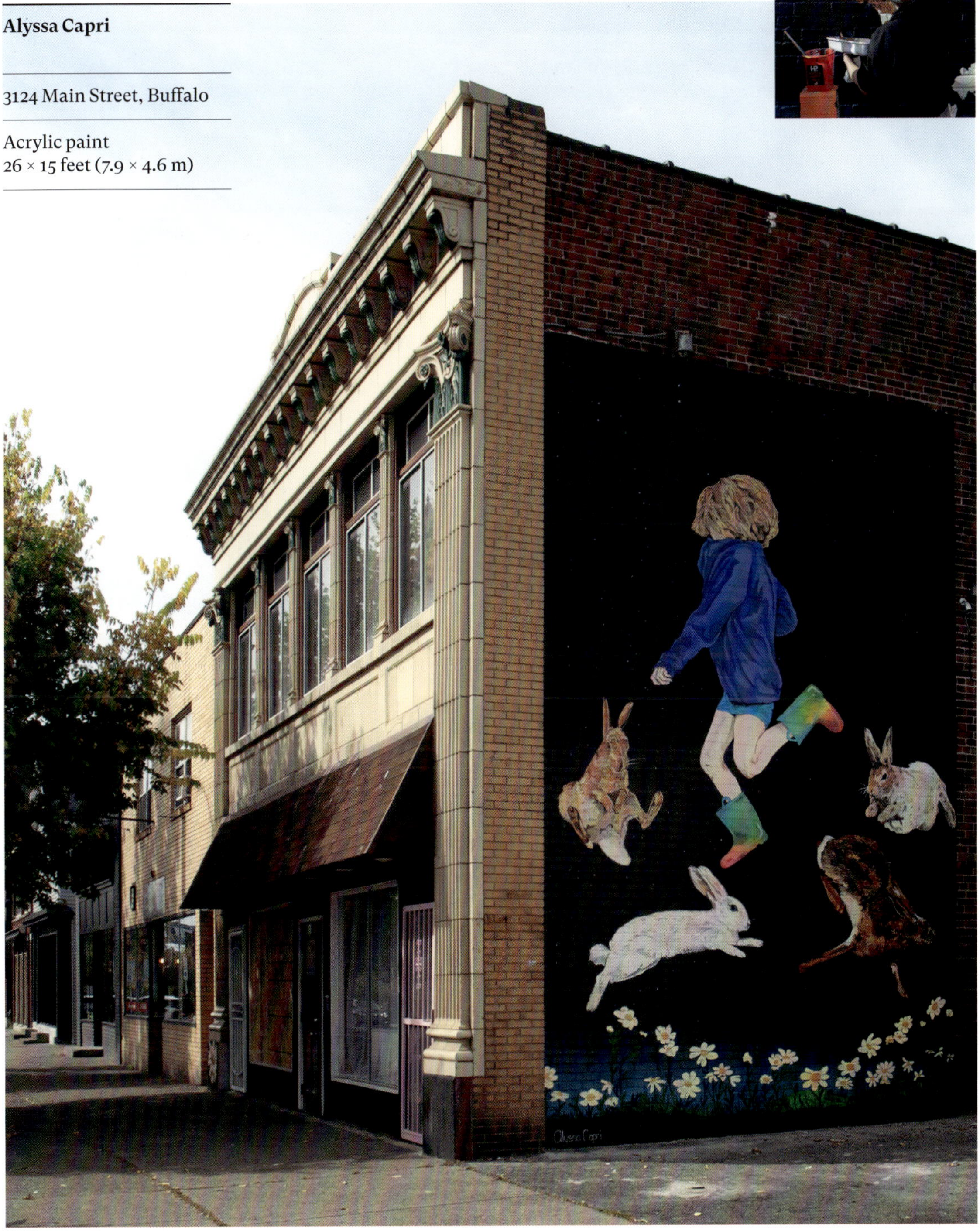

A Wish on the Wind

Mandi Caskey, aka Miss Birdie

Pearl Street & East Main Street, Springville

Acrylic and spray paint 17 × 77 feet (5.2 × 23.5 m)

Springville Center for the Arts and the Buffalo AKG Art Museum brought Caskey to live in Springville for a month-long residency, where the artist held workshops with young people (right), gave talks, and practiced her art.

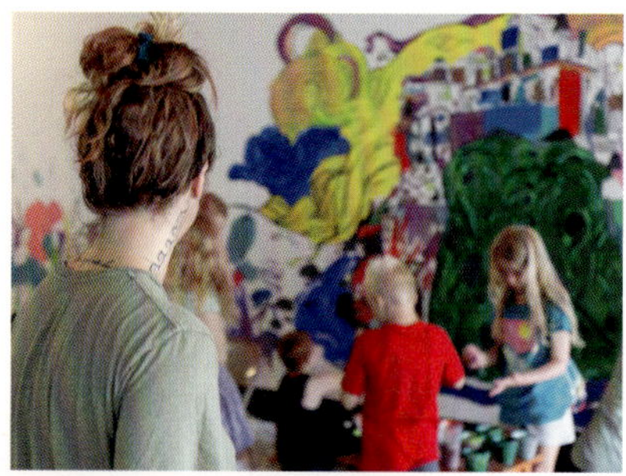

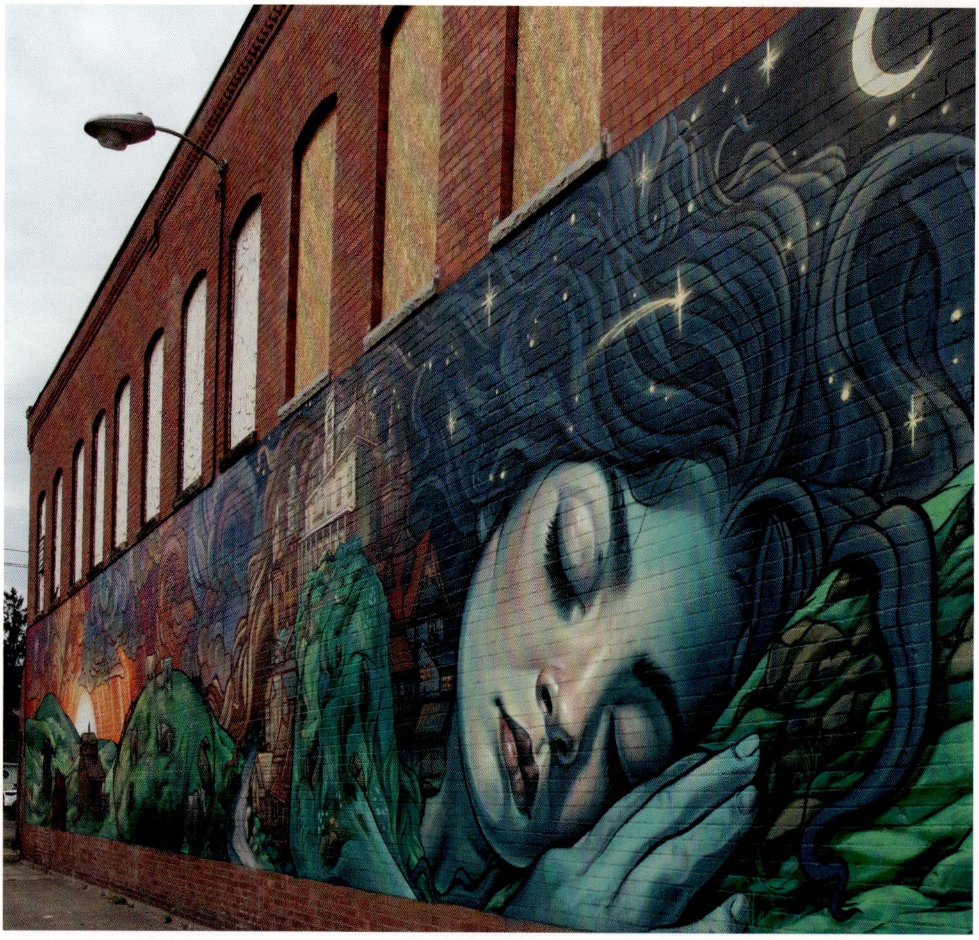

What Is Here

Aaron Li-Hill

LBJ Apartments

Acrylic paint
160 × 70 feet (48.8 × 21.3 m)

Painting on walls is a meditation on place. One engages with a canvas rooted in environment, lives, concepts, utility, and dense layers of history. When painting a wall, you get to know a space intimately. For a brief, fierce moment, you enter into the life cycle of a space. You alter a surface, which alters the rhythms of those inhabiting that space, however great or subtle. It reminds me of the mantra in *Parable of the Sower* by the genius Octavia Butler: "Everything you touch, you change, everything you change, changes you." The outcome can be profound when one is open to place.

What Is Here, the ten-story mural on the south facade of the LBJ community housing project, is one such project that effected this type of expanding change. It was created over years of consultation with the residents at LBJ and features images of residents of the buildings and Buffalonians alike. Images were taken by local photographer Pat Cray, who embedded himself in the building's goings-on. This mural is about strength amid division. Located next to the complex is the Scajaquada Expressway, which cuts through the city of Buffalo. Pre-1960 this was a tree-lined boulevard designed by Frederick Law Olmsted, which was then paved over by Robert Moses to prioritize the movement of vehicles. These changes contributed to rising divisions between the populations of Buffalo. In an attempt to acknowledge this embedded history of place, the background of the mural is symbolic of this concrete divide and the communities it affects.

At the head of the composition is an Indigenous resident of the building, Bow and Arrow. This choice, not only an acknowledgment of the original inhabitants of the land on which this building stands, but also their persistence in the face of continued oppression within the US and globally, becomes an enduring symbol of strength and survival. These are the broader concepts explored in this mural. How does one endure and create community amid division and oppression?

On the morning of the twelfth day of painting, before the cameras, vans, and officials arrive for the unveiling of the mural, I hear the beat of drums. From my eight-story vantage point, I can make out the feathers and hat of Bow and Arrow at the base of the wall. On a small stool with drums, bells, and singing, his sounds rise up to meet me. On the concrete surface of the wall, as I add the final details to his ornate portrait, his looming

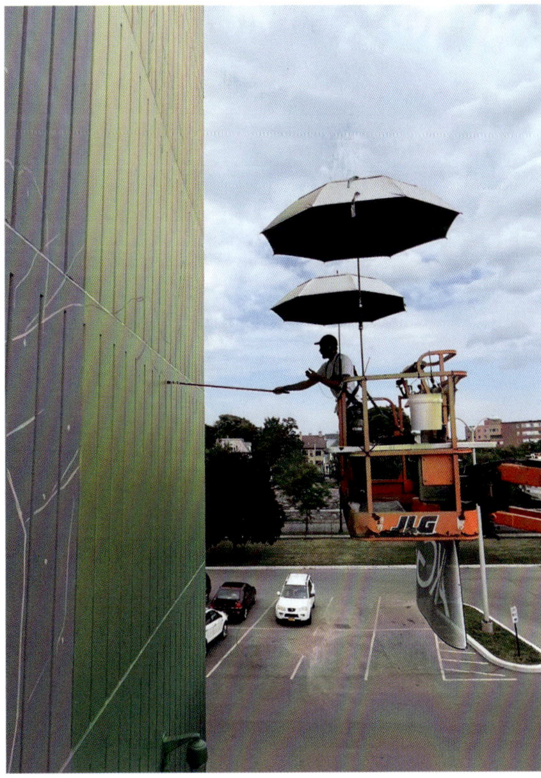

Li-Hill works more than one hundred feet in the air, completely at ease.

face, distorted out of proportion, stares back at me. He is sharing his art, just as I am, changing the vibes in and around him. In the reverberation of the beat, I am transported to Bow and Arrow's apartment, where he shows me his exuberant dream catchers, adorned with bells and shiny beads, bringing to mind Nick Cave–esque creations, and adamantly requests I take one home. I think of the face of the elderly grandmother who looks cool beyond her years, beaming at me as she recognizes herself standing like a specter over Main Street. I think of the soul singer living in the building, her fierce pose immortalized in paint. She points herself out to her incredulous grandchild. "That was me," she says. I see the children's cartwheels that are offered up as their own spectacle, the car honks, the "good jobs," the smiles and intrigues, and I see the pulse of this place in each drumbeat.

Over the project, I became close to the office manager, who one day shares what a resident told her: "You know, it's so important what he is doing, it's important because we are forgotten here, people forget we exist." I hope this wall becomes a reminder of what is here, a place of history, a place of joy, struggle, support, and love.

—AARON LI-HILL

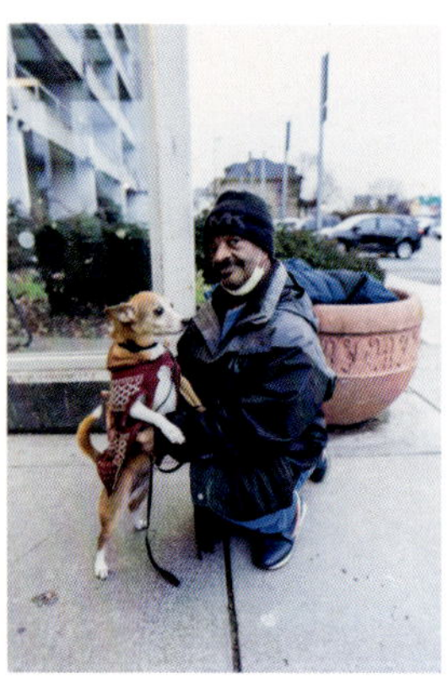

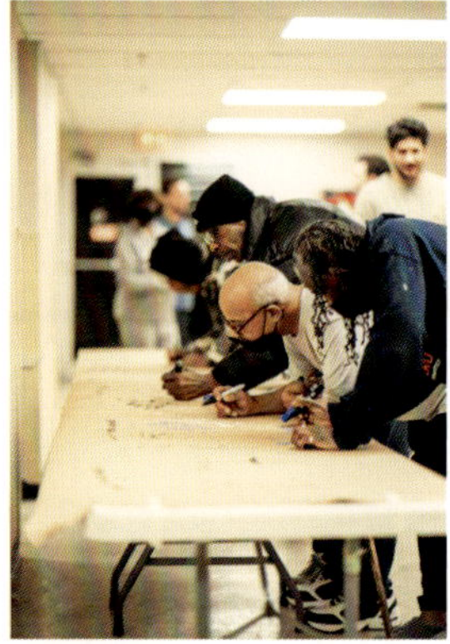

Li-Hill, with the assistance of Buffalo photographer Pat Cray, spent months getting to know residents of the building, to understand what they wanted to see and represent in the mural.

↓ Erma Ecford is one of the residents of LBJ Apartments whose likeness appears in the mural.

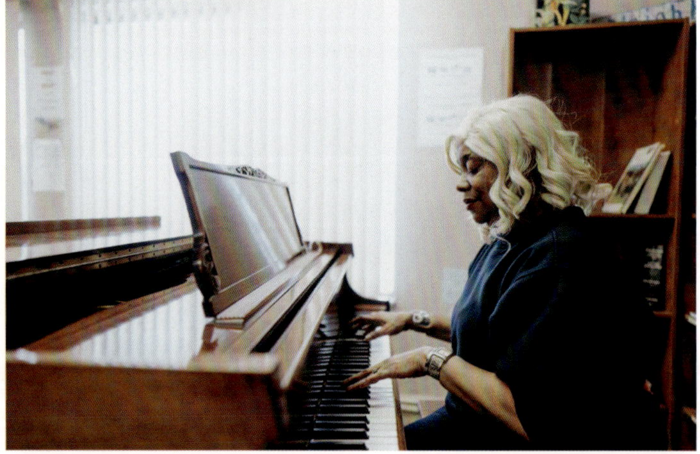

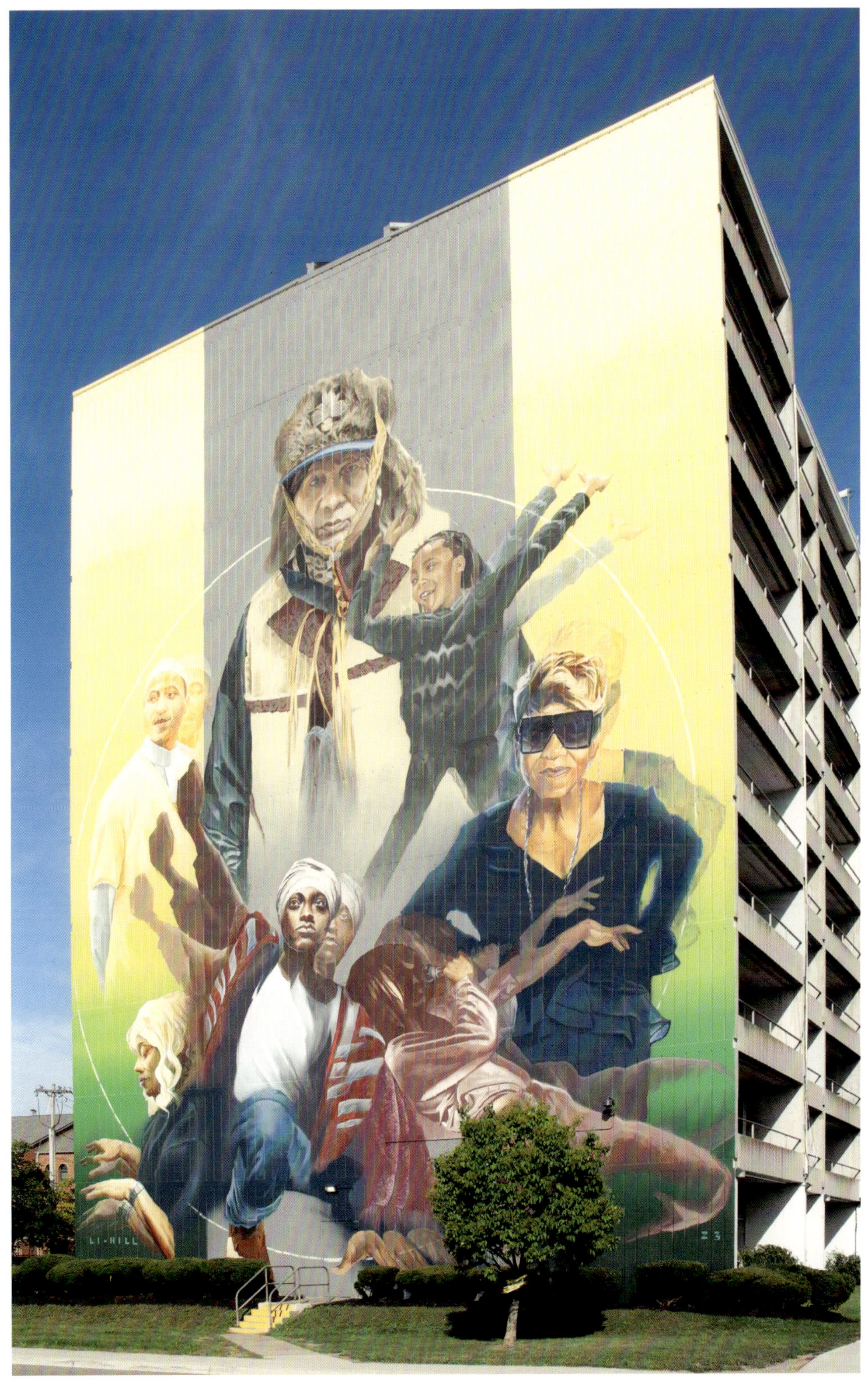

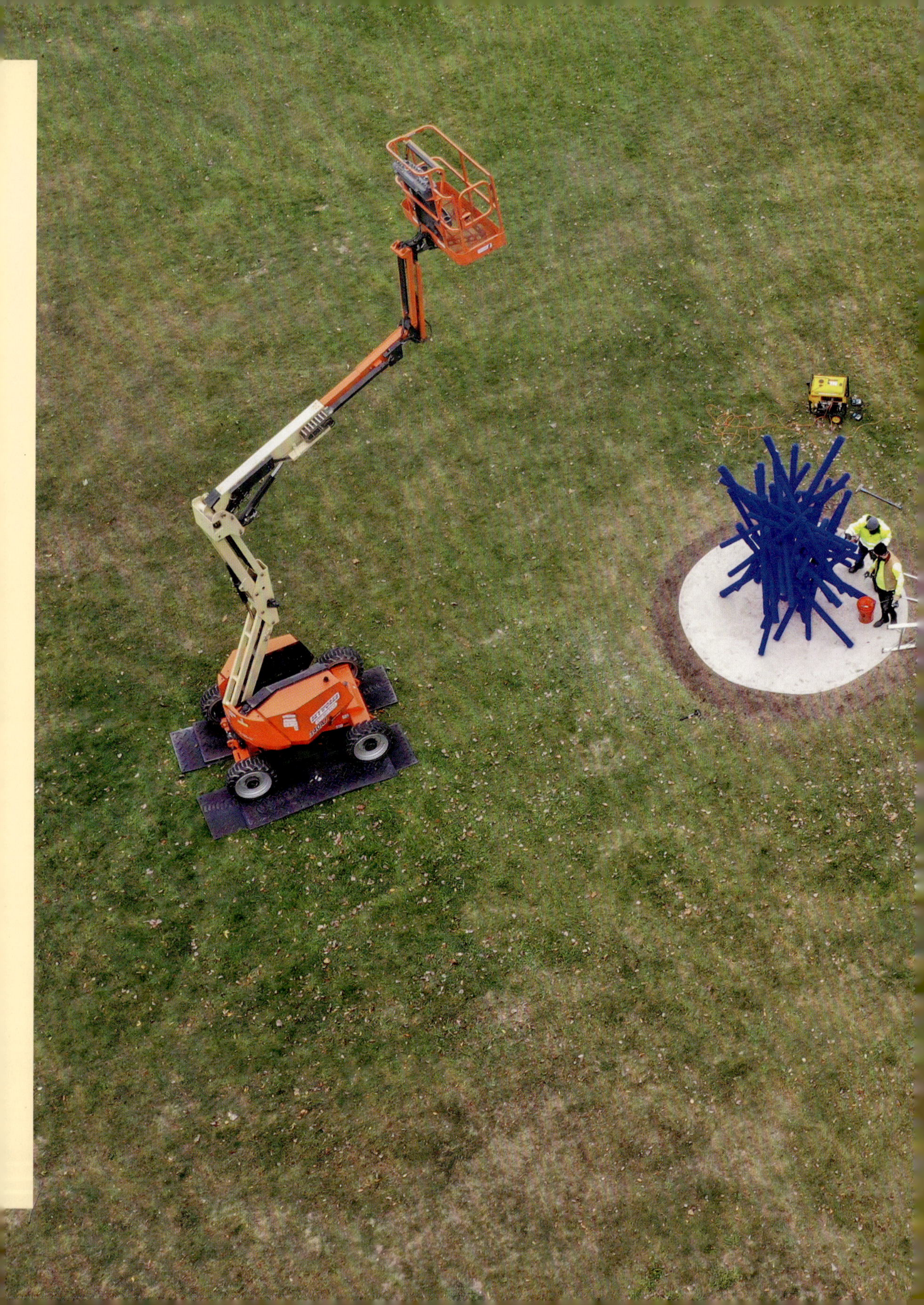

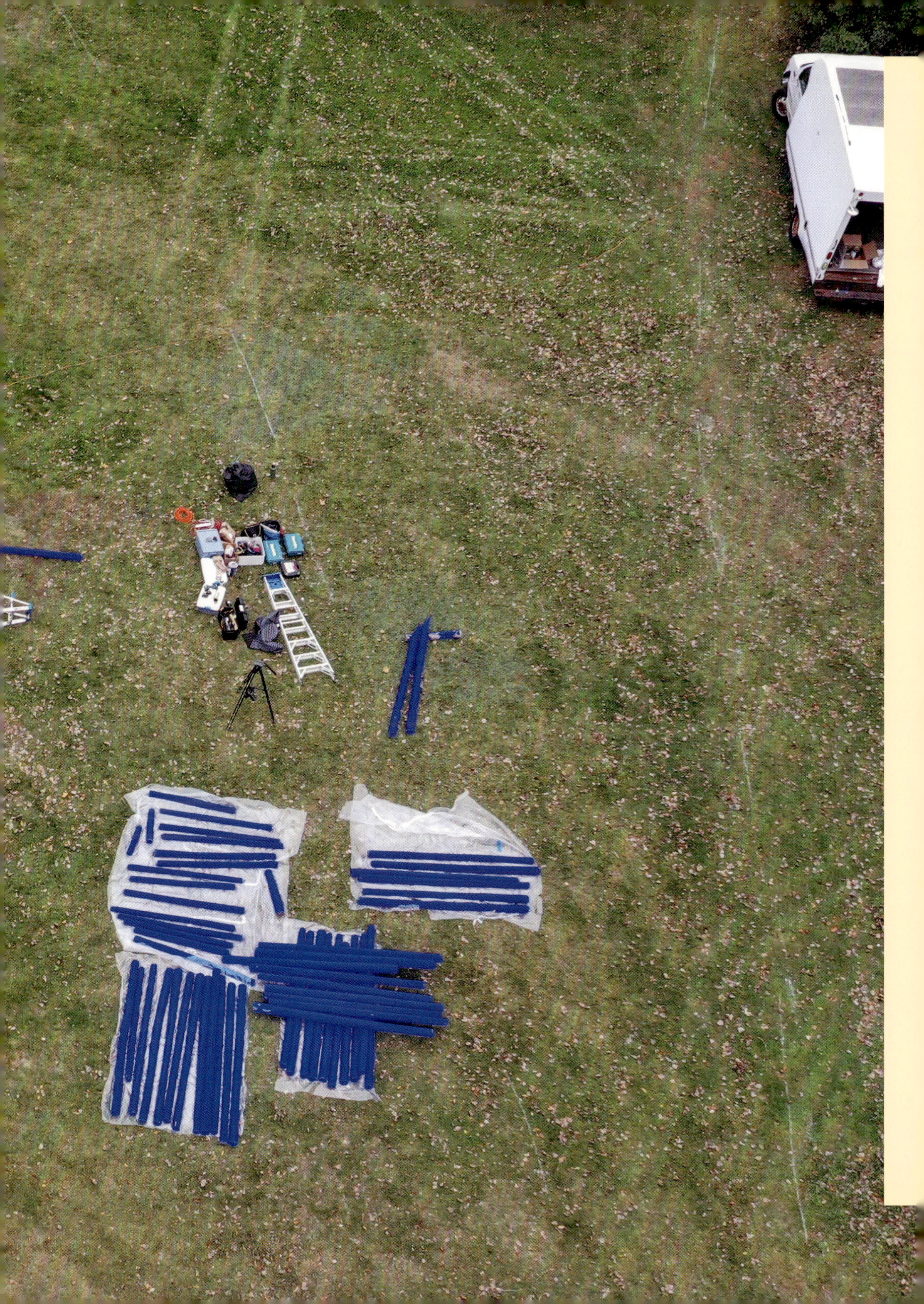

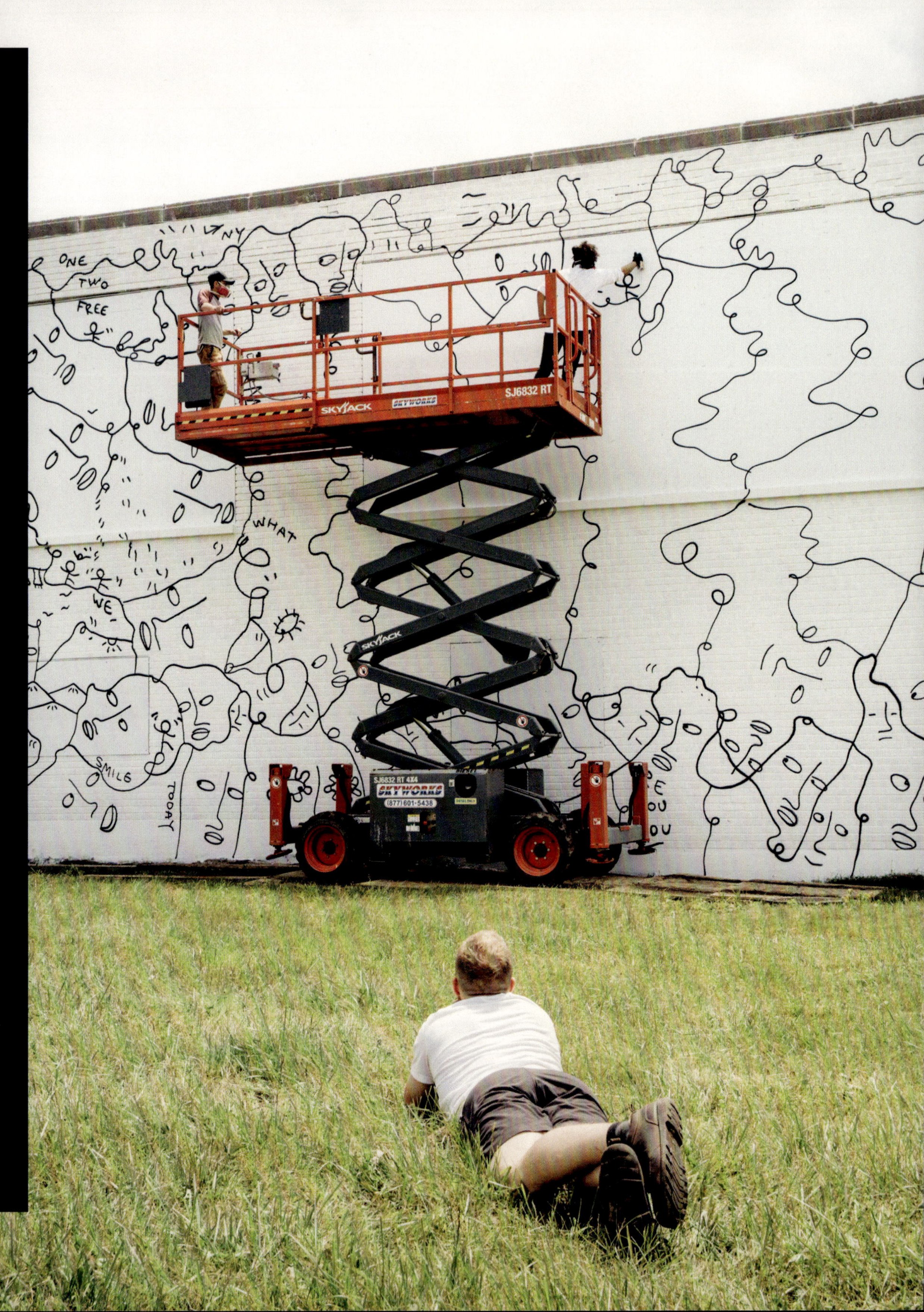

ONE
TWO
FREE
NY
WHAT
WE
SMILE
TODAY
SKYJACK
SKYWORKS
SJ6832 RT
SKYJACK
SJ6832 RT 4X4
SKYWORKS
(877) 601-5438

The Public Art Initiative was established and is supported by leadership funding from the County of Erie and the City of Buffalo.

2014

Matthew Hoffman
American, born 1979
You Are Beautiful, 2014
Forty-four billboards
Dimensions variable
Commissioned by the Buffalo AKG Art Museum Public Art Initiative
Supported, in part, by Lamar Advertising, 2014

Casey Riordan
American, born 1973
Shark Girl, 2014 (created 2013)
Fiberglass and paint
60 × 60 × 36 inches (152.4 × 152.4 × 91.4 cm)
Public Art Collection of the Buffalo AKG Art Museum
Gift of A. Conger Goodyear, by exchange, 2014

Charles Clough
American, born 1951
Hamburg Arena Painting, 2014
Acrylic on canvas
6 feet 3 inches × 16 feet 8 inches (1.9 × 5.1 m)
Public Art Collection of the Buffalo AKG Art Museum, 2014

Tape Art
American, established 1989
Buffalo Caverns, 2014
Green and blue painter's tape
Variable: approximately 50 feet at highest point × 150 feet (15.2 × 45.7 m)
Commissioned by the Buffalo AKG Art Museum Public Art Initiative, 2014

2015

Jaume Plensa
Spanish, born 1955
Silent Poets, 2015 (created 2012)
Two parts: polyester resin, stainless steel, and light element
Each overall: 26 feet 3 inches × 5 feet ¼ inch × 4 feet 3 ⅝ inches (8 × 1.5 × 1.3 m)
Temporary anonymous loan, 2015
Sponsored, in part, by the Erie Canal Harbor Development Corporation

Kaarina Kaikkonen
Finnish, born 1952
We Share a Dream, 2015
Donated apparel, rope, and wire
Two elements, each overall: 17 feet 6 inches × 138 feet (5.3 × 42.1 m)
Commissioned by the Buffalo AKG Art Museum Public Art Initiative, 2015
Made possible, in part, through the support of Corvette Cleaners

Jenny Kendler
American, born 1980
ReWilding New York (Community Seed Stations), 2015
Repurposed news boxes with vinyl flower wrap, seed packets, postcard mailer; planter and internal shelving made from reclaimed barn siding
36 × 19 × 16 inches (91.4 × 48.3 × 40.6 cm)
Commissioned by the Buffalo AKG Art Museum Public Art Initiative, 2015

Milkweed Dispersal Balloons, 2015
Performance involving mobile food cart, biodegradable latex balloons, milkweed seeds, orange hemp twine
Dimensions variable
Public Art Collection of the Buffalo AKG Art Museum, 2015

Shayne Dark
Canadian, born 1952
Tanglewood, 2015 (created 2006)
Cedar and paint
Dimensions variable
Public Art Collection of the Buffalo AKG Art Museum
Gift of the artist, 2017
The exhibition *Shayne Dark: Natural Conditions* (May 22–October 4, 2015) at the Buffalo and Erie County Botanical Gardens was made possible, in part, through the generous support of the Albright-Knox Contemporary and Modern Art Foundation Canada, Charles E. Balbach, and Margie and Sandy Nobel.

2016

Roberley Bell
American, born 1955
Locus Amoenus, 2016
Chain link fencing with powder coating, welded and forged polychrome steel urns, weathered cast-plaster birds, and concrete animal forms
Dimensions variable
Commissioned by the Buffalo AKG Art Museum Public Art Initiative, 2016

Daniel Galas
American, born 1982
72 Jewett, 2016
Acrylic paint
Approximately 28 × 200 feet
(8.5 × 61 m)
Commissioned by the
Buffalo AKG Art Museum
Public Art Initiative, 2016
Made possible through
the generous support of
Bank of America
Additional support was
provided by Tri-Main
Development LLC and Koch
Metal Spinning Co, Inc.

Alice Mizrachi
American, born 1977
Dream Keepers, 2016
Acrylic and spray paint
30 × 80 feet (9.1 × 24.4 m)
Commissioned by the
Buffalo AKG Art Museum
Public Art Initiative, 2016
Made possible by the
support of the Community
Foundation for Greater
Buffalo

Jessie and Katey is Jessie
Unterhalter, American,
born 1983, and Katey Truhn,
American, born 1983
*Noodle in the Northern
Lights*, 2016
Acrylic paint
Approximately 32 × 240 feet
(9.8 × 73.2 m)
Commissioned by the
Buffalo AKG Art Museum
Public Art Initiative, 2016
Sponsored by the County of
Erie and the City of Buffalo
with support from Gregory
and Sandra Norwood, 2016

Amanda Browder
American, born 1976
Spectral Locus, 2016
Donated fabric and steel
cable
Dimensions variable
Commissioned by the
Buffalo AKG Art Museum
Public Art Initiative, 2016
Supported, in part, by
an award from the National
Endowment for the Arts

2017

Public Art mural projects
in 2017 were generously
underwritten by the New
Era Cap Foundation.

Beverly Pepper
American, 1922–2020
Walk Through, 2017
(created 1967)
Stainless steel and baked
enamel
Two elements: 32 × 30 ×
87 inches (81.3 × 76.2 × 221
cm) and 30 × 30 × 87 inches
(76.2 × 76.2 × 221 cm)
Overall: 65 × 63 × 87 inches
(165.1 × 160 × 221 cm)
Public Art Collection of the
Buffalo AKG Art Museum
Gift of Nina Freudenheim,
2015

Bunnie Reiss
American, born 1975
Magic Buffalo, 2017
Acrylic paint
22 × 42 feet (6.7 × 12.8 m)
Commissioned by the
Buffalo AKG Art Museum
Public Art Initiative, 2017
Magic Buffalo was made
possible, in part, by City
of Buffalo Council Member
Joel Feroleto. Additional
support was provided by
Joe's Deli.
Repainted in 2022
Commissioned by the
Buffalo AKG Art Museum
Public Art Initiative, 2022

Shantell Martin
British, born 1980
Dance Everyday, 2017
Acrylic and spray paint
Approximately 22 × 200
feet (6.7 × 61 m)
Commissioned by the
Buffalo AKG Art Museum
Public Art Initiative, 2017
The exhibition *Shantell
Martin: Someday We Can*
(March 11–June 25, 2017)
at the Buffalo AKG Art
Museum and the mural
Dance Everyday were made

possible through funding
provided by the Creative
Arts Initiative of the
University at Buffalo. The
toys in this exhibition were
donated by Fisher-Price.

Keir Johnston
American, born 1979
Ernel Martinez
American, born Belize, 1975
Welcome Wall, 2017
Acrylic on Polytab
Approximately 27 × 42 feet
(8.2 × 12.8 m)
Commissioned by the
Buffalo AKG Art Museum
Public Art Initiative, 2017
Sponsored, in part, by
Broadway-Fillmore
Neighborhood Housing
Services, Inc.

Shasti O'Leary Soudant
American, born 1967
Gut Flora, 2017 (created
2016)
Six powder-coated steel
structures
Each 11 feet (3.3 m) tall
Produced by the Buffalo
AKG Art Museum Public
Art Initiative, 2016
Made possible by
the Niagara Frontier
Transportation Authority,
with additional support
provided by Colleagues,
Friends, and Family
in memory of John E.
Friedlander, First Chief
Executive Officer of
Kaleida Health, 1998–2001

Betsy Casañas
American, born 1974
*Patria, Será Porque Quisiera
Que Vueles, Que Sigue
Siendo Tuyo Mi Vuelo
(Homeland, Perhaps It
Is Because I Wish to See
You Fly, That My Flight
Continues to Be Yours)*, 2017
Acrylic on Polytab
Jersey Street side: approx-
imately 35 × 55 feet (10.7 ×
16.8 m); Niagara Street side:
approximately 35 × 45 feet
(10.7 × 13.7 m)

Commissioned by the
Buffalo AKG Art Museum
Public Art Initiative, 2017
Funding for this project
was provided by the Rich
Family Foundation and
M&T Bank.

John Baker
American, born 1964
Julia Bottoms
American, born 1988
Chuck Tingley
American, born 1983
Edreys Wajed
American, born 1974
The Freedom Wall, 2017
Spray and acrylic paint
Approximately 12 × 300 feet
(3.7 × 91.4 m)
Commissioned by the
Buffalo AKG Art Museum
Public Art Initiative, 2017
Additional support for this
mural has been provided
by Hyatt's Graphic Supply
Company.

2018

Stephen Powers
American, born 1968
Emotional Wayfinding, 2018
Fifteen billboards;
reclaimed metal sign, neon
Dimensions variable
Commissioned by the
Buffalo AKG Art Museum
Public Art Initiative, 2018
Supported by LAMAR
Outdoor Advertising

Robert Indiana
American, 1928–2018
*ONE through ZERO
(The Ten Numbers)*, 2018
(created 1980–2002)
Ten Cor-Ten steel sculp-
tures
Each overall: 96 × 96 ×
48 inches (243.8 × 243.8 ×
121.9 cm)
Private collection
Installation made possi-
ble through a partnership
with the Erie Canal Harbor

Development Corporation
Produced concurrently
with the exhibition *Robert
Indiana: A Sculpture
Retrospective* (June 16–
September 23, 2018), which
was made possible through
the generosity of M&T Bank
The museum's exhibition
program was generously
supported by The Seymour
H. Knox Foundation, Inc.

White Bicycle
American, established 2005
We Are Here, 2018
Acrylic paint
12 × 30 feet (3.7 × 9.1 m)
Commissioned by the
Buffalo AKG Art Museum
Public Art Initiative, 2018
We Are Here was made
possible, in part, by City of
Buffalo Council Member
Joel Feroleto.
Additional support has been
provided by Clover Group,
Inc. and C2 Paint.

Louise Jones
American, born 1988
Wildflowers for Buffalo,
2018
Acrylic paint
Approximately 80 × 180
feet (24.4 × 54.9 m)
Commissioned by the
Buffalo AKG Art Museum
Public Art Initiative, 2018
Made possible through
the generosity of Hodgson
Russ LLP, Nottingham
Advisors, and the New Era
Cap Foundation
Additional support for
this mural was provided
by Hyatt's Graphic Supply
Company.

Muhammad Zaman
American, born
Bangladesh, 1990
*Our Colors Make Us
Beautiful*, 2018
Acrylic paint
17 feet 6 inches × 42 feet
(5.3 × 12.8 m)
Commissioned by the
Buffalo AKG Art Museum

Public Art Initiative, 2018
Support for *Our Colors
Make Us Beautiful* has been
provided by C2 Paint
and Hyatt's Graphic Supply
Company.

Matt Grote
American, born 1984
Chuck Tingley
American, born 1983
weego, 2018
Acrylic paint
25 × 60 feet (7.6 × 18.3 m)
Commissioned by the
Buffalo AKG Art Museum
Public Art Initiative, 2018
Made possible, in part,
by City of Buffalo Council
Member Joel Feroleto
Additional support was
provided by Hyatt's
Graphic Supply Company
and the Robert Bojdak
and Sarah Williams
Foundation.

Otecki (Wojciech Kołacz)
Polish, born 1984
Work and Play, 2018
Acrylic paint
30 × 50 feet (9.1 × 15.2 m)
Commissioned by the
Buffalo AKG Art Museum
Public Art Initiative, 2018
Work and Play was
sponsored, in part, by
Broadway-Fillmore
Neighborhood Housing
Services, Inc., and M&T
Bank.
Additional support for this
mural has been provided
by Hyatt's Graphic Supply
Company.

Aakash Nihalani
American, born 1986
Balancing Act II, 2018
Steel, aluminum,
and acrylic polyurethane
Overall: 108 × 96 × 2½ inches
(274.3 × 243.8 × 6.4 cm)
Public Art Collection of the
Buffalo AKG Art Museum
Gift of the artist, 2019

2019

Felipe Pantone
Argentinian and Spanish,
born 1986
Optichromie—BUF, 2019
Spray and acrylic paint
44 × 90 feet (13.4 × 27.4 m)
Commissioned by the
Buffalo AKG Art Museum
Public Art Initiative,
2019

Hillary Waters Fayle
American, born 1987
Botanical Blueprint, 2019
Acrylic paint
13 × 48 feet (14.3 × 14.6 m)
Commissioned by the
Buffalo AKG Art Museum
Public Art Initiative, 2019
Support provided by
the Rich Family Foundation
Additional support from
C2 paint

Eduardo Kobra
Brazilian, born 1976
Untitled, 2019
Oil paint
38 × 53 feet (11.6 × 16.2 m)
Commissioned by the
Buffalo AKG Art Museum
Public Art Initiative, 2019
Made possible, in part,
by City of Buffalo Council
Member Joel Feroleto
Additional support was
provided by Drs. Andy and
Helen Cappuccino.

Nicole Cherry
American, born 1987
1800s Bikes in Vines, 2019
Acrylic paint
26 × 86 feet (7.9 × 26.2 m)
Commissioned by the
Buffalo AKG Art Museum
Public Art Initiative, 2019
Made possible by
Buffalo Spokes LLC

Tavar Zawacki
American, born 1981
Metamorphosis #5, 2019
Acrylic paint
90 × 160 feet (27.4 × 48.8 m)
Commissioned by the
Buffalo AKG Art Museum

Public Art Initiative, 2019
Metamorphosis #5 was
made possible by Sinatra &
Company Real Estate and
Bank of America.
Additional support provided
by C2 Paint

Augustina Droze
American, born 1981
Green Kaleidoscope, 2019
Acrylic paint
17 × 23 feet (5.2 × 7 m)
Commissioned by the
Buffalo AKG Art Museum
Public Art Initiative, 2019

James Cooper III
American, born 1971
John Brent Mural, 2019
Acrylic on e-panel and steel
Overall: 11 × 24 feet
(3.4 × 7.3 m)
Commissioned by the
Buffalo AKG Art Museum
Public Art Initiative, 2019
Support provided by
City of Buffalo Council
Member Joel Feroleto,
with additional support
from Drs. Andy and Helen
Cappuccino, 2019

Logan Hicks
American, born 1971
Walking Back Time, 2019
Acrylic paint
25 × 50 feet (7.6 × 15.2 m)
Commissioned by the
Buffalo AKG Art Museum
Public Art Initiative, 2019

2020

Bryan Metzdorf
American, born 1982
Before and Not Yet, 2020
Acrylic paint
20 × 24 feet (6.1 × 7.3 m)
Commissioned by the
Buffalo AKG Art Museum
Public Art Initiative, 2020

Obsidian Bellis
American, born 1993
Morgan Blair
American, born 1986

Jason Brammer
American, born 1974
Thomas Evans, aka Detour
American, born 1984
Monet Alyssa Kifner
American, born 1997
Lauren Mckenzie-Pearce
American, born 1988
James Moffitt, aka YAMES
American, born 1987
Karle Norman
American, born 1983
Ellen Rutt
American, born 1989
Miriam Singer
American, born 1976
Cyrielle Tremblay
Canadian, born 1986
Bradd Young, aka SALUT
American, born 1994
Cobblestone Commons,
2020–22
Variable: acrylic, spray
paint, and Polytab
Thirteen panels: 16 ×
21 feet each (4.9 × 6.4 m)
Commissioned by the
Buffalo AKG Art Museum
Public Art Initiative, 2020
Made possible by
the Niagara Frontier
Transportation Authority
Additional support provid-
ed by Ferguson Electric,
Labatt USA, Savarino
Companies, Lockhouse
Distillery, Pegula Sports
and Entertainment,
Port × Logistics,
Watts Architecture &
Engineering, Abbey
Mecca, CPL Architecture,
Engineering & Planning,
ECIDA, RP Oak Hill
Building Company Inc.,
Gilbane Building
Company, and Julia Spitz

Edreys Wajed
American, born 1974
James "YAMES" Moffitt
American, born 1987
Love Black, 2020
Acrylic paint
29 × 45 feet 6 inches
(8.8 × 13.9 m)
Commissioned by the
Buffalo AKG Art Museum
Public Art Initiative, 2020

Mickey Harmon
American, born 1984
Ari Moore
American, born 1953
Stonewall Nation: WNY LGBT History Mural, 2020
Acrylic paint
20 × 40 feet (6.1 × 12.2 m)
Commissioned by the Buffalo AKG Art Museum Public Art Initiative, 2020
Supported by M&T Bank

Jun Kaneko
Japanese, born 1942
The Space Between: Frank Lloyd Wright/Jun Kaneko, 2020–21
Eleven ceramic sculptures
Dimensions variable
The exhibition *The Space Between: Frank Lloyd Wright/Jun Kaneko* (June 26, 2020–October 24, 2021) was made possible by City of Buffalo Council Member Joel Feroleto, Mr. Charles E. Balbach, and Constance W. Stafford Charitable Lead Trust, with additional support from Penny and Charlie Banta, Bonnie and Nick Hopkins, Jack Walsh, Eberl Iron Works, Inc., Marvin Lunenfeld Beautification Grant, and an anonymous donor.

Obsidian Bellis
American, born 1993
Julia Bottoms
American, born 1988
Tricia Butski
American, born 1990
Fotini Galanes
American, born 1965
Jay P Hawkins, Sr.
American, born 1989
Ashley Johnson
American, born 1988
Jon Mirro
American, born 1978
MJ Myers
American, born 1982
Sarah Myers
American, born 1982
Karle Norman
American, born 1983

Omniprism
Chris Piontkowski
American, born 1986
Jennifer Ryan
American, born 1988
Jason Seeley
American, born 1983
Rachel Shelton
American, born 1988
Adam Weekley
American, born 1975
Works, from Home, 2020
Acrylic on Polytab
Sixteen works, each 2 × 3 feet (0.6 × 0.9 m)
Commissioned by the Buffalo AKG Art Museum Public Art Initiative, 2020
Made possible by the generosity of The Phyllis L. Goldman Memorial Endowment Fund

2021

Maya Hayuk
American, born 1969
Buffalo Soldier Wing Stance (The Tree of Y), 2021
Mineral paint on compressed concrete panels
60 × 96 feet (18.3 × 29.3 m)
Commissioned by the Buffalo AKG Art Museum Public Art Initiative, 2021
Sponsored by D'Youville University through a donation by Philip Perna, Linda Perna Ball, and Mary Jo Perna in honor of their late mother, Phyllis Esposito Perna, D'Youville class of 1942

Josef Kristofoletti
American, born 1980
Golden Hour, 2021
Mineral paint on Minerit panels
East panel: 69 × 62 feet (21 × 18.9 m); West panel: 47 × 57 feet (14.3 × 17.4 m)
Commissioned by the Buffalo AKG Art Museum, 2021
Sponsored by Ciminelli Real Estate Corporation

Hervé Tullet
French, born 1958
Traits points taches gribouillage (Lines dots stains scribbles), 2021
Acrylic on Polytab
25 × 85 feet (7.6 × 25.9 m)
Commissioned by the Buffalo AKG Art Museum Public Art Initiative, 2020

Julia Bottoms
American, born 1988
Tricia Butski
American, born 1990
Max Collins
American, born 1988
Fotini Galanes
American, born 1965
Rachel Shelton
American, born 1988
Phyllis Thompson
American, born 1946
Hervé Tullet: Shape and Color Resident Artist Murals, 2021
Acrylic on Polytab
Five murals: 10 × 15 feet (3 × 4.6 m); one mural: 15 × 10 feet (4.6 × 3 m)
The exhibition *Hervé Tullet: Shape and Color* and artist residencies were made possible through the generosity of Wegmans, Drs. Andy and Helen Cappuccino, and Mrs. Ralph C. Wilson, Jr. Additional support was provided by Mr. Robert M. Carey.
Additional sponsorship by Hyatt's All Things Creative and an anonymous donor
The museum's exhibition program was generously supported by The Seymour H. Knox Foundation, Inc. Albright-Knox Northland was supported by M&T Bank.
Additional support was provided by our *Hervé Tullet: Shape and Color Resident Artist Murals* sponsor BankOnBuffalo.

2022

Beau Stanton
American, born 1985
Verdant Vessel, 2022
Acrylic paint
37 × 25 feet (11.3 × 7.6 m)
Commissioned by the
Buffalo AKG Art Museum
Public Art Initiative, 2022

Sarah Braman
American, born 1970
*Sarah Braman: Finding
Room*, 2022–23
Various media
Dimensions variable
The exhibition *Sarah
Braman: Finding Room*
(July 30, 2022–March 19,
2023) commissioned
by the Buffalo AKG Art
Museum, 2022
Acquisition of *Sit* and *Stay*
made possible by the
Sherman S. Jewett Fund,
by exchange, 2023

**Adeyemi Adegbesan,
aka Yung Yemi**
Canadian, born 1982
Queen City, 2022
Digital print and acrylic
paint on Polytab
25 × 15 feet (7.6 × 4.6 m)
Commissioned by the
Buffalo AKG Art Museum
Public Art Initiative, 2022

**Julia Jamrozik and
Coryn Kempster**
Canadian, established 2003
Woven Together, 2022
Handwoven pillows
Dimensions variable
Commissioned by the
Buffalo AKG Art Museum
Public Art Initiative, 2022
Produced by Stitch Buffalo

Monet Alyssa Kifner
American, born 1997
The Divine Feminine, 2022
Acrylic paint
22 × 27 feet 6 inches
(6.7 × 8.4 m)
Commissioned by the
Buffalo AKG Art Museum
Public Art Initiative, 2022

2023

Futura 2000
American, born 1955
Bradford Reds, 2023
Acrylic and spray paint
15 × 35 feet (4.6 × 10.7 m)
Commissioned by the
Buffalo AKG Art Museum
Public Art Initiative, 2023

Robert Montgomery
Scottish, born 1972
*THE STARS PULLED DOWN
FOR REAL*, 2023 (created
2015)
Steel and LED lights
6 × 24 × 0.5 feet (1.8 × 7.3 ×
0.2 m)
Public Art Collection of the
Buffalo AKG Art Museum
Gift of the artist, 2020

Alyssa Capri
American, born 1987
Leap, 2023
Acrylic paint
26 × 15 feet (7.9 × 4.6 m)
Commissioned by the
Buffalo AKG Art Museum
Public Art Initiative, 2023

**Mandi Caskey, aka
Miss Birdie**
American, born 1993
A Wish on the Wind, 2023
Acrylic and spray paint
17 × 77 feet (5.2 × 23.5 m)
Commissioned by the
Buffalo AKG Art Museum
Public Art Initiative, 2023
A Wish on the Wind was
made possible by: the
membership of Springville
Center for the Arts; sup-
port from the Springville
Regional Coalition with
funding through the
Drug Free Communities
program; grants from
Ralph C. Wilson, Jr. Arts &
Culture Initiative admin-
istered by the Community
Foundation for Greater
Buffalo, Creatives Rebuild
New York (CRNY), a proj-
ect of Tides Center; as well
as public funds provided
by the County of Erie and
New York State Council on
the Arts with the support
of Governor Kathy Hochul
and the New York State
Legislature.

Aaron Li-Hill
Canadian, born 1986
What Is Here, 2023
Acrylic paint
160 × 70 feet (48.8 × 21.3 m)
Commissioned by the
Buffalo AKG Art Museum
Public Art Initiative, 2023
Support provided by
Buffalo Municipal Housing
Authority

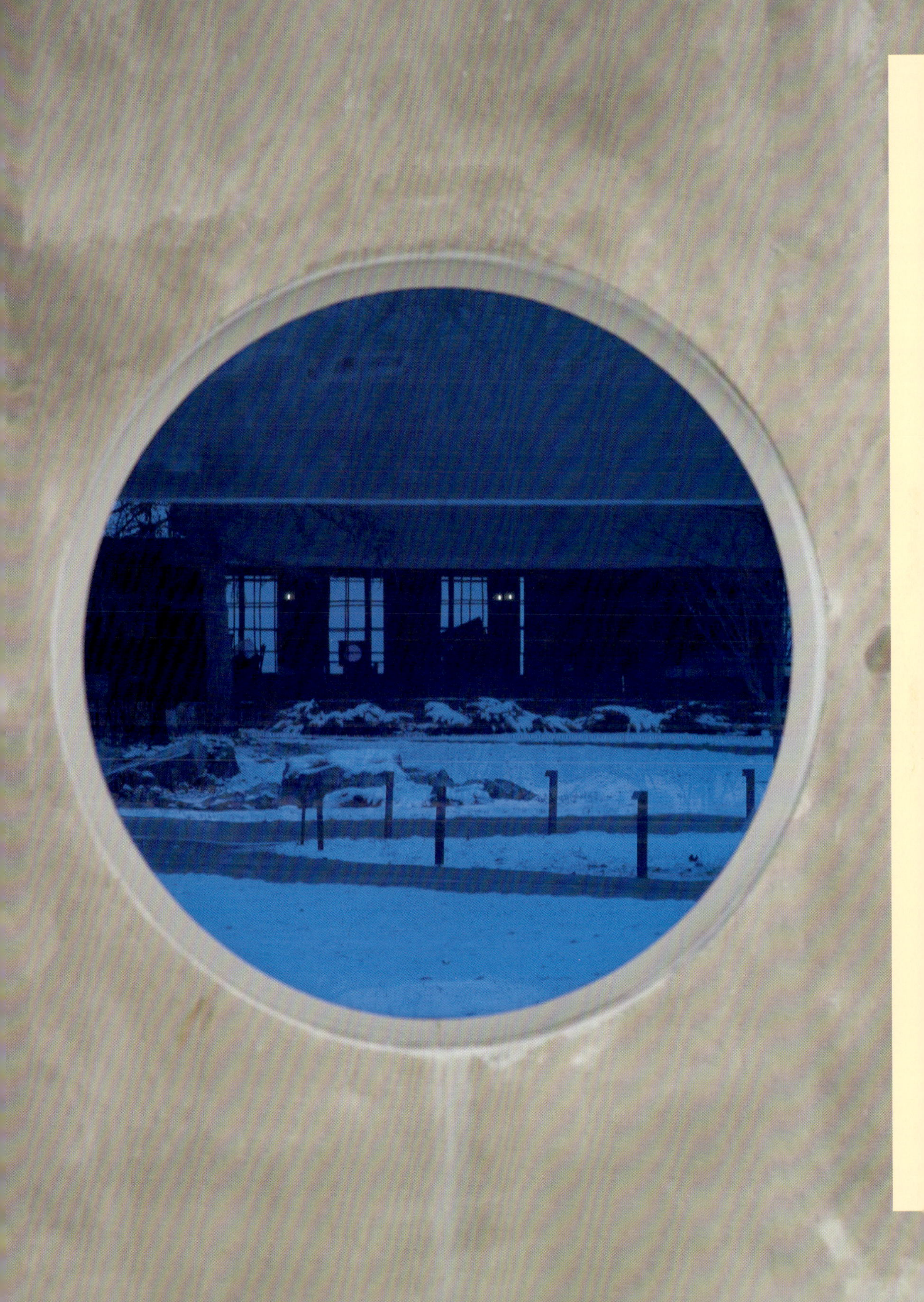

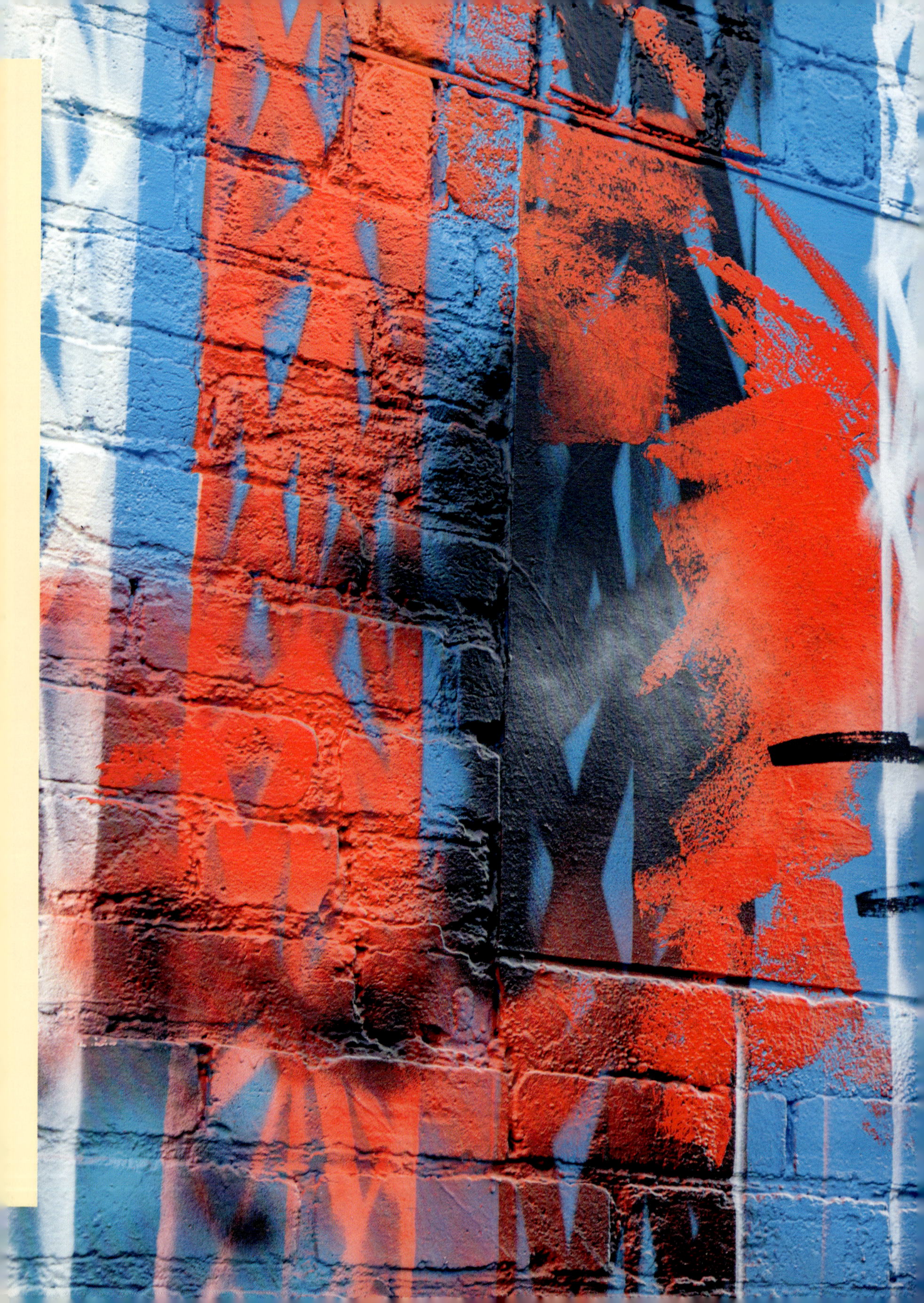

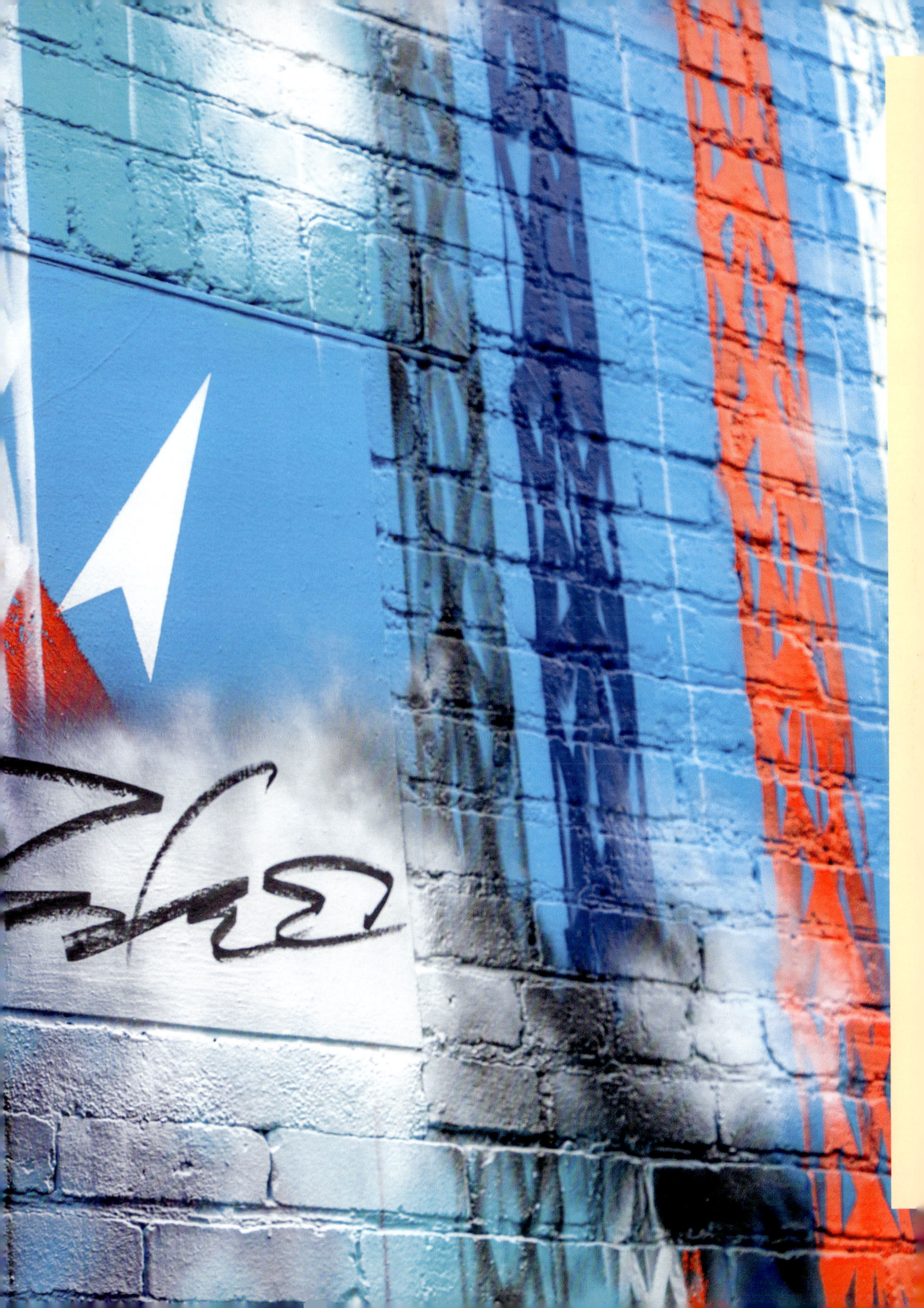

Acknowledgments

It is an honor to recognize the many individuals, artists, institutions, organizations, civic leaders, and visionaries whose participation, influence, and passion for public art have made our work in and around Western New York for the past ten years possible. We are grateful to be trusted to steward this work in our community, and our gratitude knows no end for the opportunity to create this one-of-a-kind initiative.

Without the bold inspiration of our Peggy Pierce Elfvin Director, Janne Sirén, and the leadership of Erie County Executive Mark Poloncarz, there would be no Buffalo AKG Public Art Initiative. We have had the privilege of establishing careers, families, and homes in Buffalo because these two individuals believe in the transformative power of public art and understand that the citizens of our region and visitors from all over the world deserve a lived experience rich with the opportunity to engage with creative culture in our shared landscapes.

The framing of our initiative as a public/private partnership was first established through foundational support in 2013 from the Erie County Legislature, with unanimous bipartisan agreement, which was swiftly followed in 2014 by support from the City of Buffalo through Mayor Byron Brown. Government buy-in has always been an essential component of our success, lending not only authority to our expertise but acting as connective tissue to constituents in the community who care deeply about their cities, towns, and villages throughout Erie County.

Erie County's legislators have championed our projects across a massive geographic swath amongst diverse populations. We are grateful for their foundational and ongoing support. In addition, we've had the privilege of working closely with many legislators on specific projects, including April N. M. Baskin, Patrick Burke, Lynne Dixon, Betty Jean Grant, Kevin Hardwick, Howard J. Johnson, Jr., Michael H. Kooshoian, Thomas Loughran, Barbara Miller-Williams, John J. Mills, Edward Rath III, and Peter Savage.

Buffalo City Council Member Joel Feroleto has established himself as a leader in our region for the support of public art. We are grateful for his support and that of his many current and former colleagues. We'd especially like to thank Zeneta B. Everhart, David Franczyk, Joseph Golombek, Jr., Mitch Nowakowski, Darius G. Pridgen, David A. Rivera, Christopher P. Scanlon, and Rasheed N. C. Wyatt.

We have been privileged to find support from other regional and state governmental bodies and would like to thank Governor Kathy Hochul, Congressman Brian Higgins, Congressman Timothy M. Kennedy, Senator Sean M. Ryan, Assembly Member Jonathan Rivera, Majority Leader and Assembly Member Crystal D. Peoples-Stokes, Amherst Town Supervisor Brian J. Kulpa, and former Deputy County Executive Maria Whyte. We would also like to thank the members of the Buffalo Arts Commission for their guidance and support of our projects in publicly owned spaces.

We are generously supported by the AKG Board of Directors and have been privileged to have Monica Angle serve as our Public Art Committee chair from the beginning. The effect of her leadership and advocacy cannot be overstated. Our committee has welcomed board members and citizens alike, including: Cindy Abbott-Letro, Karima Amin, Ann Bonte, Helen Cappuccino, Catherine B. Foley, Nick Hopkins, Thomas Hyde, Alice Jacobs, Jody Lippes, Catherine Gillespie, Sally Gioia, Roscoe Henderson, Victoria Beck Newman, Alphonso O'Neil-White, Deborah Russell, Christine Sabuda, Rachel Stenclik, Nicole Swift, Michael Tunkey, Kayla Zemsky, and Leslie Zemsky.

Our board continues to surprise, humble, and inspire us. In addition to the direct support from our committee members, we have found essential support from Susan O'Connor Baird, the late Charles E. Balbach, Charles Banta, Steven Biltekoff, Harold Cohen, Pamela Dinsmore, Peter Hunt, Michael Joseph, Roberta Joseph, Seymour H. Knox IV, Gerald Lippes, and Elisabeth Roche Wilmers.

The learning curve was steep in the beginning, and we have not encountered a community anywhere else so enthusiastic to embark on such a journey as the citizens of Western New York. We rely on our community's individual talents and expertise to take the ambitious ideas of a museum and artists and make them a reality. There is no greater example of this than Mike and Jeff Kolaga. From our earliest projects, these two ironworkers worked closely with us and taught our team how to operate safely, efficiently, and respectfully, with intent and care, with pride and skill. Among count-

less skills, the Kolagas taught us how to operate heavy machinery at elevation. They did this thoughtfully with attentiveness and admiration for the work that we did. We have collectively spent thousands of hours in lift buckets with the Kolagas, and we would not be as good as we are without them. It astonishes me to this day that we have been able to do some of the things we have done, and there is no doubt that without the Kolagas we would not be the professionals we are today. We are eternally grateful to them and to Clark Rigging, including Shawn Foti, for helping us achieve what would otherwise be unachievable.

Further, so many experts in their fields have greatly contributed to the success of our projects and offered their knowledge. These include all of the fabricators, makers, and skilled laborers on our projects, such as Al Wochensky, Tom Saia and Chris Beal at Iroquois Bar Corp., David Mitchell, Sean Wrafter, Chris Siano, Tom Stringham at imagineFORM, George Minasidis at Alpha Painting Services, and Michael Kistner at Kistner Concrete Products. We must thank all the artists who have worked as assistants on our projects over the years, especially James "YAMES" Moffitt, Mickey Harmon, and Max Collins. Many projects also would have not made it past the point of ideation without the time of WSP engineering, especially Joe Fonzi and Mark Bajorek.

We are proud to be an artist-centered organization, and in Public Art we are proud to support our artists every step of the way, including physically producing work with them. This means that we are a hands-on group and rely heavily on local support for products, supplies, materials, and assistance throughout the process. We would like to recognize and thank Josh Martineau at Skyworks for essentially always being on call for us and never letting us down. Tom Hill, president of C2 Paint, supplied us with critical knowledge on the materiality of paint and bolstered our work with hundreds of gallons over the years. Likewise, our friends at Golden Artist Colors, Inc., have worked with us to deliver the highest quality paints for murals. Our artists are always thrilled to be working with such quality materials. Hyatt's All Things Creative continues to be an essential source of supplies for our projects, and we are always happy to provide their products to our artists.

Two organizational partners lead the way in our region by example, the Niagara Frontier Transportation Authority (NFTA) and the Buffalo & Erie County Public Library (B&ECPL). The NFTA has a long-standing commitment to public art that predates our initiative, and Executive Director Kim Minkel and Vice President of Operations Tom George have stood as the gold standard of partners for us. Former Director at B&ECPL Mary Jean Jakubowski was a consistent champion of our efforts, notorious for always saying "yes" when we brought her projects we thought were seriously challenging. Jakubowski's enthusiasm was always matched (and still is) by Manager of Community Engagement at B&ECPL Anne Conable. These two organizations and these four people created repeated opportunities for us to do things that no other organizations would consider, and with them we completed some of our greatest successes.

The NFTA partnered with us on arguably our most celebrated and beloved project, *The Freedom Wall*.

First and foremost, our gratitude goes to our vocal and passionate community who demanded representation and trusted us to meet their reasonable requests. In addition to all those members of the community who helped steward that project to success, we thank those that participated in the challenge of taking community feedback and distilling it into the detailed documents that our artists relied on. Thank you to the guidance committee composed of local historians, community activists, and artists, including Karima Amin, Max Anderson, Cynthia Conides, Hiram Cray, Eva M. Doyle, and Henry Louis Taylor, Jr., who helped determine consensus. Claudia Carballada proved herself to be an essential community liaison for our museum and our artists during *The Freedom Wall* installation. She proved critical to our success on this and other projects, and we are thankful for her passion and commitment to fostering the best relationships possible between the museum team and our various communities.

In addition to repeat partnerships, early partnerships proved critical in our development and success. Lamar Advertising helped us establish our first broad-reach project. Erie Canal Harbor Development Corporation, a subsidiary of Empire State Development, jumped on board without batting an eye at *Shark Girl* and has since supported numerous projects.

Over ten years we have had the privilege of working with other cultural organizations throughout the county and are grateful to all of them. Among those organizations, we thank Erin Grajek, Chief Operating Officer at the Buffalo and Erie County Botanical Gardens; John Schaller, Vice President of

Development at Shea's Performing Arts Center; The Buffalo Zoo; Tifft Nature Preserve; Mary Roberts, former Executive Director at Frank Lloyd Wright's Martin House; and Anna Kaplan, Executive Director at Graycliff.

Universities have proven fertile partners, providing us with some of our most outspoken advocates, including at the University at Buffalo (UB): Kelly Hayes McAlonie, Director of Campus Planning; Robert Shibley, former Dean of the School of Architecture and Planning; and Bob Scalise, Director at UB Art Galleries; among many others. D'Youville University also supported a number of projects, and we thank President Lorrie Clemo and former Vice President of Operations Nathan Marton.

We have found significant support from like-minded civic and private organizations throughout our evolution, including from Town Ballroom, OSC Manufacturing & Equipment Services, Inc., Say Yes Buffalo, Open Buffalo, Buffalo Urban Development Corporation, the Rich Family Foundation, Historic Cobblestone District stakeholders, Ciminelli Real Estate Corporation, Sinatra & Company Real Estate, Iskalo Development Corp, Buffalove Development, Clover Group, Inc., Hispanic Heritage Council, Broadway-Fillmore Neighborhood Housing Services, Inc., Cedarland Development Group, Beautiful River Landscape, Five Points Bakery, Fitz Books and Waffles, BUREAU, Oxford Pennant, Robert Sienkiewicz, Rachel Heckl, Holly Ortman and Emily Doren, The Buffalo News, Artspace, Buffalo Center for Arts and Technology, People Inc., Springville Center for the Arts, Buffalo Niagara Medical Campus, Buffalo Place, Buffalo Municipal Housing Authority, and Joe's Deli.

Over ten years we were bound to lose some of those who provided us with critical insight. In particular, we mourn the loss of Lorna Hill, founder of Ujima Theater, who supported our projects with a fierceness only met by how she held our feet to the fire to do our work right. Gail Wells will also be deeply missed. She stood as a shining example of how to put community first. Heather Williams, an influential AKG board member deeply committed to her faith and charity, was an outspoken advocate for the vibrancy and health of our community and a tireless supporter of our work. We continue to be inspired in her absence and hope to embody her joyful spirit and dedication to improving all people's quality of life.

We are grateful beyond words to our endlessly talented colleagues throughout the museum. We have worked with the kind of people that, when they moved on, left us happy for them and devastated for ourselves. Maria Morreale was an unmatched leader, and there is not the remotest chance that we would have successfully launched our initiative without her leadership as the former Director of Communications at the AKG. Our former Deputy Director, Joe Lin-Hill, was a consummate manager who routinely protected us from our own ambition, making sure we stayed focused on what we could reasonably accomplish without burning ourselves out in an effort to serve our community. Without his leadership, we would have likely found ourselves adrift.

As the Public Art Initiative has grown, so too has the AKG itself. Our museum staff has more than tripled from the launch of the initiative, and the frank fact of the matter is that virtually everyone we have worked with has been unbelievably talented. Former Deputy Director Associate Megan Crowley, Executive Assistant to the Director Danielle Sansanese, and Executive Offices Associate Caroline Gerwitz have kept us plugged into the museum when we were far afield. Former Director of Advancement and current Deputy Director Jillian Jones has ensured that we stay true to our mission of collaboration. Carly Kirchberger, Associate Director of Advancement, has been with us the entire length of our initiative, and with her unparalleled team in Advancement she has made sure we are funded, celebrated, and recognized. She makes the difficult task look easy.

Because of the collaborative nature of what we do, we would be in the weeds without the support of our Finance Department. We are blessed to have a department led by CFO Melissa Arena and balanced by Controller Merideth Powers. These two women understand our departmental and institutional goals and are in a position to help us make them real. This is an unbelievable challenge in an organization that has grown like ours has, and they have never let us down. Our gratitude is immeasurable for their leadership and laughter.

We are spoiled to have the support of our Learning & Creativity, Community Engagement, Registrarial, Art Preparation, Information Technology, Facilities, Preservation & Safety, and Visitor Experience teams as they consistently promote, advocate for, and expand the depth of our projects.

The book team, led by Pam Hatley, Head of Publications & Digital Experience, and Editor Matt Connolly, is on full display here with the challenging task of distilling our first ten years. We cannot thank you properly. The fact that this gets to be a thing at all, let alone the thing that it is, astonishes us. Pam and Matt introduced us to our immensely talented designer Barbara Glauber of Heavy Meta, who grew up in Buffalo and has embraced this project with the enthusiasm of an insider who understands this wonderful city and all it has to offer. It is due to Barbara that the end result is so visually stunning. We also thank our co-publishing team at D Giles Ltd, led by Managing Director Dan Giles, Managing Editor Allison McCormick, Production Director Louise Ramsay, and Sales and Marketing Manager Liz Japes, who helped make this project successful with their enthusiasm and expertise.

Our gratitude is matched for our Imaging and Visual Resources department, led by Imaging, Visual Resources, and Digital Assets Manager Kelly Carpenter, who helped steward the wild task of herding the visual history of our initiative into something that could begin to be handled, not to mention assisting with the demanding task of condensing that history here. Museum photographers past and present, including Brenda Bieger, Amanda Smith, and Tom Loonan, added the documentation of these projects to their already daunting workloads, and for that we are grateful. A special thanks goes to Jeff Mace, whose dedication to documenting our work has seen him working all hours of the day and night in any number of weather conditions to capture a record of not only the finished works, but the long process of creating them. We would also like to thank the many independent photographers who have helped capture our work over the years, including MK Photo.

Janne Sirén's astounding legacy at this institution will endure. We are fortunate to have been hired under his leadership and vision. We are especially lucky to have witnessed the profound shifts in our museum culture under his direction. When he arrived at the AKG in 2013, he did so with a clear mandate: build a new building. Functionally this was necessary, and he rightly focused his energies on creating our beautiful new and renewed campus. It is not lost on us that many of the qualities that have made public art so vibrant in the region are now some of the essential qualities found in our new campus: a space where a full third of the building is free and open to the public, where there is space to play, lounge, and gather, where there is space to share and engage in meaningful, spirited dialogue, where we can see ourselves reflected in our fellow citizens.

Janne has already had generational impact through public art. We have entered an era where children at the time of our inception are now adults. They have lived with and shared public art as part of their everyday existence and understand it as an essential value in Western New York. Directors are built to take risks, and Janne took on the risk of establishing a completely novel initiative in the form of public art while simultaneously embarking on a decade-long building project. The result of his confidence is something so much bigger than the work that any one of us does in our own time, and we are grateful to be entrusted with the opportunity to work on behalf of the AKG and our public.

We could not possibly complete a list of acknowledgements without extending a deep thanks to our wives and families. Our dedication to this work has often led to extended hours, work on weekends and holidays, and missed social events. Their support of us has been crucial and their patience invaluable.

Our admiration and appreciation run deeper than these pages could possibly hold. Attempting to acknowledge everyone who has helped us over the last ten years would be impossible, and there are people we haven't been able to include here. Please know that we know our work relies on you. Your support has been essential to our success, and it continues to be the lifeblood of our work to this day. Thank you.

Aaron Ott
Eric Jones
Zack Boehler

This book was published on the occasion of the exhibition *Hi-Vis*, organized by Curator of Public Art Aaron Ott and Public Art Project Coordinators Eric Jones and Zack Boehler.

Buffalo AKG Art Museum
February 21–June 9, 2025

This publication was supported by an anonymous donor.

This exhibition is presented by the Buffalo AKG National Council.
The Public Art Initiative was established and is supported by leadership funding from the County of Erie and the City of Buffalo.

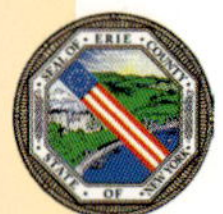 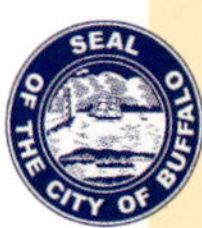

First published in 2025 by the Buffalo AKG Art Museum and GILES

BUFFALO AKG ART MUSEUM

1285 Elmwood Avenue
Buffalo, New York
14222-1096
buffaloakg.org

GILES
An imprint of
D Giles Limited
66 High Street
Lewes, BN7 1XG, UK
gilesltd.com

Designed by Barbara Glauber, Heavy Meta, New York
Edited by Matt Connolly and Pam Hatley, Buffalo AKG Art Museum

For D Giles Limited:
Proof-read by Sarah Kane
Produced by GILES, an imprint of D Giles Limited

First edition © 2025 The Buffalo Fine Arts Academy
All texts © 2025 The Buffalo Fine Arts Academy

ISBN: 978-1-913875-85-5
Library of Congress Control Number: 2024943966

Printed and bound in China

Distributed in the USA and Canada by
Consortium Book Sales & Distribution
The Keg House
34 Thirteenth Avenue NE, Suite 101
Minneapolis, MN 55413-1007
USA
www.cbsd.com

Photo Credits

Tom Loonan, Buffalo AKG Art Museum: pages 1–2, 6, 12–13, 15, 17, 20, 21 (bottom), 30–33, 35–36, 37 (top), 38, 40–42, 45–47, 49, 51, 54, 57, 67 (top), 68, 73, 75, 77, 78–79 (bottom), 79 (top), 80, 82–83, 86 (top), 87–89, 93–94, 100–1, 103, 104–5, 108 (top), 111 (top), 129, 131, 134, 135 (center and bottom), 139, 156, 171. Jeff Mace, Buffalo AKG Art Museum: cover and pages 4–5, 27, 28 (top), 60 (bottom), 61–62, 90–92, 96–99, 102, 106–7, 108 (bottom), 110–11 (bottom), 112–13, 116–17, 119 (top), 120–21, 122 (top), 126 (top), 132, 136, 138, 140, 145 (top), 146–147 (bottom), 149–51, 152 (top), 153 (top), 154–55, 157, 162 (top), 167 (bottom), 169, 172 (bottom), 174–78, 180–81, 182 (bottom), 183 (top), 184 (top), 188–89, 198–99, 207–8. Brenda Bieger, Buffalo AKG Art Museum: pages 10–11, 14, 39 (bottom), 67 (bottom), 86 (bottom), 88, 95, 100–1, 104–5, 109, 115, 118, 118–19 (bottom), 122 (bottom), 123, 124–25, 126 (bottom), 127, 145 (top), 147 (top), 148, 152–53 (bottom), 156, 158–61, 163–64, 165 (bottom), 182 (top), 183 (bottom), 184 (bottom), 187, 197. Image courtesy of Tape Art: page 21 (top). © RMN-Grand Palais/Art Resource, NY: page 23 (top). Scala/Ministero per i Beni e le Attività culturali/Art Resource, NY: page 23 (bottom). HIP/Art Resource, NY: page 24 (top). HAM/Maija Toivanen: pages 24 (bottom), 25. Aaron Ott, Buffalo AKG Art Museum: pages 34, 53, 55, 60 (top), 135 (top). MK Photo: pages 39 (top), 66, 78 (top), 79 (bottom), 84. Michael Townsend: page 21. Marco Cappelletti: page 28 (bottom). Jenny Kendler: page 37 (bottom). Image courtesy of Matthew Hoffman: page 50. Connie Tsang: pages 59, 64, 70–72, 190. Zack Boehler, Buffalo AKG Art Museum: pages 76, 167 (top). Claudia Carballada, Buffalo AKG Art Museum: page 81. Tracy M. Maybray, Springville Center for the Arts: page 114. Pat Cray: 137, 186. Amanda Smith, Buffalo AKG Art Museum: page 142–43, 146 (top), 165 (top). Adeyemi Adegbesan: page 162 (all at bottom). Seth Wochensky: page 172 (top). Image courtesy of Concord Historical Society: page 172 (center). Eric Jones: page 185.

Shark Girl photos (pages 18–19) were submitted by the following members of the public: Ivan Gonzalez, Georgia Hallinan, Julie Johnson, Judy Kosinski, Liz Midgley, Celia Vicente Pearce, Kelly C. Sedinger, Holly M. Shaw, Cooper Shreves, Kelsey Sweet, Sonia Timothy, and Zed.

On the cover: A wall prepared by the Public Art Team for Futura 2000's mural *Bradford Reds*, 2023.
Pages 1–2: Work in progress on Jessie and Katey, *Noodle in the Northern Lights*, 2016.
4–5: Work in progress on Josef Kristofoletti, *Golden Hour*, 2021.
6: Touch-ups on Tavar Zawacki, *Metamorphosis #5*, 2019.
10–1: Detail of *Hervé Tullet: Shape and Color* resident artist Max Collins's *Humboldt Parkway: Now & Then*, 2021.
12–13: Detail of Tape Art, *Buffalo Caverns*, 2014.
30–31: Detail of Kaarina Kaikkonen, *We Share a Dream*, 2015.
40–41: Installation in progress of Amanda Browder, *Spectral Locus*, 2016, at 950 Broadway Avenue.
64–65: Work in progress on Shantell Martin, *Someday We Can*, 2017.
84–85: Detail of Louise Jones, *Wildflowers for Buffalo*, 2018.
96–97: Work in progress on Tavar Zawacki, *Metamorphosis #5*, 2019.
112–13: Installation in progress of Jun Kaneko's work at Frank Lloyd Wright's Martin House, 2020.
142–43: Thomas Evans, aka Detour, works on his mural for Cobblestone Commons, 2021.
154–55: James Moffitt, aka YAMES, assists on Monet Alyssa Kifner's *The Divine Feminine*, 2022.
176–77: Work in progress on Mandi Caskey, aka Miss Birdie, *A Wish on the Wind*, 2023.
188–89: Installation in progress of Shayne Dark, *Tanglewood*, 2018, at Bassett Park.
190: A spectator looks on while Shantell Martin works on her mural *Dance Everyday*, 2017.
197: Detail view through one of Sarah Braman's works to the Frank Lloyd Wright home at Graycliff.
198–99: Detail view of Futura 2000's signature on his mural *Bradford Reds*, 2023.
207–8: Work in progress on Tavar Zawacki, *Metamorphosis #5*, 2019.

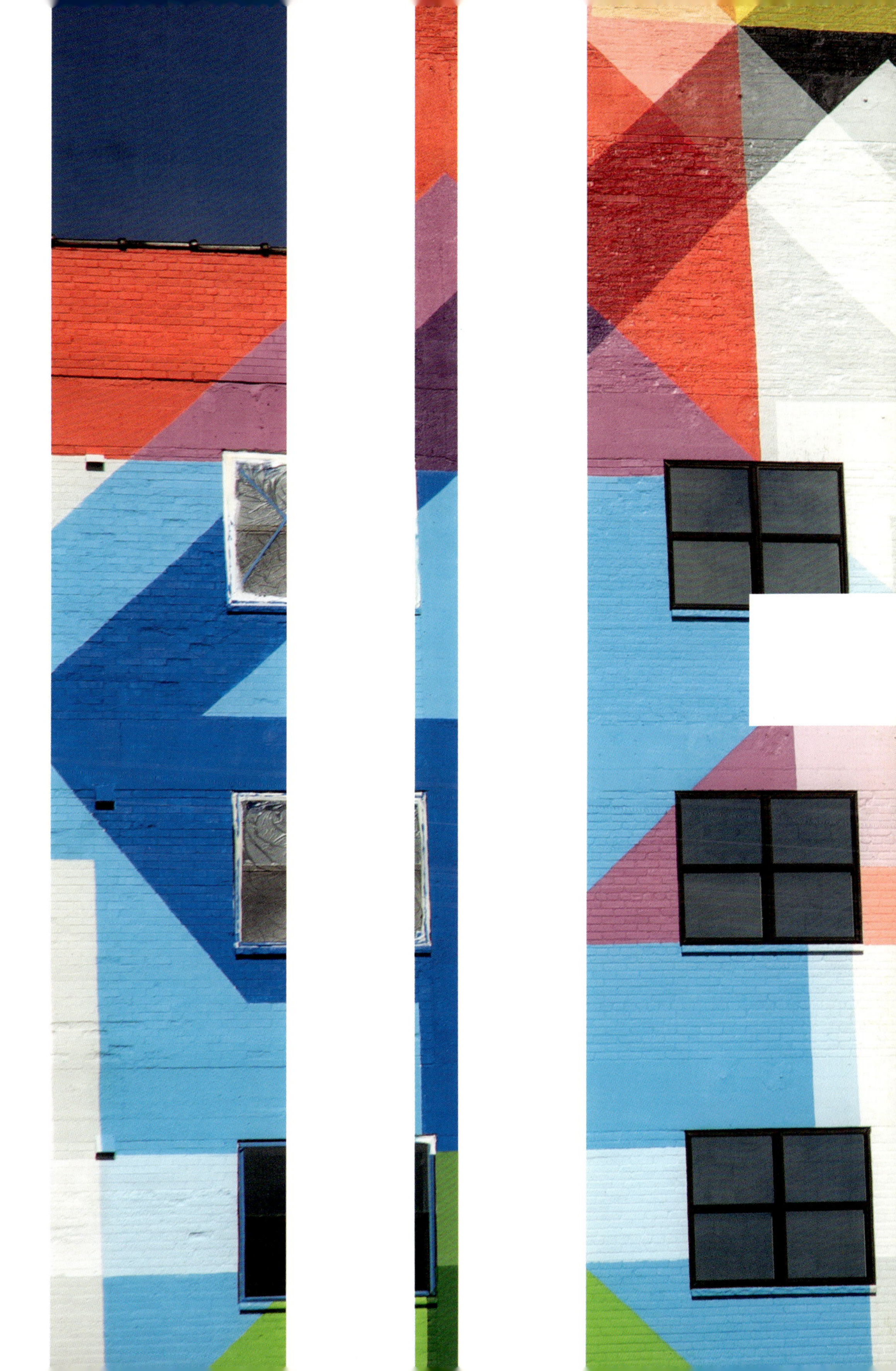

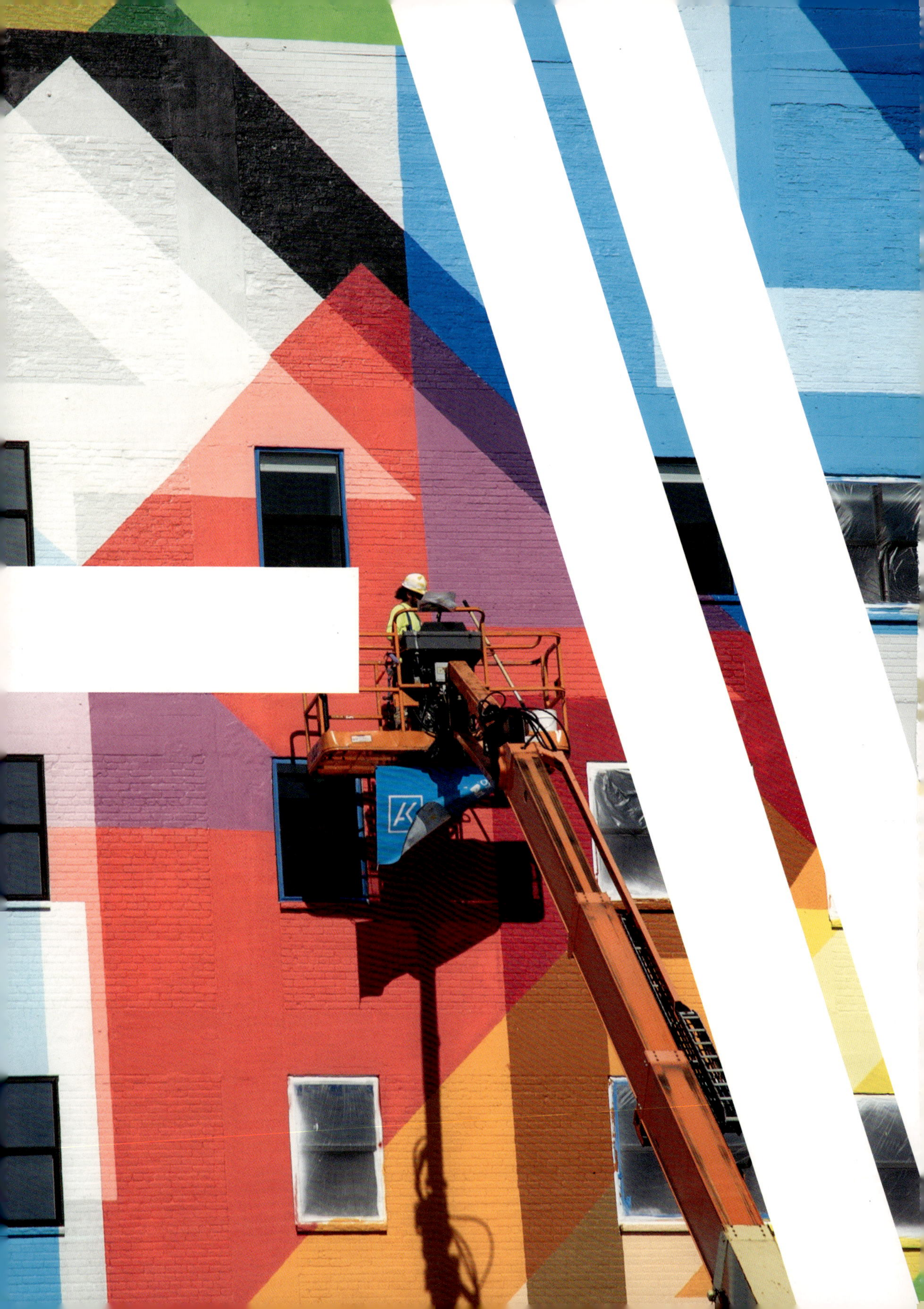